NICOLA TAYLOR

CW00705211

Behaviour, Crime and Legal Processes

A Guide for Forensic Practitioners

Edited by
James McGuire
University of Liverpool, UK
Tom Mason
Caswell Clinic, Forensic Healthcare Directorate,
South Wales, UK
Aisling O'Kane
Wirral and West Cheshire Community NHS Trust,
St Catherine's Hospital, UK

JOHN WILEY & SONS, LTD
Chichester · New York · Weinheim · Brisbane · Singapore · Toronto

Copyright © 2000 by John Wiley & Sons Ltd,
Baffins Lane, Chichester,
West Sussex PO19 1UD, England

National   01243 779777
International   (+44) 1243 779777
e-mail (for orders and customer service enquiries): cs-books@wiley.co.uk
Visit our Home Page on http://www.wiley.co.uk
or http://www.wiley.com

All Rights Reserved. No part of this publication may be reproduced, stored in a retrieval system, or transmitted, in any form or by any means, electronic, mechanical, photocopying, recording, scanning or otherwise, except under the terms of the Copyright, Designs and Patents Act 1988 or under the terms of a licence issued by the Copyright Licensing Agency, 90 Tottenham Court Road, London, UK W1P 9HE, without the permission in writing of the Publisher.

Other Wiley Editorial Offices

John Wiley & Sons, Inc., 605 Third Avenue,
New York, NY 10158-0012, USA

WILEY-VCH GmbH, Pappelallee 3,
D-69469 Weinheim, Germany

Jacaranda Wiley Ltd, 33 Park Road, Milton,
Queensland 4064, Australia

John Wiley & Sons (Asia) Pte Ltd, 2 Clementi Loop #02-01,
Jin Xing Distripark, Singapore 129809

John Wiley & Sons (Canada) Ltd, 22 Worcester Road,
Rexdale, Ontario M9W 1L1, Canada

Library of Congress Cataloging-in-Publication Data

Behaviour, crime, and legal processes: a guide for forensic practitioners / edited by James McGuire, Tom Mason, Aisling O'Kane.
        p.   cm.
    Includes bibliographical references and index.
    ISBN 0-471-99868-0 (cloth)—ISBN 0-471-99869-9 (paper)
    1. Criminal psychology.   2. Criminal behavior.   3. Criminal law.   I. Title: Behavior, crime, and legal processes.   II. McGuire, James.   III. Mason, Tom, 1950–   IV. O'Kane, Aisling.

    HV6080 .B39 2000
    364.3—dc21   00-043283

British Library Cataloguing in Publication Data

A catalogue record for this book is available from the British Library

ISBN 0-471-99868-0 cloth
ISBN 0-471-99869-9 paper

Typeset in 10/12 pt Times by Best-set Typesetter Ltd., Hong Kong
Printed and bound in Great Britain by Antony Rowe Ltd, Chippenham, Wilts
This book is printed on acid-free paper responsibly manufactured from sustainable forestry, in which at least two trees are planted for each one used for paper production.

Contents

About the Editors

James McGuire, PhD *Department of Clinical Psychology, The University of Liverpool, Ground Floor, Whelan Building, The Quadrangle, Brownlow Hill, Liverpool L69 3GB, UK*
James McGuire is a Senior Lecturer and Director of the Doctorate in Clinical Psychology at the University of Liverpool. Prior to that he held a joint post working as a clinical psychologist in Ashworth Special Hospital, and as a lecturer in the University of Liverpool where he helped to establish a new Diploma and MSc course in Forensic Behavioural Science. He has carried out research in prison and probation services, with young offenders, and in secure hospital settings. His main research and clinical interests are in applications of psychology in criminal justice; including social-cognitive skills training, programme evaluation, risk assessment, and psycho-legal issues.

Tom Mason PhD, BSc Hons, RMN, RNMH, RGN *Caswell Clinic, South Wales, Forensic Healthcare Directorate, Glanrhyd Hospital, Bridgend, Mid-Glamorgan CF31 4LN, South Wales, UK*
Tom Mason has worked in forensic mental health services for over twenty-five years, predominantly but not exclusively in high-security settings. Following seventeen years as a clinical forensic psychiatric nurse he moved to full-time research posts and later academic appointments as lecturer/researcher and senior lecturer. He has published widely on numerous issues relating to forensic mental health, with over fifty articles and six books, and has received several major research grants. He is an active member of the International Association of Forensic Nurses and won their 1999 Achievement Award. His major interests are in the management of violence, risk management, users' perspectives, and professional role development. He was awarded a Senior Robert Baxter Fellowship in 1999 and is currently based at the Caswell Clinic Bro Morgannwg NHS Trust in South Wales undertaking a five-year research programme.

Aisling O'Kane MSc   *Wirral and West Cheshire Community NHS Trust, Directorate of Psychological Services, St Catherine's Hospital, Derby Road, Birkenhead, Wirral CH42 OLQ, UK*

Aisling O'Kane is a Clinical Psychologist at Wirral and West Cheshire Community NHS Trust. Previously she has worked in high-security hospitals, in medium-secure units and at the University of Liverpool as Course Director of the MSc in Forensic Behavioural Science. Her current research interests include the relationship between psychosis and offending.

About the Contributors

Peter B. Ainsworth *School of Social Policy, Faculty of Economic and Social Studies, University of Manchester, Oxford Road, Manchester M13 9PL, UK*

Peter B. Ainsworth is originally from Blackburn, Lancashire. Upon leaving school he worked as a police cadet and later a police constable with Lancashire police. He was subsequently seconded to Lancaster University where he took a degree course in psychology. He then took up a scholarship to study psychology and sociology at Colorado University, USA. On his return from there, Peter began work on his PhD and shortly afterwards was appointed as a lecturer in the Department of Social Policy and Social Work at the University of Manchester. He has remained at Manchester until the present time and teaches courses in forensic, social and applied psychology. He is now a Senior Lecturer and Director of the Henry Fielding Centre for Police Studies and Crime Risk Management. His recent books include *Psychology and Policing in a Changing World* (Wiley, 1995), *Psychology, Law and Eyewitness Testimony* (Wiley, 1998), and *Psychology and Crime: Myths and Reality* (Longman, 2000).

Richard Bentall *Department of Psychology, The University of Manchester, Oxford Road, Manchester M13 9PL, UK*

Richard Bentall is Professor of Experimental Clinical Psychology in the Department of Psychology at the University of Manchester. He obtained his PhD in experimental psychology at the University College of Wales, Bangor, before training as a clinical psychologist at the University of Liverpool. After a brief period working as a forensic clinical psychologist he worked at the University of Liverpool until taking up his present post in 1999. Professor Bentall's main research work has concerned the psychological mechanisms responsible for particular symptoms of psychosis (hallucinations, delusions, mania) and also the development of novel psychological treatments for psychotic patients.

Ronald Blackburn   *Department of Clinical Psychology, University of Liverpool, Whelan Building, The Quadrangle, Liverpool L69 3GB, UK*

Ron Blackburn is a clinical psychologist who has spent most of his career working with mentally disordered offenders as practitioner and researcher. He has held clinical posts at Broadmoor, Rampton, and Park Lane (now Ashworth) special hospitals, and academic posts at Aberdeen and Liverpool universities. Since 1993 he has been Professor of Clinical and Forensic Psychological Studies at the University of Liverpool. His research and clinical interests centre on violent offenders and the assessment and treatment of personality disorders. He has published extensively on these topics, and is the author of *The Psychology of Criminal Conduct* (Wiley, 1993).

David Carson   *Director, Behavioural Science and Law Network, Faculty of Law, University of Southampton, Highfield, Southampton SO17 1BJ, UK*

David Carson is Reader in Law and Behavioural Sciences in the Faculty of Law at Southampton University. His research and teaching interests lie in promoting the contribution of the behavioural sciences to the law and legal system and in developing preventive applications of the law. He founded and directs the Behavioural Sciences and Law Network (1994) which provides applied courses on extant inter-disciplinary topics, and conferences on developing issues. He is an editor of the inter-disciplinary journal *Expert Evidence* (Kluwer) and the *Handbook of Psychology in Legal Contexts* (Wiley). He is author of *Professionals and the Courts* (Ventura), a practical guide to being an expert witness, and has contributed to the journals and conferences of several disciplines. He is currently developing applied work related to risk-taking.

Nigel Eastman   *Section of Forensic Psychiatry, St George's Hospital Medical School, Jenner Wing, Cranmer Terrace, Tooting, London SW17 ORE, UK*

Nigel Eastman is Head of Forensic Psychiatry at St George's Hospital Medical School, London. Qualified in both psychiatry and law, his research and publications are mainly in the field of legal psychiatry, ethics and public policy. He is co-editor of *Law without Enforcement* (Eastman, N. and Peay, J. (1999) Hart Publications, Oxford). His other field of research is in relation to services for mentally disordered offenders, again with an emphasis upon the analysis of public policy.

Adrian Grounds   *University Lecturer in Forensic Psychiatry, University of Cambridge, Institute of Criminology, 7 West Road, Cambridge CB3 9DT, UK*

Adrian Grounds has been, since 1987, University Lecturer in Forensic Psychiatry at the Institute of Criminology and Department of Psychiatry, University of Cambridge, and Honorary Consultant Forensic Psychiatrist, Addenbrookes Hospital NHS Trust. He qualified in medicine from the University of Nottingham, and trained in psychiatry and forensic psychiatry at the Maudsley and Bethlem Royal Hospitals, Broadmoor Hospital, and the Institute of Psychiatry, London. His research interests are in mentally disordered prisoners, forensic psychiatry services and the psychological consequences of long-term imprisonment.

David Heywood   *Social Work Department, Stockton Hall Psychiatric Hospital, The Village, Stockton-on-the-Forest, York YO32 9UN, UK*

David Heywood trained as a psychiatric nurse at the Maudsley Hospital in the late 1970s before working with adolescent "failures" of the child care system in Earls Court, West London. After completing the Psychiatric Social Work Course at the University of Manchester he worked for three years in child guidance in the Liverpool area. In 1986 he began work as a social worker at the Scott Clinic Medium Secure Unit where he was the Social Work Team Manager for ten years until 1998. He was able to develop an expertise in Forensic Social Work through multi-disciplinary working, fulfilling the role of Approved Social Worker, managing a team of social workers, supporting families and liaising with a wide range of agencies. He was appointed an honorary lecturer on the Forensic Behavioural Science Course at the University of Liverpool. He is currently Head of the Social Work Department at Stockton Hall Hospital near York. Stockton Hall is a private sector medium-secure facility and is in the *Partnerships in Care* group.

Julie Hird   *Edenfield Centre, Mental Health Services of Salford, Bury New Road, Prestwich, Manchester M25 3BL, UK*

Julie Hird graduated in psychology from the University College of Wales, Bangor, in 1982. She then undertook research in the same department, studying the role of language in human/animal differences and gained a PhD in 1989. In 1988 she obtained an MSc in Clinical Psychology and then worked for eight years in the Regional Forensic Psychology Service in Liverpool, where she developed a strong interest in the assessment and treatment of adolescent and adult sex offenders. This was followed by a two-year period working as a clinical psychologist in Ashworth Hospital and as a lecturer in the Department of Clinical Psychology in Liverpool University. She works at present as a Consultant Clinical Psychologist at the Edenfield Centre, a Medium Secure Unit, which is part of the Mental Health Services of Salford NHS Trust.

Jenny McEwan   *School of Law, University of Exeter, Amory Building, Rennes Drive, Exeter EX4 4RJ, UK*

Jenny McEwan was appointed as a lecturer in law at Manchester University in 1975. From there she moved to Keele University, where she held a Chair in Law until 1999. She is now a Professor of Law at the University of Exeter. Professor McEwan has published widely on various aspects of the law of evidence, as well as on criminal law and criminal justice. Her book, *Evidence and the Adversarial Process: the Modern Law* is published by Hart Publishing, and has led to involvement in some campaigning television programmes for the BBC. Her current research interest is in the concepts common to law and psychology, and, inspired by the chapter in the present collection, Hart are to publish her book on the subject.

Amina Memon *Department of Psychology, Kings College, University of Aberdeen, Old Aberdeen AB24 2UB, UK*
Amina Memon is a senior lecturer in psychology at the University of Aberdeen. She was formerly a lecturer at Southampton University (1990–99) and a visiting professor at University of Texas and Southern Methodist University, USA (1996–98). She received her post-doctoral training at the University of California at Los Angeles. Amina has been actively researching forensic issues concerning witnesses in Europe and North America since 1985 and has published widely on the subject of eyewitness accuracy, investigative interviewing and child witnesses. Her text on *Psychology and Law* (co-authored with Aldert Vrij and Ray Bull) was published by McGraw-Hill in 1998. Amina is also co-editor (with Ray Bull) of the *Handbook of the Psychology of Interviewing* (Wiley, 1999). Her current research, funded by the Economic and Social Research Council and National Science Foundation (USA) focuses on elderly witnesses. Dr Memon also holds research grants awarded by the Royal Society and the British Council to investigate the development of false beliefs and memories.

Daniel B. Wright *Department of Cognitive and Computing Sciences, University of Sussex, Falmer, Brighton, UK*
Daniel B. Wright graduated from Pomona College in the USA with a BA in mathematics, before moving to the London School of Economics for postgraduate work in psychology. He worked at the University of Bristol's Department of Experimental Psychology, where he lectured in statistical methods and psychological aspects of the legal system. His research interests are also in these areas, with a particular emphasis on how people learn statistics, on survey methodology and on eyewitness testimony. He recently moved to Sussex University to take up a readership in psychology. He enjoys sport (LA Dodgers and Arsenal FC and playing some), listening to music (Dead, Dylan, etc.) and food (cooking and eating).

Foreword

It is a great pleasure to be asked to write the Foreword for a publication as timely as this one. The Editors of this impressive book see its primary aim as being a "source book of information and concepts for use by those whose work straddles the fissures between criminal justice, mental health and social and behavioural sciences; and in the corresponding services and agencies in applied settings". The associated benefits of the book are to increase cross-disciplinary understanding of the multiple perspectives available and to demonstrate the inter-relationship of research and practice.

These are very important issues—particularly given the current context of service provision where the emphasis is very much on multi-agency working and on inter-disciplinary collaboration. There is a wide range of policy initiatives being taken forward at the moment: the National Service Framework for Mental Health; the integration of high-security psychiatric care with wider mental health services in the NHS; the Future Organisation of Prison Healthcare; Crime Reduction Strategy; Our Healthier Nation; Review of the Mental Health Act 1983; Young Offenders; and the policy proposals for Managing Dangerous People with Severe Personality Disorder. These and other developments are having, or will have, a major impact in this area. Their success partly rests on effective joint working, on a shared understanding of the system, and on a developing evidence base with clear expected outcomes for services.

The book not only covers in detail the up-to-date evidence and thinking across a number of areas, but also covers a wide range of issues. It makes for very interesting reading. The chapters have been written from the perspectives of those who are expert, yet there are common underlying themes. These include the need for a common language and a shared understanding as well as the need to appreciate the underlying ideology of each profession. In Chapter 5, Nigel Eastman writes metaphorically about two countries "Legaland" and "Mentaland"—the two countries have "different histories, cultures" and "they pursue different life purposes by different means of thinking and behaving". This is a central issue to address in determining how different agencies can work together.

When the mentally disordered offender and his or her needs are being considered, it is important for different agencies and professionals to communicate in a way that allows all concerned to understand and appreciate where individual and agency responsibilities lie in effecting the appropriate pathway of care for any particular person. Given that there may be a significant number of players, this can be challenging. One case alone may often involve police, probation, mental health services, social services and prison healthcare, not to mention the courts and probation, as well as legal advisers. Morgan (1991) describes how the "language game" can present organisational activity as little more than a "game of words, thoughts and actions" and concludes that "language is not simply communicative and descriptive: it is ontological". This is one of the mechanisms that can create barriers between agencies.

The book sets out to develop shared perceptions and to overcome barriers. It examines the specific roles of different professionals and their interaction with others; it delineates some specific responsibilities linked to each group, but it starts to outline some common objectives and themes to build on. The chapter on Risk Assessment and Prediction, by Ron Blackburn in Part II (Research and Practice), will be of interest and value to all agencies. The second part also covers explanations and causes of offending, and a broad look at systems of services and at care and interventions in a variety of settings. It continues to do so in a linked way so that the whole represents a comprehensive and coherent examination of services which suggests, where appropriate, the common interests between different agencies and professions.

The research evidence is used to make the arguments for various strategies suggested in the text. These have been carefully and thoughtfully set out and deserve considerable reflection. The question "How do we put into practice what we know?" is raised throughout the text. The findings from research, and their discussion here, create challenges for all services. One such example is the efficacy of the Sex Offender Treatment Programme within the prison system—what lessons can other services learn from this? How can we effectively share and disseminate findings across agencies? These discussions and the others in the book provide considerable food for thought and action by a wide range of practitioners, policy makers, managers and others working with offenders in terms of prevention, management and therapeutic intervention. The book deserves to be widely read and to be the basis for much debate.

Dilys Jones
Senior Policy Adviser
Home Office/Department of Health

REFERENCE

Morgan, G. (1991) Paradigms, metaphors, and puzzle solving in organisation theory. In Jane Henry (Ed.), *Creative Management*, London: Sage Publications.

Preface

We are delighted to have been able to bring together the distinguished group of authors who have contributed to this book. The area of overlapping ground between law, mental health, behavioural sciences and social service is a fascinating one in which to work. It presents difficulties that are uniquely challenging: from those which arise within the vagaries of individual "case management", to more abstract questions that are generated when different conceptual systems and "bodies of knowledge" come into contact with each other. Those professional groups who work in the field each bring something of value, indeed something indispensable, to the overall process. But as a result of specialised training, each inevitably contributes only part of the knowledge, skills and perspective required to respond to the complexities we all face. Some of the problems encountered in this area are likely to be ever-present and may by their nature be virtually insoluble. But others can be effectively addressed and some headway made in understanding them. In editing this book, our objective was to produce a volume that presented overviews of major areas and issues which must be addressed by anyone working in this intricate, multifaceted area.

The purpose behind the book is therefore primarily integrative. Readers who wish to have further detail and depth in the treatment of some of the issues raised will be able to pursue this in the background materials referenced by chapter authors. To that extent, we hope this volume can act as a sourcebook for its readership. Our key aim, however, is to enable individuals to obtain a grasp of fundamental principles, ongoing debates, and available evidence related to fields other than their own. Whether working as researchers or practitioners, by enhancing our appreciation of diverse viewpoints our thinking can become both more theoretically and empirically sound; and our practice improved thereby.

We wish to express warm thanks to all our contributors for the work they have done in preparing their chapters. We thank Dr Dilys Jones for agreeing to write the Foreword and for her helpful and insightful remarks. We are grateful to David Glasgow who was instrumental in developing the initial idea of a "forensic behavioural science". Thanks also to Mike Coombs and Lesley Valerio at John

Wiley for all their hard work and encouragement while the book was in preparation. Thanks finally to Di Brennand, Lyndsay Edmonds, Mary Gregg, and Susan Knight for all the administrative support while this work was in progress.

December 1999

James McGuire
Tom Mason
Aisling O'Kane

Part I

Behavioural Sciences and Legal Processes

Chapter 1

Behavioural Sciences Applied to Forensic and Legal Contexts

James McGuire
Department of Clinical Psychology, University of Liverpool, UK
Tom Mason
Caswell Clinic, Glanryhd Hospital, Bridgend, UK
and
Aisling O'Kane
Department of Clinical Psychology, University of Liverpool, UK

AIMS OF THE BOOK

The earth's surface, geologists tell us, is divided up into colossal sub-continental "plates" that scrape slowly and ponderously against each other. At their margins and along hundreds of fault-lines wrought by their ceaseless movement, there is constant friction and turbulence. It is usually imperceptible but intermittently produces cataclysmic side-effects: earthquakes, volcanic eruptions, tidal waves. This is the science of plate tectonics.

This book is about "plate tectonics" of a different kind. It deals with the intersection of three large land masses of human activity: the law, psychiatry and behavioural and social sciences respectively. Each involves a basic field of research and scholarship. Each is also put to extensive practical use to address a range of human problems. But often, at the meeting-points where these realms of knowledge are applied to practice, there is resistance, agitation and occasionally an outcome with, metaphorically speaking, some similarities to an earthquake. While the overall scale will be less dramatic, human lives may still at stake.

Behaviour, Crime and Legal Processes: A Guide for Forensic Practitioners.
Edited by James McGuire, Tom Mason and Aisling O'Kane.
© 2000 John Wiley & Sons Ltd.

At the points where the interests of law, medicine and social sciences come face-to-face, there is, in short, a perennial sense of disquiet.

The focus of the book is on that meeting-point. Our primary aim in editing it can be stated fairly simply. It is intended to provide a sourcebook of information and concepts for use by those whose work straddles the fissures between criminal justice, mental health, and social and behavioural sciences; and in the corresponding services and agencies in applied settings. It is hoped that two further, associated aims will flow from this: to increase cross-disciplinary understanding of the multiple perspectives available concerning common problems; and, in doing so, to illustrate the interrelationships of research and practice.

Such aims are plainly enough stated. To accomplish them however is a more formidable task. On the surface, it should be feasible for groups of often highly qualified personnel, with supposedly shared or at the very least overlapping general aims, to understand each other and work together effectively. Experience shows, however, that is not always the case: and of course it would be naive to expect things to function perfectly. Yet it is probably not an unreasonable claim that, often, publicly appointed tasks in this field are, if perhaps not wholly, nevertheless largely accomplished. At the same time, almost everyone working at the meeting-points of these fields would be likely to agree that there is still considerable room for improvement. We all, in some way or another, could do better.

DEFINING THE "FIELD"

In a formal sense, the "field" towards which this book is directed does not exist in an easily demarcated form. It tends to be denoted by hybrid names such as "psycho-legal" or "socio-forensic"; though the terrain envisaged here, which for the purpose of this book we will call *forensic behavioural science*, means more than what is conveyed by these terms. One initial reason for the difficulties likely to arise within it is that in many respects it appears as a vacuum between pre-existing, indeed firmly established, sectors of activity. Its boundaries are amorphous and its exact location is difficult to define. Medicine and law have lengthy histories and crowded collective memories—even if, in historical terms, psychiatry is a relative newcomer. As an intellectual enterprise the social and behavioural sciences are comparatively less well established. The validity of their conclusions continues to be questioned by outside observers, even though side-by-side comparisons show that research findings in these fields can be as robust as in other forms of scientific inquiry (Hedges, 1987).

The difficulty of clarifying our focus is compounded by quandaries of several other kinds. There are four principal aspects of this. First, the client problems addressed by practitioners in this area are exceedingly complex. Second, the empirical "body of knowledge" on which practitioners can draw is neither as detailed nor as coherent as in other fields. Third, public services as organised along existing lines often have difficulty responding to individuals whose problems are not straightforward. Fourth, the background training of specialists in these fields sometimes places limits on their appreciation of perspectives other than their own.

Client Problems

In many respects the client problems encountered in this domain are among the most complex found in any sector of human services. Individuals who simultaneously manifest problems of mental disorder *and* criminal or anti-social behaviour also tend to have disadvantaged lives in other respects. They all too frequently come from disrupted family backgrounds. Most endure or have endured some form of social deprivation. Many have histories of victimisation. Mental health problems themselves rarely exist in isolated form. Even relatively common types of distress such as anxiety, depression, or other troubling internal states are typically found alongside each other. In numerous instances, personal upheaval is accompanied by other problems, like substance abuse or self-harm. Stresses of all these kinds characteristically exacerbate each other and interact in extremely convoluted pathways. While diagnostic classifications systems such as the DSM-IV have been developed, there remains a significant and worrying degree of co-morbidity between many of the categories employed (Blashfield & Fuller, 1996; Clark, Watson & Reynolds, 1995).

Given these complexities, occasionally problems arise that prove insurmountable. The fate of those citizens whose misfortune it is to be beset by multiple problems is that they have to be seen by representatives of numerous agencies. A not uncommon consequence, to repeat a time-worn cliché, is for them to "fall through the net". To be the responsibility of many personnel can result in being the responsibility of none; such clients are at risk of becoming the people that "nobody owns" (Prins, 1993a).

Research and Knowledge-base

The void between legal, medical and social sciences is not an easy space in which to conduct research, with the consequence that the knowledge-base supporting the work of practitioners is often less firm than elsewhere. This originates in part from the numbers of variables to be taken into account when carrying out a study and obtaining meaningful results. Furthermore, the issues to be addressed do not easily lend themselves to experimental study in laboratory settings. While knowledge gained from such work can be of immense value for certain purposes, it leaves a gap to be bridged in deploying its findings to the explanation of occurrences in more intricate "real-world" settings.

Another factor is the legal status of the individuals whom we hope might participate in research. With regard to most health-related interventions, there is a familiar issue of "compliance" or "adherence": the degree to which the sufferer will consistently follow a course of action prescribed or suggested by a clinician.

Meichenbaum and Turk (1987) reviewed evidence concerning the extent to which individuals, despite clear health risks, will deviate from treatment regimens. For example, one study cited concerned individuals suffering from glaucoma, who were told that failure to use prescribed eye drops three times a day might result in blindness. Despite this information, an astonishing 58% did not administer the drops. Such difficulties are sharper still given the added complication of anti-social behaviour and the involvement of the law. Where there is a need for co-ercion or application of statutory procedures to maintain a hold on a recalcitrant consumer of medical or social services, the resultant obstacles may be very diffi-cult to manage and require a careful and skilled response.

Organisation of Services

Current provision of public services is still arranged in terms of massive and bureaucratic agencies each with its own specific remit: health, social services or criminal justice, not to mention education, employment or housing. These reflect apparently self-evident categories of human need and have proved administra-tively convenient for provision of mainstream services. Their evolution into their present-day form is a result of numerous historical conditions, political forces and other factors. Regrettably, some inertia is to be expected when agencies charged with particular tasks are faced with demands that do not neatly fit into their exist-ing modes of responding to need. With reference to mentally disordered offend-ers, the Butler Committee identified a "... lack of satisfactory co-ordination of the various services involved", such that they "... continued largely to work independently, each to some extent following its own objectives and limiting its responsibilities and involvement according to its own judgment" (Home Office & Department of Health and Social Security, 1975, p. 29). While recent years have seen the development of some excellent examples of multi-agency collaboration, there are many residual problems in this area. For example, despite significant improvements in resources for psychiatric assessments to be conducted at police stations, such provision is unevenly spread and facilities for diversion and com-munity care remain much more limited (Cavadino, 1999).

Divergent Perspectives

Associated with current patterns of service provision, traditional training courses in most vocational fields were intensively and narrowly focused solely on pro-ducing individuals capable of working in those fields. The arrival of cross-disciplinary training, for example the introduction of behavioural sciences teaching in medical schools, or of social sciences in nurse education, is still a com-paratively recent innovation.

When dealing with persons whose problems and predicaments are multi-faceted, there are many points at which misunderstandings can arise due to differences in perspective between the various professional groups who have a stake-holding in the "vacuum" mentioned earlier. As a consequence of all of these pressures, perhaps the most pervasive and insidious source of difficulty is the divergent ways in which individuals working for separate agencies, or with diverse backgrounds, *think* about the work they are doing. Equally problematic perhaps is the question of what they assume others think: the attributions they have concerning the ethos, the fundamental values and attitudes, of other professional groups. As is suggested in Chapter 5, it is probably not too implausible to imagine that practitioners with respective backgrounds in, for example, the fields of medicine and law, are like citizens of different countries speaking mutually unintelligible languages.

INTEGRATING PERSPECTIVES

For a combination of reasons, a consensus has emerged concerning the importance of multi-disciplinary working in this rather poorly delineated field at the borders of legal, medical and social work practice. A central concern of this book is with those client groups who become enmeshed at the juncture of these three systems of services. With respect to mentally disordered offenders, who are caught in the middle of several agencies' attempts to provide for them, this issue has been thought to be in need of remedy with some urgency.

The need for new departures in professional practice was identified over two decades ago by the Butler Committee (Home Office & Department of Health and Social Security, 1975) which reviewed services for this client group. Its report drew attention to steps that could be taken to "improve mutual understanding" (p. 252), to improve liaison and working relationships, and to establish inter-disciplinary working groups, and promote ". . . officially recognised co-ordination" (p. 261). At a later stage, the Reed Committee (Department of Health & Home Office, 1992) called for significant expansion in the numbers of staff in all of the professions working in this area. But it also affirmed the importance of ". . . a growing commonality of interests between the various professions" that could lead to ". . . greater flexibility and versatility, and a better understanding of complementary interests and skills" (1992, p. 26).

These recommendations accepted, it remains the case that staff of many professional groups adjoining this area are acutely aware of their own limitations when addressing some of the difficulties likely to arise. For example, surveys conducted in the early 1990s indicated that between 12% and 18% of the clients who constitute the caseloads of probation officers have mental health problems (Hudson, Cullen & Roberts, 1993; Roberts, Hudson & Cullen, 1995). On the basis of the evidence they collected, these authors concluded that there were ". . . large gaps in the education and training of probation officers in regard to many topics relating to mentally disordered offenders" (Roberts, Hudson & Cullen, 1995, p. 82). Unfortunately, a more recent review of this position has suggested that very little has altered in the intervening years, with "considerable deficiencies" still evident in training needs in this area (Vaughan, Kelly & Pullen, 1999, p. 110).

Clearly, members of separate disciplines need to be able to talk to each other, and to be able to understand each other, on a regular, everyday basis. This applies to both communication and liaison which may be relatively brief, circumscribed and casual, with reference to a specific case or decision; and to multi-disciplinary working, which represents a higher level of collaboration in terms of how services are designed and delivered. But whatever the extent of such contact, the need for professionals to grasp each other's approach at a theoretical, conceptual level has perhaps been all too often underestimated.

There are acknowledged advantages in adopting this approach to practice. As discussed above, clients' problems and personalities are multi-faceted. No single profession can cater for the multiplicity of their needs. Further, no single theory or perspective that is currently available is in itself sufficient to explain the phenomena or the problems under consideration. While some division of labour is essential to ensure that services work, by its very nature it can also be an encumbrance. The Reed Committee did not anticipate or recommend that professional boundaries should disappear, but did recognise there were common training needs for all the staff groups in this field. This was thought to apply both to residential settings and community-based services.

Large-scale reviews of legal frameworks or of service provision typified by the Butler or Reed reports, involving representatives of different government departments and area services, have found that there is a need for greater contact and understanding between professional groups. These needs have been heightened by a series of well-publicised catastrophes which have kept the issue of care and management of mentally disordered offenders at the centre of public attention. Evidence accumulated some years ago concerning the damage done by institutional life, as well as its considerable cost, led to the community care initiatives of recent decades, and the massive transfer of clients from hospital to "outpatient" services.

Following a number of scandals concerning maltreatment of hospital patients, it used to be thought that this was the prime focus of public anxiety in relation to mental health. However, it has recently been suggested that following calamitous incidents involving homicides committed by individuals with serious mental disorders, the focus of public concern has shifted to the risks accompanying community care (Crichton & Sheppard, 1996). In the wake of each of such incidents, formal inquiries were launched into why the events had occurred. Indeed subsequent to the inquiry into the murder of Jonathan Zito by Christopher Clunis in 1992 (Ritchie, Dick & Lingham, 1994), the conduct of such inquiries was placed on a mandatory footing by the Department of Health.

Stalwart efforts have been made to aggregate the evidence from this detailed scrutiny of separate events, and to extract as much as possible that may be learned from the process (Boyd, 1996; Peay, 1996). The Royal College of Psychiatrists assembled confidential information concerning 39 cases of homicide and 240 cases of suicide involving persons who had been seen by psychiatric services.

"It is striking that problems in communication feature so frequently in the cases reported to us" (Boyd, 1996, p. 56). "Those employed in each agency need information about working practices and liaison with other agencies" (ibid., p. 59). More recently, Reith (1998) collated details of the recommendations of 28 published inquiries, in an attempt to distil the most frequently pinpointed problems that might have contributed to the events, and with a view to avoiding their recurrence. One key point reiterated across many of the investigations was again that of communications between agencies. "One of the most consistent findings of virtually every inquiry into the failings and tragedies of our care for the severely mentally ill in the community is the need to improve communication, both within and between agencies and with families and carers" (Reith, 1998, p. 200).

It has, however, also been suggested that there is little more that can be learned from the relentless round of inquiries. One contention is that there might be a more useful higher-level exercise to be conducted, through auditing or monitoring the impact of inquiries (Eastman, 1996). It has additionally been pointed out that many practitioners and others, whether or not directly involved in an inquiry, have been overwhelmed by "inquiry fatigue" (or *inquiryitis*; Fallon, 1999).

Meanwhile, the secure hospitals have not escaped recurrent problems of their own, with major inquiries into maltreatment of patients, and other problems, during the 1990s (Blom-Cooper, 1992; Prins, 1993b; Fallon, 1999). Many of the problems identified by the most recent of these inquiries were regarded as structurally entrenched, with the "system" being held to be the "biggest villain of the piece" (Fallon, *Executive Summary*, p. 4). The structure of institutional psychiatric services in the UK has remained a controversial and politically sensitive issue. Debates concerning the form they should take are conducted in a highly charged atmosphere, in which some are calling for an abolition, or at least a sizeable reduction, of the "special" high-security hospital services while others have called for reform (Richman & Mason, 1992).

Over recent years, then, there has been a steady increase in the extent to which individuals trained in any of these adjacent fields have been enjoined to expand their horizons and adopt multi-disciplinary perspectives. It has become important, in addition, to provide explanatory frameworks grounded in evidence-based practice within their own particular professional areas. In any case, the need for individuals to work, and liaise, with colleagues from different professional backgrounds has increased substantially over recent years. This has highlighted certain limitations of confining oneself to working within traditional boundaries and knowledge-bases. It can also give rise to some perplexing ethical questions (Grisso & Appelbaum, 1992; McGuire, 1997). Given this, the familiar single discipline texts approaching the central questions in any given discipline appear progressively less adequate.

Thus, the purpose of this book is to address this deficit by focusing upon the interfaces, interconnections, and overlaps of the three public service systems and their related knowledge-bases and fields of research. This will hopefully consolidate existing bodies of research evidence from within these fields and establish the major practical lessons that can be drawn from them. Equally important, the chapters presented here are designed to link the material together in the context of legal and clinical experience to address the most urgent practical issues faced by practitioners on the many sides of what is now loosely called the "forensic" arena.

How can such an arena be accurately depicted? There is no definition that is adequate for this purpose, but in approaching it the present volume seeks to provide accounts of ongoing interconnections between separate "segments" of the arena as a whole. There are, for example, two-way processes of cross-fertilisation between psychology and law (Bull & Carson, 1995), psychiatry and law, or criminology and social work. Some of them are addressed explicitly in the chapters which follow. But there are also ways in which such interplay can take place in several directions, or on multiple levels, simultaneously. Figure 1.1 shows some of the primary interconnections to be considered in this field or meeting-place, in respect of some of which there is a relevant chapter in this volume. This also portrays, in an approximate sense, the nodes of activity and successive loci of decisions to be made concerning individuals who enter and are "processed" by the criminal justice and mental health systems of services. Were all the intricacies and potential interconnections within such a web to be shown, it could be rendered indecipherable. The figure displays only the most important linkages.

This conceptual scheme allows us to configure, with a little more fidelity, what might be considered to be an emerging study in its own right. It is addressed to the patterns of interplay between the "bodies of knowledge" represented in Figure 1.1, many of which are also allied with particular forms of professional practice. Our central contention is that there are enormous advantages to those working in any of these areas to have some acquaintance with each of the others.

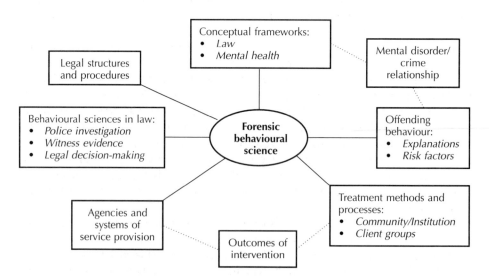

Figure 1.1   Principal interconnections between fields of research and practice

This is not a plea for a new breed of polymaths. However, it is to suggest that practitioners are better able to make use of their own perspectives and competencies when they have a broader grasp of current knowledge concerning factors which influence the progress of individuals through different phases of the interlocking networks of legal, mental health and social service systems.

HISTORICAL AND POLITICAL CONTEXTS

The current position and modes of functioning of these systems cannot be understood without also considering their historical and political contexts (Pilgrim & Rogers, 1993). Professional groups vary significantly in their relative status and power. The legal and medical professions remain in a dominant position with regard to decision-making in many services. The links between psychiatry and law are long established: however, the nature of their relationship fluctuates. Both psychiatry and law have historical origins and endorse value systems that are rooted in benevolence and compassion, in the care of the sick and in the restoration of justice (Forshaw & Rollin, 1990). Yet both have also been described as sharing a more malevolent underlying purpose grounded in a "will to power" (Mason & Mercer, 1996). To some extent their relationship has been a symbiotic one: resulting partly in a medicalisation of offending behaviour, in parallel with a criminalisation of mental illness. Part of this struggle is also carried on through the means by which different types of behaviour are represented and relevant knowledge is promulgated in the furtherance of professional interests.

Prior to the nineteenth century, little attention was paid to the state of an offender's mental health, with the more traditional focus being paid to rational and proportional punishment based on the crime and its relation to social harm (Young, 1981). However, with the rise of "scientific" criminology there was a shift in focus away from the crime as an act towards the criminal as an actor. Criminal anthropologists sought scientific respectability through such procedures as the body mapping of "criminal types". Although such crude reductionism has been largely discredited, it remains influential, albeit cast within a more sophisticated framework, in some strands of contemporary criminology. Throughout the twentieth century the expansion of criminological theories to explain offending behaviour has been wide and varied, and has drawn upon both the social and the biological sciences. Medically oriented explanations of serious anti-social behaviour have remained a powerful force, leading to the augmentation of professional territory and a growth in "experts" in ever-narrower specialisms.

Conversely, at repeated intervals throughout history, distinct stereotypical views have been held of those afflicted with mental disorder. They have variously been perceived as impulsive, violent and dangerous. This often led to unwarranted responses from the public that resulted in summary punishments, or social exclusion through incarceration. In more subtle forms this continues to the present day irrespective of evidence pointing to the fact that the majority of persons suffering with mental illnesses do not constitute a danger to others. For example, recent research has shown that the annual proportionate contribution to homicides by individuals suffering from mental disorders has declined steadily (at an average of 3% per annum) over the past four decades (Taylor & Gunn, 1999). Nevertheless, there has been no shortage of forensic "expertise" as professionals claim knowledge of this territory, while sensationalist media coverage of some cases continues to criminalise the mentally ill in terms of derangement and dangerousness (Philo, 1996).

While the two long-standing professional power-bases, law and psychiatry, have been traditionally viewed as engaged in a battle for territorial gains over each other, with the mentally disordered offender as the currency in that struggle, this perspective now needs to be re-appraised. Since the advent of the 1983 Mental Health Act (England and Wales; Mental Health (Scotland) Act 1984), legislation required the Responsible Medical Officer to make explicit the treatment plan offered to compulsorily detained patients. It was required that this should, at the very least, prevent a deterioration in the individual's condition: this gave the law a stronger basis for governing disposal of offenders at court. By setting down, through a legislative framework, parameters of this kind, a benchmark is provided for subsequent evaluation of the effectiveness of proposed interventions. Furthermore, the onus on the psychiatric profession to establish treatment plans has ensured a closer involvement with other disciplines in contributing to such programmes. This produced an added impetus towards working from a multi-disciplinary starting-point.

In the last decade this has resulted in a closer relationship developing, not only between professional groups working on all sides of the criminal justice, mental health and social service domains, but also across these systems. At present, mental health professionals may often be found working closely with police, courts and prisons. More recently, within the legal profession itself, there has been some dismay concerning the relationship between the law and those who are made subject to it, resulting, for example, in the emergence of perspectives such as therapeutic jurisprudence (discussed in Chapter 2; and see McGuire, 2000). This has made the defining boundaries between professional territories gradually less clearly demarcated. It is our contention that practitioners in any given domain need to develop greater appreciation of the work of colleagues in other disciplines while simultaneously having a clearer vision concerning the boundaries of their own.

STRUCTURE OF THE BOOK

The book is divided into two parts. Part I consists of six chapters dealing with fundamental aspects of legal frameworks and processes, and the application of behavioural sciences to aspects of their operation. In Chapter 2 David Carson outlines some fundamental features of legal structures and legal processes. Some key observations are made concerning modes of thinking employed in legal decision-making with specific reference to the nature and usage of evidence. He also highlights nodal points in which there is a demonstrable and increasing need for greater *rapprochement* between behavioural scientists and legal practitioners. The chapter concludes with a discussion of legal and behavioural perspectives on risk assessment, and of the viewpoint of *therapeutic jurisprudence* as a set of principles for evaluating the impact of legal processes upon individuals.

The three chapters which follow focus on selected meeting-points between the components of the network set out earlier in Figure 1.1 (page 10). Nowhere is the expansion of forensic behavioural science more notable than in the relationship between psychology and policing. In Chapter 3 Peter Ainsworth discusses this relationship and emphasises a gradually growing interchange of research findings and practical applications. The fact that this chapter outlines the limitations, as well as the strengths, of psychology in police investigations suggests that the conjoint effort is steadily maturing.

The examination of factors affecting the reliability of witness evidence is another extensive and well-established area in which behavioural science research has yielded findings applicable to law. In Chapter 4 Amina Memon and Dan Wright deal with the substantial volume of work available in this area, which ranges from cognitive/information processing research to studies of child development and to the social-psychological research on interaction during the process of questioning. This chapter summarises the principal directions that this research has taken and outlines the key findings of critical importance in providing admissible evidence to courts of law.

In Chapter 5 Nigel Eastman deals with key psycho-legal questions and brings into stark relief the conflicting approaches and discourses employed by lawyers and mental scientists respectively. A central focus is how this often leads to confusion and misinterpretation of each other's concepts and interpretations; and upon circumstances in which this can lead to misapplication and ultimately injustice. Elucidating the precise points at which such misunderstandings occur, there is also discussion relating to how different constructs are interpreted and operated with reference to selected types of decisions made in courts of law.

The theme of decision-making in legal settings is further developed in Chapter 6 in which Jenny McEwan draws on the available research on factors influencing legal decisions, with a particular focus on the courtroom and on the deliberations of juries. The chapter deals primarily with selected aspects of judicial decision-making, and explores the implications of studies of cognitive heuristics for how information is collected and employed for legal decision-making. There is also a discussion of different factors influencing the distinction between criminal justice and mental health "disposals" by courts. Finally, the implications of psychologically based research for an understanding of sentencing decisions are set out.

In the second part of the book, attention turns to a series of interconnected areas of research and practice. In Chapter 7 James McGuire focuses on the varieties of theories that are available to explain offending behaviour, noting first that the occurrence of acts of crime cannot be understood from any single theoretical perspective: most have "multi-factorial" causes. The field of criminology has been described as over-supplied with theoretical models. The author reviews a number of integrated accounts of the occurrence of acts of crime drawing on concepts from several levels of explanation.

The relationship between psychopathology and anti-social behaviour is the focus of Chapter 8 and consists of a review of the principal models which have been offered as explanatory frameworks of the interrelationship of psychosis and the occurrence of anti-social behaviour. Aisling O'Kane and Richard Bentall approach this first from an epidemiological standpoint, examining the prevalence of serious mental health problems in the offender population, and of anti-social behaviour among clients of mental health services. Secondly, following a litera-ture review they describe a model for the assessment and formulation of the func-tional interconnectedness of problems in the individual case.

In Chapter 9 Ron Blackburn deals with the evasive issue of risk assessment and prediction, which is now seen as a fundamental activity of professionals, and teams, in the interlinked fields of law, mental health and social work. Assessing the extent to which individuals pose a risk of serious harm to themselves or to others is an undertaking which is both practically difficult and riven with ethical consequences. This chapter provides an account of the successive generations of research which can be delineated in this area and outlines the relative strengths and limitations of statistical and clinical prediction, and of the assessment of static and dynamic risk factors. In addition, a set of guidelines is presented for system-atic assessment and communication of risk information, based upon which defen-sible practice by individuals, and policies in support of it, can be established within the relevant service agents.

David Heywood (Chapter 10) discusses the systems and agencies involved in forensic psychiatry and allied services. He outlines the referral routes into foren-sic mental health services and discusses the interface between accurate clinical assessments and the availability of resources, the lack of which can create diffi-culties for risk management strategies. The chapter deals with the mechanisms of disposal through criminal justice routes or transfer to mental health services, and with factors relating to the decisions regarding psychiatric referral including shortage of beds and accurate assessments of security requirements. He illus-trates the issues which arise by outlining six case scenarios relating to crucial decision-points in the movement of individuals between different components of these "systems".

Chapter 11 discusses contemporary moves to manage mentally disordered offenders in community settings despite a number of serious violent incidents in recent years leading to public inquiries, as outlined earlier in this chapter. Tom Mason outlines the main forms of community-based mental health treatment services for mentally disordered offenders and the multiple agencies that are involved, at one level or another, in case management. Despite the growth in community approaches it is apparent that resources are an ever-dwindling com-modity and this chapter outlines some approaches to managing patients in the community using case management, and both assertive and passive outreach programmes, and goes on to suggest that more focus ought to be paid to issues of desistance.

Next, Julie Hird in Chapter 12 addresses the issue of treatment of sexual aggression. Individuals who have committed sexual assaults are commonly regarded as among the most difficult client groups to work with and with whom to achieve effective outcomes. In this chapter the author outlines the available research on the treatment of adolescents and adults found guilty of sexual assaults. The chapter then provides an integrative, research-based theoretical account of the occurrence of sexual aggression which is followed by a systematic account of treatment–outcome research based in institutional and community settings respectively.

Adrian Grounds, in Chapter 13, outlines the range of treatment approaches in use in current work—both in institutions and in the community—with mentally disordered offenders. First, the relationship between different models of serious mental disorder is considered and a multi-faceted approach is adopted based on case formulation in which the relative importance of biological, psychological and social factors are assessed jointly in the individual case by multi-disciplinary mental health teams. Second, the author sets out the implications of this for the range of treatment options available, and their application and management is discussed. This entails a specification of what should be provided if services are to be comprehensive and effective, drawing on available evidence and applying procedures based on combining this with experience of service management.

Although, within the framework of involuntary detention and coercive treatment, there are many issues relating to ethics and civil rights, and others relating to broader professional concerns, it is ultimately the extent of further harm and re-offending rates by which services will be judged (Blackburn, 1990; Eastman, 1993). In the final chapter, James McGuire, Tom Mason and Aisling O'Kane address the question of how effective services can become in accomplishing such a goal. As outcome data with a direct bearing on this is in limited supply, this involves a process of "triangulation" using other fields of evidence, including those from mental health treatments, and reduction of offender recidivism.

REFERENCES

Blackburn, R. (1990) Treatment of the psychopathic offender. In K. Howells and C.R. Hollin (Eds) *Clinical Approaches to Violence.* Chichester: John Wiley.

Blashfield, R.K. & Fuller, A.K. (1996) Predicting the DSM-V. *Journal of Nervous and Mental Disease*, **184**, 4–7.

Blom-Cooper, L. (1992) *Report of the Committee of Inquiry into Complaints about Ashworth Hospital.* Cm 2028. London: HMSO.

Boyd, W. (Ed.) (1996) *Report of the Confidential Inquiry into Homicides and Suicides by Mentally Ill People.* London: Royal College of Psychiatrists.

Bull, R. & Carson, D. (Eds) (1995) *Handbook of Psychology in Legal Contexts.* Chichester: John Wiley & Sons.

Cavadino, P. (1999) Diverting mentally disordered offenders from custody. In D. Webb & R. Harris (Eds) *Mentally Disordered Offenders: Managing People Nobody Owns.* London and New York: Routledge.

Clark, L.A., Watson, D. & Reynolds, S. (1995) Diagnosis and classification of psychopathology: Challenges to the current system and future directions. *Annual Review of Psychology*, **46**, 121–153.

Crichton, J. & Sheppard, D. (1996) Psychiatric inquiries: Learning the lessons. In J. Peay (Ed.) *Inquiries after Homicide*. London: Duckworth.

Department of Health & Home Office (1992) *Review of Health and Social Services for Mentally Disordered Offenders and Others Requiring Similar Services* (The Reed Report). Cm. 2088. London: HMSO.

Eastman, N.L.G. (1993) Forensic psychiatric services in Britain: A current review. *International Journal of Law and Psychiatry*, **16**, 1–26.

Eastman, N. (1996) Towards an audit of inquiries: Enquiry not inquiries. In J. Peay (Ed.) *Inquiries after Homicide*. London: Duckworth.

Fallon, P. (1999) *Report of the Committee of Inquiry into the Personality Disorder Unit, Ashworth Special Hospital*. Cm. 4195. London: The Stationery Office.

Forshaw, D. & Rollin, H. (1990) The history of forensic psychiatry in England. In R. Bluglass & P. Bowden (Eds) *Principles and Practice of Forensic Psychiatry*. London: Churchill Livingstone.

Grisso, T. & Appelbaum, P.S. (1992) Is it unethical to offer predictions of future violence? *Law and Human Behavior*, **16**, 621–633.

Hedges, L.V. (1987) How hard is hard science, how soft is soft science? The empirical cumulativeness of research. *American Psychologist*, **42**, 443–455.

Home Office & Department of Health and Social Security (1975) *Report of the Committee on Mentally Abnormal Offenders* (The Butler Report). Cmnd. 6244. London: HMSO.

Hudson, B.L., Cullen, R. & Roberts, C. (1993) *Training for Work with Mentally Disordered Offenders*. London: Central Council for Education and Training in Social Work.

Mason, T. & Mercer, D. (1996) Forensic psychiatric nursing: visions of social control. *Australian and New Zealand Journal of Mental Health Nursing*, **5**, 153–162.

McGuire, J. (1997) Ethical dilemmas in forensic clinical psychology. *Legal and Criminological Psychology*, **2**, 177–192.

McGuire, J. (2000) Can the criminal law ever be therapeutic? *Behavioral Sciences and the Law*, **18**, in press.

Meichenbaum, D. & Turk, D.C. (1987) *Facilitating Treatment Adherence: A Practitioner's Guidebook*. New York, NY: Plenum Press.

Peay, J. (Ed.) (1996) *Inquiries after Homicide*. London: Duckworth.

Philo, G. (1996) *Media and Mental Distress*. London: Longman.

Pilgrim, D. & Rogers, A. (1993) *A Sociology of Mental Health and Illness*. Buckingham: Open University Press.

Prins, H. (1993a) Offending patients: The people nobody owns. In W. Watson & A. Grounds (Eds) *The Mentally Disordered Offender in an Era of Community Care*. Cambridge: Cambridge University Press.

Prins, H. (1993b) *Report of the Committee of Inquiry into the Death in Broadmoor Hospital of Orville Blackwood and a Review of the Death of Two Other Afro-Caribbean Patients: "Big, Black and Dangerous?"* London: Special Hospitals Service Authority.

Reith, M. (1998) *Community Care Tragedies: A Practice Guide to Mental Health Inquiries*. Birmingham: Venture Press.

Richman, J. & Mason, T. (1992) Quo vadis the special hospitals? In S. Scott, G. Williams, S. Platt & H. Thomas (Eds) *Private Risks and Public Dangers*. Aldershot: Avebury.

Ritchie, J., Dick, D. & Lingham, R. (1994) *The Report of the Inquiry into the Care and Treatment of Christopher Clunis*. London: HMSO.

Roberts, C., Hudson, B.L. & Cullen, R. (1995) The supervision of mentally disordered offenders: The work of probation officers and their relationship with psychiatrists in England and Wales. *Criminal Behaviour and Mental Health*, **5**, 75–84.

Taylor, P.J. & Gunn, J. (1999) Homicides by people with mental illness: myth and reality. *British Journal of Psychiatry*, **174**, 9–14.

Vaughan, P., Kelly, M. & Pullen, N. (1999) Psychiatric support to mentally disordered offenders within the prison system. *Probation Journal*, **46**, 106–112.

Young, J. (1981) Thinking seriously about crime: Some models of criminology. In M. Fitzgerald, G. McLennan & J. Pawson (Eds) *Crime and Society: Readings in History and Theory.* London: Routledge & Kegan Paul.

Chapter 2

The Legal Context: Obstacle or Opportunity?

David Carson
Faculty of Law, University of Southampton, UK

WHY?

Why are you reading this chapter? What are your expectations of it? Are you and I, reader and writer, about to frustrate each other?

Perhaps you expect an authoritative, clear, explanatory and yet concise introduction to the law and the legal system, at least as it affects people whose behaviour may be deemed criminal. Given that this is the first substantive legal chapter in this book, that would not be surprising, but it would be foolhardy. Nobody could achieve all that here. There is so much to describe and discuss—without misrepresentation—about laws and legal systems, even if we were only parochially concerned with England and Wales.

Perhaps you expect something that provides a framework, foundation or context, for the rest of the book. Well, I will try to do that, with appropriate equivocations, but given that a major rationale for the existence of this book is the lack of connections between the disciplines and professions involved with forensic behavioural science, it will have to be partial and hesitant.

Perhaps you do *not* expect, or want, something critical, something that questions many of the basic assumptions about the law, the legal system, and how it relates to mental health, criminal justice and social work practitioners. But I want to do that!

Behaviour, Crime and Legal Processes: A Guide for Forensic Practitioners.
Edited by James McGuire, Tom Mason and Aisling O'Kane.
© 2000 John Wiley & Sons Ltd.

CRITICAL PERSPECTIVES

This book was devised to inform and to facilitate inter-disciplinary studies and inter-professional communication. It grew out of increasing contact and interaction between the various disciplines and professions involved in analysing and responding to people with inappropriate or unacceptable behaviour. But those interactions and contacts, between disciplines and services, are often perceived as problematic. Co-operation and understanding are not optimal. The law is involved. It prescribes the limits of what professionals may do. It declares the responsibilities, and protects the rights, of the offenders and patients in question. An understanding of those laws will help professionals to be better technicians. They will be better able to work the system. It does not follow, however, that they would understand the law or the system, let alone have an overview of, perspective on, or insight into, how it might be developed. Also, the law is an ever-changing beast with law reform regularly on the agenda.

We all may have to be deferential in court. That is one of the rules and practices designed to demonstrate respect and encourage order. But it does not follow that we have to be intellectually deferential, beyond the canons of fair comment and rational argument. The law and the courts are certainly central to the themes of this book, but their assumptions and approaches are often radically different from those of other disciplines and institutions. Because they are courts, and because they declare and legitimate what is to happen, the appropriateness of their assumptions and methods regularly go unchallenged. In due course other disciplines and professions adopt the same or similar assumptions, methods and often values. That may be necessary when those professions have to work with or in the courts, but it should not invade the way they think about, research and/or conceptualise issues in their discipline!

Take a key example. The first problem is that lawyers regularly dichotomise inappropriately (Aubert, 1963; Campbell, 1974). The second is that other disciplines fall in line with and accept this as if it were inevitable. It is not!

Dichotomising involves splitting concepts into either/or categories. Gender, for example, is regularly divided between male and female. That is quite a useful division, but is it accurate? Are we either male or female, as the law and most other authorities insist or assume? Are we one or the other? Are we somewhere along a continuum from one paradigm to another? Is the distinction drawn by reference to genitalia, reproductive function, sexual orientation or what? Or is there a bundle of characteristics (genetic, social or whatever) that we have in different distributions, at different times and of different degrees of relevance, for different purposes? Forget about those interesting questions—well, for the moment—and consider the following key questions. Is it correct to represent gender as either male or female? Has the dichotomous nature of this distinction been useful? Or has it been responsible (at least in part) for centuries of misery to people who have not felt able to fit easily into an either/or category? If someone does not fall into one or the other category is he or she (there is that dichotomy again), somehow, "wrong"?

Lawyers may (although not necessarily) have an excuse. There may be reasons why they have to categorise, pigeonhole, dichotomise people into one or the other. If "being married" requires that the people involved are of different genders then the courts have to decide, for example, whether birth gender can be surgically altered (*Corbett* v. *Corbett* [1971] pp. 83). The media may be expected to simplistically reproduce others' ideas and ways of thinking, especially if those ideas are considered interesting, authoritative or easy to reproduce, but do other disciplines, such as yours (actual or putative) have an excuse for adopting and enforcing such dichotomies anywhere outside of the courts?

It may take time and (will take) money but the courts will always give you an answer, a decision. None of this "may" or "more research is required" stuff! They will give you a decision; e.g. guilty or not guilty, competent or incompetent, mentally ill or not mentally ill. (Did you spot any cunningly inserted questionable dichotomises in that list?) That is because the legal system is a pragmatic enterprise. It may be concerned with some very complex, indeed ultimately unanswerable, questions and issues such as those about the nature of justice, but the courts, on a very real day-to-day basis, are concerned with making decisions (see Chapter 6 by McEwan). Those decisions are authoritative; they justify action, such as the detention or discharge of patients or offenders. They are binding—subject to provisions for appeal—and can influence similar subsequent cases. Everyone has to face up to this reality. We have to accept, for example, that the courts have decided that epilepsy is a "disease of the mind" for the purposes of the defence of insanity (*Sullivan* [1983] 2 All ER 673, and see Chapter 5 by Eastman). We have to agree that that is the law, at least in England and Wales, but we do not have to approve of that, or other decisions!

Introductory, context setting, chapters on the law can be useful. They have their purposes, but they can also encourage readers to switch off their critical faculties, for example, about whether the law and legal system described are apolitical. The reader's pragmatic need to know the content of the law can lead to him or her only wanting information which, when obtained, is received and regarded uncritically. He or she has to work with that law. Knowing and understanding it provides him or her with valuable employment skills. He or she must work with the law as it is, not as it—arguably—ought to be. Indeed if the law were changed there would be a need for retraining. That would involve time and other expenses. Knowledge of, and experience in, the former law and practice would become redundant. Employment relationships built upon differential degrees of knowledge and experience of the law would become unstable. So there are vested interests in stability, in maintenance of the status quo, in not challenging the law.

But the inter-disciplinary and intra-professional problems being experienced in this area of criminal justice may be, largely, caused by the law and the legal system! Greater understanding of the law, if accompanied by uncritical acceptance, would be an obstacle towards greater inter-disciplinary and intra-professional co-operation! A questioning approach to the law and legal system recognising what the law is, but also appreciating that it does not have to be like that, provides an opportunity to discover some of the structural causes of dissension, opposition and misunderstanding, that exists within this broad topic. That is how this chapter is designed to fit into this book.

LAW AND CHANGE: IT CAN BE REFORMED

The law is the law. Because that is a "simple fact" many assume that the law and politics are separate entities. To practice and to apply the law, such as when a judge interprets the law in a particular way, is (regularly assumed) to be apolitical, but to act to change the law is political. Or so it is often (dichotomously) assumed or argued. The intense conservatism implicit in such arguments is regularly overlooked. Lawyers are technicians; they know where to find the law and how to organise its application. An intensive effort is put into honing and intellectualising that knowledge-base and those skills. Consider a textbook on any area of law. Examine the wealth of ideas and the detail of the analyses in a book on jurisprudence (legal philosophy). These are highly sophisticated systems of knowledge and skills, particularly valued for their ability to separate analysis from sentiment, but (subject to a debate about whether there are universal or natural laws that cannot be abrogated) they are not immutable. They can be changed. Parliament, or the judges, can change the meaning of "murder". The jury is often declared to be an essential foundation, bulwark (or some other romantic term), of British justice. So how do other countries manage without them? Would our legal system fall to pieces if we did not have a jury? Obviously not. In fact the vast majority of criminal trials take place in the lower courts where there are no juries. Declaring, as judges have, that people with epilepsy have a "disease of the mind" makes no scientific sense and, given the value system within which we live, is insulting. How could the courts come to such a conclusion, and why has their decision not been changed?

The surgeon (deliberately not using a psychiatrist as an example) who removes a diseased appendix is being a technician in a much more neutral sense than is a lawyer involved in applying a law, say, obtaining an injunction in a case where there has been violence within a home. Lawyers are, necessarily, involved in reinforcing an existing system of laws and procedures even if they can challenge them, at the margins, in certain appeals. Lawyers are paid to discover and to apply the existing law rather than to agitate for change. Academic lawyers may not be so directly involved as they are paid, among other things, to think independently and to make the case for different laws and systems. But they too play major roles in intellectually justifying the whole process and socialising successive generations of law students into assumptions and expectations about the law and how "to do it".

The law can be changed. New legislation can replace old. It can also, in common law countries (such as England and Wales, the USA and the old Commonwealth), alter the precedents established by the judges, often over hundreds of years, on topics untouched by legislation. This case law covers a broad range of important topics including, in England and Wales, the definition of murder and negligence. Often there is extensive consultation before new legislation is presented to a parliament. In many countries there is a Law Commission, or similar body, charged with reviewing topics that are considered relatively apolitical. For example, in England and Wales the Law Commission produced several discussion papers on the law relating to decision-making by mentally disordered people before publishing its recommendations for a new statute (1995). The government has, since then, published a green paper (Lord Chancellor's Department, 1997) outlining its ideas. Presumably a Bill with explicit proposals will be brought forward in due course.

Although often dealing with topics central to the behavioural sciences, such as capacity and competence, these official law reform bodies tend to be dominated by lawyers. This can lead to assumptions being made, for example, that "capacity" is only or best tackled by a verbally stated cognitive, rather than demonstrable behavioural or developmental test. It can also lead to relevant research not being utilised and to the topic being treated as "lawyers' law". For example, lawyers are regularly, if not automatically, appointed to head inquiries into apparent service failures which have led to personal harm—say, a discharged patient has killed someone. It is not just that those inquiries demonstrate little knowledge of decision theory or research, but that other professions, for example systems engineers, might have additional, alternative, or better tools to give us more or different insights into the possible contributing factors. It is true that decisions and distinctions have to be made. Lines must be drawn, for example, about the degree of risk there must be before someone with a mental disorder can be detained, and lawyers can quickly become frustrated with other professions' reluctance to provide clear dichotomous answers and with their continual equivocations and emphasis upon what is not—rather than what is—known about research topics. But that does not justify assuming that the legal agenda or the legal approach is the only, or the most appropriate, method to adopt.

LAW AND PHILOSOPHY: INITIAL ATTITUDES

The pragmatic orientation of lawyers is also related to the epistemological assumptions that they regularly take for granted. Consider: what is law? To most lawyers the law is the body of rules and interpretations contained in the official sources. In common law countries this involves the statutes and other legislation passed by their parliaments and the precedents developed by their courts. So, to most law students, the law is found in books and libraries. But this is just one theory. Its appeal comes from the pragmatic imperatives. Judges and officials will listen to, because they consider themselves bound by, what is stated in legislation and precedent. It is true that there may be considerable ambiguity in how those rules are stated. Some judges are capable of considerable imagination in their interpretation and development of particular rules, and lawyers are skilled in knowing, or discovering, those rules, in working with concepts.

There are, however, other theories of what law is. Some, known as realists, insist that the law is that which judges and other officials actually do. They focus on the law in action, the decisions taken, officials' behaviour, on what happens rather than the verbal rationalisations. The first viewpoint, that law is what is stated in legal sources, can be associated with positivist epistemologies which tend to see facts as independent of perceptions. For them the law is a neutral, technical, apolitical enterprise. The judge declares the correct law that applies to the facts of the case. With this approach or assumption it is misguided, for example, to criticise lawyers for confusing witnesses during examination in court. That is their job, the law. Law reform is a separate, after-hours, if at all, exercise. But realists are more akin to interpretativists who stress that finding facts, including law, is a creative process. They emphasise the discretion that is available to judges and officials when deciding which facts to find, which rules to declare applicable and which rationalisation to develop. They emphasise the relative importance of fact-finding to law-finding, by courts. Law students are taught about rules, how to find them, apply them, distinguish them; but, if they become practitioners, the vast bulk of their work will involve investigating, discovering and resolving disputed facts. Even those who concentrate upon giving legal opinions will have to stress that they are assuming that the facts can be found to be as they have been told they are. It is a rare case—outside of law student examination papers—where the parties in dispute agree the facts and only differ over the law.

Is it a law if it is not enforced? The positivist answers "yes" if there is an official rule. Realists would understand the positivist's answer but believe that when predicting what legal officials will do it is critical to take "extra-legal" factors into account. The local police force, or its Chief Constable, may not be as anxious about enforcing prostitution law as, for example, his or her neighbour. One may be developing restorative justice schemes, such as encouraging family conferences, and a neighbour not. In preparing a plea in mitigation of a crime the wise lawyer will discover whether the individual judge has any personal values or views which might affect the punishment if he or she "says the wrong thing".

This sortie into legal theories of knowledge is not just (hopefully) interesting and good for the soul. It should give some insights into the past and future development of behavioural sciences and law. Take, as an example, the studies by Loftus and Palmer (1974) into how differently worded questions affected witnesses' perceptions of an incident. Although the research subjects had all seen the same film, of a vehicle accident, those asked questions involving words like "smashed" estimated higher vehicle speeds than those where words like 'hit' were used. Thus, if such studies can be generalised the lawyer can, in part, create the "facts" of an event for a witness. It is not a neutral process. Realists will be less shocked by such studies than positivists. Realism is an approach to law associated with the United States of America rather than the United Kingdom. Perhaps this explains, in part, the different degrees of interest, between the two countries, in the development of behavioural science and law studies.

Some "realists" go further. Critical theorists emphasise the interpretative and choice components of fact- and law-finding to such an extent that they dispute whether it has any objectivity or rationality. They perceive judges as choosing their findings of fact and law rather than simply applying a mechanistic process whereby facts and law, somehow, emerge. Some argue that the law is just one, among many, competing sets of moral and/or political rules. What makes the law distinctive is the state apparatus of courts and enforcement systems behind it (e.g. Kairys, 1982; Kelman, 1987).

Also, although usually from a rather different political starting-point, there are "natural law" theorists. Some truths are self-evident. There are basic rights over and beyond those donated by parliament or the judges. The source of the argument may be a religious belief or a rationalist induction; but, whatever the source, the conclusion is that some laws cannot be made or abolished by mere parliaments or judges. Similar sentiments lead to the creation and declaration of basic principles which can override incompatible laws—for example, the European Convention on Human Rights (which will become part of UK law when the Human Rights Act 1998 comes into force). This approach emphasises "rights".

This language of rights attracts many. It has political appeal. We want rights for ourselves and for some others—for example, prisoners, people with disabilities. They are perceived as a bulwark against inappropriate action by states and their officials, but they are often vague and expressed in ways that allow exceptions—for example, states may preventatively detain people who have committed no crimes, if they have a mental disorder. Still, they are popular with many lawyers and are seen as an important tool for protecting individuals, such as patients and prisoners, who otherwise lack political power. Some organisations seek to develop "test-case strategies". This involves finding individual cases that can be taken to the courts and litigated. The hope is that the courts will establish rights for the individuals involved, say high security prisoners, which can then be generalised to others. Critics of "rights" approaches are often simply sceptical about its success as a method.

LAW AND BEHAVIOURAL SCIENCES: THERAPEUTIC JURISPRUDENCE

Disillusionment with the rights approach to mental health law was and is a major factor behind the development of therapeutic jurisprudence. This is an inherently inter-disciplinary approach to the law. It is principled, reformist, reflective and practical. It originated in relation to mental health law in the USA. It has close affinities with Restorative Justice and related ideas, which are developing in the criminal justice system. It has a considerable potential for developing understanding and co-operation between the law and related disciplines concerned with the criminal justice and mental health services. And it has emerged at a—possibly—critical juncture because it offers an egalitarian relationship between the disciplines at a time when a master (law) to servant (behavioural sciences) relationship appears to have developed in the USA, and to be developing in Europe. Behavioural scientists increasingly focus on the current needs of lawyers and the legal system, rather than developing critiques and alternative models of how the law could influence human behaviour, make better decisions, and so on.

Being an expert witness in an individual trial appears to be valued more highly than being a consultant to a law reform project. That may not be too surprising. Being recognised as an expert in order to give evidence on a topic, and hopefully surviving a battle or words and wits with questioning lawyers in a courtroom, can be prestigious, if masochistic. But it is, at least, problematic. Being a witness, in particular cases, involves all the problems related to applying research and other insights gained from studies on a large population to a specific case. And it only directly affects that one case. Law reform will affect many more people and can have a much greater effect without those methodological problems. However there are structures for funding expert witnesses. Law reform requires sponsorship or largesse.

The basic thesis of therapeutic jurisprudence (TJ) is that, even despite the best of intentions of those who make them, laws can have negative as well as positive effects. Given the initial context of mental health law these effects were conceived of in terms of being therapeutic (tending to aid recovery or minimise ill effects) or anti-therapeutic (extending or intensifying adverse reactions). Hence the title. The basic value is that laws ought to have as many, and as great, therapeutic effects and as few anti-therapeutic effects, as is possible. TJ researchers scour behavioural science research and insights to conceive of ways in which therapeutic effects may be maximised and the anti-therapeutic minimised. That research has revealed a number of counter-intuitive insights and hypotheses that have been, or may be, empirically tested. For example, some adults with a mental disorder are adjudged as being incapable of making certain legal decisions, such as ability to consent to treatment. This is a considerable interference with their basic civil rights. Hence it tends to be assumed that a good law should make provision for regular review of, or appeal concerning, that finding of incapacity. However, Bruce Winick's research (1996) suggests that incapacity hearings will often have an anti-therapeutic effect. Citing several studies approaching the problem from different perspectives, he suggests that individuals generalise from any findings that they lack a specific competence. Thus a legal tribunal's finding that an individual lacks a specific capacity will be interpreted and understood, by the individual concerned, as a general incapacity. Instead of understanding that he or she has a limited disability, the individual tends to conclude that he or she lacks general competence. In due course it becomes self-fulfilling and the individual's incapacity is perceived as general.

Therapeutic jurisprudence emphasises the law in practice. It developed from the realist tradition. It emphasises that it is what legal officials (such as judges, the police and head-teachers in school exclusion cases) do which matters—is real law—rather than what is written in law books in a library. What happens to people diagnosed as having a psychopathic disorder may depend much more upon what services are available locally, and whether local psychiatrists regard it as 'treatable', than to any official interpretation of a verbal formulation in a statute. There is no written rule that prescribes that, in England and Wales, black people should, disproportionately, receive custodial sentences or women offenders should receive psychiatric disposals. Yet that is what happens, and those working with such clients need to anticipate it if they are going to predict legal decision-makers with any accuracy. A focus upon what happens in practice will draw in the contribution of practitioners as well as researchers.

Therapeutic jurisprudence, in terms of its product, is reformist rather than radical. It is about making laws and legal processes work better. It involves co-operation between the law and the behavioural sciences, rather than the social sciences such as sociology, politics and economics. It is not designed to challenge inequality in resources or power. It will not produce extra resources, although it may highlight inefficiencies in current services. Indeed it is sometimes criticised for being paternalistic, for assuming that what is proclaimed to be "therapeutic" is good. That is unfair! TJ recognises that whether something is therapeutic, or not, involves value judgements which may differ considerably between people and by time and place. It is concerned with what is therapeutic for the individual. It emphasises that legal rights must have priority over therapeutic goals.

In terms of publications it is noticeable that most of the running, in developing TJ ideas, critiques, and applications, has come from law academics in the USA (see Wexler & Winick, 1996). However, as law is a postgraduate subject in the USA, unlike in the UK, they were more likely to have an inter-disciplinary orientation and skills. A number of US judges have "come out" and argued that they were practising TJ for years before the phrase was coined. For instance, specialist courts have been established. Some judges have almost despaired at the legal system's apparent inability to reduce the amount of domestic violence in our societies. Thus they have developed schemes which, among other things, reduce dependence upon the victim's evidence and require convicted perpetrators to participate in, and graduate from, anger management classes. Drug treatment and specialist mental health courts have been established. There are important cultural and socialisation differences between these US—and they are a minority within that country, although growing—and British judges. The arrangements for their appointment as well as the socialisation, through which they process, are very different. The US judges are also taking advantage of the positions of power that they hold. They are able to order or cajole services into doing things, such as setting up schools for excluded children in court basements, which they could not do on their own. So, to a considerable extent, TJ is an overture from lawyers to other disciplines. It needs to become more co-operative in the sense of cross-disciplinary teams undertaking more general reviews of behavioural patterns and systemic needs rather than academic lawyers "picking off" specific topics. It also needs to tackle the methods and processes that the law uses, as well as substantive topics. However, within its limits, therapeutic jurisprudence has considerable potential for developing the relationships between law and other disciplines involved in the criminal and mental health systems.

LEGAL TECHNOLOGY

A major problem with the law, which contributes to its problems in co-operating with other disciplines, is its restricted "technology". It has an underdeveloped methodology. Take legislation as an example. Passing new laws through Parliament, with provision for extensive debate, is time-consuming and expensive. Alternative forms of "law" have had to be developed. "Secondary legislation" refers to statutory instruments, rules and similar which are made by a Government Minister under the powers provided by an earlier Act of Parliament. These become law if approved on a single vote, or are not disapproved within a certain time limit. But they produce the same problems of interpretation as full Acts. The goals, when drafting legislation, include comprehensiveness and certainty. All possibilities, and problems, should be predicted and provided for. Thus the basic pattern within a section of an Act, or even a group of sections, is for the statement of a broad rule (in the first section or subsection) followed by a list of exceptions and explanations.

Legal language is complex because the writer is trying to cover all relevant cases and not to generate problems such as a "loop-hole", but in trying to encompass all cases, and provide for all permutations, legislation regularly oversimplifies and thereby falsifies issues. This problem is all the more significant and serious for the frequency and ease with which it occurs. Relative concepts are compressed into categories. Distinctions are made and dividing lines are drawn where there are none in real life, if you stop to think about it. Lots of problems arise, for example, when legislation seeks to distinguish "day" and "night". It is not lawyers' fault or their incompetence. The problems are independent of the law. They arise from the problems inherent in communication and language. Try for example, to concoct a neat definition of "night" and "day" that will work for lots of different purposes, remembering that it gets dark at different times of the year and at different places in the world. Once you have sorted that out, move on to "criminal responsibility" and "mental illness".

So how are mental disorders to be defined in legislation? It is critical that they are, given the importance of not imposing detention, treatment and other special restrictions on people without clear authority and justification. Almost every (if not every) attempt to define a mental disorder creates problems. Imposing categorical limits upon a matter of degree is bound to be difficult, if not impossible. Perhaps we should look for alternative approaches. For example, a number of authorities have argued that personality disorder should be recognised as a trait (that is, a matter of degree) and that certain dimensions can be measured (Blackburn, 1993). Instead of a single cut-off point being verbally stated in a legal test, a composite assessment could be provided for. That, nevertheless, would still involve imposing a categorical distinction upon a matter of degree. However, we too often forget the context and purpose of legal definitions. For example, dangerousness is not just something "in" the patient, client or offender. It is interactive with, *inter alia*, the setting. There is greater danger when a paedophile is near children. So legal tests could require consideration of more factors so that whether something may lawfully be done to, say, a paedophile, such as detention, is determined after considering a range of factors, or dimensions, which practitioners could act upon, such as by reducing one element, to determine a particular response.

Legislation articulates rules. That did not surprise you! But the point is what it cannot do, or cannot do easily. It proscribes what may not be done or prescribes what must be done. It lays down boundary lines. Human society, however, calls out for so much more—for example, for goals, values, diversity, standards, encouragement, examples, models, direction. And legislation, at least as currently utilised, is very poor at providing for these other aids to social cohesion and behaviour shaping. Legislation (for example, a new mental health statute) is drafted with a view to the decisions that will be made in its light, but that is less than the tip of an iceberg in terms of the effect and influence that new law will have. Services will be designed around it, working methods altered, structures generated. New legislation regularly affects how people think and act, even on topics far removed from those that are likely ever to lead to litigation. But we tend not to think about those latent effects of legislation, however important they may be in practice. It is possible to draft legislation that includes statements of goals, aspiration and values, and provides examples of what is sought. (See the US Uniform Commercial Code as an example.) But it is unusual.

A more common response to the inadequacies of legislation is to develop a code of practice. For example, there is a code relating to the Mental Health Act 1983 (section 118). This seeks to 'fill in' the detail that it is considered would be inappropriate in legislation. Can patients, who have not been detained under the legislation, be placed in wards that are locked because other patients there are detained? But codes are not law. Their legal status and power depends upon the legislation that established them. That Act may specify that the code is to be taken into account by courts and tribunals, which is tantamount to making it law. However, the courts will retain discretion when deciding whether—and if so, how—the terms of the relevant code apply to the case before them. On many occasions, as with the Mental Health Act code mentioned, there is no provision to make it legally enforceable and yet many of those working in that service will consider themselves bound by, and not just guided by, the code.

Codes of practice can be generated and regenerated in a variety of different ways. The Act can specify a group of people who are to write a code for the government of the day to adopt. Thus there can be some participation in drafting and "ownership" of the document. And codes can be re-drafted, again involving a range of people in an exercise that is educational as well as participative, without all the complexities of the drafting of legislation. If behavioural scientists do not feel it appropriate to contribute to legislation, perhaps because their knowledge is not sufficiently "clear cut" for legal categorisation, they surely can contribute to codes! Here is an important way forward.

A similar idea to the code of practice linked to legislation, but importantly different, is the protocol or professional code of practice. A professional will break the standard of care, which is one of the key ingredients in the law of negligence, if he or she acts or fails to act (which includes decision-making) in a manner which would not be supported by a responsible body of co-professionals. Thus it is helpful to know what those standards of co-professionals are, in different circumstances. So a number of people are, sensibly and preventatively, preparing documents which articulate contemporary professional standards. These are variously described as protocols, codes, standards, risk policies. If someone is alleged to have been negligent, and to have breached the standard of care that applied, then this document can be cited to a court as evidence of what the current professional standards actually are. If the individual's behaviour clearly fell within those standards then it is unlikely that any lawyer would take the case as far as the courts. While the courts are not obliged to accept that any statement of standards in a code (or a similar document) is correct or that those standards are high enough, they are likely to do so in practice (*Bolitho* v. *City & Hackney Health Authority* [1997] AC 232).

The courts enforce professional standards through the law of negligence. That has a major impact upon how people behave. The fear of being found negligent by a court, or comparably criticised by a committee or tribunal of inquiry, can have a major impact upon how people behave. For example, many practitioners have been traumatised by the experience of an inquiry being held after, as is currently required in England and Wales, a mentally disordered patient has killed a member of the public. The law only requires that a professional person exercise a (not "the") standard of care and attention that would be adopted by a substantial body of their co-professionals. Yet tests and procedures not required by that standard, and therefore an unnecessary use of time and other resources, are often undertaken by people wrongly thinking that the law requires them. Sometimes decisions are delayed or avoided in an apparent, but mistaken, belief that that would prevent liability and criticism.

Despite all the time and money put into it, this legal system of enforcing standards through the law of negligence and/or inquiries is inefficient. It depends upon people suffering losses. But there can, and often are, breaches of good practice without anyone suffering a loss. A dangerous patient may have been wrongly discharged from hospital but not gone on to injure anyone. The legal system does not pick up on the error. The "loss" may be the absence of a service, but individuals are unlikely to know that that omission could count as a "loss" in their circumstances. It depends upon victims knowing that they may have a remedy and being able to afford the risk and other costs involved in litigation. Even if they succeed, the compensation they receive will be unrelated to the degree of negligence to which they were victims (excepting deductions for their contributory negligence). The amount of compensation paid depends upon the degree of loss—for example, the extent of the injuries and their consequences for the individual and any dependants, not upon how extensive was the degree of negligence. Legal approaches to causation are categorical, and relate to notions of responsibility rather to degree. The problems involved in attributing and distributing causation and responsibility tend to get glossed over so that a decision can be made and order maintained. There are similar issues or problems with regard to criminal responsibility.

CRIMINAL RESPONSIBILITY

In essence there are four key components to criminal responsibility, from a legal perspective. There must have been proscribed behaviour, in the common law world known as an *actus reus*. That must have been accompanied by a "mental state" known as the *mens rea*. The defendant must have caused the *actus reus*, and there must be an absence of any justifying or excusing circumstances within the defendant and/or surrounding his or her criticised behaviour. But, unsurprisingly, it is a little more complex.

The *actus reus* can be behaviour, such as having sexual intercourse which is not consented to, or a consequence, such as causing someone's death. Note that possessing a controlled drug would be regarded as behaviour, for these purposes. And the factor which determines whether it is proscribed can depend upon another person—for example, whether the sex is consented to, or the age of the partner. Obviously we would prefer it if the harm proscribed did not occur. Thus, it is also criminal to attempt to commit a crime. But at what stage may the police intervene and apprehend the "offenders"? A cut-off point, involving yet another dichotomy, has to be determined. If the individuals are arrested before this point then, generally, no crime will have been committed. If apprehended after this stage, and convicted, then they will be liable to the same punishment as if they had completed the offence. The test for the sufficiency of an attempt is, in England and Wales (Criminal Attempts Act 1981), that it was "more than merely preparatory" to the completion of the full offence. So the police are obliged, if they wish to secure a conviction, to allow a crime, which they know is being prepared, to progress to a remarkably late stage before they can risk intervening. Note the generally unchallenged legalistic assumption that it is appropriate to apply a conceptual distinction to these problems of both principle and practice. And that distinction relates to external behavioural steps rather than any degrees of commitment to completing the crime which the prosecution might be able to prove. The same rule, about whether a sufficient attempt has been made, applies to all crimes irrespective of the different kinds and degree of potential risk involved. The police should allow the possible armed robber to enter the shop or bank before arresting him or her for attempted robbery (*Campbell* [1991] Crim LR 268).

Conspiracy is a particular kind of crime. The *actus reus* is an agreement of two or more "relevant" people (i.e. not spouses or people, like young children, without criminal capacity) to commit a crime, or to do something lawful in an illegal manner. This is an alternative way in which the police can intervene before criminal harm is completed. The "behaviour" is an agreement that many might prefer to think of as a state of mind rather than as behaviour. In order to prove the conspiracy, however, there will need to be some evidence of the agreement which will involve reference to some behaviour, such as planned and co-ordinated behaviour.

Some believe, explicitly or implicitly, that the degree of criminality and/or seriousness of a crime can and/or should be determined by the consequences; by what happens. They emphasise external, or more objective, factors. Causing death is always more serious, and criminal, than causing grievous bodily harm which, in turn, is more serious than causing actual bodily harm. Stealing £1000 is more criminal than stealing £100. But the amount of harm or loss can be accidental. What would cause actual bodily harm to one person might cause grievous harm to another. Whether there are any knock-on consequences and their seriousness can be accidental in relation to the original act. How far away from a hospital was the victim and how good were the staff there? And yet we regularly conceptualise a major facet of criminal responsibility in this way.

Others argue that it is, or should be, the "mental attitude", or *mens rea* that determines the degree of criminality or seriousness of particular behaviour. They emphasise the actors' subjective attitudes towards the behaviour. But this approach also has problems. Many *mens rea,* utilised by the criminal law, do not relate to "mental" states at all. For example, a very useful model of *mens rea* categories regularly utilised when defining crimes is: intention, recklessness, negligence, blameless inadvertence. While "intention" clearly refers to a state of mind, "negligence" and "blameless inadvertence" do not. Yet they are *mens rea.* Someone can be found guilty of a crime, and punished, even when they have acted conscientiously to avoid causing harm. (Prosecutors might, however, decide it is not in the public interest to proceed.) Selling diseased meat is, at least in some countries, a crime irrespective of whether the vendor intended to do so, was reckless or negligent. These are known as "strict liability" crimes.

It seems perfectly appropriate that a driver who deliberately aims his or her car at a pedestrian should be regarded as more criminal, and his or her crime as more serious, than someone who is careless and thereby kills another. Also, the driver who kills someone who runs into the road in front of him or her, not giving sufficient time to stop the vehicle, should be regarded as blameless, provided it did not occur on a pedestrian crossing. The problems arise when we look more closely. It is, for example, murder when one person intentionally kills another. It is manslaughter when the killing is reckless or grossly negligent. So the difference between "intention" and "reckless" is critical. (In England and Wales judges must sentence murderers to life imprisonment but have total discretion with those they convict of manslaughter.) Legal approaches assume that there is a distinction. But is there?

You have despised someone for decades and have enjoyed contemplating his or her death before actually getting around to hitting him or her. Someone irritates you and you strike out at him or her. Both of those acts were intentional, in legal terms. Both are sufficient to make you the perpetrator of an offence. Any differences in the duration of the experience of intending, or in the "quality" of the experience of intending, are irrelevant. The category of intending was entered and that was sufficient. But does that accord with popular conceptions of "intention" and culpability? If the criminal law is to obtain popular support and/or if offenders are to accept and work on their responsibility for their behaviour, should not the meaning of "intention" have a more realistic legal definition? Here is an important area for greater collaboration between the law and the behavioural sciences. Psychological insights, and ways of conceptualising "mental attitudes" towards criminal conduct, need to be developed and offered to the legal system. For example, ways of examining and "measuring" the duration and quality of "intention" should be developed. For instance, to what extent did the individual focus on the consequences of the behaviour and choose the means towards achieving them? How much choice and control were exercised? How cognitive—contrasting degrees of learnt, socialised or automatic responses—was the experience of committing the crime? It is not just, it is submitted, that these considerations reflect real differences in perceptions of criminal responsibility but such information is important for those treating, or otherwise responding to, the criminal behaviour.

A useful and common distinction between "reckless" and "negligent" criminal behaviour is that, when being reckless, the individual is aware of the possibility of harm. Behaviour is "negligent" if reasonable people would regard it as such. It is "grossly negligent" if, because of the degree of harm or the degree of likelihood involved, reasonable people would have regarded it as entailing an obvious risk. "Recklessness" requires proof that the defendant had a degree of knowledge about the consequences. Thus lawyers refer to it as being a subjective *mens rea*. Negligence does not, so lawyers consider it to involve an objective test. So the presence or absence of some degree of knowledge is critical. It appears to be a neat, categorical, distinction. But is this distinction descriptive or normative?

To make the points through an example, consider the law of rape. At least within England and Wales the male perpetrator must be proved to have intended that the sex was without the victim's consent, or that he was reckless to that consent. If he believes that she or he consented, however unreasonable that belief might be (provided not intoxicated), he cannot be guilty. Did he contemplate that she or he might not be consenting? It appears to be a simple question of fact. And it is a very controversial rule. It appears easy for a man to simply claim that he believed the victim consented, although the jury may not agree, but it satisfies the legal approach which emphasises these dichotomous cognitive categories. Perhaps the behavioural sciences might produce alternative approaches to produce better rules or more rigorous methods of investigating what the individual's *mens rea* was at the time. Surely any *mens rea* which relates to concepts of risk, such as recklessness and negligence, could be informed by work on decision-making. What was the nature and quality of the man's decision that the victim was consenting? What systems did the company, accused of corporate manslaughter, have in place to avoid the kind of tragedy which occurred?

Whatever the *mens rea* involved, the defendant must have caused the *actus reus*, for example the death. This is the requirement for causation. The legal requirements, however, have more to do with notions of moral responsibility for the events than degrees of association or connection with them. You injure someone and that person is taken to hospital where he or she is negligently treated and a doctor switches off the life-support machinery, or refuses treatment in the full knowledge that the person will die. Did you kill that person? Yes. What if you began to sexually molest someone and she or he jumped out of a window, to her or his death? Yes, if that behaviour was reasonably foreseeable. So you can be a very minor factor in the end result and it could still have happened without your contribution, but you are deemed to have caused the result (although others could also be liable for their contributions). Lawyers are excused an understanding of statistics, let alone probability theories and scientific tests of causal connection.

And, for criminal responsibility to be complete there must be no defence. There may be factors about the defendant or the circumstances in which the crime was committed which excuse or reduce responsibility for the criminal conduct. If the behaviour is "justified" then no crime was committed. If there is a "defence" or "excuse" then there was a crime but responsibility is removed or reduced for the particular offender. If there is "mitigation" then there was a crime, and responsibility is in no way reduced, but there are circumstances, which are raised after the finding of guilt, which are thought to justify a reduced punishment.

Many of the recognised defences are little more than a denial of the existence of the *mens rea* for that offence, although the textbooks deal with them differently. For example, in England and Wales, intoxication, whether by drink and/or other drugs, is a defence to a "specific intent" crime. But specific intent crimes are those which can only be committed with intention. For example, murder can only be committed if the offender intended to kill or cause serious harm. If he or she was only reckless about it then there is no *mens rea* for murder, although there would be for manslaughter. Thus if the individual was intoxicated it cannot be murder, but it can be manslaughter as that does not require intention (recklessness will do). The real problem is the definition of "intoxication". If ever there was a good example of the problem with inappropriate dichotomies it is between "drunk" and "not drunk". The implicit model is that alcohol and other drugs remove the capacity to intend. Certainly there is a relationship between intoxication and cognitive ability but it is not that simplistic! Most drunks can still intend to order another round.

There are a number of defences that relate to features of the individual. The defence of insanity, based upon the nineteenth-century decision of *McNaughton* ((1843) 1 Car & Kir 130) provides a defence to all crimes. However, psychiatric disposals were, until recently in England and Wales, required and are still possible so it was used relatively rarely for the more serious offences. It required that the defendant prove (contrary to the normal rules of responsibility for proving) that: he or she was suffering from a "defect of reason" which was due to a "disease of the mind". This had to produce the result that he or she "did not know the nature and quality" of his or her acts or "did not know that they were wrong".

The definition of "disease of the mind" has always been legal rather than medical. It includes epilepsy, diabetes and sleepwalking, all because they have an effect upon, or relation to, the operation of the brain. And "defect of reason" is a cognitive test. Thus those with impulse control problems have not been able to utilise this defence.

Other defences, related to capacity, have had to be developed. In England and Wales there is the defence of diminished responsibility (Homicide Act 1957, section 2). This provides a defence where the offender has such an abnormality of the mind as substantially impairs a person's responsibility for his or her acts. While "abnormality of the mind" is broad, this defence only applies to charges of murder and only reduces the conviction to manslaughter. It encompasses behavioural as well as cognitive problems but requires psychiatrists to give evidence on questions of responsibility, in which they have no special skill or knowledge.

Some defences relate to features of the offending behaviour. Provocation, which also is only a defence reducing a murder charge to manslaughter, requires proof that the offender lost his or her self-control in circumstances in which a reasonable person, with the same relevant characteristics, would also have so acted. It has been condemned as sexist as men have regularly relied upon the defence when they respond with explosive and impulsive anger. But it has been unavailable to women whose response to prolonged provocation has been perceived to have been planned and cold-blooded because it did not occur during, or immediately after, a provocative act (even though they would have been assaulted had they responded as the law implicitly assumes is normal). Battered wives' syndrome, which tends to medicalise the problem and blame the woman, has been developed as a response to this legal problem. It has been admitted and utilised by certain courts despite its questionable scientific credentials.

Other defences concerning the capacity of the offender include infancy and infanticide. Defences concerning the criminal conduct include duress, necessity and mistake. If a defendant has made a mistake, provided (at least in England and Wales) it is not based upon intoxication, then he or she should be judged on the basis that the facts were as he or she thought them to be. For instance, if he or she anticipated being attacked and responded with violence, even though it was in fact a friendly overture, the mistake would enable self-defence to be argued. It does not matter how unreasonable the mistake was, provided it was made. Well that is the theory; a jury might think and act otherwise.

EVIDENCE: RULES AND PROBLEMS

You might expect the study or science of proof to be an integral part of a law degree. You would be wrong. The closest that a traditional law course would get to that would be courses on the laws of evidence and procedure. While changes are occurring with the work of Schum (e.g. 1994), Anderson and Twining (1991), and their importance has been dangerously under-appreciated, most evidence courses concern the rules about how lawyers may go about seeking to prove their clients' accounts of events. For example, there are rules about when, and on what topics, expert witnesses may express an opinion. For instance, they may not give evidence on matters which are within the ordinary knowledge of judges and jurors. But how do we know what that is, assure ourselves that they are correctly informed and deal with instances of counter-intuitive knowledge? Critical issues, such as what should be recognised as a scientific theory, have been tackled in some jurisdictions, such as the US (e.g. see *Daubert et al.* v. *Merrell Dow Pharmaceuticals, Inc.* 113 S.Ct. 2786 (1993) and *United States* v. *Shonubi* (1995), WL 472704 EDNY), but not in others, such as the UK.

In Germany, and some other countries, evidence about the credibility of particular witnesses—such as that derived from Statement Based Content Analysis (SBCA; for an introduction and further references see Memon, Vrij and Bull, 1998)—is not just permitted but regularly relied upon by the courts. But it is inadmissible in common law countries such as England and Wales because of a rule prohibiting evidence about the credibility of individual witnesses; witnesses must not interfere with the jury or judge's role of assessing the evidence. However, even if these sorts of questionable rules are not challenged and changed, there are alternative ways of getting experts' valuable information and knowledge before a court. For example, if a professional is satisfied, say after having applied SBCA, that a client is telling the truth (and does not confuse that with accuracy), then he or she could explain his or her conclusion to the lawyer who will be presenting the case in court. SBCA, as do many other forms of behavioural science analyses such as syndrome evidence, provides an intellectual rationalisation for behaviour which might otherwise be interpreted differently. Using these analyses the story, or evidence, becomes more comprehensible (to the extent that it does not, the theory should then be challenged). Thereafter the lawyer can use that explanation to help him or her to rationalise the witness's explanation to the court. For example, the witness may have used different language to describe an event. That can, very easily in courts, lead to suggestions that the witness is unclear or is changing his or her evidence. But the alternative insight, that truthful people will change the way in which they describe an event as they discover better words with which to do so, can help a jury and judge to believe that version.

If it is a criminal trial then, with very few exceptions, the prosecution side is obliged to prove their allegations beyond reasonable doubt. If it is a civil case then the party bringing the case, the claimant or plaintiff, must prove his or her version of events on a balance of probabilities. It is tempting to reduce these statements to statistical terms. For example, the civil claimant's version of events must be more than 50% believable. But to what do these figures refer? All the evidence, in a civil case, may be highly improbable, but the party with the better version is entitled to the decision. There are no baseline standards. In a criminal case, however, the defence lawyer can emphasise the existence of doubt. Theoretical doubt is insufficient. It must be reasonable doubt. What makes a doubt reasonable? Legal reasoning is so much more about persuasion rather than strict proof.

CRITICAL REFLECTION

This basically, is where this chapter began. Can the law and behavioural sciences, lawyers and the professions concerned with offenders and mentally disordered people, co-operate when their starting-points and methods are so different? The answer is "Yes", provided everyone is prepared to be critically reflective about their own professions and disciplines and about the others. "Yes" if we are prepared to seek progressively better ways of working together and give up on the myths of the attainability of perfect tests and distinctions verbally formulated. "Yes" if we have a practical focus on what does, and should, happen in practice. Understanding, predicting and shaping human behaviour, which is what the law and behavioural sciences have in common, is a practical enterprise. The future lies in being critically reflective about our mutual systems of thinking and working, not in uncritically using those systems and pretending that we are victims of others' assumptions and approaches and simply earning our daily bread.

REFERENCES

Anderson, T. & Twining, W. (1991) *Analysis of Evidence*. London: Weidenfeld & Nicolson.
Aubert, V. (1963) The structure of legal thinking. In J. Andenaes (Ed.) *Legal Essays: A Tribute to Frede Castberg on the Occasion of His 70th Birthday*. Boston, MA: Universitetsforlaget.
Blackburn, R. (1993) *The Psychology of Criminal Conduct: Theory, Research and Practice*. Chichester: John Wiley & Sons.
Campbell, C. (1974) Legal thought and juristic values. *British Journal of Law and Society*, **1**, 13–31.
Kairys, D. (Ed.) (1982) *The Politics of Law: A Progressive Critique*. New York: Pantheon.
Kelman, M. (1987) *A Guide to Critical Legal Studies*. Cambridge, MA: Harvard.
Law Commission (1995) *Mental Incapacity* (Law Com. 231). London, HMSO.
Loftus, E.F. & Palmer, J.C. (1974) Reconstruction of automobile destruction: An example of the interaction between language and memory. *Journal of Verbal Learning and Verbal Behaviour*, **13**, 585–589.
Lord Chancellor's Department (1997) *Who Decides? Making Decisions on Behalf of Mentally Incapacitated Adults*. London: HMSO.
Memon, A, Vrij, A. & Bull, R. (1998) *Psychology and Law: Truthfulness, Accuracy and Credibility*. Maidenhead, Berkshire: McGraw-Hill.
Schum, D.A. (1994) *Evidential Foundations of Probabilistic Reasoning*. New York: John Wiley & Sons.
Wexler, D.B. & Winick, B.J. (1996) *Law in a Therapeutic Key; Developments in Therapeutic Jurisprudence*. Durham, NC: Carolina Academic Press.
Winick, B.J. (1996) The side effects of incompetency labelling and the implications for mental health law. In D.B. Wexler & B.J. Winick, *Law in a Therapeutic Key: Developments in Therapeutic Jurisprudence*. Durham, NC: Carolina Academic Press.

Chapter 3

Psychology and Police Investigation

Peter B. Ainsworth
Faculty of Economic and Social Studies,
University of Manchester, UK

INTRODUCTION

For anyone who has watched the British television series *Cracker*, or seen films such as *Silence of the Lambs*, there may be a belief that a large number of psychologists are employed by the police to help with major investigations. Techniques such as offender profiling capture the public's imagination, and the portrayal of such methods has been partly responsible for an increase in the number of students wishing to study psychology at British universities. While offender profiling provides a striking example of the way in which police officers and psychologists can work together, there are a large number of areas in which psychology can and does offer help to the police in their day-to-day work. Furthermore, the value of techniques such as offender profiling may have been over-stated, and in reality its use is restricted to a relatively small number of serious and difficult cases.

THE RELATIONSHIP BETWEEN POLICING AND PSYCHOLOGY

There are a number of areas of psychology which may be relevant to policing. Indeed some psychologists would want to argue that their subject can be applied to many areas of contemporary policing duties (Ainsworth, 1995a; Baldry, 1998; Brewer & Wilson, 1995; Brown, 1998). As Kapardis (1997, p. 265) notes:

Behaviour, Crime and Legal Processes: A Guide for Forensic Practitioners.
Edited by James McGuire, Tom Mason and Aisling O'Kane.
© 2000 John Wiley & Sons Ltd.

> The domain of policing offers ample opportunity for psychological research . . . psychologists will come to play a more significant part in contributing to knowledge about and influencing developments in a broad range of policing issues.

While this is certainly true in many parts of the USA, British police forces have generally been more reluctant to embrace the findings of psychological research and to incorporate them into their training or their day-to-day operations. Many police officers may believe that the subject area has something of value to offer, while at the same time being reluctant to accept that "outsiders" such as psychologists should be part and parcel of the police organisation.

In a survey of British police officers carried out almost 20 years ago (Ainsworth, 1982, 1983) the majority of police officers questioned believed that the subject did have something of value to offer in their work (though there were some misunderstandings as to what exactly psychology involved). Many respondents to the survey tended to focus on areas in which they felt psychology might help to solve more crimes or to arrest more offenders. Psychologists (and indeed sociologists) who openly criticise oppressive interviewing techniques (Gudjonsson, 1992) or who suggest that some officers are prejudiced (Holdaway, 1994) may be greeted less warmly.

One important breakthrough in the UK came in 1981 when London's Metropolitan Police introduced "Human Awareness Training" as an integral part of initial training (Bull & Horncastle, 1988). This was a significant departure from normal recruit training which had traditionally laid a heavy emphasis on the rote learning of law and police powers (Southgate, 1988). It is interesting to note that only a few years after its introduction, the title of the module was changed from Human Awareness Training to "Policing Skills". Such a change was significant in that it removed the obvious link with psychology and implied that policing had its own core of essential skills which could be taught by those inside the organisation.

The reluctance to fully embrace the many areas in which psychology may be of value can be partly explained by reference to the organisation itself. Since the 1960s, a number of sociologists have drawn attention to the closed nature of the police organisation and highlighted officers' suspicion of outsiders (Bittner, 1967; Holdaway, 1989). Many writers have commented on the so-called "canteen culture" in which the lower ranks in particular establish norms of behaviour in dealing with the public and with other agencies (Fielding, 1988; Mitchell & Munro, 1996).

The perspective of many police officers would appear to be one of suspicion and cynicism in which rigid lines are drawn between "us" and "them". (Stratton (1984) and Graef (1990) provide some excellent examples.) An illuminating illustration of the possible tension between police officers and psychologists is provided by Canter (1994). Canter describes an occasion on which he was discussing the possible contribution which psychology could make to the detection of crime. Canter (1994, p. 12) quotes an erudite detective sergeant who asked: "Why do we need all this new-fangled stuff professor? After all we've got

150 years of police experience to draw upon." Such words should perhaps be borne in mind by those psychologists who would wish to influence the police organisation!

The canteen culture appears to be a powerful agent of socialisation within the police service and one which may frustrate management's attempts to introduce change. One example of this is the way in which some British chief constables have recently admitted that there is "institutionalised racism" within their own forces despite considerable effort to eliminate the problem. The reasons for the persistence of the canteen culture may be found partly in psychological theory. For example, Tajfel's Social Identity Theory (Tajfel, 1971) suggested that assigning people to groups tends to produce in-group favouritism and out-group hostility. If the group to which a person belongs is perceived to be under constant threat, this will tend to result in a greater reliance on the group for support, personal pride and even identity (Ainsworth, 1995a, p. 71). Although the police service is not unique in this tendency towards ethnocentrism, in the case of the police it has proved to be a formidable obstacle to improving relationships with other agencies, and in challenging institutional prejudice (Ainsworth, 1995a, ch. 12; Thomas, 1994).

It should also be borne in mind that the police service still largely meets its training needs by expertise drawn from within the organisation. Thus even when psychologists do have valuable contributions to make, there is a reluctance to have such people come along and teach recruits directly. Rather, the norm will be for a small number of police officers to receive training from a psychologist and for these officers to then become the "experts" who will pass on the information via internal training courses. Such a tendency is unlikely to result in trainees acquiring a full, detailed or even accurate knowledge of the intricacies of psychological methods and theories (Ainsworth, 1995a, ch. 8).

It is against this background that psychologists have started to work with police officers and, in some cases, attempted to influence the police organisation. While interactions have improved significantly over the last 20 years there remains a doubt in many police officers' minds as to the real value of inputs from professionals such as psychologists. Most police forces do now have psychology departments within the organisation, but the range of duties that the psychologists are expected to perform is often somewhat restricted. Psychologists who are employed directly by police forces, tend to have a background in occupational psychology and, as such, they work largely with management and in developing appropriate assessment and selection procedures (Reese, 1995; Blau, 1994). When the police force requires the services of, say, a psychological profiler it is most likely that someone from outside the organisation will be called upon.

We can thus see that relationships between psychologists and the police organisation are not as close as a first glance might suggest. Having said that, there are a number of important areas in which psychologists can and do have a significant impact. We will review a number of these areas, focusing in particular on the interviewing of witnesses and victims, the interviewing of suspects, recruitment and selection, and crime analysis and investigation.

INTERVIEWING WITNESSES AND VICTIMS

One of the major advances made by psychologists over the last 20 years has been the development of more appropriate interviewing methods, especially with regard to the interviewing of witnesses. (See Chapter 4, this volume.) Work by Beth Loftus (1979) and her colleagues established the importance of appropriate question wording if memories were not to become altered. Interviewing methods, such as the Cognitive Interview Technique (CIT) developed by Fisher and Geiselman (1992), have had a major impact on police procedures and provide one of the best examples of police-psychologist interaction.

The impact of the technique should not be underestimated. Prior to its implementation, the police paid little attention to the way in which witnesses should be interviewed. As has been noted elsewhere (Ainsworth, 1995a, p. 20):

> Many police officers will take the view that there are good witnesses and bad witnesses and that any difference in the quality of their statements can be put down to the individual witness rather than the interviewing technique used.

Traditionally, a great deal of time and effort was spent in training police officers how to interview suspects, but very little space was given over to the interviewing of eyewitnesses and victims. The little attention that was given to the subject tended to focus on the evidential points which should be contained within witness statements rather than on learning good interviewing procedures. This is perhaps surprising given the central role which witnesses often play in securing the conviction of an accused person.

The vast majority of crimes are not witnessed by the police themselves nor captured on CCTV. For this reason, the quality of eyewitness accounts can have a major bearing on the outcome of a case (Rand Corporation, 1975). Perhaps the reason why witness interviewing has been given such scant attention is that it is seen as a less glamorous activity than the interviewing of suspects. Interviews with suspects provide the individual officer with far more opportunity to demonstrate his or her prowess than does simple statement-taking. (See below.)

However, a growing number of police forces have now accepted that witness interviewing is one area in which appropriate training can produce tangible benefits. Many forces have adopted the methods advocated in the Cognitive Interview Technique and we will discuss these briefly below. (The interested reader may wish to consult Ainsworth (1998, ch. 7) for a more detailed review.)

Unlike some developments in cognitive psychology, the CIT was always seen as a practical tool which would have immediate applications in the "real world". Its originators developed the methods partly as a result of research in the laboratory, but also as a result of working with police officers and witnesses in the field. The two main emphases of the technique are *memory* and *communication*— not only must witnesses retrieve the details from their memory, but they must also translate the memory into words, and communicate the information to the interviewer. The technique relies on a process of guided retrieval in which the interviewer encourages and assists the witness to access all the appropriate information held in the memory store. The interviewee is thus put in the dominant position, and the interviewer's role becomes one of facilitator. This is a departure from the more traditional form of interview in which the police officer assumes control of the situation and asserts his or her authority.

Fisher and Geiselman suggest a number of techniques which will assist in the successful retrieval of information. These include establishing good rapport with the witness, and encouraging his or her active participation in the interview process. These steps can be particularly important if the witness has undergone a traumatic experience and finds the retrieval of information painful or embarrassing (Ainsworth & May, 1996). In trying to exert control over the situation, police officers may previously have used techniques which were counterproductive. For example, one study found that, on average, the police officer would interrupt the witness only seven and a half seconds after he or she had started to speak (Fisher et al., 1987). If the witness does experience anxiety when recalling details of the crime, then Fisher and Geiselman suggest that some time should be spent on appropriate relaxation techniques.

The four main techniques which the CIT uses to aid retrieval are:

1. *Recreating the context*. Fisher and Geiselman suggest that whenever a witness views a crime, his or her memory will be affected by the context which existed at the time. Thus the person's mood, where he or she was going, etc., may all affect the memory trace. Fisher and Geiselman believe that context plays a crucial role in the way in which memory is stored, and for this reason it is vital to recreate that original context in some detail when attempting recall. This might be achieved by simply asking the witness to think about how he or she was feeling or about what he or she was doing just before the crime occurred.
2. *Focused concentration*. Fisher and Geiselman believe that the interviewer must persuade the witness to concentrate hard on the task and thus to recall more and more detail. They suggest that the interviewer should encourage the witness to pay particular attention to the more detailed sensory representations in all the sensory systems. Thus not only should the witness try to recall an assailant's appearance but he or she should also think about what was said and, perhaps, even whether the person had a distinctive smell.
3. *Multiple retrieval attempts*. Fisher and Geiselman liken memory retrieval to a search process. If a person wishes to find a lost object he or she might start by looking in the most likely places, then look again more thoroughly, and then perhaps widen the search to other possible locations. It is suggested that a similar strategy is appropriate when attempting to retrieve information from memory. Fisher and Geiselman acknowledge that a witness who has failed to retrieve information once may be somewhat reluctant to make further attempts. However, encouraging the witness to do so may produce beneficial results, providing of course that the information is actually in the person's memory. There is a danger that too much "encouragement" may lead

the witness to fabricate information for which there is no original memory (Ainsworth, 1998, p. 105).

4. *Varied retrieval.* When witnesses are asked to describe what happened they will normally tell their story in chronological order and entirely from their own perspective. However, Fisher and Geiselman believe that additional information might be produced if a witness is asked to recall details in a different order, or even from a different perspective. In the former case, witnesses do sometimes produce additional information but mainly for peripheral details. Encouraging a witness to recall from a different perspective (e.g. from that of someone else at the scene) may, however, be rather less desirable. There is a real danger that a witness who is asked to try to recall from a different perspective may simply guess as to what the other person "should" have seen. Fisher and Geiselman did come to accept the dangers inherent in this strategy, and in the revised version of the technique placed far less emphasis on this aspect (Fisher et al., 1987).

The CIT has been adopted so extensively simply because it works. The vast majority of studies evaluating the technique have demonstrated that it produces more information than a "standard" interview, but with no increase in the amount of false information (Ainsworth, 1998, p. 108; Boon & Noon, 1994; Memon, 1998). As such it is today much more likely to be used than techniques such as hypnosis. Its success has been demonstrated both in the laboratory and in the field. It has also been shown to be effective with a wide range of different witnesses. It has also been used with children, although this can present some difficulties (Memon, 1998; Smithson & Ainsworth, 1999).

Despite the benefits which the CIT appears to offer, this has by no means guaranteed its complete adoption for all witness interviewing. The fact that the technique tends to take longer than the more traditional type of interview means that an ever-pressed police service may shy away from its general adoption and tend to resort to its use in only the more serious cases. It has also been found that police officers may experience some difficulty in applying the technique correctly (Memon, Bull & Smith, 1995). Poor training, particularly when the training is given by non-psychologists, may partly account for this difficulty although it must also be acknowledged that some individuals seem better able than others to conduct cognitive interviews (Memon, 1998, p. 183).

The CIT is a good example of the way in which psychology and policing can come together and bring practical benefits. As noted by Memon (1998, p. 183):

> The cognitive interview (CI) emerges as probably the most exciting development in the field of eyewitness testimony in the last 10 years.

Although there are still some unanswered questions about the effectiveness of the CIT, its correct use can have significant and tangible benefits in the investigation of crime.

INTERVIEWING SUSPECTS

If witness interviewing has undergone significant changes in recent years, then the same is also true of interviews with suspects. While psychologists have been partly responsible for these changes (Gudjonsson, 1992) other events and legislation such as the Police and Criminal Evidence Act (PACE) 1984 have also conspired to bring about significant transformations in practice. Although we are dealing with witness interviewing and suspect interviewing separately, it should be borne in mind that some writers see the processes as very similar and deal with the two under the one heading of "investigative interviewing" (Moston, 1991).

As was noted above, the interviewing/interrogation of suspects has usually been seen by police officers, especially detectives, as one way of demonstrating their professional prowess. A great deal of kudos will be gained by the police officer who is able to persuade an initially reluctant suspect to finally "cough" and admit to his or her part in a crime. Fans of the American television series *NYPD Blue* will be aware of the high priority given to such tactics, at least in fictional television series!

Police officers tend to see this type of interview mainly as a way of obtaining a confession from a suspect who is "obviously" guilty. In many police officers' minds, the suspect would not have been arrested unless he or she was guilty, and so the interview is seen simply as a way of obtaining further evidence of that guilt (Ainsworth, 1995b). Such views are not helped by the sort of advice offered in one American book on interviews and interrogation (surprisingly, written by a psychologist). In this, the author states that:

> Experienced interrogators agree that most offenders want to confess and have a psychological and emotional need to do so. (MacHovec, 1989, p. 119)

This same source advocates that "Stress, Pressure, Threat" can all be applied in interviews and states:

> These behaviors increase fear, anxiety, guilt or anger, depending on the interviewee's attitude, personality and mental state. If the person is a suspect this technique can test for "guilty knowledge". (MacHovec, 1989, p. 110)

The possible effects of such techniques on an innocent suspect are, unfortunately, not discussed by this writer. It is, however, rather worrying that in this case a psychologist is supporting rather than challenging the use of some of the more questionable techniques which some police writers have themselves advocated (Inbau, Reid & Buckley, 1986).

One British study (Moston, Stephenson & Williamson, 1992) sheds some light on police officers' assumptions about suspects who are to be interviewed. This research found that in almost three-quarters of cases, the police interviewer was already "sure" of the person's guilt before the interview began. Furthermore, in almost 80% of cases, the aim of the interview was said to be simply to obtain a confession. McConville and Hodgson (1993) similarly found that in 83% of the 157 interviews which they studied, the main aim appeared to be to secure a confession. In such a situation we should not be surprised if the interview rarely serves two of its supposed aims, i.e. to obtain valuable facts, and to eliminate the innocent (Swanson, Chamelin & Territo, 1988).

A detective who fails to elicit a confession from a suspect will be unlikely to come away admitting that he or she "must have the wrong man". Such an admission would produce tension (or, in psychological terms, dissonance) in the officer concerned (Festinger, 1957). Rather, the lack of a confession may well be put down to the suspect's shrewdness, perhaps stemming from his or her previous experience of interrogations. It is interesting to note that suspects who choose to exercise their right to silence during the interview may be more likely to be charged with an offence than those who deny the charge throughout (Moston, Stephenson & Williamson, 1992).

When the interview situation is viewed so rigidly by police officers, it is unlikely that the genuinely innocent suspect will be able to persuade the interviewer that he or she really did not commit the crime in question. Whatever methods the suspect uses will be reinterpreted as further evidence of guilt. A suspect's anxiety, for example, will be assumed to stem from guilt rather than from nervousness about the interview situation (Ainsworth, 1995a, pp. 43–47; Vrij, 1998a). Police officers often firmly believe in their own ability to spot when a person is lying (Oxford, 1991) though research suggests that this faith may be misplaced (Vrij 1998a; Vrij & Winkel, 1993; Ekman & O'Sullivan, 1989).

The available research evidence suggests that even experienced detectives are usually no better than civilians at detecting deception, and invariably perform no better than at chance level. One reason for this appears to be that police officers are likely to attend to the wrong cues when attempting to spot whether a suspect is lying (Vrij, 1993; Ekman & O'Sullivan, 1989). In Vrij and Winkel's (1993) study it was found that police officers tended to focus on the person's clothing and general appearance when trying to decide whether or not he or she was lying. Such cues are in fact unreliable indicators of deception. However, such inappropriate attempts to categorise others largely by their appearance may be an example of police officers' tendency to stereotype and categorise most of those with whom they come into contact (Stratton, 1984; Ainsworth, 1995a, p. 10).

Legislation such as PACE may have curtailed some of the worst excesses of persuasion used previously by police officers by, for example, insisting that all suspect interviews are now tape recorded. However, the introduction of such safeguards may have done little to change officers' attitudes towards the interview situation once the person in the interview room has been labelled "a suspect". We should also bear in mind that although formal interviews are now tape recorded, there may be other opportunities for the police officer to "work on" the suspect outside the interview room. Thus the officer may discuss the situation with the suspect in the police car on the way to the station. When the formal interview then begins, each participant may simply act out a scenario agreed upon earlier.

This may partly explain one rather surprising finding from the work of Baldwin (1990, 1993). Baldwin (1993) claimed that in only 10% of the cases he studied did the suspect show any change in his or her original story over the course of the interview. Further, only 3% of suspects who originally denied the charge made a full confession eventually. This low rate of acquiescence was confirmed by other research by Pearse and Gudjonsson (1996). One explanation that has been offered for this low figure is that many police officers are actually not very good at conducting interviews with suspects. This is perhaps surprising given the cultural prestige surrounding the elicitation of confessions. Many researchers (e.g. Baldwin, 1993; Moston, 1995; Pearse & Gudjonsson, 1996; Shepherd, 1993) conclude that the police are invariably ill prepared when it comes to conducting interviews and often behave in unprofessional ways.

The mismatch between interviewing officers' intentions and their abilities has been partly explained by Moston, Stephenson and Williamson (1992). These writers suggest that the police may continue to believe, mistakenly, that it is their own skilled techniques which will produce a confession. However, research evidence suggests that confessions are most likely to come as a result of the suspect's perception of the amount of evidence there is against him or her.

The other rather surprising finding from recent research concerns the behaviour of most suspects. Fictional police television series (e.g. *NYPD Blue*) and perhaps even police folklore, would lead one to believe that the majority of suspects are unco-operative, suspicious and aggressive. However, research suggests that most suspects are in fact polite and compliant, and often give full answers to questions posed by the interviewer (Pearse & Gudjonsson, 1996).

False Confessions

Despite the fact that many suspects are co-operative there are occasions when the police may use inappropriate interviewing techniques. The main reason why we should be concerned about heavy handed or blinkered interviewing tactics is that they may lead to false confessions and the subsequent conviction of an innocent person. Until relatively recently, most juries would have had little hesitation in convicting an accused person if a signed confession was produced in court (Underwager & Wakefield, 1992). Even now it may be difficult for ordinary members of the public to accept that a genuinely innocent person would ever sign a confession and admit to a crime which he or she had not committed. However, this somewhat naive view may be misplaced and fail to acknowledge the powerful situational forces which are present in the interview room.

One of the most important developments within social psychology in recent years has been the study of attributions which people make about the behaviour of others (Heider, 1958). One consistent finding is that people tend to underestimate situational (or external) forces when explaining others' behaviour, and instead assume that the person behaved the way he or she did because of dispositional (i.e. internal) factors. This tendency has been labelled the Fundamental Attribution Error (Jones & Nisbett, 1972).

Thus, according to attribution theory, the person who makes a confession would be presumed by others to have done so because he or she really was guilty. In making this judgement, people may well try to imagine themselves in the suspect's position and feel that if they were innocent, no amount of pressure would make them sign a false confession. However, this conclusion may be misplaced and simply be an example of the Fundamental Attribution Error discussed above. It is interesting to note that most police officers (who will be very familiar with the interview situation) still do not believe that an innocent person would or could ever confess (Williamson, 1990).

History tells us that some people do make false confessions, and that there are a number of reasons why they do so (Gudjonsson, 1992; Vrij, 1998b). Kennedy (1986) suggests that the most common cause of such confessions is over-zealousness by the police officer carrying out the interview. Starting with the belief that they must have the right person in the interview room, police officers may adopt a primarily accusatorial or confrontational questioning style (Moston, 1991). This serves to exert pressure on the individual until he or she sees confession as perhaps the only way to escape from the oppressive and aversive situation (Irving & Hilgendorf, 1980). The tape recording of such interviews at least now allows jurors to make up their own mind as to whether unreasonable coercion or force was used. It is interesting to note that when the tape recording of interviews was first proposed, its introduction was opposed vigorously by most police forces. However, many police officers have now accepted the situation and are often pleased to be able to demonstrate to the court that undue coercion was not used to elicit a confession from an accused.

Research suggests that following the introduction of PACE, the number of manipulative and persuasive tactics used by detectives fell dramatically (Irving & McKenzie, 1989) although some of this initial large fall was reversed in later years. Williamson (1990) supported Irving and McKenzie's early research, finding that police officers are today more likely to use professional rather than coercive tactics in the interview room. Williamson also highlights other positive changes which resulted from the introduction of PACE, including the fact that there were fewer interviews at night, fewer repeat interviews and that suspects now had easier access to a solicitor. All these changes are likely to lessen the chances of a false confession being made.

Nevertheless, some people may still make false confessions, even if they are not subjected to the more coercive type of interview described above. Following the announcement of many major crimes, police interview rooms tend to fill up with people wanting to confess to the crime in question. Many individuals who display this somewhat unusual behaviour may do so in order to achieve some degree of notoriety or to enhance their self-esteem. However, others may choose to confess freely because of specific or even more generalised guilt complexes— they might wish to relieve themselves of the heavy burden of guilt over something else, and achieve this by confessing to the crime in question. Such behaviour may be more likely in the mentally ill, especially those suffering from schizophrenia (Gudjonsson, 1992).

There are at least two other reasons why people may make false confessions. First, the person may confuse fantasy with reality. Thus a person who fantasises about killing an ex-lover may be driven to confess if the ex-lover is subsequently murdered, but by someone else. A second possibility is that a person may confess in order to save the real perpetrator from being punished. This is perhaps most likely to occur within families when one family member lies in order to protect another. Such cases may be difficult for the police to recognise, especially if a conspiracy has previously been agreed between the family members.

While these latter types of false confession are extremely worrying, of perhaps even more concern are those in which a suspect confesses falsely because of the pressure exerted on him or her in the interview room. Gudjonsson refers to this type of confession as *coerced-compliant*. In these cases, the person seeks to end the ordeal of the interview by admitting guilt. To the casual observer this may seem a strange act; however, the pressure which a suspect feels at the time may prompt him or her to try to reduce this immediate stress and do what the interviewer wants. The fact that such a course of action may have serious long-term consequences may not be the most urgent concern at the time—bringing an end to the intolerable stress is the more pressing need.

With this type of confession, the person is likely to try to retract the admission once he or she has escaped the aversive conditions. However, such attempts at retraction may not always be believed. Earlier we noted that most jurors will find it hard to accept that a genuinely innocent person would ever confess. As such, an attempt at retraction may be viewed as simply the action of a guilty person who is now trying to save his or her own skin rather than the action of an innocent person who gave in to intolerable pressure in the interview room.

Gudjonsson has identified another type of false confession which he labels *coerced-internalised*. In these cases, the suspect may initially believe that he or she is innocent but will subsequently come to admit and accept that he or she did commit the crime. Such a change may come about largely as a result of tactics used by the interviewing police officer. (See Ofshe (1989) for an interesting description of some of these tactics.) In such cases, the suspect may have little if any memory of the original incident or may come to distrust his or her own memory. Eventually the person may come to accept that the version of events which the police are giving "must" be true.

Such acceptance is most likely to happen if the police officer can convince the suspect that there is irrefutable evidence linking him or her to the crime. The officer must also provide the suspect with a plausible explanation as to why he or she has no recollection of the event or why the recollection is inaccurate (Ofshe, 1989). Although none of the cases which Ofshe examined appeared to involve people who could have been described as mentally ill, there were certain personality variables which were relevant. For example, those individuals who trusted in authority, lacked self-confidence, and were highly suggestible were most likely to confess and to then internalise the belief that they did commit the crime. Police officers who elicit such admissions may not even be aware that the confession is false. It will be hard for many police officers to accept that the same techniques which might persuade a guilty person to confess might also lead to a confession by an innocent person.

Although coerced-internalised confessions may lead to a permanent change in the person's belief about his or her involvement in the crime, this is not necessarily the case. The person may have accepted the police officer's version of events while he or she was in the interview room and have signed a confession. However, when he or she is removed from such a pressured environment there will be an opportunity to reassess the "evidence" and the person may revert to his or her original story.

Suggestibility

One recurring theme in many discussions of confessions is the notion of suggestibility. It was pointed out earlier that those individuals who are highly suggestible are more likely to confess falsely and to then perhaps accept their guilt as "fact". For this reason it would be desirable to be able to test levels of suggestibility, perhaps ideally before interviews commence.

Gudjonsson (1989) has spent some time developing appropriate psychometric tests in an effort to identify those individuals who may be particularly vulnerable to forceful interviewing techniques. Gudjonsson identifies two important variables which he entitled *suggestibility* and *compliance* and makes a distinction between the two. In the former case, the individual may come to believe and internalise the suggestions made by the interviewer. However, the individual who is merely compliant may simply go along with the version of events suggested by the interviewer, but never fully believe in them.

Gudjonsson claims that his scales do enable distinctions to be made between suggestible/compliant individuals and those who are non-suggestible/compliant. As such the scales may help to explain the behaviour of those individuals who make what are later claimed to be false confessions. Gudjonsson cites the case of the Birmingham Six, all of whom were falsely convicted of killing 21 people by planting bombs in pubs in Birmingham. Gudjonsson claims that the four accused who did (falsely) confess showed higher scores on his suggestibility and compliance scale than did the two individuals who did not confess.

Gudjonsson sees suggestibility as a personality trait which will tend to make some people more vulnerable than others. However, Gudjonsson and other writers have suggested that mood may also have a powerful effect on susceptibility to suggestion. According to Vrij (1998b), this creates a problem. If, for example, the person's mood when he or she completes the test is different from his or her mood when interviewed by the police, then the suggestibility score may not be an accurate reflection of vulnerability.

While considering vulnerability to police questioning, we should also bear in mind that there are now provisions for certain individuals (e.g those with communication difficulties or learning disabilities and the mentally disordered) to be interviewed in the presence of an "appropriate adult" (Gudjonsson et al., 1994; Pearse & Gudjonsson, 1997; Bull, 1995).

We can see from this section that psychologists have done a great deal to help us to understand the effects of some common police interviewing techniques. Psychologists have also been able to point out the potential dangers when inappropriate techniques are used. Perhaps the most important contribution made by psychologists such as Gudjonsson is a better understanding of how and why some suspects come to make false confessions. Like any large organisation, the police service may be slow to change its methods, but change has taken place and will continue to do so. In some cases this has only been brought about as a result of the growing number of wrongful convictions which have now come to light (Gudjonsson, 1992). Police officers have also had to accept that a signed confession is no longer the guarantee of conviction that it may once have appeared to be.

RECRUITMENT AND SELECTION

It has been suggested so far that some of the tactics and techniques used by the police might well be counter-productive. The reason why such methods are still used can be explained partly by reference to the organisation itself, but may also have something to do with the sort of person who applies to join the police service. For this reason we will next consider some relevant issues concerning the recruitment and selection of police officers.

The police service has long since recognised the importance of recruiting the "right" sort of person to the organisation. Mistakes at the earliest stage of selection can have serious consequences for the organisation, both in terms of wasted training, and in terms of the reputation and efficiency of the force. As psychologists have spent a great deal of time and effort developing a wide range of psychometric tests, this would appear to be an area where co-operation would prove to be extremely fruitful. However, the development of psychometric tests specifically for the selection of police officers has proved to be a rather demanding task (Ainsworth, 1995c; Gowan & Gatewood, 1995).

The first dilemma concerns whether testing should be used primarily as a means of screening out unsuitable applicants, or as a way of ensuring that the "best" applicants are identified and then recruited, i.e. screening in. These two approaches might not necessarily produce the same results. For example, an applicant may score very highly on almost all dimensions tested, yet show some evidence of racism in his or her attitudes. For this reason, a decision may be taken to reject this person in favour of one who has scored lower on many of the dimensions tested but does not show the same racist tendencies. Alternatively, the organisation may choose to recruit the prejudiced applicant, believing that suitable training will challenge and then change such prejudiced views.

A further problem concerns the very wide range of duties which a police officer may be called upon to perform. At a time when "multi-tasking" is becoming a buzz word for many organisations, police officers have always needed to have a wide range of skills in order to help them perform the many duties asked of them. Police work is one of the most varied occupations to be found, and indeed the job appeals to many applicants because of its wide variety. However, knowing that a police officer must be capable of carrying out a very large number of different tasks, each of which may require slightly different skills, makes the identification of core attributes difficult. Although it may be possible to break down required qualities into "Knowledge, Skills and Attributes" (Gowan & Gatewood, 1995), the exact specifications can prove to be rather more elusive.

Things have moved on since the early days of policing when the only requirements of a (virtually always male) police constable were that he be below a certain age, above a certain height, and be of "good character" (Tobias, 1972; Reese, 1995). Educational qualifications are now seen to be important, though a belief remains that only interviews can identify the "right" sort of person for the job (Ainsworth, 1995a, p. 138).

By helping to identify suitable (and unsuitable) applicants, psychologists can offer some help to the police organisation, though this is by no means a straightforward task. Should we really expect the police dog handler, the community constable, the drug squad detective, and the future chief constable all to exhibit identical characteristics at the time of recruitment? Should an applicant who shows good leadership qualities be encouraged to join the organisation or be rejected? While such an individual may be good "officer material", he or she may not take kindly to following orders from less competent people who have nevertheless risen through the ranks. This is clearly a dilemma for any organisation which selects its managers entirely from within. The police organisation with its rigid rank structure and ethnocentrism may thus be slow to introduce change, especially change advocated by those outside the mainstream of the force.

Part of the problem in selection is that a detailed job analysis of the role of "police officer" is hardly ever carried out. Thus specifying the exact requirements for a recruit can prove to be difficult. When serving officers are asked about the essential qualities required in a recruit, they are inclined to talk about things like "common sense" or "a sense of humour" (Ainsworth, 1995a, p. 136). Interestingly, these attributes may prove rather difficult to measure through established psychometric tests.

Promotion and Assessment

If psychologists' input into recruitment decisions is problematic, the same may not be true of promotion or selection for specialist roles within the organisation (Wigfield, 1996). To take one example, British police officers, unlike their counterparts in most other countries, do not routinely carry firearms (McKenzie, 1996). However, those who are authorised to do so will have been required to pass a number of tests which today includes some form of psychological assessment. This serves to eliminate those applicants considered unsuitable (Mirrlees-Black, 1992).

Brown (1998) suggests that implementation of such a specific assessment policy was a landmark in British policing. She notes (p. 541):

> Despite the attempts at civilianization, many police personnel departments were headed by senior police officers with no specialist qualifications in human resource management. Methods of recruitment and selection . . . were, by and large, unsystematic and procedures were undocumented.

Brown goes on to note how concerns over equal opportunities, especially with regard to career advancement, has led many forces to examine their procedures and to employ consultants to improve the situation. These consultants have helped to develop more systematic methods, including Assessment Centres (Gowan & Gatewood, 1995; Wigfield, 1996). Assessment Centres allow a standardised evaluation of a number of different aspects of behaviour, thereby allowing a better assessment to be made of each person's strengths and weaknesses. As such, Assessment Centres appear to have a number of advantages over more subjective methods such as interview panels. However, Assessment Centres are expensive to run, and are often used in conjunction with other selection criteria. This can tend to diminish the influence of the more objective Assessment Centre results (Wallace, 1994).

CRIME ANALYSIS AND INVESTIGATION

Two other major areas in which psychologists would appear to have made an impact on the work of the police are in the analysis of crime trends and patterns, and in offender profiling. In the remainder of this chapter we will consider some examples of where collaboration appears to have been the most fruitful, looking in particular at repeat victimisation and psychological profiling.

In recent years there has been increasing pressure on the police to demonstrate their effectiveness and efficiency, and we have witnessed the introduction of performance indicators and other forms of monitoring (Ainsworth, 1995a, ch. 9). Such moves have forced the police to prioritise their activities and to set targets against which their performance can be measured. The problem for the police is that demonstrating effectiveness is not always easy (Reiner & Spencer, 1993). The public have expectations about what the police should be doing, but the police's performance cannot always rise to the level which the public might expect.

If the police's role is seen as the prevention and detection of crime, then it could be argued that they have been failing in their primary duties for a long time. For example, the number of officially recorded crimes rose from about half a million in 1950 to over five million by the early 1990s (though, in fairness, official levels have fallen yearly throughout the 1990s). Victim surveys suggest that in reality the true level of crime may be almost double the figure recorded officially (Mirrlees-Black et al., 1998). If we again look at the official figures for recorded crime, the police appear to solve only about a quarter of the total number of offences. Again, if we take the figures revealed by studies such as the British Crime Survey, then the police detection rate may actually be nearer one in eight. Even this figure may, however, be misleading as many crimes are solved not by clever detection work by the police, but rather by people telling the police who was responsible. Domestic assaults are one example of such cases.

The police will of course claim that low manpower levels, and an ever more demanding but unhelpful public, account for at least some of the increase in crime and the poor detection rate. However, forcing the police to set priorities and to achieve targets has led to a more careful consideration of what they are doing and how they are doing it. We may wish, for example, to consider the way in which the police might deploy their meagre resources. The police have traditionally relied on their local knowledge when making decisions on, for example, the deployment of their officers. Thus the police may have noticed what appears to be a series of burglaries on one estate, and decide to target this area for additional patrolling and surveillance. However, the police service's relatively unsophisticated methods of data collection may mean that their analysis of the situation is inaccurate and that their resources are not targeted sufficiently well, but by the use of techniques such as crime pattern analysis, a much clearer picture can often be produced (IALEIA, 1998). Crime pattern analysis can serve to establish links between crimes and help to predict when and where future offences might occur.

An example of what can be achieved through careful analysis of crime data is provided by Forrester et al. (1990). Forrester and colleagues carried out a study of burglary on the Kirkholt estate in Greater Manchester. Kirkholt had long been recognised as a "problem" estate with high crime levels which the police seemed incapable of tackling. However, researchers quickly established that a large proportion of burglaries on the estate were "repeats" in that it was the same houses which were being targeted over and over again. In fact it was found that homes which had been burgled once were four times more likely to be burgled again than were homes which had not been targeted previously. It was further recognised that the repeat attacks tended to follow quite soon after the first attack—in most cases within six weeks.

Once these facts had been established, it became possible to target resources on those properties which were the most likely to become victimised in the future. Cocoon Neighbourhood Watch schemes were set up which typically involved only the six households which were closest to the targeted home. The council also made the vulnerable premises more secure through the installation of better locks, etc. Utility companies were also persuaded to remove the coin meters from within the homes, thus removing one ready source of cash for the burglars. The police were also able to target their efforts directly on the most vulnerable homes, rather than just patrolling the estate generally.

The Kirkholt project was incredibly successful. Burglaries on the estate had been reduced by a remarkable 75% by Phase II of the project—this figure is significantly higher than the vast majority of crime prevention initiatives. Although there are a large number of reasons for this dramatic fall, the ability to identify and then protect likely future targets was a major breakthrough. The recognition that a large number of crimes are repeat victimisations spurred many researchers to examine the concept in much greater detail (Farrell & Pease, 1993). It now appears that repeat victimisation is a remarkably robust phenomenon, occurring as it does across a very wide range of crimes (Ellingworth, Farrell & Pease, 1995). In fact Pease (1996, p. 3) has gone so far as to suggest that in most cases the best single predictor of whether or not a person will become a victim in the future is whether or not they have been a victim in the past.

A recent review of repeat victimisation research (Pease, 1998) has drawn out a number of important implications for policing. The report's author (one of the leading researchers on repeat victimisation) suggests that an understanding of repeat victimisation will allow the police to improve their efficiency levels significantly. Pease (1998, pp. v–vi) suggests that preventing repeat victimisation is an important crime control strategy for a number of reasons:

1. Focusing on repeats automatically concentrates efforts on the highest crime areas.
2. Focusing on repeats automatically concentrates on those individuals who are at greatest risk of future victimisation.
3. The predictable time course of repeats allows resources to be targeted temporally as well as spatially.
4. The roles of victim support and crime prevention can be fused.
5. Because a series of repeat offences is often committed by the same person it is likely that arrest will lead to a larger number of clear-ups and to the recovery of significant amounts of property.
6. Because early research suggests that repeat offenders tend to be the more prolific offenders, targeting of repeat offences is likely to result in the arrest of the most prolific offenders.

From this one example of repeat victimisation research we can see just how important the proper analysis of crime can be. The police are slowly beginning to accept that crime analysts, many of whose academic background is in psychology, do have a role to play within the organisation. Taking on board the suggestions made by psychologists such as Ken Pease can help police forces to become significantly more effective and efficient.

Offender Profiling

Offender profiling is one area in which it would appear that psychology and police investigation can be brought together to produce worthwhile results. (The reader may wish to note that in the literature on the subject, offender profiling is also referred to by other names including *Psychological Profiling* and *Specific Profile Analysis*.)

The popularity of many recent fictional television series and films may well have led the public to believe that psychologists spend a great deal of time in this activity and help the police to solve a large number of serious cases. However, as was pointed out at the start of this chapter, there would appear to be a mismatch between the public's perception and reality. This is certainly the case if people's picture of a typical psychological profiler has been taken from images portrayed in the television series *Cracker*. In this series, a maverick character named Fitz (played by Robbie Coltrane) solves many serious crimes, partly through some rudimentary (if flawed) psychological insight, and partly through flashes of inspiration and logical deduction. This is a long way from the reality of real-life offender profilers. Gudjonsson and Copson (1997) suggest that misunderstandings about profiling are perhaps understandable. They note that:

> Profiling is neither a readily identifiable nor a homogeneous entity . . . Little has been published to shed light on what profilers actually do or how they do it.
> (Gudjonsson & Copson, 1997, p. 76)

One of the main misunderstandings about psychological profiling is that it can somehow identify the exact person whom the police should arrest. Contrary to the image presented by Fitz (see above), this is certainly not the case. What a profile can often do is to generate hypotheses about the offender's most likely demographic and physical characteristics, and about his or her behavioural habits and personality. As such it can perhaps assist the police in suggesting where they might start looking for a perpetrator. In addition, the profile may allow the police to eliminate a number of possible suspects who do not match any of the identified characteristics. A profiler may also be able to advise the police as to the most appropriate interviewing methods to be used with a particular suspect.

An appropriate note of caution regarding the usefulness of profiling is sounded by Jackson and Bekerian (1997, p. 3):

> . . . the answers that are offered are *not* solutions. Offender profiles do not solve crimes. Instead . . . profiles should be viewed as simply one more tool that can be extremely useful in guiding strategy development, supporting information management, and improving case understanding.

While there had been isolated attempts at psychological profiling for a number of years (Brussel, 1968) it was the FBI's Behavioral Science Unit (now called the Investigative Support Unit) which first built up a body of knowledge and expertise in the USA (Hazelwood, 1983). More recently, researchers in Britain and elsewhere have extended this work, and in some cases developed their own distinctive techniques and methods of offender profiling (Canter, 1994; Jackson & Bekerian, 1997). We should also point out that not all profilers have a psychology background—some have a training in, for example, psychiatry (Badcock 1997).

Although researchers may disagree about the exact definition of offender profiling, underlying most approaches is a belief that offender characteristics can be deduced from offence characteristics. In other words, it is believed that a careful analysis of the way in which a crime was carried out may tell us something about the characteristics of the offender. To take one example, early work by the FBI sought to make a distinction between organised and disorganised murderers. Thus some crime scenes suggested that the crime had been well planned, that the offender showed control at the scene, and that he had been careful not to leave clues. By contrast other killings showed no evidence of pre-planning and there appeared to be little attempt to conceal evidence. Similarly with rape, the FBI's unit sought to classify rapists' behaviour as "power assurance", "power assertive", "anger retaliatory" or "anger excitation". These attempts at classification led to the development of the *Crime Classification Manual* (Ressler et al., 1992).

One reason why such a classification system is used is that it helps investigators to establish possible links between different crimes. This can be helpful for at least two reasons. First, it is obviously important for the police to establish whether they should be looking for one perpetrator or a number of different people. Second, each crime scene might in itself reveal only a few clues, but if information from a number of different scenes can be combined then the police may be able to build up a better picture of the perpetrator.

Classification of crimes also allows investigators to focus on the type of person they should be seeking. In this respect it differs from the more normal type of forensic evidence gathered at the scene (e.g. fingerprints, clothing fibres) which may later be used to prove that a suspect had been in contact with the victim. Although such evidence can be crucial in subsequently securing a conviction, in most cases it does not help the police to identify the type of person they should be looking for in the first place. By contrast, psychological profiling can sometimes provide information of this type.

To take an example, it has been argued that the four different types of rape identified above may each be carried out by a different personality "type" (Hazelwood & Burgess, 1987). Thus, if the police do not even know where to start looking in their search for a perpetrator, advice from a profiler may help them at least to narrow down the field of possible suspects. Alternatively, if the police have a number of possible suspects in mind, advice from a psychological profiler may help them to decide which suspect they should target in their search for further evidence.

The FBI's approach to offender profiling has been criticised by a number of academics (e.g. Rossmo, 1996; Oleson, 1996; Canter, 1994) not least because it is based on the analysis of a very small number of cases, and on interviews with a small number of serial murderers and rapists. Furthermore, as Canter and others have noted, it has been subject to very little formal scientific evaluation. The FBI may well choose to publicise the cases in which its methods have proved to be successful, but may be less willing to bring their failures to public attention. Jackson and Bekerian (1997, p. 6) have noted:

In spite of this not only has investigative support, research and training in behavioural analysis continued unabated in the USA since 1978 but many, if not all, of the psychological profiling units in other countries . . . have been modelled to a large extent on the FBI approach.

In Britain the police have only recently started to accept offender profiling as a way of helping to solve some of the more serious crimes. Although the FBI's approach has had some influence on practice, British experts have also been brought in as consultants and advisers. Foremost in this work has been Professor David Canter from Liverpool University. (See Ainsworth, 1995a, ch. 10, for a review of Canter's approach.)

Canter has labelled his subject *Investigative Psychology* and has developed a number of important hypotheses concerning criminals' behaviour. Canter has taken issue with the FBI's approach and has developed his own system of crime analysis and profiling which appears to have more in the way of a scientific foundation. In particular, he has developed a methodology based on aspects of Facet theory (House, 1997, p. 181).

Canter's early work led him to believe that there were five important characteristics which can help in investigations:

- Residential location
- Criminal biography
- Domestic/social characteristics
- Personal characteristics
- Occupational/educational history

Although all can be important variables, the first two have proved to be particularly useful in helping to identify perpetrators. Canter's work on the distance between a typical offender's residence and the location of his or her crimes has been especially helpful. He has been able to show that most criminals commit crime within a two-mile radius of their home, and that their choice of target is governed partly by their own "mental maps" of the neighbourhood (Ainsworth, 1995a, p. 191).

In order that a profiler can collect as much information as possible, it might be presumed that he or she should visit the crime scene as soon as possible and look for clues which might reveal something about the characteristics of the perpetrator. A careful examination of crime scenes will also allow investigators to compare, and possibly link, different crimes. It is then surprising to learn that (in Britain at least) psychological profilers may not always be brought into an investigation until long after the crime scene has been discovered (Copson, 1995; Smith, 1998).

In Britain, despite the media coverage given to certain prominent cases, profilers are seldom called upon. When their help is sought, they tend to be consulted about the more unusual types of crime, or where more conventional police investigation methods have failed. We should also be aware that while profiling is suitable for certain types of crime, it would be less useful in other cases. The

FBI's view is that property crimes and robberies are perhaps the least suitable crimes for profiling, as the criminal is unlikely to reveal his or her underlying personality when committing such offences.

It has proved to be rather difficult to establish the "success rate" of profiles provided by psychologists (Smith, 1998; Gudjonsson & Copson, 1997, p. 73). If half of the information a profiler provides is found to be accurate, should we count this as a success? If, as was suggested earlier, profilers tend to be brought in only after other methods have failed, should we expect a high success rate? In attempting to measure "success" we should also be aware that some senior detectives might be unwilling to admit that it was the profiler who played the major part in solving the crime. In order to protect his or her own reputation, the senior detective may play down the role of the profiler and instead claim most of the credit for having solved the case personally (Smith, 1998). The limited amount of British data on the subject found that many senior detectives are not very complimentary or enthusiastic about the services provided by profilers (Copson, 1995; Copson & Holloway, 1997; Smith, 1998). Data provided by Copson and Holloway (1997) suggest that profiling helped to solve only 16% of crimes in which it was used, and led to the identification of an offender in less than 3% of cases.

Jackson and Bekerian (1997) suggest that for offender profiling to realise its potential, two things must happen. First, profilers must better understand the requirements and needs of police investigations, and second, the police must better understand the nature and use of profiles. At present it would appear that there are misunderstandings on both sides and this has led to some disillusionment with the process. It should also be recognised that profiling is not one technique but several. While such variation may be understandable in the early stages, it may have a longer term negative impact. As Jackson and Bekerian (1997, p. 209) note: ". . . too much diversity can result in the field becoming fragmented theoretically, and therefore less accessible to application."

We can thus see that while offender profiling might fire the public's imagination, and have intuitive appeal, there are limits to its usefulness. Having said that, there is no doubt that the use of more scientific attempts to understand crime and the criminal can have long-term beneficial effects.

CONCLUDING COMMENTS

We have seen in this chapter that there are a range of opportunities for psychologists to bring their expertise into the police arena. While such inputs may not always be welcomed warmly in the first instance, there is no doubt that the police service can benefit from a closer working relationship with psychologists. Police work continues to be a demanding and challenging occupation requiring a large range of skills. If psychologists can tailor their expertise to meet the demands of the police service, their influence will no doubt grow in years to come.

REFERENCES

Ainsworth, P.B. (1982) *British police officers' perceptions of psychology*. Paper presented to the International Conference on Psychology and Law, Swansea, July.

Ainsworth, P.B. (1983) *Sex differences amongst British police officers' perceptions of psychology*. Paper presented to the British Psychological Society Conference, London, December.

Ainsworth, P.B. (1995a) *Psychology and Policing in a Changing World*. Chichester: Wiley.

Ainsworth, P.B. (1995b) *Police folklore and attributions of guilt: Can psychology challenge long held assumptions*? Paper presented to the 5th European Conference on Law and Psychology, Budapest, 2nd September.

Ainsworth, P.B. (1995c) Psychological testing and police recruit selection: Difficulties and dilemmas. In G. Davies, S. Lloyd-Bostock, M. McMurran & C. Wilson (Eds) *Psychology, Law and Criminal Justice: International Developments in Research and Practice*. Berlin: Walter de Gruyter.

Ainsworth, P.B. (1998) *Psychology, Law and Eyewitness Testimony*. Chichester: Wiley.

Ainsworth, P.B. & May, G. (1996) *Obtaining information from traumatised witnesses through the Cognitive Interview Technique*. Paper presented to the Trauma and Memory International Research Conference, Durham NH, 27 July.

Badcock, R. (1997) Developmental and clinical issues in relation to offending in the individual. In J.L. Jackson & D.A. Bekerian (Eds) *Offender Profiling: Theory, Research and Practice*. Chichester: Wiley.

Baldry, A.C. (1998) Is psychology "all fangled stuff" for the police? *Forensic Evidence*, **53**, 20–26.

Baldwin, J. (1990) Police interviews on tape. *New Law Journal* (May), 662–663.

Baldwin, J. (1993) Police interview techniques: Establishing truth or proof. *British Journal of Criminology*, **33**, 325–352.

Bittner, E. (1967) The police on Skid Row: A study of peace keeping. *American Sociological Review*, **32**(5), 699–715.

Blau, T. (1994) *Psychological Services for Law Enforcement*. Chichester: Wiley.

Boon, J. and Noon, E. (1994) Changing perspectives in cognitive interviewing. *Psychology, Crime and Law*, **1**, 59–69.

Brewer, N. & Wilson, C. (Eds) (1995) *Psychology and Policing*. Hillsdale, NJ: Lawrence Earlbaum.

Brown, J. (1998) Helping the police with their enquiries. *The Psychologist*, **11**(11), 539–542.

Brussel, J.A. (1968) *Casebook of a Crime Psychiatrist*. New York: Simon & Schuster.

Bull, R. (1995) Interviewing people with communication difficulties. In R. Bull & D. Carson (Eds) *Handbook of Psychology in Legal Contexts*. Chichester: Wiley.

Bull, R. & Horncastle, P. (1988) Evaluating training: The London Metropolitan Police's recruit training in Human Awareness/policing skills. In P. Southgate (Ed.) *New Directions in Police Training*. London: HMSO.

Canter, D. (1994) *Criminal Shadows: Inside the Mind of the Serial Killer*. London: Harper Collins.

Copson, G. (1995) *Coals to Newcastle? Part 1: A Study of Offender Profiling* (Paper 7). London: Police Research Group Special Interest Series, Home Office.

Copson, G. & Holloway, K. (1997) *Offender profiling*. Paper presented to the Annual Conference of the British Psychological Society's Division of Criminological and Legal Psychology, Cambridge, England.

Ekman, P. & O'Sullivan, M. (1989) Hazards in detecting deceit. In D.C. Raskin (Ed.) *Psychological Methods in Criminal Investigation and Evidence*. New York: Springer.

Ellingworth, D., Farrell, G. & Pease, K. (1995) A victim is a victim is a victim: Chronic victimization in four sweeps of the British Crime Survey. *British Journal of Criminology*, **35**, 360–365.

Farrell, G. & Pease, K. (1993) *Once Bitten Twice Bitten: Repeat Victimization and its Implications for Crime Prevention.* Crime Prevention Unit Paper 46. London: Home Office.

Festinger, L. (1957) *A Theory of Cognitive Dissonance.* Evanston, IL: Row, Peterson.

Fielding, N. (1988) Socialisation of recruits into the police role. In *New Directions in Police Training.* London: HMSO.

Fisher, R.P., Geiselman, R.E., Raymond, D.S., Jurkevitch, L.M. & Warhaftig, M.L. (1987) Enhancing enhanced eyewitness memory: Refining the cognitive interview. *Journal of Police Science and Administration,* **15**, 291–297.

Fisher, R.P. & Geiselman, R.E. (1992) *Memory Enhancing Techniques for Investigative Interviewing.* Springfield, IL: Charles C. Thomas.

Forrester, D., Frenz, S., O'Connor, M. & Pease, K. (1990) *The Kirkholt Burglary Prevention Project: Phase II.* Crime Prevention Unit Paper 23. London: Home Office.

Gowan, M.A. & Gatewood, R.D. (1995) Personnel selection. In N. Brewer & C. Wilson (Eds) *Psychology and Policing.* Hillsdale, NJ: Lawrence Earlbaum.

Graef, R. (1990) *Talking Blues: The Police in their own Words.* London: Fontana.

Gudjonsson, G.H. (1989) Compliance in an interrogation situation: A new scale. *Personality and Individual Differences,* **10**, 535–540.

Gudjonsson, G.H. (1992) *The Psychology of Interrogations, Confessions and Testimony.* Chichester: Wiley.

Gudjonsson, G.H., Clare, G., Rutter, S. & Pearse, J. (1994) Persons at risk during interviews in police custody: The identification of vulnerabilities. *Research Bulletin,* **35**, 31–32. London: Home Office Research and Planning Unit.

Gudjonsson, G.E. & Copson, G. (1997) The role of the expert in criminal investigation. In J.L. Jackson & D.A. Bekerian (Eds) *Offender Profiling: Theory, Research and Practice.* Chichester: Wiley.

Hazelwood, R.R. (1983) The behaviour oriented interview of rape victims: The key to profiling. *F.B.I. Law Enforcement Bulletin,* **59**, 1–8.

Hazelwood, R.R. & Burgess, A.W. (1987) *Practical Aspects of Rape Investigation: A Maltidisciplinary Approach.* New York: Elsevier.

Heider, F. (1958) *The Psychology of Interpersonal Relations.* New York: Wiley.

Holdaway, S. (1989) Discovering structure: Studies of the British police occupation culture. In M. Weatheritt (Ed.) *Police Research: Some Future Prospects.* Aldershot: Gower.

Holdaway, S. (1994) Recruitment, race and the police subculture. In M. Stephens & S. Becker (Eds) *Police Force, Police Service.* Basingstoke: Macmillan.

House, J.C. (1997) Towards a practical application of offender profiling: The RNC's criminal suspect prioritization system. In J.L. Jackson & D.A. Bekerian (Eds) *Offender Profiling: Theory, Research and Practice.* Chichester: Wiley.

IALEIA (1998) *Successful Law Enforcement Using Analytic Methods.* South Florida, USA: International Association of Law Enforcement Intelligence Analysts.

Inbau, F.E., Reid, J.E. & Buckley, J.P. (1986) *Criminal Interrogations and Confessions.* Baltimore, MD: Williams & Wilkins.

Irving, B.L. & Hilgendorf, L. (1980) *Police Interrogation: The Psychological Approach.* Research Study No. 1, Royal Commission on Criminal Procedure. London: HMSO.

Irving, B.L. & McKenzie, I.K. (1989) *Police Interrogation: The Effects of the Police and Criminal Evidence Act, 1984.* London: The Police Foundation.

Jackson, J.L. & Bekerian, D.A. (eds) (1997) *Offender Profiling: Theory, Research and Practice.* Chichester: Wiley.

Jones, E.E. & Nisbett, R.E. (1972) The actor and the observer: Divergent perceptions of the causes of behaviour. In E.E. Jones, D.E. Kanouse, H.H. Kelly, S. Valins & B. Weiner (Eds) *Attribution: Perceiving the Causes of Behaviour.* Morristown, NJ: General Learning Press.

Kapardis, A. (1997) *Psychology and Law: A Critical Introduction.* Cambridge: Cambridge University Press.

Kennedy, L. (1986) Foreword. In N. Fellows (Ed.) *Killing Time.* Oxford: Lion.

Loftus, E.F. (1979) *Eyewitness Testimony.* Cambridge, MA: Harvard University Press.

MacHovec, F.J. (1989) *Interview and Interrogation: A Scientific Approach.* Springfield, IL: Charles C. Thomas.

McConville, M. & Hodgson, A. (1993) Custodial legal advice and the right to silence. *Royal Commission on Criminal Justice Research, Research Study No. 16.* London: HMSO.

McKenzie, I.E. (1996) Violent encounters: Force and deadly force in British policing. In F. Leishman, B. Loveday & S. Savage (Eds) *Core Issues in Policing.* London: Longman.

Memon, A. (1998) Telling it all: The Cognitive Interview. In A. Memon, A. Vrij & R. Bull (Eds) *Psychology and Law: Truthfulness, Accuracy and Credibility.* Maidenhead: McGraw-Hill.

Memon, A., Bull, R. & Smith, M. (1995) Improving the quality of the police interview: Can training in the use of cognitive techniques help? *Policing and Society*, **5**, 53–68.

Mirrlees-Black, C. (1992) *Using Psychometric Personality Tests in the Selection of Firearms Officers.* Home Office Research and Planning Unit Paper 68. London: Home Office.

Mitchell, M. & Munro, A. (1996) The influence of the occupational culture on how police probationers learn to deal with incidents of sudden death. In N.C. Clark & G.M. Stephenson (Eds) *Psychological Perspectives on Police and Custodial Culture and Organization.* Leicester: British Psychological Society.

Mirrlees-Black, C., Budd, T., Partridge, S. & Mayhew, P. (1998) *The 1998 British Crime Survey, England and Wales.* Home Office Statistical Bulletin 21/98. London: Home Office.

Moston, S. (1991) *Investigative Interviewing* (Vol. I). London: Metropolitan Police/ACPO.

Moston, S. (1995) From denial to admission in police questioning of suspects. In G. Davies, S. Lloyd-Bostock, M. McMurran & C. Wilson (Eds) *Psychology, Law and Criminal Justice: International Developments in Research and Practice.* Berlin: Walter de Gruyter.

Moston, S., Stephenson, G.M. & Williamson, T.M. (1992) The effects of case characteristics on suspect behaviour during police questioning. *British Journal of Criminology*, **32**, 23–40.

Ofshe, R. (1989) Coerced confessions: The logic of seemingly irrational action. *Cultic Studies Journal*, **6**, 1–15.

Oleson, J.C. (1996) Psychological profiling: Does it actually work? *Forensic Update*, **46**, 11–14.

Oxford, T. (1991) Spotting a liar. *Police Review*, 328–329.

Pearse, J. & Gudjonsson, G.H. (1996) Police interviewing techniques at two south London police stations. *Psychology, Crime and Law*, **3**, 63–74.

Pearse, J. & Gudjonsson, G.H. (1997) Police interviewing and mentally disordered offenders: Changing the role of the legal advisor. *Expert Evidence*, **5**, 49–53.

Pease, K. (1996) *Repeat Victimization and Policing.* Unpublished Manuscript: University of Huddersfield.

Pease, K. (1998) *Repeat Victimization: Taking Stock.* Crime Prevention and Detection Series Paper 90. London: Home Office Police Research Group.

Rand Corporation (1975) *The Criminal Investigation Process.* Volumes 1–3. Santa Monica, CA: Rand Corporation.

Reiner, R. & Spencer, S. (1993) *Accountable Policing: Effectiveness, Empowerment and Equity.* London: IPPR.

Reese, J.T. (1995) A history of police psychological services. In M.I. Kirke & E.M. Scrivner (Eds) *Police Psychology in the 21st Century.* Hillsdale, NJ: Lawrence Earlbaum.

Ressler, R.K., Douglas, J.E., Burgess, A.W. & Burgess, A.G. (1992) *Crime Classification Manual.* New York: Simon & Schuster.

Rossmo, D.K. (1996) Targeting victims; serial killers and the urban environment. In T. O'Reilly-Fleming (Ed.) *Serial and Mass Murder: Theory Research and Policy.* Toronto: Canadian Scholars Press.

Shepherd, E. (1993) Resistance in interviews: The contribution of police perceptions and behaviour. In E. Shepherd (Ed.) *Aspects of Police Interviewing*. Leicester: British Psychological Society.

Smith, G.E. (1998) *Offender profiling: Its role and suitability in the investigation of serious crime*. Unpublished MA dissertation, University of Manchester.

Smithson, H. & Ainsworth, P.B. (1999) *Too young to tell? A comparison of the revised cognitive interview and standard interview with three and four year old children*. Paper presented to Law and Psychology International Conference, Dublin, July 1999.

Southgate, P. (1988) *New Directions in Police Training*. London: Home Office.

Stratton, J.G. (1984) *Police Passages*. Manhattan Beach, CA: Glennon.

Swanson, C.R., Chamelin, N.C. & Territo, L. (1988) *Criminal Investigation* (4th edn). New York: McGraw-Hill.

Tajfel, H. (1971) Social categorization and inter-group behaviour. *European Journal of Social Psychology*, **1**, 149–178.

Thomas, T. (1994) *The Police and Social Workers* (2nd edn). Aldershot: Ashgate.

Tobias, J.J. (1972) *Nineteenth Century Crime in England: Prevention Punishment*. New York: Barnes & Noble.

Underwager, R. & Wakefield, H. (1992) False confessions and police deception. *American Journal of Forensic Psychology*, **10**, 49–66.

Vrij, A. (1993) Credibility judgements of detectives: The impact of nonverbal behaviour, social skills and physical characteristics on impression formation. *Journal of Social Psychology*, **133**, 601–611.

Vrij, A. (1998a) Nonverbal communication and credibility. In A. Memon, A. Vrij & R. Bull (Eds) *Psychology and Law: Truthfulness, Accuracy and Credibility*. Maidenhead: McGraw-Hill.

Vrij, A. (1998b) Interviewing suspects. In A. Memon, A. Vrij & R. Bull (Eds) *Psychology and Law: Truthfulness, Accuracy and Credibility*. Maidenhead: McGraw-Hill.

Vrij, A. & Winkel, F.W. (1993) Objective and subjective indicators of deception. *Issues in Criminological and Legal Psychology*, **20**, 51–57.

Wallace, W. (1994) *The value of assessment centres as a determining element in the police promotion process*. Unpublished MA dissertation, University of Manchester.

Wigfield, D. (1996) Competent leadership in the police. *Police Journal*, **LXIV**, 99–107.

Williamson, T.M. (1990) *Strategic changes in police interrogation*. Unpublished PhD thesis, University of Kent.

Chapter 4

Factors Influencing Witness Evidence

Amina Memon
Department of Psychology, University of Aberdeen, UK
and
Daniel B. Wright
Department of Cognitive and Computing Sciences,
University of Sussex, UK

Justice often depends on the reliability of eyewitness testimony. Criminals are released because eyewitnesses fail to identify them. Innocent people are convicted on the basis of errant eyewitness testimony. In the USA, the FBI has carried out DNA testing on people convicted of rape and other crimes which leave biological evidence (Connors et al., 1996). Wells et al. (1998) describe 40 of these cases, in which the most prominent evidence that convicted the person was eyewitness identification, often by the victim. The DNA tests showed that none of these "criminals" was in fact the culprit, and all were (eventually) released. Huff, Rattner and Sagarin (1996) estimate that there are approximately 10 000 false convictions in the USA each year. Agreeing with Brandon and Davies' (1973) findings from the UK, Huff and colleagues believe that eyewitness misidentification is the leading cause of false convictions.

Consider the case of Ronald Cotton, one of the people discussed in the DNA report and recently the focus of the Frontline documentary *What Jennifer Saw* (Frontline, 1998; additional information gathered from *http://www.pbs.org/wgbh/ pages/frontline/shows/dna/*, all quotes are from interviews gathered for the *Frontline* programme). In one night in July 1984, in separate but similar incidents, the apartments of two women were broken into and the women raped. Ronald Cotton, a black man, was arrested. The first victim, Jennifer Thompson (a white woman), identified Cotton in a photo-spread, in a live line-up (called an identi-

Behaviour, Crime and Legal Processes: A Guide for Forensic Practitioners.
Edited by James McGuire, Tom Mason and Aisling O'Kane.
© 2000 John Wiley & Sons Ltd.

fication parade in the UK) and at trial. She said he had "a really distinctive nose". The second victim did not identify Cotton. The positive identification by the first victim, along with a torch found at Cotton's house being similar to one used in the crimes and the rubber of Cotton's trainers being consistent with traces found at one of the crime scenes, was enough for the jury to convict Cotton of raping Jennifer Thompson.

That jury did not hear that the other rape victim did not identify Cotton in either the photo-spread or a live lineup. A re-trial was ordered in 1987. At this trial, but not seen by the jurors, was Robert Poole. Poole, an inmate with Cotton, had allegedly told Cotton he did the crimes. This information was not allowed as evidence but Jennifer Thompson saw both men. She told the Frontline programme, "I never remember looking at Bobby Poole thinking, 'I've got the wrong person. I mean I've made this huge mistake. Now I remember'."[1] By the time of the second trial, the second victim now believed that Cotton was the culprit. Ronald Cotton was convicted of both rapes and sentenced to two life sentences.

In 1995, DNA tests showed that Robert Poole's confession was legitimate. Ronald Cotton was released and pardoned entitling him to $5000 compensation (less than 2p per day that he was incarcerated).

Numerous other cases exist in the literature of miscarriages of justice because of faulty eyewitness testimony (for example, Huff, Rattner & Sagarin, 1996; Loftus & Ketcham, 1991). In a survey of lineups in London approximately 20% of the time the eyewitness identified an innocent foil chosen by police to stand with the suspect (Wright & McDaid, 1996). While these foils were not charged with the crime, it demonstrates the extent of eyewitness errors; errors which can as easily be made of an innocent suspect taking part in an identification parade. Levi (1998) used the London line-up data to estimate that when a suspect is picked in a lineup, about 25% of the time that person is not guilty. This is a disturbingly high figure. It is likely that many of these innocent suspects were convicted.

Despite these erroneous identifications, much of what is recalled is accurate. Eyewitness testimony can play a profound role in the apprehension and prosecution of criminal offenders. The eyewitness is probably the single most common form of witness in criminal trials (Penrod, Fulero & Cutler, 1995). Our concern is that given the fallibility of some eyewitness reports, this form of evidence is weighted too highly by police in their investigations and by jurors in their decisions. A recent survey of British police officers found that the police believe that eyewitnesses are accurate and reliable most of the time (Kebell & Milne, 1998). This could lead them down investigative avenues that other more reliable evidence contradicts. With respect to the Cotton case, so much weight was put on the identification by Thompson that Poole's confession was not allowed to be presented to the jurors in the second trial.

The weight that jurors place on eyewitness identification has also been

---

[1] Compare this with "Nancy Von Roper" (not her real name), who identified Steve Titus as her rapist, when she saw her actual rapist: " 'Oh, my God,' she said, sobbing, 'What have I done to Mr. Titus?' " (Loftus & Ketcham, 1991, p. 51).

demonstrated to be too high. Loftus (1979, p. 10) gave people one of three versions of a crime. When there was only circumstantial evidence against the suspect 18% of the people opted for conviction. However, when there was an eyewitness the conviction rate rose to 72%. Critically, this dropped to only 68% when the eyewitness testimony was discredited due to extremely poor eyesight.

In this chapter we examine factors that are likely to result in inaccurate eyewitness memory and the conditions under which an eyewitness is more likely to produce a reliable identification. We begin by discussing the way in which memories can be distorted and how memory operates for traumatic events. Next we discuss the extent to which we can improve eyewitness recall through the use of a Cognitive Interview. We conclude with a discussion of the usefulness of various types of identification procedures.

THE MALLEABILITY OF EYEWITNESS MEMORY

There are many metaphors that have been used by scientists and the populace for memory processes (Roediger, 1980). One popular metaphor is that of a video recorder. Providing the correct tape is found, and the physical apparatus is working, then an accurate representation of the original event can be played. Research has demonstrated that this metaphor is highly misleading. Memories are reconstructions. The exact way in which memories are reconstructed is debated, but that they are not complete accurate representations of the past is agreed throughout the scientific psychology community. A more suitable metaphor comes from Neisser's (1967) seminal textbook, *Cognitive Psychology*, where he likened memory construction to a palaeontologist creating a model of a dinosaur from a few pieces of evidence but also from theories about dinosaurs. Memories can be constructed from a few fragments of recollection coupled with the scripts or schema which guide the encoding, the storage and the reconstruction of memories. Much of the research dismantling the video recorder myth has been conducted as part of eyewitness testimony research.

Imagine that you have just seen a car accident. In an attempt to determine culpability and cause, an officer asks you: "About how fast were the cars going when they hit each other?" If you are like Loftus and Palmer's (1974, exp. 2) participants who saw a video of a car crash, you might have said about 8 mph. However, if you were asked "About how fast were the cars going when they smashed into each other?" your estimate is likely to have been higher, about 10 mph. The information in the question influences the estimate of speed. More interestingly it can even influence participants' responses to whether there was shattered glass at the scene of the accident. Only 14% of the "hit" participants thought that there was shattered glass, against 32% of the "smashed" participants. Loftus and Palmer's seminal paper was one of the early studies on the influence of post-event information (PEI) on memory. Here the PEI was delivered as part of a biasing question.

While Loftus and Palmer (1974) used a leading, or biasing, question, other researchers have presented errant information, sometimes called *misinformation*. The basic misinformation effect (Loftus, Miller & Burns, 1978), that people shown misinformation are more likely to report the misinformation than controls who have not been presented with misinformation, has been replicated in numerous studies with both adults and children (see Ceci & Bruck, 1993, for review). However, there is still much debate regarding the role of PEI in reconstructing memories (for example, Ayers & Reder, 1998; Brainerd & Reyna, 1998; Wright & Loftus, 1998). One important aspect of misinformation research is that once a person comes to believe in a memory, whether true or false, it can be difficult to change (Brainerd & Poole, 1997). The memory becomes a valued "possession" and part of the person's autobiography (Wright & Gaskell, 1995). This appears to have happened with Jennifer Thompson. After identifying Ronald Cotton in a photo-spread, seeing (and identifying) him again in a line-up and then seeing him in court, his face was part of her memory of the incident. Even when confronted with the DNA evidence she had difficulty updating her memory.

One possible reason for the misinformation effect is that participants remember the misinformation but they do not remember where they heard it. Cognitive psychologists refer to this as a *source monitoring error* (Johnson, Hashtroudi & Lindsay, 1993). It can happen when you confuse what is real and what is fantasy, or what you experienced directly with what you saw on TV or heard about from someone else. An example of source monitoring errors comes from Crombag, Wagenaar and Van Koppen's (1996) study of memories for the case of an El Al Boeing 747 crashing into apartment buildings in Amsterdam. Crombag et al. asked people if they remembered seeing the film clip of the crash. No one had filmed this crash, yet 60% said that they saw the plane crash on television. Some even answered detailed questions about the crash. Participants presumably had heard numerous reports about the plane crash and may have used this information to form an image of what had taken place. Under these conditions, it becomes relatively easy to suggest to them that they may have actually seen a video of the crash on TV.

One way in which source monitoring errors affect eyewitness testimony is by *unconscious transference*. This involves remembering something seen in one context when it was encoded in another context. A vivid example of unconscious transference comes from one of the key witnesses in the Oklahoma bombing, where, on 19 April 1995, 168 people died and over 600 were injured (see Memon & Wright, 1999, for further details). On 17 April, Timothy McVeigh, who was convicted of the bombing, rented a Ryder truck from Elliott's Body Shop. One of the employees at Elliott's, Tom Kessenger, gave the FBI a description that helped to lead to McVeigh's conviction. However, Kessenger also reported another man who, he remembered, was with McVeigh and gave the FBI a description. This person became known as John Doe 2 and the FBI began a massive manhunt for a person meeting this description. What they found was a man resembling the description who was at Elliott's on 18 April. It appears that Kessenger may have accurately remembered this other man, but mistakenly remembered him being with McVeigh.

When viewing a crime, you may encode certain details. These fragments are held together, in a sense, into a coherent memory by your mental theories about events, what cognitive psychologists often call scripts or schemata. This can bias a person's memory. Further, after viewing a crime you may encounter further information, some of which could be misleading. This misinformation is often subtle and goes undetected: "The new information invades us, like a Trojan horse, precisely because we do not detect its influence" (Loftus, 1993, p. 530). Other events, and even our own thoughts, become entangled in the mind and can play their roles in the reconstruction of a memory.

THE CHILD WITNESS

In the last two decades the increase in reports of child abuse has led researchers working in the area of children's testimony to focus on the vulnerability of child witnesses in interview situations. For example, a large body of research has set out to identify how easily children may succumb to misleading suggestions provided by an authority figure (Ackil & Zaragoza, 1995; Ceci & Bruck, 1993, 1995; Leichtman & Ceci, 1995; Poole & Lindsay, 1995).

Leichtman and Ceci (1995), in their study of pre-schoolers' (3–6 year olds) eyewitness reports, examined the effects of repeated interviews with different degrees and types of suggestive influences. Following the visit of a stranger (Sam Stone) to their nursery, some children were interviewed with suggestive questions about the event once a week for the four weeks following the visit. The fifth interview experienced by all children was conducted ten weeks after the event by a new interviewer who was not present during the visit of the stranger or during the prior four interviews. In this final interview all children were asked for a free report and then probed with questions. The basic finding was that prior repeated suggestions increased false reporting. The effects were observed both in the free report and in the question phases of the final interview.

The Leichtman and Ceci (1995) study is one of the first to have noted effects of suggestions on free recall performance, which is generally assumed to produce an uncontaminated account (but see Warren & Lane, 1995; Poole & Lindsay, 1995). Moreover, the Leichtman and Ceci study demonstrated that an event which is inaccurately reported in free recall will continue to be inaccurately reported when probed with questions. In other words, a prior erroneous report increases the likelihood of making a subsequent inaccurate report. Furthermore, the children in the Leichtman and Ceci study tended to embellish their statements with more and more confabulated details after a series of interviews. The Leichtman and Ceci procedure is an example of quite intense suggestion. Although this may happen in real cases (see Ceci & Bruck, 1995, and Ceci et al., 1994, for examples) it would also be relevant to look at the effects of one inappropriate interview (i.e. containing some suggestive questions). This may, for example, happen if parents are suspicious that their child had been sexually abused and then try to verify this suspicion. Since they are unlikely to be experienced interviewers, the chances are that they will ask at least some suggestive questions. The question then is whether or not a single suggestive interview or an interview with a few suggestive questions will have the same devastating effects on the quality and evidential value of a later statement as the repeated suggestions of the Leichtman and Ceci type.

Using the "logic of opposition" procedure, several recent studies have shown that when participants (children and adults) are explicitly instructed not to report anything encountered in the misleading phase of the experiment (because it is wrong), they continue to report such misinformation. In other words, they believe they saw details that were merely suggested to them (e.g. Lindsay, Gonzales & Eso, 1995). There is some evidence to suggest that children who are made aware of the purpose and relevance of reporting details of the original event, may be able to disregard misleading information (Newcombe & Siegal, 1995; Thierry, Spence & Memon, 1998).

EMOTION AND MEMORY

Jennifer Thompson was raped at knife point. It was clearly a traumatic experience that continues to haunt her. She tried hard to position herself so that she could see the rapist, and engaged him in conversation in the hope that some useful information could be gathered to assist with the police investigation. Even more than a decade later, when being interviewed by Frontline, she could vividly recount some details. The question is: How does memory work when placed in these circumstances? Ideally, when encoding a highly emotional and consequential event the mind/brain would encode everything. Brown and Kulik (1977) described such a mechanism and said it produced "flashbulb memories". Research since then has concluded that while people have good memories for some events, and usually emotion and consequentiality are correlated with memory clarity, there is no mechanism that records everything (see Conway, 1994, and Wright & Gaskell, 1995, for a discussion of flashbulb memories).

Brown and Kulik (1977) said it would be important, from an evolutionary standpoint, to have good memory for emotive and consequential events. They gave the example of encountering a dangerous carnivore and stated that it would be an advantage to have a flashbulb mechanism to record details of the event. However, it is likely that the increased encoding and accuracy would be at the cost of additional time.

If the flashbulb memory hypothesis is at one extreme, then at the other end is the notion that memories for highly emotive events are repressed (see Loftus & Kaufman, 1992, for a comparison of these hypotheses). The validity of this repression hypothesis is hotly debated and entangled in the recovered memory debate. As discussed below, it is very difficult to study memory for very traumatic events using strict experimental controls for obvious ethical reasons. Instead people who are known to have experienced trauma are questioned about the events. Pope, Oliva and Hudson (1999) recently reviewed 33 studies of memory for traumatic events and found reports of traumatic amnesia to be very rare and explainable by other causes. From this we would predict, as is observed, that witnesses to violent crimes are aware of the event unless there are non-psychological explanations for their not being so (such as severe head injuries, alcoholic blackouts, being too young, etc.). Obviously for minor and non-consequential crimes, like any minor event, people will forget. The point is that the increased level of emotionality does not make the person forget.

What appears to happens is something between the two extremes. The memory system is efficient (Easterbrook, 1959). In situations where both accuracy and rapid processing are desirable, it focuses attention on central aspects of the scene (Christianson et al., 1991). This creates good memory for these details at the cost of memory for peripheral objects. This is almost exactly the opposite of Brown and Kulik's (1977) hypothesis, where increased emotion supposedly led to good memory for peripheral details. The flashbulb memory studies, however, have consequential (or important) confounding emotion. These are almost always correlated. It seems likely that heightened emotion improves memory for central details, but that the importance of certain events/memories encourages people to reconstruct their memories for peripheral details to make a better story (which does not mean that the story is inaccurate).

With relation to eyewitness testimony, this focusing of attention is often called *weapon focus* (Loftus, Loftus & Messo, 1987). When a threatening object, such as a gun or knife, is present at the scene of a crime, it can capture people's attention and promote memory for the weapon at the expense of other details such as the suspect's face (see Stelbay, 1992, for a review). It is worth noting that recent data suggest that novel items also create this narrowing of attention. Mitchell, Livorsky and Mather (1998) and Pickel (1998) found that memory for a perpetrator's appearance was affected more by the person holding an unusual object (like a stalk of celery) than by the person behaving threateningly.

Real world research seems to support the idea that memory for emotive events is fairly good. In Wright and McDaid's (1996) study, it was estimated that identification accuracy was better for violent than for non-violent crimes. In fact, Tollestrup, Turtle and Yuille (1994) compared robberies with and without a weapon. They found "the presence of a weapon does not appear to have a detrimental influence on the amount of descriptive information or accuracy of that information" (p. 158). However, Tollestrup et al. are careful in pointing out the difficulties of making firm conclusions, given the complexities dealing with real crimes. With their comparison, for example, it is likely that the police put more effort into solving crimes involving guns.

Given the difficulties of studying memory for emotional events, we agree with Tollestrup et al., and others (see below), that a combination of laboratory, archival and field simulations are necessary to create theories of memory for emotional events that will be able to disentangle the various hypotheses about how memory operates in situations of extreme emotion. It is worth noting, though, that not all eyewitnesses are in a highly emotive state. The Oklahoma bombing witness, Tom Kessenger, for example, was simply observing what he felt was a routine transaction.

It has been shown so far that cognitive psychologists have some understanding of the factors that may influence encoding and retrieval of eyewitness events. How can that knowledge be used to improve the performance and obtain more detailed and accurate reports? The Cognitive Interview (CI) may be one answer.

GETTING MORE DETAIL: THE COGNITIVE INTERVIEW

The CI is a forensic tool that comprises a series of memory retrieval techniques designed to increase the amount of information that can be obtained from a witness. The CI may help police officers and other professionals to obtain a more complete and accurate report from a witness. The CI can only be used with a co-operative interviewee and therefore may be most suitable in interviews where the witness is not a suspect. The effectiveness of the CI in improving the quality and quantity of information from an eyewitness, and as a way of improving the skills of interviewers, has been tested empirically. To date, some 45 studies have been conducted, including two studies conducted in the field using real-life witnesses and police officers trained in the CI technique (Koehnken et al., in press).

The CI was initially developed by the psychologists Ed Geiselman (University of California, Los Angeles) and Ron Fisher (Florida International University) in 1984 as a response to the many requests they received from police officers and legal professionals for a method of improving witness interviews. The CI is based upon known psychological principles of remembering and retrieval of information from memory. Police detectives trained to use this technique enabled witnesses to produce over 40% more valid information than detectives using their traditional interviewing techniques. In fact university students using this new procedure obtained more information from witnesses than did experienced police officers who interviewed in their normal way! (See Memon & Higham, in press).

The CI represents the alliance of two fields of study. The original version drew heavily upon what psychologists know about the way in which we remember things. Revisions of the procedure focused more heavily on the practical considerations for managing a social interaction and this was led by a desire to improve communication in police interviews and alleviate some of the problems described above. The "cognitive" components of the CI draw upon two theoretical principles. The first is that a retrieval cue is effective to the extent that there is an overlap between the encoded information and the retrieval cue and that reinstatement of the original encoding context increases the accessibility of stored information (Tulving & Thomson's Encoding Specificity Hypothesis, 1973). Thus one of the most frequently used components of the CI is for the witness to mentally reconstruct the physical (external) and personal (internal) contexts which existed at the time of the crime. The second theoretical perspective that influenced the development of the CI was the Multiple Trace Theory (Bower, 1967). This suggests that rather than having memories of discrete and unconnected incidents, our memories consist of a network of associations and, consequently, there are several means by which a memory could be cued. It follows from this that information not accessible with one technique may be accessible with another (Fisher & Geiselman, 1992). An example of a CI technique that draws upon this principle is the instruction to make retrieval attempts from different starting points. Witnesses usually feel they have to start at the beginning and are usually asked to do so. However, the CI encourages witnesses to recall in a variety of orders from the end, or from the middle, or from the most memorable event.

The original version of the cognitive interview resulted in substantial gains in the amount of correct information that was elicited from eyewitnesses without any apparent increases in errors (Geiselman et al., 1985). However, in order to be able to implement the use of the "cognitive" components of the CI effectively, it is necessary to provide interviewers with the necessary social skills and communication strategies that are required to build rapport with a witness. The enhanced version combines the four cognitive techniques with some strategies for improving interviewer–witness communication and flow of information in the interview (Fisher & Geiselman, 1992; Memon & Stevenage, 1996). Several techniques are used to facilitate the communication including the "transfer of control" of the interview from the interviewer to the witness. This technique is put into place during the rapport-building phase in several ways— for instance, through the use of open questions which request an elaborated response from the witness (thereby allowing the witness to do most of the talking), and by not interrupting witnesses, by timing questions carefully so that they are related to witnesses' retrieval patterns and not to a protocol that an interviewer may be using. For example, if a witness is describing a suspect's face, an appropriate question would be to ask about eye colour rather than the suspect's shoes.

The CI generally compares favourably with other interview procedures such as the typical police interview (standard interview), the Guided Memory Interview (Malpass & Devine, 1981), the Structured Interview (SI; Memon et al., 1997, but see Memon & Stevenage, 1996), and hypnosis (Geiselman et al., 1985). There is, however, some evidence to suggest that the cognitive interview does not work well unless police interviewers are sufficiently trained (Memon et al., 1994). With children, the CI has been found to increase errors in reporting (Memon et al., 1997) although there is some controversy over how much we should be concerned about a small increase in errors when accuracy rates are equivalent across the CI and the SI (see Memon & Stevenage, 1996; Memon & Higham, in press).

IDENTIFICATION: THE RELIABILITY OF WITNESS DESCRIPTIONS AND LINEUPS

Tyrone Briggs, a black 19-year-old high school basketball star, was arrested in January 1987 for a series of rapes on white and Asian professional women in the Seattle area. Tyrone's defence attorney Hansen describes the case as a Tragedy of Errors. First of all Tyrone had a terrible stutter, something that none of the five victims mentioned. Tyrone also has a distinctive mole that went unnoticed until the police drew attention to it. Nor did the initial descriptions given by the victims match Tyrone. The most detailed description came from a victim who described her assailant as 22–25 years of age, with yellow crooked teeth with gaps at the front and bushy Afro hair that was tinted red. Tyrone was barely 19, wore his hair in "Michael Jackson" like Jeri curls, weighed 155 pounds and has white evenly spaced teeth and a prominent mole above his right lip (Loftus & Ketcham, 1991). Upon Tyrone's arrest, victims were called to the police station to attempt a live identification. They were told, however, that this was not possible because they did not have enough people who resembled the suspect to conduct a lineup. Instead the police made a photo montage which included Tyrone and drew a mole on each of the foils in an attempt to create a fair photo lineup. It wasn't too difficult for witnesses to assume from this that the suspect held in custody had a mole (post-event information). All five victims identified Tyrone from the photographs but each had reservations (Loftus & Ketcham, 1991).

On 12 December 1987, Tyrone was sentenced to 16 years, 3 months in prison. This conviction was later reversed following evidence of jury misconduct. Two further trials resulted in hung juries and the third in a mistrial with the jury split 10–2 on the side of acquittal. On 14 June 1990, the case was dismissed (Loftus & Ketcham, 1991).

The purpose of a lineup is to add information to the guilt or innocence of the suspect. In order to help their investigation, the police will often ask witnesses to view a book of photographs or a live (sometimes video) lineup of the suspect with several members of the public. Psychologists have researched many of the factors that can influence the validity of identifications made from a lineup (for reviews, see Cutler & Penrod, 1995; Memon, Vrij & Bull, 1998; Sporer, Malpass & Koehnken, 1996). Most lineups are composed of a police suspect among some foils or people known to be innocent of the crime. The foils should all resemble the suspect (see Wells, Leippe & Ostrom, 1979; for guidelines for assessing lineup fairness). The lineups can be presented in different ways. Most common is when a witness is exposed to all lineup members together (*simultaneously*) and they then try to identify the one that looks *most* like their memory for the culprit. The task becomes a relative judgement. By showing witnesses lineup members one at a time (*sequentially*) they are forced to make an absolute judgement. Lindsay and Wells (1985) found significantly fewer false positive identifications in the sequential lineup condition (18.3%) than in the simultaneous (35%). Sequential lineups do not, however, seem to aid the identification of child witnesses (Lindsay et al., 1997) or the elderly (Searcy, Bartlett & Memon, in press).

Sometimes a witness is just shown a photo of one suspect and asked if that person is the culprit. This is called a "showup". Showups are considered prejudicial (Yarmey, Yarmey & Yarmey, 1996) because witnesses may feel obliged to make an identification because they believe that the police would not be showing them the picture unless "they got their man". Witnesses may feel that it is their social responsibility to protect society and see the guilty person punished; they may be under great pressure to confirm the hypotheses of the investigating officer. Thus, the risk of false identification in showups is high.

THE EFFECTS OF PRIOR EXPOSURE TO A MUGSHOT

Research has shown that seeing the suspect previously (in the media, in mugshots, in an earlier lineup) influences identification accuracy in subsequently presented lineups. The mechanisms responsible for this (source monitoring and unconscious transference) were discussed earlier. Several experiments (Brown, Deffenbacher & Sturgill, 1977; Gorenstein & Ellsworth, 1980) have shown that when witnesses view a lineup after having looked at mugshots, they are more likely to identify a person whose mugshot photograph they have previously seen (regardless of whether that person is the perpetrator) than people not shown that mugshot. In the case of Tyrone Briggs, this problem was accentuated by the fact that witnesses had earlier been presented with a lineup in which all suspects had a mole. When witnesses were shown a second lineup some weeks later, only one person from the original lineup reappeared (Tyrone) and he was the only one with a mole (Loftus & Ketcham, 1991).

In the Gorenstein and Ellsworth (1980) study of all the people who were previously shown the mugshots, 44% identified the mugshot person and 22% identified the real intruder. Of those who did not participate in the mugshot phase, 39% correctly identified the intruder. There are two possible reasons for this *repeated identification* effect (Koehnken, Malpass & Wogalter, 1996). It occurs because the witness recognizes the photo but forgets the circumstances in which he or she originally saw it (resulting in source confusion and the "unconscious transference" effect, discussed earlier). An alternative explanation is that once a witness comes to a decision and expresses it, he or she feels committed and may be less willing to change the decision later (so-called "commitment" effect; Kiesler, 1971). Both effects can account for why witnesses identified Tyrone in the second lineup.

CROSS-RACE IDENTIFICATIONS

Another variable affecting eyewitness accuracy is the racial similarity of the witness and suspect. Cross-race identifications are more difficult than same race identifications (Brigham & Ready, 1985). Differences in frequency and quality of contact may account for these effects (Chance & Goldstein, 1996). Dunning, Li and Malpass (1998) conducted an interesting study of basketball fandom. They tested the hypothesis that European American basketball fans, because they have spent years watching African Americans play the sport, would achieve higher rates of identification accuracy in a recognition memory test for African faces than would European Americans who did not follow the game. This is what they found: the basketball fans were just as accurate at identifying African faces as European ones and were more accurate in identifying African faces than their basketball novice counterparts. Finally, the basketball fans were better able to discriminate previously seen African faces from novel ones. Overall measures of intra-interracial contact only predicted performance for African American subjects: those who reported high levels of own race contact more accurately recognised own race faces.

The cross-race effect may have influenced witnesses' identification of Tyrone Briggs (Loftus & Ketcham, 1991). Three of the victims were Caucasians, two were Asians and the assailant was black. One of the victims who positively identified Briggs is also black. However, this victim had previously encountered Briggs (they had mutual friends) and had come into casual contact with him several times prior to the incident. In other words, the face of Briggs was already familiar to this witness. An unconscious transference effect cannot be ruled out. Similarly, that Jennifer Thompson is white and her rapist is black, could have influenced the unreliability of her identification.

CONFIDENCE–ACCURACY RELATIONSHIP

Most people believe that a confident witness is an accurate witness. To what extent is this the case? Early reviews of the literature showed that inaccurate witnesses are just as confident in their memory as are accurate witnesses (Bothwell, Deffenbacher & Brigham, 1987). Similarly, field and laboratory studies consistently demonstrate that the accuracy of verbal descriptions of once seen suspects or other targets are uncorrelated with accuracy of later facial identifications (e.g. Wells, 1985).

Recent reviews have indicated that when a confidence–accuracy relationship is measured only for choosers (those who pick someone from a lineup) the relationship is stronger (Sporer et al., 1995). More recently, it has been shown that the relationship between confidence in an identification and accuracy depends in part on the participant's ability to identify the target. Gruneberg and Sykes (1993) have also questioned the ecological validity of laboratory studies of confidence and accuracy relationships. They argue that laboratory studies invariably involve placing subjects under specific conditions designed to produce variability in responding. Gruneberg and Sykes argue that in real-life situations an aspect of the situation may be so salient that everyone who witnesses it is likely to be correct. Both accuracy and confidence are higher under conditions that lead to good memory of the target than under conditions that lead to poor memory (Lindsay, Read & Sharma, 1998). This fits with the optimality hypothesis put forward by Deffenbacher (1980) which states that the more optimal the viewing conditions are, the higher is the relationship between confidence and accuracy. Lindsay, Read and Sharma (1998) also noted that those conditions that lead to higher confidence in correct identifications also lead to higher confidence in false identifications.

CONCLUSION

"The scientific study of eyewitness testimony has been one of the most successful applied research topics in scientific psychology over the last two decades" (Wells et al., 1998, p. 604).

In this chapter we focused on current scientific literature on the reliability of eyewitness testimony under different conditions. The significance of eyewitness research was highlighted with references to cases where identification errors have resulted in miscarriages of justice. The malleability of eyewitness memory was illustrated by showing how memory is reconstructed and altered during the process of retrieval. We compared child and adult witnesses and young adults with seniors. We examined whether memories for emotional events were retained any better than memory for trivial events. The evidence is not clear cut but some studies have shown that novel or emotionally arousing events may narrow attention so that we encode some details at the expense of others. Recent research on the Cognitive Interview was used as an example of how eyewitness memory may be enhanced. The final section highlighted some of the problems that can arise with eyewitness identification procedures.

There is no doubt that eyewitness testimony is among the most important forms of evidence that can be presented in a criminal case. As our knowledge of the factors influencing eyewitness performance continues to improve and research is translated into good practice with respect to eyewitness identification procedures, the chances of a wrongful conviction as a result of an identification error will to be reduced.

REFERENCES

Ackil, J.K. & Zaragoza, M. (1995) Developmental differences in eyewitness suggestibility and memory for source. *Journal of Experimental Child Psychology*, **60**, 57–83.

Ayers, M.S. & Reder, L.M. (1998) A theoretical review of the misinformation effect: Predictions from an activation-based memory model. *Psychonomic Bulletin and Review*, **5**, 1–21.

Bothwell, R.K., Deffenbacher, K.A. & Brigham, J.C. (1987) Correlations of eyewitness accuracy and confidence: Optimality Hypothesis Revisited. *Journal of Applied Psychology*, **72**, 691–695.

Bower, G. (1967) A multicomponent theory of memory trace. In K.W. Spence & J.T. Spence (Eds) *The Psychology of Learning and Motivation*, Vol 1. New York: Academic Press.

Brandon, R. & Davies, C. (1973) *Wrongful Imprisonment*. London: Allen & Unwin.

Brainerd, C. & Poole, D. (1997) Long-term survival of children's false memories: A review. *Learning and Individual Differences*, **9**, 125–151.

Brainerd, C.J. & Reyna, V.F. (1998) Fuzzy-trace theory and children's false memories. *Journal of Experimental Child Psychology*, **71**, 81–129.

Brigham, J. & Ready, D.R. (1985) Own race bias in lineup construction. *Law and Human Behaviour*, **9**, 415–424.

Brown, R., Deffenbacher, K. & Sturgill, W. (1977) Memory for faces and the circumstances of encounter. *Journal of Applied Psychology*, **62**, 311–318.

Brown, R. & Kulik, J. (1977) Flashbulb memories. *Cognition*, **5**, 73–99.

Ceci, S.J. & Bruck, M. (1993) Suggestibility of the child witness: A historical review and synthesis. *Psychological Bulletin*, **113**, 403–439.

Ceci, S.J. & Bruck, M. (1995) *Jeopardy in the Courtroom*. New York: American Psychological Association.

Ceci, S.J., Loftus, E.F., Leichtman, M. & Bruck, M. (1994) The role of source misattributions in the creation of false beliefs among preschoolers. *International Journal of Clinical and Experimental Hypnosis*, **62**, 304–320.

Chance, J.E. & Goldstein, A. (1996) The other-race effect and eyewitness identification. In S.L. Sporer, R.S. Malpass & G. Koehnken (Eds) *Psychological Issues in Eyewitness Identification* (pp. 153–176) Mahwah, NJ: Lawrence Erlbaum.

Christianson, S.-Å. (1992) Emotional stress and eyewitness memory: A critical review. *Psychological Bulletin*, **112**, 284–309.

Christianson, S.-Å., Loftus, E.F., Hoffman, H. & Loftus, G.R. (1991) Eye fixations and memory for emotional events. *Journal of Experimental Psychology: Learning, Memory and Cognition*, **17**, 693–701.

Connors, E., Lundregan, T., Miller, N. & McEwen, T. (1996) *Convicted by juries, exonerated by science: Case studies in the use of DNA evidence to establish innocence after trial*. NIH Research Report: US Department of Justice.

Conway, M.A. (1994) *Flashbulb Memories*. Hillsdale, NJ: Lawrence Erlbaum Associates.

Crombag, H.F.M., Wagenaar, W.A. & Van Koppen, P.J. (1996) Crashing memories and the problem of "source monitoring". *Applied Cognitive Psychology*, **10**, 95–104.

Cutler, B.L. & Penrod, S.D. (1995) *Mistaken Identification: The Eyewitness, Psychology and Law*. New York: Cambridge University Press.

Deffenbacher, K.A. (1980) Eyewitness accuracy and confidence: Can we infer anything about their relationship? *Law and Human Behaviour*, **4**, 233–260.

Dunning, D., Li, J. & Malpass, R. (March, 1998) *Basketball fandom and cross-race identification among European-Americans: Another look at the contract hypothesis*. Paper presented at the American Psychology–Law Society Biennial Conference, Redondo Beach, CA. 24.

Easterbrook, J.A. (1959) The effect of emotion on cue utilization and the organization of behavior. *Psychological Review*, **66**, 249–280.

Fisher, R.P. & Geiselman, R.E. (1992) *Memory Enhancing Techniques for Investigative Interviewing: The Cognitive Interview*. Springfield, Ill.: Charles C. Thomas.

Geiselman, R.E., Fisher, R.P., MacKinnon, D.P. & Holland, H.L. (1985) Eyewitness memory enhancement in the police interview: Cognitive retrieval mnemonics versus hypnosis. *Journal of Applied Psychology*, **70**, 401–412.

Gorenstein, G.W. & Ellsworth, P. (1980) Effect of choosing an incorrect photograph on a later identification by an eyewitness. *Journal of Applied Psychology*, **65**, 616–622.

Gruneberg, M.M. & Sykes, R.N. (1993) The generalisability of confidence-accuracy studies in eyewitnessing. *Memory*, **1**, 185–190.

Huff, C.R., Rattner, A. & Sagarin, E. (1996) *Convicted But Innocent: Wrongful Conviction and Public Policy*. Thousand Oaks, CA: Sage.

Johnson, M.K., Hashtroudi, S. & Lindsay, D.S. (1993) Source monitoring. *Psychological Bulletin*, **114**, 3–28.

Kebbel, M. & Milne, R. (1998) Police officers' perceptions of eyewitness performance in forensic investigations. *The Journal of Social Psychology*, **138**(3), 232–330.

Kiesler, C. (1971) *The Psychology of Commitment*. New York: Academic Press.

Koehnken, G., Malpass, R. & Wogalter, M.S. (1996) Forensic applications of lineup research. In S.L. Sporer, R.S. Malpass & G. Koehnken (Eds) *Psychological Issues in Eyewitness Identification* (pp. 205–232). Mahwah, NJ: Lawrence Erlbaum.

Koehnken, G., Milne, R., Memon, A. & Bull, R. (in press) A meta-analysis of the effects of the cognitive interview. *Psychology, Crime and Law*.

Leichtman, M.D. & Ceci, S.J. (1995) The effects of stereotypes and suggestions on pre-scholars' reports. *Developmental Psychology*, **31**, 568–578.

Levi, A.M. (1998) Are defendants guilty if they were chosen in a lineup? *Law and Human Behavior*, **22**, 389–407.

Lindsay, D.S., Gonzales, V. & Eso, K. (1995) Aware and unaware uses of memories of post-event suggestions. In M. Zaragoza, J.R. Graham, G.C.N. Hall, R. Hirschman & Y.S. Ben-Porath (Eds) *Memory and Testimony in the Child Witness* (pp. 86–108). Thousand Oaks, CA: Sage.

Lindsay, D.S., Read, J.D. & Sharma, K. (1998) Accuracy and confidence in person identification: The relationship is strong when witnessing conditions vary widely. *Psychological Science*, **9**, 215–218.

Lindsay, R.C.L., Pozzulo, J.D., Craig, W., Lee, K. & Corber, S. (1997) Simultaneous lineups, sequential lineups and showups: Eyewitness identification decisions of adults and children. *Law and Human Behaviour*, **21**, 391–404.

Lindsay, R.C.L. & Wells, G.L. (1985) Improving eyewitness identifications from lineups: Simultaneous versus sequential lineup presentation. *Journal of Applied Psychology*, **70**, 556–564.

Loftus, E.F. (1979) *Eyewitness Testimony*. Cambridge: Harvard University Press.

Loftus, E.F. (1993) The reality of repressed memories. *American Psychologist*, **48**, 518–537.

Loftus, E.F. & Kaufman, L. (1992) Why do traumatic experiences sometimes produce good memory (flashbulbs) and sometimes no memory (repression)? In E. Winograd & U. Neisser (Eds) *Affect and Accuracy in Recall: Studies of "Flashbulb" Memories* (pp. 212–223). Cambridge: Cambridge University Press.

Loftus, E.F. & Ketcham, K. (1991) *Witness for the Defense: The Accused, the Eyewitness, and the Expert Who Puts Memory on Trial*. New York: St Martin's Press.

Loftus, E.F., Loftus, G.R. & Messo, J. (1987) Some facts about weapon focus. *Law and Human Behavior*, **11**, 55–62.

Loftus, E.F., Miller, D.G. & Burns, H.J. (1978) Semantic integration of verbal information into a visual memory. *Journal of Experimental Psychology: Human Learning and Memory*, **4**, 19–31.

Loftus, E.F. & Palmer, J.C. (1974) Reconstruction of automobile destruction: An example of the interaction between language and memory. *Journal of Verbal Learning and Verbal Behavior*, **13**, 585–589.

Malpass, R. & Devine, P. (1981) Guided memory in eyewitness identification. *Journal of Applied Psychology*, **66**(3), 343–350.

McCloskey, M. & Zaragoza, M. (1985) Misleading post-event information and memory for events: Arguments and evidence against memory impairment hypotheses. *Journal of Experimental Psychology: General*, **114**, 1–16.

Memon, A. & Higham, P. (1999) A review of the cognitive interview. *Psychology, Crime and Law* (Special issue) **5**, 177–196.

Memon, A. & Wright, D. (1999) The search for John Doe 2: Eyewitness Testimony and the Oklahoma Bombing. *The Psychologist*.

Memon, A. & Stevenage, S. (1996) Interviewing witnesses: what works and what doesn't? *Psycholoquy*, 96.7.06.witness-memory.1.memon.

Memon, A., Wark, L., Holley, A., Bull, R. & Koehnken, G. (1994) Towards understanding the effects of interviewer training in evaluating the cognitive interview. *Applied Cognitive Psychology*, **8**, 641–659.

Memon, A., Wark, L., Holley, A., Bull, R. & Koehnken, G. (1997) Eyewitness performance in cognitive and structured interviews. *Memory*, **5**, 639–655.

Memon, A., Vrij, A. & Bull, R. (1998) *Psychology and Law: Truthfulness, Accuracy and Credibility of Victims, Witnesses and Suspects*. Hemel Hempstead: McGraw-Hill.

Mitchell, K., Livosky, M. & Mather, M. (1998) The weapon focus effect revisited: The role of novelty. *Legal and Criminological Psychology*, **3**, 287–303.

Niesser, U. (1967) *Cognitive Psychology*. New York, NY: Appleton-Century-Crofts.

Newcombe, P.A. & Siegal, M. (1995) *Where to look first for suggestibility in young children*. Paper presented at the biennial meeting of the Society for Research in Child Development, Indianapolis, March.

Pickel, K.L. (1998) Unusualness and threat as possible sources of "weapon focus". *Memory*, **6**(3), 277–295.

Penrod, S.D., Fulero, S.M. & Cutler, B.L. (1995) Expert psychological testimony on eyewitness reliability before and after Daubert: The state of the law and the science. *Behavioural Sciences and the Law*, **13**, 239–259.

Poole, D.A. & Lindsay, S. (1995) Interviewing Preshcoolers: Effects of non-suggestive techniques, parental coaching and leading questions on reports of non-experienced events. *Journal of Experimental Child Psychology*, **60**, 129–154.

Pope, H.G., Oliva, P.S. & Hudson, J.I. (1999) The scientific status of research on repressed memories. In D.L. Faigman, D.H. Kaye, M.J. Saks & J. Sanders (Eds) *Modern Scientific Evidence: The Law and Science of Expert Testimony*, Vol. 1 (pp. 112–155). St. Paul, MN: West Group.

Roediger, H.L. (1980) Memory metaphors in cognitive psychology. *Memory and Cognition*, **8**, 231–246.

Searcy, J.H., Bartlett, J.C. & Memon, A. (1999) Age differences in accuracy and choosing rates on face recognition and eyewitness identification tasks. *Memory and Cognition*, **27**, 538–552.

Sporer, S., Malpass, R. & Koehnken, G. (1996) *Psychological Issues in Eyewitness Identification*. Mahwah, NJ: Lawrence Erlbaum.

Sporer, S., Penrod, S., Read, J.D. & Cutler, B.L. (1995) Choosing, confidence and accuracy: A meta-analysis of the confidence-accuracy relation in eyewitness identification studies. *Psychological Bulletin*, **118**, 315–327.

Steblay, N. (1992) A meta-analytic review of the weapon focus effect. *Law and Human Behaviour*, **16**, 413–424.

Thierry, K., Spence, M. & Memon, A. (1998) *Effect of repeated source monitoring on preschoolers' eyewitness suggestibility*. Paper presented at The American Psychology Law Society meeting, Redondo Beach, CA, March 5–7, 1998.

Tollestrup, P.A., Turtle, J.W. & Yuille, J.C. (1994) Actual victims and witnesses to robbery and fraud: An archival study. In D.F. Ross, J.D. Read & M.P. Toglia (Eds) *Adult Eyewitness Testimony: Current Trends and Developments* (pp. 144–160). Cambridge: Cambridge University Press.

Tulving, E. & Thomson, D.M. (1973) Encoding specificity and retrieval processes in episodic memory. *Psychological Review*, **80**, 353–370.

Warren, A. & Lane, P. (1995) Effects of timing and type of questioning on eyewitness accuracy and suggestibility. In M. Zaragoza, J.R. Graham, G.C.N. Hall, R. Hirschman & Y.S. Ben-Porath (Eds) *Memory and Testimony in the Child Witness*. Thousand Oaks, CA: Sage.

Wells, G.L. (1985) Verbal description of faces from memory: Are they diagnostic of identification accuracy? *Journal of Applied Psychology*, **70**, 619–626.

Wells, G.L., Leippe, M.R. & Ostrom, T.M. (1979) Guidelines for empirically assessing the fairness of a lineup. *Law and Human Behavior*, **3**, 285–293.

Wells, G.L., Small, M., Penrod, S., Malpass, R., Fulero, S.M. & Brimacombe, C.A.E. (1998)

Eyewitness identification procedures: Recommendations for lineups and photospreads. *Law and Human Behaviour*, **23**(6), 603–647.

Wright, D.B. & Davies, G.M. (1999) Eyewitness testimony. In F.T. Durso, R.S. Nickerson, R.W. Schvaneveldt, S.T. Dumais, D.S. Lindsay & M.T.H. Chi (Eds) *Handbook of Applied Cognition* (pp. 789–818). Chichester: John Wiley & Sons.

Wright, D.B. & Gaskell, G.D. (1995) Flashbulb memories: Conceptual and methodological issues. *Memory*, **3**, 67–80.

Wright, D.B. & Loftus, E.F. (1998) How misinformation alters memories. *Journal of Experimental Child Psychology*, **71**, 155–164.

Wright, D.B. & McDaid, A.T. (1996) Comparing system and estimator variables using data from real line-ups. *Applied Cognitive Psychology*, **10**, 75–84.

Yarmey, A.D. (1998) *Elders and the Criminal Justice System*. New York, NY: Springer.

Yarmey, A.D., Yarmey, M.J. & Yarmey, A.L. (1996) Accuracy of eyewitness identifications in showups and lineups. *Law and Human Behavior*, **20**, 459–477.

Chapter 5

Psycho-legal Studies as an Interface Discipline

Nigel Eastman
St. George's Hospital Medical School, London, UK

The relationship between two disciplines such as mental sciences and law can be approached by viewing legal provisions through the eyes of one or more of the mental science disciplines. By analogy, imagine two lands, each respectively called "Legaland" and "Mentaland". The terrains of the two lands are very different and they have very different histories, cultures and, perhaps most obviously, their inhabitants speak different languages. Indeed the "whole reason for being" perceived by the inhabitants of each land is entirely different from that of the other; they pursue different life purposes by different means of thinking and behaving. Usually, their two different life purposes determine that the inhabitants of the two lands have little to do with each other. However, the purposes of the inhabitants of one land, usually Legaland, sometimes determine that they require the skills and knowledge of some of the inhabitants of the other, Mentaland. Some of the latter are therefore invited briefly to help Legaland to answer some of its own questions, albeit always in its own terms. Mentaland visitors to Legaland are immediately aware of the very different context in which they are being asked to operate, and the very different way in which questions are put to them causes them to suffer cognitive dissonance (itself a concept with which Mentalanders are very familiar but which, when they try to explain it to Legalanders, leaves the latter rather baffled). Even the very language of the visitors confuses the hosts. Indeed, although it often sounds, within its words, similar to Legalanguage, Mentalanguage seems to be based on very different constructs, and also ways of thinking, from those with which Legalanders are familiar. In any event, ultimately the Legalanders make it plain to the visitors that what matters is the way that things are done in Legaland and that, somehow, the visitors must try to adapt their language and constructs to those used within the "problem formation" approaches

Behaviour, Crime and Legal Processes: A Guide for Forensic Practitioners.
Edited by James McGuire, Tom Mason and Aisling O'Kane.
© 2000 John Wiley & Sons Ltd.

used in Legaland. The relationship is, therefore, both somewhat unbalanced and also distorting of the way of thinking of the Mentalanders.

The inhabitants of Mentaland do sometimes have need, even within their own country, of the authority of rules developed in Legaland. Indeed, although Mentaland has developed, for example, its own ethics it does not *have* any body of *legal* rules of its own and is therefore governed by Legaland. In utilising such rules, Mentalanders sometimes find that, again, they have actually to go to Legaland (called colloquially "going to law") in order to be clear about the rules and how they apply to particular Mentaland circumstances. In so doing, they sometimes therefore use the authority of Legaland rules. However, even if they *never* "go to Legaland" in this context the rules they necessarily use are designed as "tools for Mentaland" and have to be seen in terms of their likely effectiveness towards the life purposes of Mentaland and its inhabitants.

Whether we are dealing with the application of mental science expertise to particular legal questions or with attempts to understand better the true public policy implications of particular legal measures, the nature of the relationship between law and mental sciences is, like any interface discipline, that it is concerned with the frontier between two lands. Interface disciplines such as "socio-legal studies" or "psycho-legal studies" transcend each discipline as it normally operates on its own. Application of the knowledge of one discipline, e.g. psychiatry, to the issues of the other, e.g. law, casts light from a particular angle. So in relation to legal "nervous shock", this would not amount to a simple description of the relevant psychiatry, for example, of the diagnosis "post-traumatic stress disorder" (PTSD). Rather, it might amount to the use of a psychiatric construction in order to understand better what, from a psychiatric perspective, is the nature of a particular legal rule or construct; or what are its implications, in terms of public policy, for mentally disordered people or for the clinicians and services which deal with them. The approach of such an interface discipline may not be, therefore, to offer a great deal about the epidemiology and aetiology of PTSD but, rather, to analyse the law relating to "nervous shock" *in terms of* the detailed diagnostic constructs, as well as the broad life effects and prognosis, of PTSD. Such an approach offers, therefore, a study of construct relations.

Law can, and should, be subject to analysis in its own terms, in order to determine whether it is technically well-constructed law, and clearly that does not come within any interface discipline. However, consideration of whether a piece of law is capable of delivering its intended public policy purpose does come within one or more interface disciplines, for example, socio-legal or psycho-legal studies. Hence, there is another aspect of psycho-legal studies which is concerned with the practical *operation* of law. At times such operation depends upon interpretation by the courts or by the police. Sometimes, however, the law depends for its effect on mental science or on mental scientists. This most obviously applies in relation to mental health care law, where the operation of the law "on the ground" depends very much upon its interpretation and usage (including the potential for *non*-usage) by practitioners. The fact that discretion is given to practitioners to invoke or not invoke the Mental Health Act 1983 means that mental sciences, and their practice, take on crucial significance in determining the practical effect of law. If clinicians decide not to use the Act then it is "useless". Such law is essentially "law without enforcement" (Eastman & Peay, 1999). Of course, the police or clinicians can similarly import their own (mis)understandings of any law, as well as their own ethical attitudes, into their decisions about whether and how to use that law. Even judges may be less (or perhaps more) than legal robots in their interpretation of the law. This type of approach to the operation of the law can, therefore, clearly be extended beyond *a priori* theoretical analysis so as to encompass an empirical aspect of psycho-legal studies. This chapter will deal with both theory and practice.

In their interactions with the justice system mental scientists commonly experience greater construct relation difficulties than is experienced by experts offering evidence from other scientific fields. This arises from the fact that—unlike in relation to forensic pathology, for example—when the law allows the introduction of mental science evidence it allows in a science which takes an interest in similar matters to some of the interests of the law itself. Hence, when the pathologist gives evidence the court simply uses that evidence *towards* its own questions (for example, using the nature of injuries towards determining a defendant's guilt or innocence), but when a psychiatrist gives evidence it is often *directed at* the very same aspects of human behaviour and motivation with which the law is itself concerned. Although psychiatry does not directly address such notions as "intention" or "motive", its own constructs do sit very closely alongside such legal constructs. As a result, there is often an uneasy tension between expert and court, since the rules relating to the admissibility of expert evidence require the expert not to give an opinion about the ultimate legal issue (for example, whether the defendant intended to do something) *and*, even where he or she is not (wrongly) attempting to address the ultimate issue, the expert is not allowed to give evidence at all where he or she speaks on some issue which is within the jury's natural understanding (*R* v *Turner* [1975]). Since ordinary people (including jury members) have knowledge and opinions concerning much of the stuff of mental sciences (whereas they usually have no knowledge of forensic pathology, beyond television drama), this again can be a basis for the exclusion of mental science evidence, often rightly so but sometimes based upon a misunderstanding by trial judges of what *is* "normal" human functioning (which can therefore be "known" by a jury person) and what is not.

So, the law sometimes uses mental science towards its own purposes, which are often unrelated to mental health-related purposes, while some law represents an instrument of public policy which is directed specifically at mental health outcomes and at the regulation of care. Where the purposes of the law are unconnected to mental health care the relationship is inherently unbalanced against mental science, with Mentalanders feeling decidedly "foreign" when they visit Legaland. However, when mental health sciences themselves use the law in order to effect care, the imbalance is somewhat reversed, given that such law is discretionary. It is also reversed (in a different sense) by any attempt to apply the knowledge of mental science to the constructs and thinking of the law, where the intention is to offer a "reality testing" critique of the law, either narrowly in its own terms or as a means towards better understanding of the public policy goals which lie behind them. In summary then, each aspect of psycho-legal studies implies neither a legal nor a mental science treatise. Rather, it represents an analysis of a particular section of the frontier between Mentaland and Legaland.

METHODS OF INVESTIGATING THE PSYCHO-LEGAL INTERFACE

For Gunther Teubner, an important theoretician of jurisprudence, law is entirely "autopoietic" or "self-referential" (Teubner, 1993), such that it cannot admit within its processes and thinking the constructs of any other science. Hence the differing purposes of law and mental science determine very different sets of constructs and the law, it can be argued, is incapable of acknowledging those of mental science. Rather, it makes its own constructs fashioned for its own purposes, occasionally trying crudely somehow to take note of mental science constructs which are offered to the courts by way of expert evidence. Some core aspects of psycho-legal research methodology, therefore, touch upon matters of the philosophy of science. As a result, although Teubner's critique will be seen to cast its influence over much that follows in the chapter, some simplification needs to be imposed on any methodological discussion.

In turning a mental science microscope on to the law, an analogy can be drawn between the investigation of old or new clinical therapies *and* the investigation of existing, new or even proposed legal measures. Illustrations might include investigation of the therapeutic effect (or not) of "supervised discharge orders" under the Mental Health (Patients in the Community) Act 1995, or, taking an administrative rather than a legal measure, of "supervision registers". Such investigation can properly begin with theoretical studies, from clinical "first principles", offering hypotheses for empirical investigation of the measures as they operate "in practice". However, that type of "therapeutic jurisprudence" (Wexler & Winick, 1991) attitude to legal measures, which perceives legal instruments largely as "clinical tools", must be distinguished from a civil rights legal attitude, which is potentially at profound variance with it (we shall return to this tension later). That attitude implies very different types of theoretical and empirical investigation.

The availability of new techniques in science commonly spawns a wide-ranging search for new applications of its power. Within mental health sciences, the recent availability of increasingly sophisticated brain-imaging techniques, or genetic marker techniques, has underpinned whole new theories of mental disease aetiology, or even new classifications of disease. Again by analogy, there can be new ways of "imaging" even legal and administrative measures, by way of an interface discipline which specifically addresses such measures through "mental science eyes". For example, a particular legal definition of "mental capacity" or of "disease of the mind" can be newly perceived when subjected to being viewed psychiatrically (see further below). By analogy, the development of "socio-legal studies" amounted to a new way of viewing law, the discipline of social science being used to analyse and/or demonstrate empirically the social origins and effects of particular laws or legal traditions. A similar approach is possible with regard to the inferences for, or effects upon, the mentally disordered, or their professional or family carers, of particular criminal and civil legal provisions.

Going one step further, both theoretical and empirical investigation can be pursued beyond consideration of the nature of individual clinical or legal phenomena, by addressing phenomena as a group in order to identify common threads. This may offer further illumination, by giving a new perspective ("from the group") of an individual construct *or* by demonstrating patterns (or their absence) "across the group". For example, we may better understand (or interpret) public policy lying behind individual legal or administrative measures concerned with mental disorder by looking for themes, including disparities in themes. Hence, if we discover that the legal approach to mental disorder differs between circumstances where the purpose is to protect the public, and where what is at issue is whether individuals retain (or not) the legal capacity to carry out a range of civil legal activities for themselves, then this must be of both policy and ethical interest.

Mental Science Investigatory Perspectives

Within medicine, and mental sciences more generally, there are often several perspectives by which description or understanding of observed phenomena are approached. Hence, the cell can be described biochemically, genetically or by way of electron-microscopic imaging. Each offers a "representation" of the cell which can be both valid in its own right and contribute corporately to an understanding of the cell. Similarly, legal or administrative phenomena can be viewed differently by way of the various mental sciences. Thus, individual legal measures can be subjected to analysis from a variety of mental science perspectives, so as to approach its clinical and service implications from different angles. There can also be an *ethical* analysis of any legal measure, both generally (from a "social ethic" viewpoint) and specifically (from a "mental science professional ethical" perspective). However, such an ethical analysis sometimes first requires "reconstruction" of the legal measure in mental science terms, so that its true effect, including therefore its true ethical effect, can be seen. Even concepts of disease themselves can, of course, be subjected to ethical analysis, perhaps obviously so if they are mental diseases and massively so if the disorder is "personality disorder", where the subjective aspects of diagnosis are very substantial.

Static and Dynamic Descriptions and Analyses

The cell can be described or analysed either statically, by means of some particular perspective snapshot, or dynamically. Similarly, legal measures can be viewed statically "as they read", or dynamically "as they operate". So, one particular way of approaching psycho-legal investigation is to ask "how does the law think and how is it therefore likely to function?" *or* "how does the law think on the evidence of how it is likely to function?". Again, attempts can be made to answer such questions from the perspectives of the mental sciences. By way of simple illustration, as will be seen later, the McNaughton Rules concerning legal insanity can be seen to be highly, and indeed exclusively, cognitive (in mental science terms). They are therefore rejecting of any relevance of affect, or impulse. Of course, that may reflect aspects of Victorian understanding of mental functioning or notions of culpability (from a narrowly legal perspective) or other aspects of Victorian culture (of less, or no direct relevance). However, *all* such alternative explanations (perhaps except the first, because it is inextricable from the mental science critique itself, albeit historical in nature) are beyond the scope of psycho-legal research since they necessarily invoke historical (including political, social and cultural) theory and knowledge. Hence, psycho-legal research is *restricted* to questions concerning definition, likely implications and empirical operation.

However, the static/dynamic analogy is somewhat stretched since, as already suggested, the law only *has* its real importance in how it operates *in practice*. Herein lies the origin of the potential for dispute between the legal scholar and the socio-legal or psycho-legal empiricist. In a court setting, such a practical application depends, first, upon how the individual courts interpret the legal rules *per se* (in decisions "in law") and, second, upon how judges (in most civil cases) or juries (mainly in criminal cases) first find facts relevant to the law (decisions "on the facts") and then fit the facts in their particular case into those legal rules. The distinction is apparently clear but, in reality, is often less 20. For example, as we shall see, the rules relating to "provocation" would seem almost to exclude from that defence a severely abused woman who kills her provocative abuser if she waits for a prolonged period of time before attacking, rather than doing so suddenly (Eastman & Mezey, 1997); she is also likely only rarely to have an arguable "abnormality of mind" in terms of Section 2 of the Act. Such women would seem to have little hope, therefore, on the legal rules, of avoiding a murder conviction, and yet, as is apparent from an unpublished study by the author, both juries (sometimes) and the Court of Appeal (frequently) behave in ways which appear greatly to stretch the legal rules, albeit perhaps towards achieving "natural justice". In fact, the tighter the legal definition of a particular rule (for example, the McNaughton Rules), the less inherently able are juries and judges to pursue "natural justice" in spite of the rules; the looser they are (for example, as with the definition of "abnormality of mind" within Section 2 of the Homicide Act 1957) the more can latitude be applied. However, where strict legal definitions may often exclude any potential impact of expert psychiatric testimony, loose definition may still require the collusion of mental science testimony in order for the "naturally just" result to be achieved, perhaps at the expense of mental science validity or ethics.

So, within psycho-legal studies, there can be a description of how the law is constructed and what its operation infers for patients, civil litigants, defendants or mental health professionals. But psycho-legal research does *not* include among its perspectives that of political science. It is not concerned with the processes and forces by which particular laws are made, be it in Parliament or in the courts. Rather, it is concerned with the substance and operation of such laws and with what they variously infer is the public policy lying behind them (whether or not the law-makers intended it to be so). Psycho-legal research does not study political process but political and judicial effect, perceived via mental sciences.

ETHICS AT THE INTERFACE

Welfare and Justice

There is an inherent tension between the principles of welfare and justice, as it is represented in the respect for autonomy in relation to much law relating to mental disorder. This is most obviously represented in mental health care law, where the patient suffers, by way of compulsory detention and treatment, civil rights diminution (perceived injustice) in order for there to be (welfare) gain in terms of his or her advantage or that of the public. The aim of public policy *should* be to attempt to integrate the achievement of both welfare *and* justice. However, often the two may seem irreconcilable. This irreconcilability is reflected in the conflict between the two major approaches to the role specifically of mental health care law. Proponents of therapeutic jurisprudence argue that law should be designed and operated towards therapeutic ends (Wexler & Winick, 1991). By contrast, civil rights lawyers argue that such an approach is profoundly misplaced, since the purpose of law is solely the determination of rights and duties; this includes, therefore, the right not to be detained for treatment except in specified (and rights based) circumstances. The apparent inherent irreconcilability of civil rights and therapeutic jurisprudence approaches to mental health law has often determined profound differences of approach between (particularly) doctors and lawyers, resulting in both conflict and misunderstanding.

It is important to note, however, that considerations of welfare and justice thread through other branches of law which are relevant to mental disorder; although the balance between the two is, for example, very different within criminal law compared with mental health law, and it is to the criminal law field that we now turn.

Mental Scientists and the Criminal Justice System

The ethics of psychiatric and other mental science involvement specifically in the criminal justice system is particularly highlighted by a recent change of emphasis in psychiatric jurisprudence in Britain away from the traditional welfare model and towards a model, focusing particularly on public protective sentencing. This is represented by the Crime (Sentences) Act 1997, the Sexual Offences (Amendment) Act 1999, and Sections 2(2)b and 4 of the Criminal Justice Act 1991, as well as by moves by the present government to introduce "reviewable orders" for people exhibiting "severe personality disorder" where they represent a grave danger to the public (Home Office, 1999). Measures in these statutes and proposals all have implications for both individual and corporate professional ethical policy, specifically in relation to degree of involvement in punishment. In this context, there can be a juxtaposition of the role of individual "clinician as clinician" versus "clinician as citizen".

We shall return to the public protection role of mental scientists later in the text.

MENTAL SCIENCE-RELATED LEGAL ARTIFACTS IN DIFFERENT LEGAL FIELDS

There are substantial and observable disparities between the way in which law reflects mental disorder across different fields of law. Such disparities reflect, in turn, compartmentalised approaches to public policy which achieve their various ends by defining and reflecting mental disorder in law in different ways. Hence, constructs designed towards determining the liability of a defendant for psychiatric injury of a plaintiff are very different from those designed to detain patients in the interests of their own health or safety or for the protection of the public. Aside from the law's insensitivity in its definition and operation of a variety of legal mental constructs to mental sciences *per se*, such an inconsistency of approach can, of course, potentially do a disservice not only to psychological reality but also, in a domino fashion, to civil and criminal rights, again often expressed in terms of the tension between welfare and justice.

One important legal core of this chapter is (civil) "capacity", others are (criminal) "culpability" and (civil) "responsibility". However, reference to Teubner's view of the nature of law will have made it clear that, since each of these constructs must be seen as a *legal* construct, self-referentially generated by the law without much ability to introduce relevant (real) mental constructs, it is not necessarily to be expected that its use (each is, of course a group of "its") will bear any relation to relevant mental science constructs. Rather, in Teubnerian terms, what we will view is a number of artifacts created by the law for its own various purposes. These artifacts include capacity, culpability or responsibility-related artifacts but go far beyond them. Hence, there are many other constructs relevant to the law relating to mental disorder, some of which are not necessarily defined explicitly by the law but which are nonetheless present within it. We may expect, therefore, to encounter such "persona-artifacts" (albeit attached to "real people" in "real cases") as *on trial man* (in relation to fitness to plead); *legally punished man* (in relation to the ethics of medical involvement in punishment); *the vulnerable mentally disordered witness* (in relation to fitness to be examined and cross examined); *diminished culpability man* (in relation to mental condition trial defences); *victim of poor care man* (in connection with negligence law, and, relatedly, with inquiries after homicides or complaints to the General Medical Council of professional inadequacy); *treatment refusing man* (in relation to community treatment or supervision orders); the *mentally disordered offender* (broadly as perceived by the criminal courts in relation to potential "diversion" and "discontinuance"), not to be confused within the NHS discourse with the man of the same name but who is very differently perceived by the NHS from the perception adopted by the criminal justice system; *psychiatrically injured man* (in relation to "nervous shock" or personal injury litigation); *untreatable detained man* (in relation to tribunal rules concerning discharge); and *private man* (in relation to confidentiality rules as they apply to both third party risks and trial proceedings), and so on. That is, there is a multitude of legal artifacts which are applicable across a wide range of fields. Of course, often more than one legal artifact will simultaneously apply to one (real) man; for example, Christopher Clunis (Ritchie, Dick & Lingham, 1994) has been (at least) "on trial man", "punished man", allegedly "victim of poor care man", and probably many others.

In summary, therefore, the legal constructs which are at the heart of psycho-legal studies relate mainly to capacity, culpability and responsibility and they range across many legal fields and many aspects of any given legal field. Sitting above such artifactual legal constructs are the ethical constructs of welfare and justice, by which both law and mental sciences can be judged.

PSYCHIATRIC AND PSYCHOLOGICAL PURPOSES AND MODELS[1]

The purposes of all mental sciences are focused on the welfare of the patient or client, albeit in forensic mental health sciences there is concern for potential third party victims. The models used by all the sciences are therefore directed at identifying and, if possible, rectifying "disorder". How they pursue these purposes varies somewhat between the mental sciences, but their core purposes are identical.

For doctors or psychiatrists, diagnosis is the core concept. However, athough to the non-clinician the purpose of diagnosis may appear obvious, it does bear some unpacking. Indeed, understanding some of the incongruities between mental sciences and law requires it, since artifacts within either discipline are determined by the core purpose of that discipline. The purposes of diagnosis are: (1) description, classification, and taxonomy; (2) predicting prognosis; (3) deter-

---

[1] The essence of the argument presented in the following four sections of the chapter, as well as substantial parts of the text, is a reproduction of an earlier paper published by the author (Eastman, 1992).

mining therapy; and finally, and infrequently in reality, (4) pathological under-standing. Some would argue that there are also "unscientific" and value-laden social purposes (Szasz, 1963, 1974) and this suggestion has particular relevance where diagnosis is applied to the overtly social purpose of legal process.

All such psychiatric activities are firmly rooted in the tradition of the medical model, which, in turn, is embedded in (a particular approach to) the concept of *disease*. Although there is a highly entangled relationship between diagnostic purposes and disease concepts (largely in terms of a particular disease concept providing the *assumptions* lying behind classificatory, prognostic, therapeutic, and psychopathological purposes) any attempt to characterise varying implied psy-chiatric models of man must specifically address the variety of disease concepts applied. Varying concepts of disease, therefore, have specific relevance in deter-mining specific psycho-legal incongruities and their degree.

Disease Concepts

Most medical classificatory systems, especially uniaxial ones (notably ICD-10), appear to presume a disease entity already there, or waiting to be identified. Perhaps only the DSM-IV, which adopts a multi-axial approach, *seems* to waver from a disease model but, even there, the primary axis does appear to relate to diseases, albeit modified somewhat in significance by the other axes. Such systems often also presume the concept of disease as *a lesion* (Szasz, 1961; Virchow, 1958). Close cousins of the latter concept are *disease as disturbance of part function* (Lewis, 1953), *disease based in reductionism* (Engel, 1977), and *phenomenologi-cal disease* (Jaspers, 1963), itself essentially amounting to *categorical disease* (as distinguished from *dimensional disease*) and evinced by notions of "inter-rater reliability" and various forms of "validity". These aspects of the disease concept are clustered together as a family which might be nicknamed *the psychiatric or phenomenological approach*, and it *is* a family by virtue of the distinction of its members from other families.

The *psychiatric phenomenological approach* recognises its theoretical limita-tions characteristically by resorting to a variety of simple "dichotomies"—most notably those of organic/functional, psychotic/neurotic, (neurotic) mental illness/personality disorder, acute/chronic, and endogenous/exogenous.

An "alternative family" of approaches is best termed the *psycho-understanding approach*. It most clearly has its representation in the psychody-namic tradition but is by no means limited to it (in the sense I shall use the term). It includes a cluster of models of human psychological dysfunction which have, at their core, rejection of the medical model and the lesion-based, categorical, scientific, reductionist, and phenomenological aspects thereof. The approach varies from the psychiatric phenomenological approach not only in its assump-tions about the nature of psychopathology *per se*, but in its basis of validation. It rejects the notion that truth is defined solely according to the population hypoth-esis testing methodology defined by science (classically represented in the "randomised controlled clinical trial" model), but suggests, rather, that hypothesis testing can be conducted with one patient and that detailed explanations of psychological cause and effect are valid in spite of their lack of availability to "scientific" invalidation through attempted replication. Further, it admits psychological content as centrally valid and enlightening, in contrast to abnormality of form being seen as crucially (perhaps, for many practitioners solely) valid in the phenomenological approach.

According to a third approach—a dimensional approach—there is a presumption that disease entities do not exist and that the pursuit of the categorical disease classification of psychopathology is both hopeless and spurious. It therefore shares some ground with the psycho-understanding approach. However, it goes further in alleging that disorder exists both on multi-axial (not uniaxial) and dimensional (not categorical) bases. Such a model of man will tend to produce greater psycho-legal incongruity than do models of man deriving from the disease model, phenomenological approach. According to this *psychometric approach*, man is on a continuum and disorder is defined not according to "abnormality from a previous or ideal state", but rather only according to "statistical abnormality against a population of others". Such an approach argues that it avoids forcing dimensional reality into categorical fiction.

The eclectic tradition in Western psychiatry is an escape from the failure to identify wished-for disease entities, implying specific cures. It functions as an approach aimed at pragmatic solutions to real clinical problems and variously applies psychopathological explanatory and therapeutic approaches, based on the recognition that no "disease cure" model has been identified. Operated by clinicians from more than one discipline, this "case formulation" approach of practised eclecticism often operates in stark contrast to the theoretical psychiatry (or psychology) which purports to be its foundations. Eclecticism, by definition, *has no* single model of man, even for any individual situation. However, there is a danger that involvement of practical (eclectic) psychiatrists in legal proceedings is likely to force them to *pretend* a belief in the models of man[2] originating in theoretical, especially phenomenological psychiatry.

In summary, mental science models of man vary according to their theoretical approach (psychiatric phenomenological, psycho-understanding, and psychometric) and according to the practical abandonment (or not) of single model theories.

LEGAL PURPOSES AND MODELS

In Teubnerian terms, legal models of human behaviour are derived self-referentially within a distinct and ring-fenced discourse. Indeed, the absence of a clear welfare function of criminal law, at least during the trial stage of a hearing directed towards verdict, will tend to maximise any "Teubner effect". This is

---

[2] The term "model(s) of man" is used throughout to connote man as a species and not as a particular gender.

because there the law is concerned solely with justice, in contrast to the highly welfare-directed discourses of mental health sciences which may form the basis of some expert evidence in a criminal trial. Welfare seems to have no place, yet the courts admit evidence from welfare-based sciences. However, as was apparent from the specific case type of "the battered woman who kills", even at the "trial to verdict" stage at least some notion of natural justice might sometimes be pursued by the court, *in spite of* the law's own (strictly narrower) discourse. Technically, this modifies justice rather than introduces welfare to the trial stage. In the sentencing stage of criminal proceedings, there is, of course, some potential and explicit pursuit of both "natural justice" and (perhaps even) welfare which may tend to modify the otherwise untrammelled effects of justice at trial. Hence the degree of incongruity operating between law and expert mental science evidence will vary according to the model characteristics arising from law and from mental science in any particular "case type" or situation. Finally, incongruence can only be minimised by both encouraging legal rules which put the two disciplines into inherently least incongruent model interactions *and* by encouraging law and mental sciences (and their practitioners) coincidentally to recognise the implicit varying purposes and models which they apply and the character of case-specific incongruities.

More generally, however, in direct contrast to the (stated) purposes and methods of medicine and psychiatry, law is essentially moral and value laden. It also tends to be binary, unifactorial, artificial, and adversarial in its substance and process. Further, it often allows the possibility of *several* conceptual fictions as potentially applicable to a *single* real event—for example, a particular homicide defendant *might* have a defence in all three categories of insanity, automatism and diminished responsibility, as well as coincidentally being able to argue liability only to the lesser charge of infanticide.

The criminal law applies not only different *specific* models in different legal situations but also different *general* models. Hence, where the law is binary, unifactorial, fictional, and adversarial in its method towards issues of verdict, it all but abandons such strictures in relation to issues of disposal. The model shift which is implied as occurring between trial and sentencing has particular relevance to the degree of psycho-legal incongruence, as well as to questions concerning whether there is/can be a welfare purpose in sentencing.

The law most obviously defines models of man in relation to mental capacity and responsibility (civil and criminal, respectively). Considering only criminal law, the heart of the definition of most crimes (*actus reus* plus *mens rea*) incorporates the requirement of (varying degrees of) intention, that is, it invents *intentional man*. It implies a model of human behaviour which tends to be largely or exclusively cognitive in nature, unitary (in relation to each defined crime), and based on a presumption of free will rather than scientific determinism. Further, it appears to pursue a dualistic Cartesian body/mind philosophy, most obviously in the defence of "automatism" through distinguishing the absence of *mens*.

The law, sometimes apparently and sometimes consciously, purports to incorporate "terms of art" from the sciences, including psychiatry. For example, it includes scientific "psychopathic disorder" in Section 1 of the English Mental Health Act (1983). Less obviously, solely scientific notions are "disease of the mind" (*R* v. *McNaughton* [1843]), "abnormality of mind" (Homicide Act 1957; *R* v. *Byrne* [1960]) and "disturbed balance of mind" (Infanticide Act 1938). However, even where the concept can clearly be seen to originate in mental science, the law tends either immediately to redefine it or to distort it through interpretation such that it rapidly drifts away from its original scientific meaning and its parentage becomes unrecognisable. A notable example is the judgement of Lord Denning (in *Bratty* v. *Attorney General for Northern Ireland* [1963]), in which he stated that

> any mental disorder which has manifested itself in violence and is prone to recur is a disease of the mind. At any rate it is the sort of disease for which a person should be detained in hospital rather than be given an unqualified acquittal.

This definition of "disease of the mind" clearly incorporates elements that are totally unrelated to it.

PSYCHIATRIC, PSYCHOLOGICAL AND LEGAL MODEL INCONGRUITIES

The incongruities between legal and mental science models of man are greatest in relation to verdict issues.

The law allows the mental element of a crime to be negated by evidence that the (normal) rational "intentional man" model is inappropriate to the defendant and that a deterministic, expertly available abnormal man is the appropriate standard. However, although it admits the latter *as if* it derived from psychiatric reality it does so by defining not *psychological* abnormal men but (of course) *legal* ones. It is several of these (legal) abnormal men, or artifacts, that we shall consider in a little detail, as well as juxtaposing them with the (normal) "reasonable man" which is explicit in the different (though, in psychological reality, often related) defence of provocation.

"Automatic Man"

A defendant who was in an automatism at the time of the offence had no *mens rea* or did not effect a willed *actus reus* because his mind was not operating. The paradigm case is actions deriving from a complex partial seizure arising not from the mind but from the brain. Hence, automatic man has "the ultimate psychiatric defence". The law here operates a dualistic and necessarily binary model of man in that there is no intention, or lack of a willed action. The English courts have also included "somnambulistic man" and the "night terrorist", as well as the "(fugue) dissociated man", the "hypnotised man", and the "(involuntarily) intoxicated man" among automatons. Although the courts have continually narrowed down the circumference of specifically "non-insane automatic man", the core notion of automatic man is still present in English law.

Psychiatry views medical automatic man variously but many argue that only actions based upon abnormal cerebral electrical activity are truly automatic (Fenton, 1972). Even with such a tight definition it is not clear that *only* the brain is operating (to adopt dualistic terminology). *Somnambulistic man* is variously understood as organically and hysterically neurotically determined, as is the *night terrorist* (see Howard & D'Orban, 1987; Oswald & Evans, 1985). Hence, the psychiatrist may tend to see somnambulistic man solely as having a brain (sleep) disorder, or may perhaps suggest that he has (at least partly) a neurotic basis for his activity, while the psycho-understanding expert may (by definition) tend solely to postulate the latter; similar positions might apply in relation to the night terrorist. *Dissociated man* is even more likely to be the subject of dispute since (some) psychiatrists would not accept that his consciousness and intention are qualitatively abnormal (in relation to malingering) but only quantitatively different (again in relation to malingering). Hence, the incongruity between legal and medical automatic man will depend, in this case, on *which* psychiatric model of man is offered. Even where a qualitative definition is offered, there is the immediate potential for medico-legal confusion and incongruence, arising out of differing legal and psychological notions of "unconscious", "preconscious", and "subconscious".

Legal automatic man, as classically perceived in epilepsy or post-head injury concussion, is, of course, most congruent with a "disease as lesion" model of abnormality and, therefore, with the medical psychiatric approach. Other, possibly neurotic, automatons give rise to greater potential model incongruities. Intermediate cases perhaps occur in relation to conditions thought by some to be on a continuum between the two poles of complex partial epilepsy and personality disorder (for example, explosive personality disorder, pathological drunkenness, and episodic dyscontrol syndrome).

"Irrational Man"

Responsible man is variedly (albeit normally) intelligent but rational. The primary root of "McNaughton man" (*R* v. *McNaughton* [1843]) is irrational and, although further and restrictively qualified, his insanity *amounts to* his "defect of reason". Further, his culpability is not merely diminished by such irrationality but abolished thereby. In psychological terms, only cognition is recognised as determining non-culpability, and the final "two limbs" of the McNaughton rules ("not *knowing* the nature or quality of the act or not *knowing* it was wrong") reinforce the sole relevance of cognition.

Such a legal model does not even admit the possibility of introducing psycho-understanding or psychometric approaches (except by definition of the "level" of intellectual functioning in the latter case), and even the phenomenological psychiatrist is permitted to address only cognition-related phenomena. The McNaughton rules are thus exemplary of direct legal limitation of the "admissibility", by form, of psychological evidence. Indeed, it was the recognition of the psychological incompleteness of McNaughton man which was a major spur towards the introduction into English law of another model ("mentally abnormal man") which, through its very broad definition (*R* v. *Byrne* [1960]), is exemplary of the almost limitless admissibility of psychological evidence; not only not being restrictive of other elements of phenomenology but also potentially allowing of both psycho-understanding and psychometric models.

"Mentally Diseased Man"

Restriction of the insanity defence to defects of reason arising from a *disease of the mind* would suggest, through its wording, psycho-legal congruence. Conversely, however, the incongruity between legal and psychological epistemologies is well illustrated by viewing legal precedent defining "disease of the mind" through medical and psychological spectacles.

The case precedents appear to bear little relation to any but the psychiatric phenomenological approach and, further, the primary "test" of disease of the mind appears to be defined almost exclusively in terms of a "disease as lesion" model, if indeed it is defined with any eye on medical constructs. In Quick's case (*R* v. *Quick* [1973]), automatic man is only mentally *non*-diseased if the cause of his disorder was "external" to him—specifically, in that case, caused by injected insulin. Hence, diseased man has an internal abnormality. This apparently simple and sensible test appears to derive from medical reality. However, it is less than robust when it is *viewed* medically; in medical and psychological reality the internal/external distinction is ill defined. Hence, where a seizure disorder is defined in law as being a disease of the mind, immediate confusion arises if an externally (e.g. insulin) induced (internal) seizure occurs, particularly if an abnormally low seizure threshold can be demonstrated in the defendant. Further, a defendant with a profound personality disorder, which results in his or her using insulin overdoses towards manipulative personal interactions, may be variously viewed as suffering, or not, from a disease of the mind, according to whether the cause or the route of his or her behaviour is taken as definitive. In any event, where excess insulin can also be produced *inherently*, albeit not cerebrally (by an insulinoma), the internal/external test might cause "disease of the mind" and "disease of the pancreas" to coincide (Eastman, 1986).

Additionally, a number of other accepted non-insane automatisms have previously been seen as "non-mind diseases" in spite of obvious inherency, most notably somnambulism and night terrors (although the *Quick* test is being applied increasingly restrictively now in the English courts). Narrowing the ambit of pure automatism by apparently recognising such (medical) inherency has clearly been driven, however, by public policy objectives rather than by the law wishing better to incorporate medicine.

The alternative "disease of the mind" test, the *Bratty* test, is clearly structurally unrelated to any psychological or medical notion of disease and, in light of the verdict implications, overtly incorporates criteria of social consequences, perhaps where the line of cases more clearly traceable back to *Quick* is more covert in its public purpose. Social policy is thus pursued through distortion of a "model of man" via the explicit introduction of constructs not necessarily related to diseased man.

"Mentally Abnormal Man"

Whereas "irrational man" and "mentally diseased man" are tightly and restrictively defined in terms of the implied limitation on the admissibility of psychological approaches, "mentally abnormal" man is so broadly defined, and moreover defined in lay terms, as to admit potentially almost *any* form of psychological evidence. The defence to murder of "diminished responsibility", defined by Section 2 of the English Homicide Act 1957, requires only that there be an "abnormality of mind (whether arising from a condition of arrested or retarded development of mind or any inherent causes or induced by disease or injury) as substantially impaired his mental responsibility". "Abnormality of mind" is elaborated (*R* v. *Byrne* [1960]) as "a state of mind so different from that of ordinary human beings that the reasonable man would term it abnormal". Hence, the model is a lay model and is qualitatively undefined. This definition, and its elaboration, imply a number of aspects and classes of models. Only the parenthetic clause is inherently psychological in character.

Impairment of mental responsibility is not *directly* related, as a construct, to abnormal psychology or even brain function; however, the attempt to limit the boundaries of psychological expertise to description of *only* the parenthetic clause (perhaps with inclusion of determining the presence an "abnormality of mind") is often, in legal practice, difficult. English courts not uncommonly misapply the law and invite the expert to make (or reject) "a diagnosis of diminished responsibility". The, admittedly intimate, relationship between the definition and determination of an "abnormality of mind" *and* "impairment of mental responsibility" commonly gives rise to definitional circularity, thus, "he is mad because he was not responsible, he is not responsible because he is mad" (Wootton, 1959). More generally, mental responsibility is seen not as a binary construct (as in relation to "irrational man") but as a graded one. Here, almost at last, therefore, is an example of the law adopting a definition of a mental capacity construct which is consistent with the approach of an ethical balance model (Eastman & Hope, 1988), albeit there is no balancing of welfare and justice, only pursuit of justice through the grading of degrees of culpability.

The coincidence of a lay definition of abnormality, the very broad legal definition of that abnormality (implicitly also in psychological terms), and the consequent admissibility of almost any psychological approach to abnormality, is likely to give rise to apparent inter-case inconsistency as regards what psychological models are accepted by the courts. Hence, juries largely can decide what psychological model they will allow as being indicative of mentally abnormal man with only limited judicial restraint in terms of definition *in law* of what may constitute the notion. The only real restraint on the jury is the requirement that the defendant falls into one of the elements of the parenthetic clause of Section 2.

In spite of the potential flexibility of the defence, it is diminished responsibility that, in practice, gives rise most frequently to psycho-legal incongruence (because of the much greater frequency with which it is pleaded by comparison with other defences). The degree of incongruence is likely to vary with the particular psychological approach being offered to the court. Most simply, where the approach presents apparent dichotomisation there is, in the necessarily binary legal context, likely to be least incongruity. Hence, the *psychiatric-phenomenologist* is most easily incorporated into the legal process since he or she purports to define the presence of objective mental signs and to derive a categorical diagnostic conclusion therefrom. His or her categorical diagnostic structure commonly implies, or overtly describes, dichotomies which the court is probably apt to regard as legally acceptable. Hence, "organic" contrasts nicely with "functional" and the former is more likely to be readily accepted by the courts as mental abnormality (the law thus being most congruent with "disease as a lesion"). Similarly, "psychotic" and "neurotic" (within "functional" illness) are moderately easily legally distinguished and incorporated, again the former being seen as more obviously congruent with legal notions of mental abnormality. Further down the hierarchy still, even the distinction between (neurotic) mental illness and personality disorder *appears* to offer a basis for determining the presence or absence of an abnormality of mind.

The *psychometric approach* would eschew any such dichotomisation. False psycho-legal congruence, it would likely be argued, arises out of the spurious attempt to define qualitatively distinct disease entities where reality is merely quantitative. It can also be argued more generally that, even if dichotomisation is a realistic clinical psychiatric approach, psychiatry falsely incorporates into legal proceedings (because it is forced so to do by those proceedings) one of several possible dichotomies as definitive whereas, in its own terms, it would tend to use a number of dichotomies *together*, where any of these might conflict with the legal result implied by using a single dichotomy. Practical psychiatry uses eclecticism as an escape and eclecticism, by definition, is incongruous with dichotomisation.

Even ignoring false dichotomisation as a problem, the very foundation of the psychiatric-phenomenological approach, that is, the pursuit of value free objectivity, may be in question in such a fashion that expert evidence veers towards moral philosophy. Hence, it *could* be expertly argued that, because alcohol dependence syndrome (as a recognised psychiatric disease) incorporates psychological, physiological and histo-pathological changes, which directly influence the threshold for ingestion, then intoxication in a defendant suffering from that disorder should not be adjudged as voluntary intoxication. Indeed, that *has* been argued in a case (*R* v. *Tandy* [1988]). However, voluntariness is, of course, a moral and not a medical concept.

The *psycho-understanding approach* is not naturally dichotomous. However, it is inherently explanatory (as compared with the phenomenological descriptive approach) and may, through its particularly strong presumption that all persons have psychopathology, be at risk of purporting to over-identify abnormality. Hence, it is not uncommon for contested personality disorder cases to juxtapose a psychoanalyst for the defence and a phenomenologist for the prosecution, most famously in the trial of Dennis Nilsen (Masters, 1986). Even in the context of psychosis there is a clear distinction between expert evidence that describes the coincidence, for example, of instructional auditory hallucinations and the *actus* on the one hand, *and* evidence that explains the *actus* by way of those hallucinations on the other.

"Unbalanced Woman"

There is a long and international tradition of recognising puerperal mental illness as a legal excuse for infanticide. This is perhaps the only clear example of intentional incorporation into law of a specific psychiatric diagnosis (in the Infanticide Act 1938), where the legal definition appears to be highly congruent with mental or medical constructs. Even here, however, psychiatry has moved on, so as to cause blurring of the picture psycho-legally, since it appears now that a puerperal illness commonly represents an illness to which the woman is, in any event, predisposed and the puerperium represents only a (perhaps hormone-specific) stressor towards illness. Hence, since the law has remained static, incongruence has been created.

"Reasonable Man"

In contrast to the cause of an offence of homicide being seen to lie solely in the abnormal defendant, the defence of provocation defines a normal ("reasonable man") defendant who reacts to the abnormal (unreasonable) provocation of the victim (*R* v. *Duffy* [1967]). Here also, potential psycho-legal incongruence is obvious. The test of whether the reasonable man would have reacted as did the defendant appears to imply a notion of normality, and perhaps even statistical normality. Even taken in the latter sense, this must certainly be a legal fiction, since it is not the case that most respond even to substantial provocation by homicide; taken in the more general sense of normality, again it cannot be seen as "normal" to kill. It is clear that these falsehoods arise out of the law's need to find a route to its purpose of recognising that provoked homicide is not morally equivalent to the unprovoked variety, not therefore warranting the mandatory life sentence for murder.

A further difficulty concerns the law's recognition that the reasonable man's susceptibility is not that of the *perfect* man but of the man with the characteristics of the defendant (*R* v. *Camplin*). Little difficulty arises in relation to physical characteristics (classically, the psychological hunch-back, *Bedder* v. *DPP* [1954]) but logically a defendant should be no more culpable of being susceptible to taunts against his mental characteristics than against his physical ones. The law's caution about admitting mental characteristics is understandable in psychological terms since, unlike with physical characteristics, it must surely be very difficult to distinguish between the operation of those characteristics in relation to his susceptibility and their operation in relation to his reaction, which latter only the jury can legally address. However, distinguishing between the physical and the mental may itself, at times, be difficult. Hence, a man may be impotent because of a diabetic neuropathy (which would clearly be allowed as a characteristic), yet alternatively be impotent through the character trait of anxiety, clearly a mental characteristic (which might not be so allowed).

More generally, the law's model of the reasonable man appears to amount to the use of some notion of a corporate human normality, inferring an underlying spectrum in order to derive moral normality.

"Unfit man"

The Criminal Procedure (Insanity) Act 1964 does not state the test to be applied to decide whether a person is "unfit to plead" and the legal criteria for "fitness" are derived most authoritatively from Alderson B in *R* v. *Pritchard* [1836]. They require that the defendant "can plead to the indictment, be of sufficient intellect to comprehend the proceedings so as to make a proper defence, know that he might challenge any one of the jurors to whom he may object and comprehend the details of the evidence". The Butler Report (1975) suggested modification of *Pritchard* to include pleading *with understanding* and the addition of the ability to "give adequate instructions to Counsel". Amnesia as a sole criterion (*R* v. *Podola* [1960]) and failure of the defendant to "act in his own best interest" (*R* v. *Robertson* [1968]) are specifically excluded as criteria.

It can be argued cogently that the current legal criteria are too narrow to represent adequately all true psychological disabilities in relation to undergoing trial. Amnesia for events relevant to the offence *may*, in psychological if not in legal reality, be a marked defence handicap and not merely "equivalent to other adventitious difficulties affecting the defence" (Butler, 1975). Delusions specific to the offence *may*, similarly, significantly disadvantage a defendant and yet may be excluded as a basis for unfitness because they imply no more than "failure to act in one's own best interest" (*R* v. *Robertson* [1968]). Mood abnormalities *may* also fall into a similar category. Hence, Teubner's notion of autopoietic legal artifacts appears to apply to unfitness.

HOW CONSTRUCTS ARE ACTUALLY INTERPRETED AND OPERATED

In spite of all the foregoing consideration of legal definitions of models of human behaviour, the practical effect of any legal construct is dependent, as we have already observed, not only upon how it is defined but also upon how it is operated. This is obviously so for loosely defined artifacts but it is true even for those which have tight legal definitions. Such operation of the law can amount, for example, to deciding whether an available defence is to be pleaded by a defendant, whether (and how) an expert mental scientist might refer to a particular legal construct, how a judge might interpret the same construct and in what circumstances he or she might allow it to be addressed or, finally, how a jury might interpret the construct. There is insufficient space to allow a comprehensive review of how a wide range of constructs can be variously interpreted and used, both by lawyers and mental scientists. Indeed, such a review could be the subject of a book in its own right. However, it may be helpful to address two examples in order to illustrate the importance of the potential range of operation of legal constructs generally.

Insanity

As with unfitness (see again below), it seems likely that, before the 1991 Act, the effects of a finding of insanity substantially limited its use. The fact of an automatic direction to hospital on a finding of insanity heavily deterred it from being pleaded. The Criminal Procedure (Insanity and Unfitness to Plead) Act 1991 altered this situation (except in relation to a charge of murder) such that a range of disposal options is now available to the court. However, despite the new Act, there is evidence of only slightly increased use of insanity since 1991 (Mackay, 1995). It is unclear whether this arises from ignorance of the altered legal situation on the part of counsel and judges or from the continuing effect of a very narrow definition of insanity. This said, the situation *could* now substantially change as a result of the 1997 Crime (Sentences) Act, which all but mandates a life sentence on a finding of guilt of a second "serious offence".

Certainly, any attempt there may be in future to increase the use of insanity will, as with the *Pritchard* rules in relation to unfitness (see below), still be substantially limited by the highly restrictive *McNaughton* rules. Hence, although there may now be an even greater *incentive* to plead insanity (because the inflexible disposal to hospital with a restriction order was removed by the 1991 Act and because of the shift somewhat away from welfare and towards justice sentencing represented by the 1997 Act) the definition of insanity is too narrow to allow more than a handful of mentally disordered defendants through it. In terms of an aggregate effect on justice, this reflects a far bigger justice issue than arises out of inadequate unfitness criteria, for example. Even if there were to be somewhat broader unfitness criteria, it seems likely that fewer defendants could or would be found unfit by comparison with the total number of mentally disordered defendants who should properly have access to a psychiatric defence which is adequate, so as to reflect their disordered functioning in the degree or nature of culpability which is attached to them at trial. So, put simply, many severely mentally ill or learning disabled defendants will fail (perhaps *just* fail) to pass the McNaughton test, which is their only escape from (full) conviction of a charge less than murder. If they are therefore found guilty, they will then either be at risk of a penal disposal or will automatically (bar indeterminate "exceptional circumstances") receive a life sentence. In either case the sentence will be without a hospital direction (because such a direction is currently, in England and Wales, available only for psychopaths). It seems highly likely that this situation will result not only in more frequent attempts somehow to fit defendants into the McNaughton rules but also in clarion calls for redefinition of the insanity defence (so as to make it broader), in order more adequately to reflect justice for such defendants and to facilitate the securing of their subsequent welfare.

Unfitness

As already suggested, any inadequacy of strict legal definition may be modified in its effects by medical and/or judicial practice. This is of some importance in determining the practical relevance for justice of such inadequate definitions, for example in relation to the justice impact of so-called "hybrid orders" and of extension of the mandatory life sentence in the Crime (Sentences) Act. Unlike in relation to most legal models of man, which have been little researched as regards medical knowledge and interpretation of them, there *is* some empirical evidence concerning psychiatrists' interpretation of unfitness. This is useful as an illustration of the "real" operation of law, particularly law which is highly psycho-legally incongruent, which can usefully be read in the light of the foregoing analysis of the relationship between legal and mental science models of human behaviour and capacity.

A reasonable review of the relevant literature runs as follows. Apart from evidence of a general failure to use the unfitness criteria, or to use them adequately, their interpretation by psychiatrists was, before the passage of the amending 1991 Act, almost certainly not independent of the impact upon the defendant of a *finding* of unfitness (Grubin, 1991). It seems highly likely that there was deliberate false negative determining of unfitness by psychiatrists, specifically *because of* the perceived unjust impact of "indefinite detention untried". That is, there was probably deliberate psychiatric distortion towards the finding of fitness arising because of the law's rule about disposal. Unusually, therefore, psychiatry distorted the criminal law, rather than reverse. Indeed, it probably did so because it took both (perhaps) a moral welfare and (probably) a clinical stance; that is, it was thought unjust to incarcerate an untreatable unfit defendant long term *and* he or she would (certainly) present a therapeutic problem. The nature of any injustice is of particular interest in relation to juxta-posing welfare and justice sentencing models since the earlier 1964 Act clearly reflected a welfare intention (at least if the charge was not a very serious one) and yet, in its effect of detaining a defendant potentially indefinitely (albeit in hospital), it had had a clearly punitive result. Further, as regards how psychia-trists might have perceived, and been influenced by, these effects of a finding of unfitness on *their* evidence, Grubin (1991) interestingly poses the question: "Are psychiatrists acting in their client's/patient's best interest when they recommend a finding of unfit to plead, or are they, with the best of intentions, using an archaic legal philosophy which, in the end, does more harm than good?" The basis of the question is that doctors will wish to seek to do "more good than harm", rather than merely give an honest clinical opinion, irrespective of its legal implications. To the extent that this *may* reflect how doctors decide their opinions,[3] it empha-sises potential medical distortion of a justice-based legal process, directed towards a medical welfare purpose. However, Grubin's reference to "an archaic legal philosophy" seems to go much further since it can be interpreted to include the criteria for a finding of unfitness *per se*.

Even with the much greater flexibility of disposal on a finding of unfitness in the 1991 Act and the introduction of a required "trial of the facts", the current criteria remain a potential bar to justice. Hence, defendants who, on fairer, or more mental science realistic, criteria of unfitness, would be adjudged unfit and who could, thereby, go to hospital under the Mental Health Act (1983), even in spite of extension of the mandatory life sentence in the 1997 Act, are unable to do so. This welfare disadvantage is, of course, compounded by the justice effect (in fact "*in*justice") of conviction *per se*. Similarly, defendants who, even though at risk of only a determinate sentence, would be the potential subjects of a hybrid order (in essence a penal disposal) might not be so if the unfitness criteria were broader.[4] Similar effects concerning to the impact of the 1997 Act apply in rela-tion to the narrow definition of "insanity", also dealt with under the 1991 Act but, again, solely in terms of disposal.

One further effect of the Crime (Sentences) Act 1997 will likely be that, whereas before the 1991 Act, psychiatrists may well have distorted their view about unfitness in order to *avoid* unfitness, since the 1997 Act they may be tempted to do the reverse, so as to avoid the automatic life sentence for someone charged with a second "serious offence". As already suggested, there may be a similar tendency to try to expand psychiatric findings of insanity, for similar reasons.

---

[3] Grubin's (1991) other finding that "many individuals who are found unfit to plead seemed little dif-ferent from the majority of mentally disturbed or mentally handicapped defendants who come before the courts" suggests that chance, or factors unrelated to unfitness *per se*, determine findings of unfit-ness and that, therefore, doctors may well take their "own view". It also suggest substantial under-finding of unfitness.

[4] See Eastman and Peay (1998) for discussion of this and the similar effect in relation to the narrow definition of insanity.

CLINICAL INVOLVEMENT IN THE CRIMINAL JUSTICE SYSTEM

In the criminal justice system, consideration of the ethical implications of clinician involvement goes beyond posing the question of whether a clinician should, on ethical principle, avoid the system if its constructs fail to reflect mental science reality. That is an important ethical question, but there are less erudite and fundamental ethical issues to consider.

Section 4(1) of the Criminal Justice Act 1991 requires a trial judge to ensure that a psychiatric report is provided to the court on anyone who is or appears to be mentally unstable. Clearly this can be seen potentially as facilitating a welfare aspect of sentencing. However, Section 2(2)b also *requires* the court to impose a "longer than normal sentence" (LTNS), that is, longer than the usual tariff justified by the offence *per se*, if, in the opinion of the judge, it "is necessary to protect the public from serious harm". Since "irrationality of the behaviour, the selection of vulnerable persons, or a particular class of persons, or target, unexplained severe violence, unusual obsessions or delusion, any inability on the part of the offender to appreciate the consequences of his or her actions . . . (and) lack of remorse or unwillingness to accept medication" have been defined as factors relevant to the decision (*R* v. *Fawcett* [1994]), and since guidance on the Act (Leng & Manchester, 1991) lists "mental impairment" as evidence directly relevant to passing a LTNS it seems clear that psychiatric factors and evidence are directly relevant to passing an LTNS. Hence, as Solomka (1996) points out from a study of the first 35 Court of Appeal cases on Section 2(2)b, a medical report prepared for one purpose (assessing possible admission to hospital) can be used for another (a LTNS). As a result, a potential welfare function of psychiatric evidence is translated into a punitive justice function. Again, as Solomka also emphasises, the factor which determines, on psychiatric evidence, *non*-hospital admission, that is, untreatability, becomes the factor which determines greater punishment, and, as Fitzgerald (1995) points out, without any right to treatment potentially ameliorating of the offending dangerousness. Indeed, Fitzgerald also suggests that, apart from failure to provide for regular judicial testing of the continuing basis for preventative detention and failure to require clear specification of the portion of the sentence which is preventive (both of which, he argues, contravene Article 5 of the European Convention on Human Rights), the *absence* of a right to treatment contravenes the Convention. Related to this, Solomka's study identifies factors connected with diagnosis, treatability and suitability for medical disposal as determining of trial and appeal decisions on Section 2(2)b and, essentially, finds that "untreatable psychopathy or personality disorder" can result in very substantial premiums being added to tariff sentences (double on occasions),[5] with "lack of insight, denial, minimisation, refusal to accept treatment

---

[5] In one case where two co-defendants were jointly convicted of an offence one who was determined to have an untreatable personality disorder received a five-year sentence against his (normal) co-defendant who received 30 months (*R* v. *Bestwick and Huddlestrom* [1994]).

and repeated failure of hospital treatments as factors taken into account". Of course this assumes a medical model, or positivist criminological model, of offending and dangerousness rather than acceptance of the important role of situational variables and the usual model of risk management of such circumstances. Indeed, as Fitzgerald suggests, it is the apparent assumption in the Act, expressed by way of *fixing* a preventive sentence in advance (rather than allowing Butler's (1975) "renewable sentences") on the basis of *prediction* (sometimes even with relatively little offending *per se* (*R* v. *Fawcett*), which may also contravene the ECHR.

More broadly, clearly one result of Section 4(1) is that reports prepared under it can be used alternatively by the courts towards determining a Section 41 restriction order under the Mental Health Act 1983, a hospital and limitation directive under the 1997 Act or a LTNS under Section 2(2)b of the 1991 Act. As Solomka says, this means that neither psychiatrist nor offender can predict, before the assessment is made, to what purpose it will ultimately be applied (either because the relevance cannot be known in advance of the assessment or because, in any event, court use of the report cannot be predicted or controlled). This has ethical implications, not only in terms of direct involvement of the psychiatrist in sentencing[6] but also for the defendant's consent and the risk basis on which he or she agrees to be interviewed.[7]

The sentencing and ethical implications, as well as the ECHR aspect, of Section 2(2)(b), are well dealt with in Solomka's and Fitzgerald's papers. However, perhaps a few more points remain to be made, by placing the 1991 Act alongside other government provisions. In one sense, Section 2(2)b represents the "opposite" of the hybrid order. That is, whereas Section 2(2)b effectively *juxtaposes* punitive and welfare sentencing (in that it uses psychiatric data or opinion to impose a LTNS *because* the defendant cannot/will not be treated in hospital), the hybrid order *combines* welfare and justice, albeit that the punitive element is the trump aspect (a prisoner-patient who becomes well and who then has to serve the remainder of his sentence is hardly likely, at that point, to see the disposal as one which "mixes", rather than "combines" welfare and justice). Hence, whereas the hybrid prisoner-patient may well perceive a "double message" in the nature of his detention ("am I being punished to prevent me doing it again or being treated, towards that same purpose?"), the LTNS prisoner, if he is denying the need for treatment of the disorder which justified a LTNS, will *not even see* a double message. Rather the LTNS, in the absence of a right to treatment, is both likely to reinforce the disorder and to be a recipe for hopelessness. Also, the mentally disordered offender's (MDO's) trust in psychiatry as a route to (his) welfare is likely to have been severely damaged if he originally perceived

---

[6] It can be postulated that one difference between use of a report for deciding on a restriction order against a LTNS is that, at least in the former case, the restriction is attached to a *medical* disposal.

[7] One "solution" is the use of a "confidentiality contract" basis for the relationship between clinician and client, with maximal openness of information about how reports might be used. This is particularly relevant to this "multiple potential purpose" situation.

assessment as aimed at possible treatment but then experienced it ultimately as justifying of greater punishment. This highlights the importance of "openness" on the part of psychiatrists, both for its own sake and in order to bolster the position of psychiatry as a welfare discipline, particularly in a public policy climate which is tending to emphasise the involvement of psychiatry in state punishment and public protection.

Solomka deals at length with the boundary of psychiatric expertise in relation to Section 2(2)b, and clearly this can be distinguished into strict *legal* definition of the boundary, that is, on what issues the doctor is allowed to give an opinion (*R* v. *Turner* [1975]; *R* v. *Chard* [1992]), and the *ethical* boundary (Chiswick, 1985). However, further related issues are important. First, should not the judiciary be explicitly educated (in general and in individual cases) as to the mental science knowledge and science base, including the inadequacies of risk assessment, offered by its practitioners. Indeed, it is of particular broader public policy interest that, whereas in relation to verdict issues, the "Turner boundary" is commonly closely guarded by judges (where it is juries who will be listening to psychiatric expertise), and there is indeed a healthy scepticism about what psychiatry can offer to legal decision-making, when it comes to disposal (reserved for the judges) psychiatry is much more legally validated and far more heavily relied upon. One explanation may, of course, be that judges trust themselves to be sceptical but have less confidence in juries to be so. Another is that sentencing is an altogether softer science in itself than trial to verdict. However, given the increasingly wide sentencing ranges which are applicable in relation to risk, with points on the range for mentally disordered defendants influenced substantially by "dangerousness" and by psychiatrists, the *impact* of the sentencing mechanism and decision can hardly be seen as substantially less important than determining the verdict.

Of course, responsibility for such judicial education rests partly on those giving evidence, but there may be an argument for more formal safeguards, for example, always requiring *two* reports (one for each side) and importing into the sentencing stage a far more adversarial approach (from counsel). This might be seen in the UK as "too American". However, is not the problem arising because our courts are moving towards America in allowing doctors more influence in punitive sentencing? The scenario is, if the psychiatric opinion is hostile to the defendant, little different in its ethics and effect from the "Dr Death" role of some American psychiatrists. Any argument of English judges that *they*, and not the doctor, ultimately take the decision is less than reassuring since, where the sole determinant of a LTNS is danger arising out of mental disorder, the judge is bound, by virtue of his relative ignorance of mental disorder, to rely heavily on the doctor.[8]

Across a broad front psychiatric evidence is likely to be used increasingly to address all three sentencing criteria—mitigation of culpability, public risk and

---

[8] Solomka's study supports the importance of the role of psychiatric opinion in determining LTNSs, as well as the role of the "negative factors for treatability" listed earlier.

(more traditionally) welfare medical disposal. Indeed, psychiatry seems to be used increasingly, across an even broader front, as a means of social control.[9] However, whereas psychiatry is increasingly encouraged, or even required, to apply its expertise to the purpose of prisoner or patient control and public safety, it is still heavily excluded from a proper (perhaps even reciprocal) role in influencing the determination of culpability which, in relation to sentencing, leads in turn to punishment and public protection. That is, in Teubnerian terms, the law increasingly embraces the psychiatric discourse at the expense of its own discourse when addressing punishment and public protection, but holds strongly to its autopoietic nature when addressing culpability.

CONCLUSIONS

Convicted man is subjected to a very different legal model from that which he faced during his trial. A binary approach gives way to a graded one and the general potential for psycho-legal incongruence greatly diminishes. The need, specifically, for the psychiatric-phenomenological approach to force itself into its non-eclectic, uni-theoretical framework largely disappears, and the other two approaches may similarly be more at home. Psychiatric evidence, particularly phenomenological psychiatry, can therefore avoid confronting its own model uncertainty or avoid pressing itself into greater protestations of dichotomous and general categorical certainty than is warranted. In recognition that not even the general disputes between the three approaches will even be validly settled, it can embrace its customary, and perhaps solely valid, eclecticism in the court room. A generally applicable solution to most (inherent) psycho-legal incongruence lies, therefore, in the removal of psychiatric evidence uniquely to the disposal stage. Resistance to such a move lies in the legally perceived unfairness of conviction on the basis of an "automatic", "irrational", "mentally diseased", "mentally abnormal", or "mentally unbalanced" *mens*. That perceived unfairness has also now been given an added twist by virtue of the substantial change of sentencing philosophy represented by the "hospital direction" in the Crime (Sentences) Act 1997 and by inclusion of the mentally disordered in extension of the mandatory life sentences within the same Act. The road to abandoning the mandatory life sentence now seems, therefore, firmly closed. The 1997 Act also further emphasises the (in)justice implications of the highly restricted nature of psychiatric defences.

Psychiatry and psychology are likely, therefore, to be increasingly pressed into evidence towards issues of verdict, and so the impact of incongruence with their legal host's constructs will be emphasised. This points to the importance of minimising the impact of such inherent incongruence through clarity of defini-

---

[9] Interestingly, the one piece of recent legislation which might be seen as *not* within this trend is the Criminal Procedure (Insanity and Unfitness to Plead) Act 1991 which increased the welfare of mentally disordered offenders, and that legislation originated and passed through parliament via a private member.

tion of psychiatric and psychological models and through allowing courts to take verdict decisions in full knowledge of the real construct uncertainty that such expertise harbours. Perhaps the very least that should be required of psychiatric and psychological expertise, therefore, is that it applies the same diagnostic procedures and uncertainties to defendants as it does to patients and that, in particular, it avoids legally derived distortions of its constructs, of their reliability, and of the probability of their being valid. Hence, such expertise should continue at least to pursue non-value-ladenness even in the highly value-laden legal context. This touches on the ethics of clinician involvement in the criminal justice system *per se*.

REFERENCES

Butler, Lord (1975) *Report of the Committee on Mentally Abnormal Offenders*. Cmnd 6244. London: HMSO.

Chiswick, D. (1985) Use and abuse of psychiatric testimony. *British Medical Journal*, **290**, 975–977.

Eastman, N.L.G. (1986) Defending the mentally ill: Psychiatric aspects of insanity and automatism. In R. Mackay & K. Russell (Eds) *Psychiatry and the Criminal Process*. Leicester: Leicester Law Monograph.

Eastman, N.L.G. (1992) Psychiatric, psychological and legal models of man. *International Journal of Law and Psychiatry*, **15**, 157–169.

Eastman, N. & Hope, R. (1988) The ethics of enforced medical treatment: The balance model. *Journal of Applied Philosophy*, **5**, 49–59.

Eastman, N.L.G. & Mezey, G. (1997) *Abused women who kill their abusing partners*. Unpublished paper.

Eastman, N. & Peay, J. (1998) Sentencing psychopaths: Is the "Hospital and Limitation Direction" an ill-considered hybrid? *Criminal Law Review*, February, 93–108.

Eastman, N. & Peay, J. (Eds) (1999) *Law without Enforcement: Integrating Mental Health and Justice*. Oxford: Hart Publications.

Engel, G.L. (1977) The need of a new medical model: A challenge for biomedicine. *Science*, **196**(4286), 129–136.

Fenton, G. (1972) Epilepsy and automatism. *British Journal of Hospital Medicine*, January, 57–64.

Fitzgerald, E. (1995) The Criminal Justice Act 1991: Preventative detention of the dangerous offender. *European Human Rights Law Review* (Launch volume), 39–48.

Grubin, D.H. (1991) Unfit to plead in England and Wales, 1976–88: A survey. *British Journal of Psychiatry*, **158**, 540.

Home Office (1999) *Managing Dangerous People with Severe Personality Disorder. Proposals for Policy Development*. London: Home Office.

Howard, C.H. & d'Orban, P.T. (1987) Violence in sleep: Medico-legal issues and two case reports. *Psychological Medicine*, **17**, 915–925.

Jaspers, K. (1963) *General psychopathology* (trans. J. Hoenig & M.W. Hamilton). Manchester: Manchester University Press. (Original work published 1913.)

Leng, R. & Manchester, C. (1991) *A Guide to the Criminal Justice Act 1991*. London: Fourmat.

Lewis, A. (1953) Health as a social concept. *British Journal of Sociology*, **4**, 109–124.

Mackay, R. (1995) *Mental Condition Defences in the Criminal Law*. Oxford: Clarendon Press.

Masters, B. (1986) *Killing for Company*. London: Coronet Books.

Oswald, I. & Evans, J. (1985) On serious violence during sleep-walking. *British Journal of Psychiatry*, **147**, 689–691.

Ritchie, J.H., Dick, D. & Lingham, R. (1994) *The Report of the Inquiry into the Care and Treatment of Christopher Clunis*. London: HMSO.

Solomka, B. (1996) The role of psychiatric evidence in passing "longer than normal" sentences. *Journal Forensic Psychiatry*, **7**, 239–255.

Szasz, T.S. (1961) *The Myth of Mental Illness*. New York, NY: Harper & Row.

Szasz, T.S. (1963) *Law, Liberty and Psychiatry*. New York, NY: Macmillan.

Szasz, T.S. (1974) *The Myth of Mental Illness: Foundations of a Theory of Personal Conduct* (revised edition). New York, NY: Harper & Row.

Teubner, G. (1993) *Law as an Autopoietic System*. Oxford: Blackwell.

Virchow, R. (1958) Standpoints in scientific medicine. In *Disease, Life and Man: Selected Essays* (trans. L.J. Rather). Palo Alto, CA: Stanford University Press. (Original work published 1847.)

Wexler, D.B. & Winick, B. (1991) *Essays in Therapeutic Jurisprudence*. Durham, NC: Carolina Academic Press.

Wootton, B. (assisted by Seal, V.G. & Chambers, R.) (1959) *Social Science and Social Pathology*. London: Allen & Unwin.

LAW CASES

Bedder v. *DPP* [1954] 2 All ER 201.

Bratty v. *the Attorney General for Northern Ireland* [1963] AC 386.

R v. *Byrne* [1960] 2 QB 396; 3 WLR 440; [1960] 3 All ER 1.

R v. *Bestrick and Huddlestrom* [1994] Criminal Law Review, pp. 771–772 October, Unreported; [1995] (CA) No. 16 Cr App R (5168K).

R v. *Camplin* 1 Car & Kir 746.

R v. *Chard* [1992] 56 Cr App R268 (CA).

R v. *Duffy* [1967] 1 QB 63.

R v. *Fawcett* [1994] (CA) (unreported) *Criminal Law Review* September, pp. 704–705; [1995] 16 Cr App RS at p. 55.

R v. *McNaughton* [1843] 10 Cl & Fin 200.

R v. *Podola* [1960] 1 QB 325.

R v. *Pritchard* (1836) 7 C. and 303.

R v. *Quick* [1973] QB 910; [1973] 3 WLR 26; [1973] 3 All ER 347.

R v. *Robertson* [1968] 1 WLR 1767; [1968] 3 All ER 557; [1968] 52 Cr App R 690.

R v. *Tandy* [1988] 87 Cr App R 45.

R v. *Turner* [1975] 1 QB 834.

Chapter 6

Decision-Making in Legal Settings

Jenny McEwan
School of Law, University of Exeter, UK

JUDGES AND JURIES

Psychological research into decision-making in court is limited in terms of what it can achieve, yet there seems no shortage of attempts to try to analyse judicial and jury thinking. The methodological problems surrounding such endeavours are many, and largely self-evident. Laboratory simulations are hard put to match the issues, atmosphere and responsibility surrounding court-made decisions, and it is rare that the sample of subjects has much in common with the average jury, since researchers tend to rely on hard-up undergraduates as mock jurors (King, 1986; Lloyd-Bostock, 1996; Hastie, Penrod & Pennington, 1983). However, given the lack of opportunity to ask real jurors to explain their verdicts, or to ask judges the basis of their reasoning, laboratory experiments and mock trials appear to be the best alternative psychologists can adopt. It would, clearly, be dangerous to make too much of their findings. It should be borne in mind, also, that the vast majority of criminal cases in England and Wales are tried before lay magistrates, who generally sit over a number of years. It would be simplistic to assume that judges, magistrates and jurors, mock or actual, reason in the same way. Apart from the obvious differences in training and experience, their roles differ significantly during a trial.

Juries are used nowadays in only about 12 to 14 civil trials a year (Lloyd-Bostock, 1996) in the United Kingdom, and thus a judge sitting alone must decide on facts as well as law in the same way as magistrates in summary criminal trials. This happens also in the "Diplock Courts" of Northern Ireland, where there is no jury. In general, however, the role of the jury is to be the arbiter of fact, while

Behaviour, Crime and Legal Processes: A Guide for Forensic Practitioners.
Edited by James McGuire, Tom Mason and Aisling O'Kane.
© 2000 John Wiley & Sons Ltd.

the judge is the arbiter of law and decides on sentence. This involves very different reasoning processes. In deciding on guilt or innocence, a jury is directed to the past, to settling disputed claims as to what happened on a particular occasion. In determining sentence, a judge (or magistrate) may to some extent be involved in the prediction of future behaviour. In those cases where a judge must resolve disputed facts, such as in civil trials, the level of activity and intervention bears no resemblance to the muted role of the jury when it fulfils such a role: "The ideal juror is characterised as a relatively passive record keeper who encodes the events of the trial verbatim" (Hastie, Penrod & Pennington, 1983). Judges are far more active during the course of a trial, and the relationship between judge and advocate which develops as a consequence may colour the final outcome (Jackson & Doran, 1995). Jurors are excluded from the interaction between the participants in the trial, but apparently may be influenced by the relationship between the protagonists (Kerr, 1982).[1] Another striking difference between a verdict arrived at by a single judge and one reached by a jury is that the latter is the product of group discussion, and may be influenced by group dynamics. Research on the effect of deliberation in groups has examined everything from the effect of a strong personality to the shape of the table (summarised in Hastie, Penrod & Pennington, 1983, ch. 3). Probably the most interesting finding in this context is that an individual reaction to evidence prior to discussion is quite a good predictor of verdict. There are possibilities for change, however, and more usually away from conviction, after group deliberation, although it may be that the individual juror who changes vote to satisfy colleagues retains his or her original opinion (Arce, Fariña & Sabral, 1996). Views, however, tend to polarise less if the prosecution case is strong; the few jurors initially against conviction are likely to be won over. It appears that the gender of the juror has little effect on the verdict. There may be differences in rape cases, where all-women juries are more likely to convict for rape. Overall, women have been found to be much less active during the group discussion in jury simulations (Arce, Fariña & Sabral, 1996).

The structure of trials presents jurors with problems that judges do not share. Juries listen to evidence sometimes over considerable periods of time without having a legal context in which to place it. By the time an explanation of its legal relevance is provided—when the judge gives the final summing up—the evidence has all been heard and must be recalled to mind and fitted within the legal framework (Jackson, 1996; Kassim & Wrightsman, 1988). It is scarcely surprising, therefore, to find that if a judicial summing-up simultaneously reminds jurors of some evidence they heard but instructs them to disregard it, the admonishment appears to be counter-productive (Wolf & Montgomery, 1977; Tanford, 1990; Hastie, Penrod & Pennington, 1983). Another problem arising from the last-minute legal instructions is that when people recall information, they are often unable to recall its source, which, during the course of a trial, could have been an advocate, a

---

[1] Curiously, a cold, relentless prosecutor achieved better results than one who displayed any warmth towards the defence.

witness, or the judge (Johnson, Bransford & Solomon, 1973; Johnson & Kaye, 1981). Confusion about the meaning of judicial instructions is particularly understandable in those cases where jurors have returned to the judge to ask for elucidation. Frequently, judges will do no more than repeat what was said in the first place, refusing to explain or paraphrase (Severance & Loftus, 1982). Yet Judge Jerome Frank dismissed the efforts of the jury:

> While the jury can contribute nothing of value so far as the law is concerned, it has infinite capacity for mischief, for twelve men can easily misunderstand more law in a minute than the judges can explain in an hour.
> (*Skidmore* v. *Baltimore and Ohio Railroad* 167 F 2d 54 [2d Cir 1948])

Studies of juror comprehension of legal instructions have produced conflicting results. In a study by Heuer and Penrod (1995), who questioned jurors who had participated in real trials, the jurors became less confident that their verdict complied with judicial instructions as the quantity of information increased. However, they were still content with the fairness of the proceedings, although they were more confident of that where they were able to question witnesses. Belfast jurors reported that judicial interventions and requests for elucidation where an expert witness was giving evidence were helpful to them (Jackson, 1996). These juries also reported high levels of comprehension. In complicated trials, jurors may receive some legal education as they go along; in the Maxwell fraud trial, the prosecutor supplied them with a booklet explaining the nature of limited companies during his opening address. Nevertheless, mock jurors presented with the same evidence in the same way as that at the Maxwell trial itself seemed, in the main, to understand it reasonably well. During regular interview sessions with the researchers, most mock jurors were found to employ good quality reasoning (Honess, Levi & Charman, 1998).

Kalven and Zeisel (1966) conclude, having compared jury verdicts in real cases with the opinion of the trial judge as to guilt, that juries do not operate significantly differently from judges in their assessment of evidence. But Stephenson (1992) points out that although in this study agreement on convictions is high, there is less unanimity on acquittals. Judges and juries may agree that a majority of defendants is guilty, but they do not agree on whom to find not guilty. In an English study conducted by Baldwin and McConville (1979) real verdicts were similarly compared with the opinions of professionals involved in the case and a high level of what were deemed perverse acquittals were discovered.[2] There were also some perverse convictions which amazed even the police. Sometimes the jury ignored a virtual direction to acquit, and were more likely to do this where the defendant was black. There have been a few instances of really alarming jury behaviour. In *Stephen Young* ([1988] 2 WLR 430), a conviction for murder delivered by a British jury had to be set aside when it was discovered that four jury members had been influenced by a seance they had conducted in order to receive a posthumous message from the victim. In the USA, the defence of demonic

---

[2] Doubted by at least two professionals.

possession was accepted by a jury, 11 members of which believed in possession by the devil (Kassim & Wrightsman, 1988, p. 99).

DECIDING CASES

Whom to Believe?

The common law traditionally lays great stress upon the importance of a witness's physical presence in court, and the opportunity of the trier of fact to observe his or her demeanour. This is a key part of the rationale of the hearsay rule (see McEwan, 1998). Yet it seems that courtroom inquiries are far from ideal settings in which to evaluate a witness's honesty. Experimental subjects regard as persuasive those communicators who are extraverted, involved, positive and moderately relaxed (Mehabrian & William, 1969; Blumenthal, 1993). Those who will be believed tend to use a great deal of eye contact, to speak in clear, steady tones, and to appear confident (Ekman, 1985; Deffenbacher & Loftus, 1982). Miller and Burgoon (1982) note that the factors associated by observers with dishonesty are equally as consistent with apprehension or anxiety. This may be associated with a general difficulty the subject has in communicating, or problems in communicating in a particular context, such as testifying in a court of law. Some people, consequently, are believed whether they are lying or not, others the opposite (Hocking et al., 1979; Kraut, 1978). There is also a problem with body language associated with a particular culture which may be misunderstood by observers from a different background (Winkel & de Winter, 1996; Ekman, Sorenson & Friesen, 1969). Although some psychologists claim that the rate of sucess people have in detecting deception is better than chance, Miller and Burgoon (1982) concluded that their "observers would probably have done as well had they flipped a coin to determine if the communicator/deceiver were lying". Some speech styles are more persuasive than others, and there is some slight evidence that narrative rather than interrupted testimony is the more credible account (Lloyd-Bostock, 1996; Dane & Wrightsman, 1982). Also, arrangements in a courtroom are hardly compatible with the delivery of testimony in the most credible manner. Jurors who are directed to pay close attention to a witness's demeanour are thus presented with an inappropriate task. Apart from that, they must rely on the general character of the witness, his or her personal background, and qualities such as ulterior motive, if any (Kassim & Wrightsman, 1988; Beaumeister & Darley, 1982).

MAKING SENSE OF THE EVIDENCE

Bennett and Feldman (1981) argue that evidence is fitted together by jurors within a story framework which dictates a chronology. However, they have to contend with evidence presented to them in the manner and order dictated by a constellation of procedural and evidential rules. Research has shown

(Pennington & Hastie, 1986) that if a party presents evidence in story order, it is more readily believed than if it is presented out of sequence. Clearly, the serial calling of individual witnesses prevents events from being described in the sequence in which they originally occurred. In a well-known study designed to discover how jurors react to this problem, 69 different mock juries were asked to assess the same case on video. It was a murder case based on a real trial. According to legal experts, the only proper verdict was second-degree murder, but there were three other possible verdicts, and 38% of jurors selected those. When the jurors explained what they thought had actually happened, it was found that this depended on which facts they recalled (Hastie, Penrod & Pennington, 1983). They had selected facts to make a plausible story, and then the story itself filled any gaps in the evidence. In fact 45% of the components of the story they accepted were mere inferences. Hastie and his colleagues concluded from this that deviant verdicts are associated with poor comprehension and poor memory for the salient facts of the case, for the legal definitions of the crimes, and for the details of the evidence of individual witnesses. Their explanation of the differences among their mock jurors was that different stories had been recalled.

A narrative is accepted as true, according to Bennett and Feldman, if it presents a coherent central action, and a setting that makes the action understandable. The research led by Professor Hastie has elaborated on Bennett and Feldman's story thesis and provided empirical evidence for it. Wagenaar has developed it further to show that, in addition to these qualities, a story must, if it is to be accepted, be tied to reality by means of evidence (which is itself only another narrative which may or may not be true). One of his examples is that of a person shot dead, with a gun by the body which bears John's fingerprints. This in itself cannot incriminate John unless some other evidence suggests that this gun was the murder weapon. This additional evidence may be scientific in nature (and, to be accepted, probably rests on an assumption that forensic experts generally tell the truth). Or the link between the gun and the killing may simply be a belief that, in general, guns found by the corpses of those shot dead are the ones used for the killing. A commonly held belief of this kind may be described as a "heuristic". Heuristics are reasoning mechanisms often employed by people who find themselves required to make judgements on insufficient information— for example, where they need to interpret or predict the behaviour of others. Wagenaar argues that triers of fact like to anchor stories in evidence which is supported by general rules or common-sense propositions; judges have been seen to do this in jury-less cases in Northern Ireland (Jackson & Doran, 1995). A judge or jury will assess the quality of the alternative narratives offered and try to anchor them to generally accepted beliefs. These are usually stated in uncertain form, e.g. "Most ballistic experts tell the truth." Therefore, they can be displaced in a particular case. In Wagenaar's study of anomalous cases, he shows how the strength of a narrative[3] may lead to erroneous verdicts. A story may be so plau-

---

[3] Wagenaar's review of decided cases is assisted by the fact that, in the Netherlands, judges gave reasons (although often quite briefly) for their decisions on the facts.

sible that it is anchored directly to the belief structure without any intermediate level of evidence. Hence there may be the occasional conviction where there is another possible, or even more likely, suspect. Just as alarmingly, very diagnostic evidence can be omitted from the anchoring structure without affecting the perceived strength of what remains. Wagenaar observes that judges will explain the evidence that convinced them, but not the common-sense assumptions they relied on. Yet the strength of the evidence depends entirely on the rule chosen as anchor, whether it be that forensic scientists make few mistakes, or that innocent men do not confess (Wagenaar, van Koppen & Crombag, 1993).

One of the cases used to illustrate this is that of a person called Henkemans, who said he had come to Amsterdam on a ticket given to him by a friend whose name and address he could not remember. The police, acting on a tip-off, observed his arrival and his immediate meeting with two Chinese professional drug-dealers in a hotel. These men left, carrying a suitcase. Their house was searched, and heroin was discovered, but no trace of heroin could be found in the suitcase or on the defendant. Henkemans was convicted of supplying heroin, although the *actus reus*[4] of the offence was not anchored at all. Anchored narratives as a theory predicts that an attempt will be made to make the narrative convincing, although not necessarily providing anchors on those issues which are key from a legal point of view in a criminal case, namely, identification, *actus reus* and *mens rea*.[5] Here, the lack of evidence in these areas was not crucial, because the story was so good. The theory is also said to explain how evidence which suggests that the defendant is not guilty, and even that someone else is, may be disregarded. The anchoring construction consists of evidence that connects the narrative to general beliefs. In a case where a major portion of the evidence does not fit with the narrative, only that evidence that fits this purpose is selected. It thus may be that only a small portion of the evidence can be used in this manner, and the rest will be disregarded.

Judicial heuristics are acquired by judges generally or individually through their work. They differ from everyday heuristics because they are not part of the pool of "knowledge" shared by the community at large. Some assumptions may be shared with others who have wide experience of the criminal process, for instance social workers and probation officers who compose social enquiry reports for the sentencer. One of these appears to be that women rarely "intend" criminality (Stephenson, 1992; Allen, 1988). Males who kill are much more likely to be regarded as the instigators of action. Stephenson suggests that this may explain the high proportion of mentally-ill male offenders to be found in the prison system (Stephenson, 1992, p. 216). In the case of women who kill, a link between mind and action seems to be ruled out. They are thought to find themselves in situations rather than to create them. Court decisions tend to amount to

---

[4] Criminal act contained in the definition of the offence.
[5] State of mind contained in the definition of the offence.

reinforcement of popular notions about women: that they are not fully responsible for what they do, that their problems are not social but individual and so require attention from helping agencies, and that when they do take deliberate action (commit crimes) such behaviour is an irrational manifestation of "crime disturbance". (Pearson, 1976, p. 273)

The continued survival of the Infanticide Act 1938, the provisions of which are no longer considered to have any basis in medical science, is probably a testament to the widely held belief that any mother who kills her baby cannot be mentally well (see O'Donovan, 1984; Mackay, 1993). With female criminality in general, psychological reports may be requested in cases where there is no particular reason to suspect mental disturbance (Pearson, 1976). Allen (1988) shows why it is that women are more likely to be dealt with by psychiatrists than by penal means. "We are sorry to see you here" is a phrase men rarely hear from the court.

FORESEEABILITY

There are numerous instances of the law requiring finders of fact to adjudicate on the probability of an event or outcome. The issue of probability to some extent determines the question of whether or not the defendant intended the harm, or was reckless as to whether or not the harm occurred, in criminal cases (*R* v. *Hancock and Shankland* [1986] AC 455; *R* v. *Caldwell* [1982] AC 341). In the law of torts, a key factor in determining whether or not a defendant has been guilty of negligence is whether the outcome of his or her conduct would have been foreseeable by the reasonable man (*Blyth* v. *Birmingham Waterworks Co.* (1856) 11 Ex 781). Judges or juries[6] are expected to provide an answer to the question, "How probable was the harm?"; that is, would the reasonable man have thought it was likely to occur? Lawyers do not regard this judgement as a wild stab in the dark. The fact-finder is expected in this regard to reach the right answer by employing that mysterious instrument, "common sense"; arguably, this opens the door to the influence of prejudice and stereotyping. As seen above, to psychologists all these mental structures are known as "heuristics".

When required to estimate the probability of an event occurring, people are found, in the absence of other information, to rely heavily on the "availability heuristic". The frequency and therefore the probability of events is measured by the ease with which instances or occasions come to mind (Tversky & Kahneman, 1973; Kahneman, Slovic & Tversky, 1982). An event is therefore regarded as more likely or frequent if it is easy to imagine or recall instances of it. Generally, it is easier to recall instances of frequent rather than infrequent events, so this heuristic normally works quite well. However, media coverage and other factors may cause a distorted picture. People may exaggerate the probabilities of events that

---

[6] In the United Kingdom negligence cases are not tried by jury.

are particularly recent or vivid or disturbing. Sentencing decisions which require assessment of risk may be influenced by this process, and consequently may be based on utterly inaccurate predictions.[7] Judges differ from juries in the content of their heuristics, in that to some extent it is a product of their experience on the Bench. In *Shonubi*, Judge Weinstein observed, "Every sentencing judge receives daily education in criminology" (1993, *US* v. *Shonubi* (Court of Appeals): 998 F.2d; 1993 US App.; Referred for sentence: 895 F. Supp 460; 1995 US Dist). The defendant had been arrested at an airport in New York, having in his stomach 103 balloons, the contents of four of which were analysed and found to contain heroin. The judge's experience had taught him that "No one carries sugar in balloons from Nigeria to New York" and so he concluded that all 103 balloons contained heroin. A further common-sense deduction was that a smuggler would carry at least the minimum quantity required to make him a profit, and so expert evidence on the economics of heroin smuggling was given by a witness from the FBI.

The "simulation heuristic" posits that decision-makers rely on the ease with which scenarios can be imagined that match the attributes of similar situations in the external world (Kahneman & Tversky, 1982). In the case of stories with adverse outcomes, the more easily people are able to imagine an alternative outcome, the more likely they are to judge that the resulting outcome could have been avoided. Wiener and Small (1992) hypothesise that jurors base their judgements of negligence on the ease with which they are able to imagine alternative outcomes independent of the probability and seriousness of risk of injury. Here the common-sense notion of coincidences, likely and unlikely, comes into play. In one case of obstruction of the highway, the plaintiff's daughter was killed by a passing car while she was walking in the road around the obstacle. He recovered damages (*O'Neill* v. *City of Port Jervis* (1930) 253 NY 423). But in a similar case, the pedestrian was forced to detour close to a landing ground, and was struck by an aeroplane trying to land. No damages were awarded; the outcome was too improbable, and was dismissed as coincidence (*Doss* v. *Town of Big Stone Gap* (1926) 134 SE).

Psychologists have shown that hindsight tends to produce inflated perceptions of foreseeability. Merely admonishing people to disregard the hindsight effect does not eliminate it. Meanwhile, subjects tend to deny that hindsight would affect their own judgement. Juries have been accused of applying hindsight to the foreseeability issue. In the USA, it is alleged, they are far too ready to believe harms to be reasonably foreseeable as consequences to given actions. Wexler and Schopp (1991) contend that juries are over-eager to award damages against psychiatrists whose patients commit suicide subsequent to treatment. It is possible that the hindsight effect may be a consequence of the availability heuristic (Nisbett & Borgida, 1975). In a study which concerned potentially illegal police searches, mock jurors had to decide whether the searches in various

---

[7] For example, sentences under the tariff taking account of the "prevalence" of particular offences, which is seen as an aggravating factor.

hypothetical cases were justified by there being reasonable and probable cause. In those instances where they were told what the police actually found, their assessments were affected by hindsight. This occurred irrespective of judicial warning to ignore the guilt or otherwise of the plaintiff (Casper, Benedict & Perry, 1988).

It may be that judges are more alert to the danger—"After the event even a fool is wise" (*Wagon Mound* [1961] 1 All ER 404, Viscount Simonds at 411). In *Walker* v. *Northumberland County Council* ([1995] 1 All ER 737), Colman J strenuously avoided the use of hindsight. Although he held that the defendant Council knew that social work is particularly stressful and that personnel were overstretched and under-resourced, it had no reason initially to know that the mental health of their employee, Mr Walker, would be damaged by the admittedly intolerable load he bore. Once he had had a breakdown, however, the risk of further mental damage resulting from the lack of support was eminently forseeable. A graphic illustration of the rejection of hindsight is provided in the old American case, *Palsgraf* v. *Long Island Railway* (248 NY 339; 16 2 NE 99 (1928)). The defendant's servants negligently pushed X, who was attempting to board a moving train, and caused him to drop a package containing "fireworks", leading to an explosion which caused some scales to fall on to the plaintiff, injuring her. It was held that the railway was not liable. Although the defendant was negligent in relation to the man who carried the package, there was nothing to suggest that it would explode and that therefore the plaintiff would be injured.

Judges may, because of awareness through experience of the influence of hindsight on the perception of risk, be more cautious than juries in finding negligence. Wagenaar, on the other hand, argues that judicial assessment of negligence in industrial accidents and disasters, such as the capsizing of the *Herald of Free Enterprise* and the stranding of the *Esso Valdez*, is very much affected by hindsight (Wagenaar, 1992; Wagenaar & Groeneweg, 1987). Accidents in complex systems do not occur as a result of one error, but out of a series of coincidences with which personnel are ill-equipped to deal. Wagenaar accuses courts of wisdom after the event; "those who are running risks cannot always be said to have taken those risks, because they are simply not in a position to make the appropriate analysis" (Wagenaar, 1992).

THE REASONABLE MAN

The question of foreseeability depends very heavily upon the concept of the reasonable man (and now woman) and the standard of behaviour he employs himself and expects from others (*Blyth* v. *Birmingham Waterworks Co.* (1856) 11 Ex 781). He is frequently described as "ordinary"—"the man on the Clapham omnibus", or, in the USA, "the man who takes the magazines at home, and in the evening pushes the lawn-mower in his shirt sleeves". It has been claimed that the reasonable man is "neither a perfect citizen nor a paragon of circumspection"

(*AC Billings* v. *Riden* [1958] AC 240, Lord Reid at 255). In the law of negligence, the infliction of a penalty is said to be morally justified by the defendant's failure to take the proper care which other ordinary citizens, including the reasonable man, would have taken. This may be a generous view of "normal" behaviour. For every accident on the roads there are 122 near misses (Austin, 1966, p. 33), and, in an American study, even "good" drivers committed an average of nine driving errors every five minutes in normal conditions (Automobile Insurance and Compensation Study, 1970). Yet the number of road accidents is proportionately very small, and the average car driver may expect to be involved in an accident which causes personal injury only once in 25 years. "Thus, it seems that whether an act of negligence ends up in the accident statistics or as a near miss is almost pure chance; it has little to do with the defendant's culpability" (Atiyah, 1975, p. 415). Jorgensen (1988) found that if traffic lights were switched to amber as a motorist approached in the "dilemma zone"—that is, it was not clear that they would pass before the light changed to red—not one car attempted to brake. There were similar findings in a University of Nottingham study (Howarth, 1988); fewer than 10% of drivers took any action to allow for the fact that there were children crossing an intersection. The avoidance behaviour had to come from the children themselves. Wagenaar (1992) suggests that drivers engage in fixed behaviour from which they deviate only where there is certain to be an accident. This behaviour seems to be universal, but it is not, we are told, the behaviour of the reasonable man. Almost any driving error is treated as negligence without argument (Atiyah, 1975, p. 421). This willingness to find fault despite the absolute ordinariness of drivers' behaviour might be explained by awareness of the defendant's ability to compensate through insurance cover (Lloyd-Bostock, 1979b).

If the person who caused the harm did so while exercising a profession or calling, the test is not what actions might be expected from the reasonable layman. The relevant standard is the degree of skill or competence normally associated with efficient discharge of that professional function. This standard is absolute; in medical negligence cases, it does not depend on the skill or experience of the particular doctor, nor the pressure long hours might place upon him.[8] It depends on the qualities normally associated with that post. Again the law of negligence is out of step with any fault principle. Once it falls to judges to identify the standard of care, reported decisions cause judicial observations on conduct to be "endowed with pervasive generality", generating complex and detailed guidelines as to what is reasonable in a given context (Fleming, 1985, p. 24). Professionals attempt to help themselves in this climate through guidelines issued by professional bodies. Together with the reported decisions, these direct the law towards set standards which enable professionals such as clinicians to predict tort liability (Schopp & Wexler, 1991).

Courts are equally unwilling to take account of the defendant's personal limitations, even where it is impossible for him or her to achieve the required standard of performance. Learner drivers are expected to drive to the standard

---

[8] Although an overworked hospital doctor might be able to recover damages if an excessive workload results in stress or depression (*Johnstone* v. *Bloomsbury Health Authority* [1991] 2 All ER 213).

of an experienced driver at once (*Nettleship* v. *Weston* [1971] 2 QB 691; an approach rejected by the Australian courts), and the courts have an erratic policy on physical disability.

> If, for instance, a man is born hasty and awkward, is always having accidents and hurting himself or his neighbours, no doubt his congenital defects will be allowed for in the courts of heaven, but his slips are no less troublesome to his neighbours than if they sprang from guilty neglect. His neighbours accordingly require him, at his proper peril, to come up to their standard, and the courts which they establish decline to take his personal equation into account. (Holmes, 1871, p. 540)

They may be more lenient where the defendant was not indulging in dangerous activities. One example is a case where the defendant was not able-bodied and therefore could not put out a fire which occurred on his land through no fault of his. Similarly, if a driver is overtaken by a sudden, unexpected, and disabling illness, he is not liable for the damage he does (*Waugh* v. *James K. Allan Ltd* [1964] 2 Lloyd's Rep 1). Even the reasonable man can have a heart attack, Fleming points out, but he can see no difference between that and an insane delusion which causes a driver to cross red traffic lights to escape an imagined enemy (Fleming, 1985, p. 225). Children receive rather different treatment from the law. A young child may be incapable of the necessary mental state for liability (Fleming, 1985, p. 26); the plaintiff must show that the defendant's behaviour would be unreasonable for a child of his age:

> We are prepared to tolerate the mistakes and failings of childhood as a condition to which everyone is heir in contrast to insanity, which, besides being rare and creating administrative difficulties enough in the criminal context, is perhaps still beset with an atavistic attribution of sin from which modern man has not yet succeeded in emancipating himself. (Fleming, 1985, p. 26)

Although the law of torts seems content to judge the action of someone with a mental illness or disorder against the standards of the man of phlegm, the criminal law has attempted to adjust the definition of the reasonable man to accommodate these individual problems. The result is not a happy one. Where the defendant in a murder case raises the defence of provocation, which, if successful, would reduce the conviction to one for manslaughter (Homicide Act 1957, s. 3), the jury must decide whether a reasonable man would have reacted as the defendant did to the event which constitutes the provocation. In *Thornton* (*No. 2* ([1996] 2 All ER 1023)), the Court of Appeal held that, in performing this function, a jury should take account of the defendant's characteristics including psychological disorders. Subsequently, the Judicial Committee of the Privy Council doubted whether the jury could be expected to think themselves into the shoes of someone suffering from such a disorder (*Luc Thiet Thuan* v. *R* [1996] 2 All ER 1033). Yet *Thornton* was followed in *Smith* ([1998] 4 All ER 387),[9] where

---

[9] Although the Law Lords sit on the Judicial Committee, the decisions are of persuasive authority only and not binding on the Court of Appeal.

the defendant was alleged to have been suffering from depression at the time of the attack. Not only does the notion of a psychologically disturbed reasonable man seem absurd, and not only does it ask the jury to perform impossible mental gymnastics in asking itself how the reasonable depressed man would have responded to the provocation, but it brings the provocation defence into head-on collision with the provisions on diminished responsibility (Homicide Act 1957, s. 2), also a limited defence to a murder charge.

RESPONSIBILITY: WHO TO BLAME?

Within attribution theory, the concept of defensive attribution grew out of find-ings that subjects are more likely to attribute blame to the actor where the harm caused is serious. It was developed to explain the unexpected results of Walster's study (1966). Subjects were told that a young man, Lennie, had left a car at the top of a hill, whereupon the handbrake failed and the car rolled downhill. The kinds of damage caused varied across different versions of the story. Significantly more responsibility was assigned to him for the severe accidents than for the mild ones, even if only Lennie suffered. Defensive attribution holds that if the outcome of an accident is minor, the observer can feel sympathetic towards the victim and attribute his misfortune to chance, that is, attribute less responsibility towards the actor, whether or not he is the victim. But if a serious harm occurs, merely to view the victim as unlucky carries the threatening implication that the observer too, by bad luck, may suffer a grave accident. Walster found, however, that her sub-jects did not impute more *carelessness* to Lennie in the severe examples where he was held responsible. Because of the ambiguity of the word "responsibility" in this context, it is not clear whether Walster's subjects found that consequences were more *foreseeable* where the damage is considerable. They found Lennie more *responsible*, but no more careless, in such cases. The key element appears to be that of causation (see Hamilton, 1978). Severe consequences might have made subjects readier to believe that Lennie *caused* the harm.

In the law of negligence, the test for causation is also one of foreseeability, and so similar to that for breach of the duty of care. Lloyd-Bostock (1979a) argues that quite often in psychological research the term attribution is used quite gen-erally to refer to the mental process of organising events and interpreting a set of information, without it being intended to analyse all the elements that deter-mine responsibility in law. In law, the seriousness of the harm should have no effect on the decision whether a duty of care exists (*Hill* v. *Chief Constable of South Yorkshire* [1988] 2 All ER 238; *M (a minor)* v. *Newham London Borough Council* [1995] 4 All ER 602). However, it does have a role in the evaluation of whether the defendant was negligent. The nature of the risk being run depends partly on the extent of the possible damage: "The more serious the damage which will happen if an accident occurs, the more thorough are the precautions which an employer must take" (*Paris* v. *Stepney Borough Council* [1951] 1 All ER 42 per Lord Morton). The scale of the potential damage is weighed against the cost and practicability of preventing the risk (*Wagon Mound (No. 1)* [1961] 1 All ER 404 per Viscount Simonds at 414; *British Railways Board* v. *Herrington* [1972] 1 All ER 749).

Efforts to replicate Walster's findings have been numerous; the introduction of other variables and the reporting of the results has generated an impressive volume of literature, but inconclusive results. Fincham and Jaspars (1980, p. 86) said scathingly of this: "The continued popularity of the defensive attribution research is perhaps surprising in view of the increasing number of constraints imposed on the hypothesis, which suggests that such defensive attributions are indeed rare." Shaw and Skolnick (1973) failed to find a correlation between the seriousness of an accident and ascriptions of responsibility. Their subjects ascribed the more serious accidents to chance, and the minor ones tended to be regarded as the actor's fault.[10] Shaver (1970) introduced a new variable into Walster's methodology, namely, similarity between the actor and the subject. The results contradicted defensive attribution; the greater the similarity between subject and actor, the less responsible the actor was thought to be. Where fault was a virtually inevitable conclusion, the subject tended to deny the similarity. Thus it may be, as Shaver concludes, that the greater concern is to avoid blame for the accident rather than to avoid the accident itself.

Defensive attribution suggests that subjects identify themselves as potential victims of a harm similar to the harm done. In contrast, the Just World theory detaches subject from victim and actor in the sense that it holds that attributions of responsibility are affected by a more personal issue. Lerner (1965) posited the theory that, for sanity's sake, people need to believe that the world is a just and predictable place; they anticipate a reasonable fit between merit and reward. Thus one might be able to tolerate the prospect of minor accidents befalling people at random, but the possibility that one could suffer a severe accident without being oneself somehow responsible threatens the belief that the world is just. The Just World hypothesis is thought to be borne out by research into cases of genuine victims of permanently disabling accidents, all having the elements of chance (that is, were not clearly the fault of some other person; these might be diving, football or car accidents). These patients tend to blame themselves if they class the accident as avoidable (Bulman & Wortman, 1977). Those who blamed themselves were coping better than those who blamed others, according to nursing staff. It seems that the best prospects for psychological survival of major injury is where it occurred during a leisure activity and there is absolutely no one else involved who could be blamed. Rape victims also have a tendency to blame themselves. They make a better psychological recovery when this self-blame does not act to exonerate the rapist, but to identify actions of their own that made them vulnerable to the rape. By avoiding repetition of this behaviour, whether it was accepting a lift or walking home at night, the victim can feel relatively safe from

---

[10] There was a difference between male and female subjects, the latter having a tendency to claim that they would have made the same judgement, suggesting they have an extremely low self-concept.

a further attack. Janoff-Bulman (1979) describes this reaction as "behavioural self-blame".

It may be consistent with defensive attribution rather than Just World, however, that in her study of accident victims, Lloyd-Bostock (1979b) found greater willingness to blame employers and other organisations in her study. She concluded that this was linked to some extent with their ability to compensate. If observers identify with the victim or see themselves as potential victims of harm, it would be reassuring for them to believe that compensation would be available. The law, however, does not rush to impose liability upon a defendant with the means to compensate. In fact, the approach of the legal system to negligence by public bodies carrying out statutory duties is sympathetic. A higher level of negligence must be shown in such cases, because unenviable tasks such as managing convicted and incarcerated criminals (*Home Office* v. *Dorset Yacht Co. Ltd* [1970] AC 1004) or dealing with child abuse within the family (*Wilsher* v. *Essex Area Health Authority* [1988] AC 1074) were imposed on, not chosen by, these bodies.

Reactions to "contributory negligence" by victims of crime may offer support for a Just World theory. Various studies show that mock jurors regard offences as less serious where the victim has made even a mild contribution (Miller et al., 1976). In a hypothetical rape case, a longer sentence was proposed by subjects in a scenario where the rapist forced his way into the victim's apartment, as opposed to when he persuaded her to let him in to make a telephone call (Field, 1979). In Howard's study (1984), subjects watched a videotaped interview ostensibly of a crime victim by a detective. The crime described would be either rape or robbery, and the circumstances varied. Female victims tended to be blamed more than male victims for the crime, irrespective of the nature of the offence. Most blame of all was attached to a female victim who had been hitchhiking at the time she was robbed. The least blame of all attached a female rape victim who had been jogging. The more likely a particular assault was perceived to be, the more blame was attributed to the victim. This kind of reasoning is consistent with that of genuine rape victims.

Doubts have been cast on the "Just World" by Chaikin and Darley (1973). Each of their subjects were given future roles of either worker or supervisor. Some were told that workers would be paid strictly according to output, others that the supervisor had a discretion on pay. They then watched a video in which blocks which the worker had assembled were sent flying by the supervisor who knocked the table accidentally. Future workers were more likely to ascribe the accident to chance if it caused no loss to the worker. When it did, they tended to find the supervisor at fault whether the consequences were mild or severe. Future supervisors tended to attribute the accident to chance. When the consequences were severe, the accident was less likely to be attributed to chance, but was blamed "not on the supervisor, who bumped the table, which toppled the blocks, which docked the pay of the worker; and not on the worker, who was obviously pretty innocent, but on the person who chose such a rickety table in the first place". These findings conflict with "Just World" in that workers should derogate victims in order to maintain a belief in justice. To blame the supervisor does not restore justice if the worker is the one penalised. The subjects attributed blame in a way that avoided casting it on the person with whom they identified, supporting Shaver's version of defensive attribution.

A belief in a Just World is threatened by cases where the victims of crimes contributed in no way to the harm they suffered. In such cases, according to the theory, observers are forced to derogate, or devalue, the victim in order for the belief to be maintained. Some evidence of this was provided by Lerner's famous study, in which a "victim" was observed apparently receiving painful electric shocks. In the "martyr" condition, observers had encountered the victim earlier, when they heard her expressing reluctance to participate in the experiment, then being persuaded to take part. Here the most severe derogation of the victim occurred (Lerner & Simmons, 1966). But contradictory results were obtained in a study where subjects watched videotaped interviews in which "patients" described their injuries to "doctors". The injuries were said to have been suffered in some cases during a car accident, and in others during a forcible rape in various conditions which might or might not attach a degree of fault to the "patient". All the victims were women. The greatest derogation (the subjects liked her less and thought her less intelligent) occurred where the victim was culpable and least when she was innocent (Stokols & Schopler, 1973).

Judges might be thought, during their careers, to have encountered too many innocent victims of harm to be able to maintain any belief in a Just World. Yet, when confronted with a victim who is not only innocent but positively heroic, they seem anxious to create a world in which virtue is rewarded. "Where . . . a person has been killed in a heroic attempt to rescue another, judges will strain every nerve to find someone at fault if they possibly can" (Atiyah, 1975, p. 426). An example is the case of a heroic railwayman who sacrificed himself to save his young child (*Videan* v. *British Transport Commission* [1963] 2 QB 650). Here the Court of Appeal managed to decide at one and the same time that the presence of a toddler on the railway line at a small station was not reasonably foreseeable, but that his father the stationmaster's leap (at the cost of his own life), to save him from a rapidly approaching trolley, was. The child was a trespasser, but "it is surely . . . remarkable how readily the focus expanded at the sight of a rescuer" (Fleming, 1985, p. 54).

DECIDING OUTCOME

Case-based reasoning involves a comparison between the current case and a specific case of which the decision-maker has knowledge. A sentencer whose decision entails prediction of consequences to some extent may use a case, the outcome of which he or she recalls, to assess the risk in the present case (Kahneman, Slovic & Tversky, 1982). There is a danger that the earlier case was not typical. If there is no relevant case available for comparison, decision-makers have to rely on other heuristics to estimate probability. The likelihood is that they will rely on the availability heuristic, which could lead to even greater error because the knowledge relied on is even less specific. It has also been found that judgements of risk are impaired by pressure to reach a decision quickly (Christiansen Szalanski, 1980). Legal proceedings will normally exert such pressure on decision-makers. Psychological literature is full of the difficulty of prediction, but courts and tribunals keep asking expert witnesses, particularly medical witnesses, to attempt it (Webster, Menzies & Hart, 1995). The Floud Report rejected any optimistic acceptance of a prediction formula for assessing the likelihood of future dangerous behaviour (Floud & Young, 1981), and those who regularly make decisions of this kind rarely follow them up to discover whether their forecasts were accurate. Even if they did, it will never be known how many of those subject to restriction would *not* have committed further offences (von Hirsch, 1998).

Despite the difficulties, the test for imposition of a restriction order under section 41 of the Mental Health Act 1983 is the risk of the offender committing further offences. This is a mandate for clinicians to estimate future behaviour despite their own admitted limited competence to do so. Prediction accuracy levels are only about 33% (Monahan, 1984). There is research claiming that clinical factors can produce accurate predictions, but they tend to concern civil patient populations and are methodologically unsatisfactory (Monahan, 1988). Clinical expertise does not appear to enhance the reliability of these assessments. The best predictors of violent re-offending are those which apply with non-disordered offender populations, namely prior criminal history, age, gender, and social class. Yet, although courts sometimes disregard the advice of medical witnesses (*Birch* 90 Cr App R 78), judges are unlikely to substitute their own opinion of the defendant's mental state for that of the experts. The factors which may prevent the making of a recommended restriction order may be practical problems such as the non-availability of a hospital place (*Howell* (1985) 7 Cr App R(S) 360: *Birch* (1989) 11 Cr App R (S) 202). When imprisonment is used *faux de mieux*, all pretence at assessment of risk is abandoned. The Court of Appeal has said that in those cases the sentence must be proportionate to the harm done.[11] There seem to be a large number of people who drift between prisons and hospitals. Some of the time they have spent in psychiatric hospital will have not been consequent to any court order (Prins, 1990). Meanwhile, prison is still being used in preference to psychiatric hospital as a remand institution pending medical reports.[12]

The difficulty of assessment is demonstrated by the finding that the majority of those defendants found unfit to plead are little different from the majority

---

[11] Not in cases which may be dealt with by life imprisonment, nor in some cases which suggest that prevention of future harm may justify fixed-term sentences which exceed the norm for the kind of offence committed (*Scanlon* (1979) 1 Cr App R(S) 60: *Gouws* (1981) 3 Cr App R(S) 325).

[12] The 1983 Mental Health Act was intended to direct mentally disordered offenders to hospital pre-trial, but judges have been slow to respond (Department of Health & Home Office, 1991).

of mentally disturbed or mentally handicapped defendants who come before the court on a regular basis. Two-thirds of those found unfit to plead had on previous occasions been dealt with by courts in a normal manner, and some went on to be convicted of further offences while still technically unfit to plead on a previous charge (Grubin, 1991). The test for unfitness to plead is in *Pritchard* ((1836) 7 C and P 303)—has the prisoner sufficient understanding to comprehend the nature of the trial, so as to make a proper defence to the charge? Grubin (1991) found that some of those deemed unfit for trial fulfilled these criteria, but regards the test itself as a confusing muddle between intellectual ability and mental state.

In general, sentencing does not require the court to engage in the prediction of future behaviour. Sentencing guidelines have been authoritatively described by David Thomas (1979), who demonstrates that sentencing courts operate a dual system. The judge first decides whether to select a tariff sentence emphasising the seriousness of the offence, or an individualised measure, maximising the offender's prospects of rehabilitation. The tariff is the appropriate response to crimes of seriousness, or where there is little prospect of reform. Once the tariff is selected, the process of sentencing becomes formulaic. Because this system is so well established, personal attributes such as the gender of the sentencer seem to have little effect on sentence (Kette & Konecni, 1996). The system is not open to testing. A previous Lord Chief Justice halted a major Crown Court Study by forbidding judges to co-operate. His view was that sentencing is an art not a science; the further judges were pressed to articulate their reasons the less realistic the exercise would become (Ashworth et al., 1984).

Although the British system retains a degree of flexibility that is much less in evidence in the 1994 Federal Guidelines in the USA, judges and magistrates who operate the tariff can justify their decisions solely in terms of their consistency with other sentencing decisions. Also, as Hebenton and Pease (1995) note, this representation of sentencing automatically forestalls criticism based on inconsistency. Courts can point to a number of different factors which might aggravate or mitigate the seriousness of the offence. However, the reality seems to be that sentencers cannot cope with the combined effect of a great many factors. The impact of each is reduced where it is part of several indications in one or other direction. In contrast, the individualised measure is selected as part of a predictive exercise. First, it is considered that the offender is capable of reform; secondly, the court chooses the sentence thought most conducive to this end. In fact, the recommendation of the probation officer is usually the source of this selection (Konecni & Ebbesen, 1979). Where the individualised measure is selected on the grounds that it might rehabilitate the defendant, courts are in the happy position that they are not criticised for any error in their prediction should it prove to be wrong (Kette & Konecni, 1996). Sentencers rarely follow up the actual outcome of their own decisions in order to learn from their mistakes (Michon & Pakes, 1995).

REFERENCES

Allen, H. (1988) One law for all reasonable persons? *International Journal of the Sociology of Law*, **16**, 419–432.

Arce, R., Fariña, F. & Sabral, J. (1996) From juror to jury decision making: A non-model approach. In G. Davies, S. Lloyd-Bostock, M. McMurran & C. Wilson (Eds) *Psychology, Law and Criminal Justice*. Berlin: de Gruyter.

Ashworth, A.J., Genders, E., Mansfield, G., Peay, J. & Player, E. (1984) *Sentencing in the Crown Court: Report of an Exploratory Study*. Occasional Paper No 10. University of Oxford, Centre for Criminological Research).

Atiyah, P. (1975) *Accidents, Compensation and the Law* (2nd edn). London: Weidenfeld & Nicolson.

Austin, M. (1966) *Accident Black Spot; A Critical Study of Road Safety Policy and Practice*. Harmondsworth: Penguin.

Automobile Insurance and Compensation Study (1970) *Driver Behaviour and Accident Involvement: Implications for Tort Liability*. Washington, DC: US Government Printer.

Baldwin, J. & McConville, M. (1979) *Jury Trials*. Oxford: Clarendon Press.

Beaumeister, R.F. & Darley, J.M. (1982) Reducing the biasing effect of perpetrator attractivenes in jury simulation. *Personality and Social Psychology Bulletin*, **5**, 286–293.

Bennett, W.L. & Feldman, M.S. (1981) *Reconstructing Reality in the Courtroom*. London: Tavistock.

Blumenthal, J.A. (1993) A wipe of the hands, a lick of the lips; the validity of demeanor evidence in assessing witness credibility. *Nebraska Law Review*, **78**, 1157–1173.

Bulman, R. & Wortman, C.B. (1977) Attributions of blame and coping in the real world: Severe accident victims react to their lot. *Journal of Personality and Social Psychology*, **35**, 351–363.

Casper, J.D., Benedict, K. & Perry, J.L. (1988) The tort remedy in search and seizure cases; a case study in juror decision making. *Law and Social Inquiry*, **13**, 279–303.

Chaikin, A.L. & Darley, J.M. (1973) Victim or perpetrator: Defensive attribution of responsibility and the need for order. *Journal of Personality and Social Psychology*, **25**, 268–275.

Christiansen Szalanski, J.J. (1980) A further examination of the selection of problem-solving strategies: The effects of deadlines and analytic aptitudes. *Organisational Behavior and Human Performance*, **25**, 107–122.

Dane, F.C. & Wrightsman, L.S. (1982) Effects of defendants' and victims' charactistics on jurors' verdicts. In N.L. Kerr & R.M. Bray (Eds) *The Psychology of the Courtroom*. London: Academic Press.

Deffenbacher, K.A. & Loftus, E.F. (1982) Do jurors share a common understanding concerning eye-witness behavior? *Law and Human Behavior*, **6**, 15–30.

Department of Health & Home Office (1991) *Review of Health and Social Services for Mentally Disordered Offenders and Others Requiring Similar Services* (Reed Report). London: HMSO.

Ekman, P. (1985) *Telling Lies*. New York, NY: Norton.

Ekman, P., Sorenson, E.R. & Friesen, W.V. (1969) Pan-cultural elements in facial displays of emotion. *Science*, **164**, 96–98.

Field, H. (1979) Rape trials and jurors' decisions: A psychological analysis of the effects of victim, defendant and case characteristics. *Law and Human Behavior*, **3**, 261–284.

Fincham, F.D. & Jaspars, J.M. (1980) Attribution of responsibility: From man the scientist to man as lawyer. *Advances in Experimental Psychology*, **13**, 82–140.

Fleming, J.G. (1985) *Introduction to the Law of Torts*. Oxford: Clarendon Press.

Floud, J. & Young, W. (1981) *Dangerousness and Criminal Justice*. Institute of Criminology: Cambridge Studies in Criminology.

Grubin, D.H. (1991) Unfit to plead in England and Wales 1976–1988: A survey. *British Journal of Psychiatry*, **158**, 540.

Hamilton, V.L. (1978) Who is responsible? Towards a social psychology of responsibility attribution. *Social Psychology*, **41**, 316–328.

Hastie, R., Penrod, S. & Pennington, N. (1983) *Inside the Jury*. Cambridge, MA: Harvard University Press.

Hebenton, B. & Pease, K. (1995) Weighing the pound of flesh: The psychology of punishment. In R. Bull & D. Carson (Eds) *Handbook of Psychology in Legal Contexts*. Chichester: John Wiley & Sons.

Heuer, L. & Penrod, S.D. (1995) Jury decision-making in complex trials. In R. Bull & D. Carson (Eds) *Handbook of Psychology in Legal Contexts*. Chichester: John Wiley & Sons.

von Hirsch, A. (1998) The problem of false positives. In A. von Hirsch & A. Ashworth (Eds) *Principled Sentencing*. Oxford: Hart Publishing.

Hocking, J.E., Baucher, J., Karminski, E.P. & Miller, G.R. (1979) Detecting deceptive communication from verbal, visual, and paralinguistic cues. *Human Communication Research*, **6**, 33–66.

Holmes, O.W. (1871) Book Review. *American Law Review*, **5**, 539.

Honess, T.M., Levi, M. & Charman, E.A. (1998) Juror competence in processing complex information: Implications from a simulation of the Maxwell trial. *Criminal Law Review*, 763–773.

Howard, J. (1984) The "normal" victim: the effects of gender stereotypes on reactions to victims. *Social Psychology Quarterly*, **47**(3), 270–281.

Howarth, C.I. (1988) The relationship between objective risk, subjective risk, and behaviour. *Ergonomics*, **31**, 527–535.

Jackson, J. (1996) Juror decision-making in the trial process. In G. Davies, S. Lloyd-Bostock, M. McMurran & C. Wilson (Eds) *Psychology Law and Criminal Justice*. Berlin: de Gruyter.

Jackson, J. & Doran, S. (1995) *Judge Without Jury: Diplock Trials and the Adversary System*. Oxford: Clarendon Press.

Janoff-Bulman, R. (1979) Characterological and behavioral self-blame: Inquiries into depression and rape. *Journal of Personality and Social Psychology*, **37**, 1748–1809.

Johnson, M.K., Bransford, J.D. & Solomon, S.K. (1973) Memory for tacit implications of sentences. *Journal of Experimental Psychology*, **98**, 203–205.

Johnson, M.K. & Kaye, C.L. (1981) Reality monitoring. *Psychological Review*, **88**, 67–85.

Jorgensen, N.O. (1988) Risky behaviour at traffic signals: A traffic engineer's view. *Ergonomics*, **31**, 657–661.

Kahneman, D., Slovic, P. & Tversky, A. (1982) *Judgment under Uncertainty: Heuristics and Biases*. Cambridge: Cambridge University Press.

Kahneman, D. & Tversky, A. (1982) The simulation heuristic. In D. Kahneman, P. Slovic & A. Tversky, *Judgment under Uncertainty*. Cambridge: Cambridge University Press.

Kalven, H. & Zeisel, H. (1966) *The American Jury*. Boston, MA: Little, Brown & Co.

Kassim, S.M. & Wrightsman, L.S. (1988) *The American Jury on Trial*. New York, NY: Hemisphere.

Kerr, N.L. (1982) Trial participants' behaviors and jury verdicts: An exploratory field study. In V.J. Konecki & E.B. Ebbeson (Eds) *The Criminal Justice System: A Socio-Psychological Analysis*. San Francisco, CA: W.H. Freeman.

Kette, G. & Konecni, V.J. (1996) Commuication channels and gender differences in decoding and integration of cues in legal decision-making. In G. Davies, S. Lloyd-Bostock, M. McMurran & C. Wilson (Eds) *Psychology, Law and Criminal Justice*. Berlin: de Gruyter.

King, M. (1986) *Psychology In or Out of Court*. Oxford: Pergamon.

Konecni, V.J. & Ebbesen, E. (1979) External validity of research in legal psychology. *Law and Human Behavior*, **3**, 39–70.

Kraut, R.E. (1978) Verbal and non-verbal cues on the perception of lying. *Journal of Personality and Social Psychology*, **36**, 380–391.

Lerner, M.J. (1965) Evaluation of performance as a function of performer's reward and attractiveness. *Journal of Personality and Social Psychology*, **1**, 355–366.

Lerner, M.J. & Simmons, C.H. (1966) Observers' reactions to the "innocent victim"; compassion or rejection? *Journal of Personality and Social Psychology*, **4**, 203–210.

Lloyd-Bostock, S. (1979a) The ordinary man and the psychology of attributing causes and responsibility. *Modern Law Review*, **42**, 143–168.

Lloyd-Bostock, S. (1979b) Common sense, morality and accident compensation. In D.P. Farrington, K. Hawkins & S. Lloyd-Bostock (Eds) *Psychology, Law and Legal Processes*. London: Macmillan.

Lloyd-Bostock, S. (1996) Juries and jury research in context. In G. Davies, S. Lloyd-Bostock, M. McMurran & C. Wilson (Eds) *Psychology Law and Criminal Justice*. Berlin: de Gruyter.

McEwan, J. (1998) *Evidence and the Adversarial Process: The Modern Law*. Oxford: Hart Publishing.

Mehabrian, A. & William, M. (1969) Non-verbal concomitants of perceived and intended persuasiveness. *Journal of Personality and Social Psychology*, **13**, 37–58.

Michon, J.A. & Pakes, F.J. (1995) Judicial decision-making in perspective. In R. Bull & D. Carson (Eds) *Handbook of Psychology in Legal Contexts*. Chichester: John Wiley & Sons.

Miller, G.R. & Burgoon, J.K. (1982) Factors affecting assessments of witness credibility. In N.L. Kerr & R.M. Bray (Eds) *The Psychology of the Courtroom*. London: Academic Press.

Miller, F.D., Smith, E.R., Ferree, M.M. & Taylor, S.E. (1976) Predicting perceptions of victimisation. *Journal of Applied Social Psychology*, **36**, 1490–1500.

Monahan, J. (1984) The prediction of violent behavior: Toward a second generation of theory and policy. *American Journal of Psychiatry*, **141**, 10–15.

Monahan, J. (1988) Risk Assessment of violence among the mentally disordered: Generating useful knowledge. *International Journal of Law and Psychiatry*, **11**, 249–257.

Nisbett, R.E. & Borgida, E. (1975) Attribution and the psychology of prediction. *Journal of Personality and Social Psychology*, **32**, 932–943.

O'Donovan, K. (1984) The medicalisation of infanticide. *Criminal Law Review*, 259–284.

Mackay, R.D. (1993) The consequences of killing young children. *Criminal Law Review*, 21–30.

Pearson, R. (1976) Women defendants in magistrates' courts. *British Journal of Law and Society*, **3**, 265–273.

Pennington, N. & Hastie, R. (1986) Evidence evaluations in complex decision making. *Journal of Personality and Social Psychology*, **51**, 242–258.

Perrow, C. (1984) *Normal Accidents*. New York, NY: Basic Books.

Prins, H. (1990) Mental abnormality and criminality: An uncertain relationship. *British Medical Journal*, **297**, 338–357.

Schopp, R.E. & Wexler, D.B. (1991) Shooting yourself in the foot with due care: Psychotherapists and crystallized standards of tort liability. In D.B. Wexler & B.J. Winick (Eds) *Essays in Therapeutic Jurisprudence*. Durham, NC: Carolina Academic Press.

Severance, L. & Loftus, E.F. (1982) Improving the ability of jurors to comprehend and apply jury instructions. *Law and Society Review*, **17**, 153–197.

Shaw, J.I. & Skolnick, P. (1973) Attribution of responsibility for a happy accident. *Journal of Personality and Social Psychology*, **18**(3), 380–383.

Shaver, K.C. (1970) Defensive attribution: effects of severity and relevance on the responsibility assigned for an accident. *Journal of Personality and Social Psychology*, **14**, 101–113.

Stephenson, G.M. (1992) *The Psychology of Criminal Justice*. Oxford: Blackwell.

Stokols, D. & Schopler, J. (1973) Reactions to victims under conditions of situational detachment: The effects of responsibility, severity and expected future interaction. *Journal of Personality and Social Psychology*, **5**, 199–209.

Tanford, J.A. (1990) The law and psychology of jury instructions. *Nebraska Law Review*, **69**, 71–111.

Thomas, D.A. (1979) *Principles of Sentencing*. London: Heinemann.

Tversky, A. & Kahneman, D. (1973) Availability: A heuristic for judging frequency and probability. *Cognitive Psychology*, **5**, 207–232.

Wagenaar, W.A. (1992) Risk-taking and accident causation. In J.F. Yates (Ed.) *Risk-Taking Behaviour*. Chichester: John Wiley & Sons.

Wagenaar, W.A. (1996) Anchored narratives: A theory of judicial reasoning and its consequences. In G. Davies, S. Lloyd-Bostock, M. McMurran & C. Wilson (Eds) *Psychology, Law and Criminal Justice*. Berlin: de Gruyter.

Wagenaar, W.A., van Koppen, P.J. & Crombag, H.M. (1993) *Anchored Narratives: The Psychology of Criminal Evidence*. Hemel Hempstead: Harvester Wheatsheaf.

Wagenaar, W.A. & Groeneweg, J. (1987) Accidents at sea: Multiple causes and impossible consequences. *International Journal of Man-Machine Studies*, **27**, 587–598.

Walster, E. (1966) Assignment of responsibility for an accident. *Journal of Personality and Social Psychology*, **3**, 73–79.

Webster, C.D., Menzies, R.J. & Hart, S.D. (1995) Dangerousness and risk. In R. Bull & D. Carson (Eds) *Handbook of Psychology in Legal Contexts*. Chichester: John Wiley & Sons.

Wexler, D.B. & Schopp, R.F. (1991) How and when to correct errors of juror hindsight bias in mental health malpractice litigation. In D.B. Wexler & B.J. Winick (Eds) *Essays in Therapeutic Jurisprudence*. Durham, NC: Carolina Academic Press.

Wiener, R.L. & Small, M.A. (1992) Social cognition and tort law. In D.K. Kagehiro & W.S. Laufer (Eds) *Handbook of Law and Psychology*. New York, NY: Springer Verlag.

Winkel, F.W. & de Winter, S. (1996) The perceived credibility of rape victims during a police interview: An experiment among victim assistance workers. In G.M. Davies, S. Lloyd-Bostock, M. McMurran & C. Wilson (Eds) *Psychology, Law and Criminal Justice*. Berlin: de Gruyter.

Wolf, S. & Montgomery, D.A. (1977) Effect of inadmissable evidence on the decisions of simulated jurors: A moral dilemma. *Journal of Applied Social Psychology*, **3**, 213–216.

Part II

Research and Practice

Chapter 7

Explanations of Criminal Behaviour

James McGuire
Department of Clinical Psychology, University of Liverpool, UK

At some point in our lives, most of us become victims of a crime. Evidence suggests that virtually all of us, at some stage, also commit one. Directly or indirectly, crime is a familiar, almost ubiquitous feature of daily life. It is a recurrent item of casual conversation and the habitual focus of media attention. This omnipresence has an unfortunate degenerative effect on our capacity to understand it.

Whereas most non-specialists will readily admit to their perplexity when molecular biology or gothic architecture are under discussion, the moment conversation touches upon crime almost everyone turns out to be an expert. Criminal acts are then typically perceived as having been carried out for a perfectly obvious motive (e.g. acquisition of money). If no such motive is instantly apparent, crimes are ascribed to more vaguely defined causes (e.g. "mindlessness"). More serious violent crimes are often portrayed as resulting from a larger, malevolent presence or force ("evil"). These common-sense theories of crime often supersede more systematic attempts to comprehend what is a formidably complex problem.

The overall aim of theory in criminology, as with its counterparts in other fields of inquiry, is to contribute to a coherent explanatory account of a phenomenon, in this case the activity designated as "crime". Again, as elsewhere, what might begin as a purely intellectual endeavour is linked with a practical goal: the urge to reduce the prevalence of the activity. It is perhaps that need which drives us so readily towards simplistic explanations. But the possibility that any single set of ideas can furnish all the conceptual tools we need to elucidate the causation of crime is extremely remote. Disputes abound concerning the definition, meaning and usage of the word "crime" itself.

Behaviour, Crime and Legal Processes: A Guide for Forensic Practitioners.
Edited by James McGuire, Tom Mason and Aisling O'Kane.
© 2000 John Wiley & Sons Ltd.

Associated with this is another problem. It is well known that the data of criminology, such as published crime rates, can be unreliable and difficult to interpret (Conklin, 1992; Glick, 1997; Walker, 1995). Official criminal statistics are the end product of many filtering processes. Social definitions of crime vary between societies and across historical epochs; as indeed do the very ways in which laws are created. On a more mundane level, there are variations in the rates of reporting of crimes by citizens. Police officers exercise discretion over how crimes are recorded and subsequent action taken. Eventual rates of detection, conviction and incarceration of offenders vary according to type of offence, police division, and court area. Cumulatively this means that we cannot be sure of the exact relationship between measured crime and the prevalence and nature of those activities which have been socially defined as illegal. If we adopt a different approach and assume we can develop a theory of crime by researching adjudicated offenders, there are problems here also. The study of, say, convicted prisoners may be very misleading as they are not necessarily a representative sample of those who commit most crimes. The entire science of criminology is thus beset at its outset with fundamental questions concerning the value of the basic information on which it is founded.

These caveats concerning its evidence-base granted, criminological theory is far from being a dry and forbidding abstract exercise. For whether based on "lay theories" like those referred to above (see Furnham, 1989), or developed more formally and rigorously, ideas concerning the causes of crime have a powerful influence on what citizens believe should be society's most appropriate response to it. That in turn sets the context for public policy in criminal justice (colloquially, the "law and order debate"). Theoretical models are also pressed into practical service by those whose responsibility it is to assess and manage persons charged with or convicted of criminal offences. When attempting to make sense of an individual's behaviour, professionals in criminal justice, social service or mental health settings will wish to apply validated approaches to the causation of the behaviour or of its nature and patterning over time.

This chapter is based on the proposition that, despite undoubted conceptual and empirical obstacles, there is sufficient consensus about what is referred to as "crime" for there to be a valid task to be undertaken in attempting to furnish a systematic, empirically based account of it. The chapter is divided into four main sections. In the first, the nature of theoretical explanation in criminology will be briefly characterised, and some of the more enduring concepts within it identified. Second, an account will be given of several of the most influential criminological theories arranged in a conceptual scheme according to "levels of explanation". Next, a number of contemporary integrative approaches to understanding crime will be surveyed, and the overall standing of this innovation appraised. Finally, the utility of broad-ranging theoretical models and concepts will be evaluated in terms of their applicability to individual acts of crime, and to patterns of crime committed by persistent offenders. Part of this will be cast in terms of a framework for the assessment of "risk-needs" factors associated with continued re-offending.

THE DEVELOPMENT OF CRIMINOLOGICAL THEORY

For centuries, most thinking on issues such as crime remained at what nowadays would be considered a "pre-scientific" stage. There is evidence that early peoples interpreted natural disasters as the recriminations of spirits for human wrong-doing. In the medieval period in Europe, most attempts at explanation of mis-fortunes were rooted in spiritual or religious beliefs. Their axis was an assumed universal conflict between powers of good and evil; for example, criminals might be believed to be afflicted or even possessed by demonic forces. Such thinking underlies what was known as *trial by ordeal*, which rested on the assumption that, if innocent, an accused person would be saved from punishment by divine intercession.

During the European Renaissance and throughout the ensuing two centuries, the physical and biological sciences began to evolve progressively into the forms in which they exist today. Their development in turn created conditions in which, from approximately the late eighteenth century onwards, the application of methods of systematic empirical investigation to human social and psychological phenomena gradually came to be seen as a legitimate mode of inquiry. As earlier forms of thinking gave way to a more analytical approach during the period of the Enlightenment, such questions were explored first at a philosophical and metaphysical level.

Crime as an Outcome of Individual Decisions

The first view to emerge concerning why crimes are committed was a product of what is known as the "classical school" of criminology. This emanated from the work of the Italian scholar Cesare de Beccaria in the second half of the eigh-teenth century, and was characterised by the application of philosophical rea-soning to enquire into the likely causes and consequences of human action. Human beings were regarded as possessing "free will", which they exercised on the basis of principles of pleasure and pain. Thus individuals were thought to cal-culate the likely benefits and costs of different courses of action, such as whether or not to commit a crime. Beccaria's book *On Crimes and Punishments* was published in 1764. His ideas found a resonance in the thinking of the English utilitarian philosopher, Jeremy Bentham. Their argument that punishment in itself was undesirable, should be proportionate to the crime and applied only as a means of deterrence, became widely influential in instigating reforms in penal practices in some European countries. It was on these grounds that the regular practice of torture of criminals was discontinued.

Crime as a Product of Social Forces

Modern scientific criminology, however, is generally considered to be less than two hundred years old. Some authors (e.g. Vold, Bernard & Snipes, 1998) have traced its origins to the publication, in France in 1827, of the first national crime statistics. This enabled André-Michel Guerry, a French lawyer, and Adolphe Quetelet, a Belgian mathematician and astronomer, to carry out a new type of study utilising criminal statistics, maps and charts and so examine the geographical distribution of crime. In books published in the early 1830s by what has since been called the "cartographic school", these authors searched for an association between crime and poverty. While they discovered no simple, direct link of the kind they had anticipated, important relationships were detected between crime rates and factors such as age, sex, population density, urban development, illiteracy, and drinking habits. The rate of crime appeared to be particularly high where there were adjacent areas of relative poverty and affluence.

Crime as a Function of Differences between Individuals

Later in the nineteenth century, paralleling the ideas of Charles Darwin and evolutionary theory, other criminologists presupposed that crime could be understood on the basis of biologically rooted differences between individuals. An Italian army doctor, Cesare Lombroso, studied physical features of groups of habitual criminals. He observed a much higher rate of anomalies in the structure of the skull than were found among a comparison group of soldiers. Lombroso proposed that repeated criminality was an indication of atavistic character: persistent criminals exemplified an earlier stage of human evolution. This viewpoint has sometimes been called the "anthropological school". A replication of this study by Charles Goring with prisoners and soldiers carried out in Britain between 1901 and 1913 failed to support the theory. While Lombroso's reputation rests almost exclusively on this widely cited aspect of his work, in his later studies he developed his views to take account of many environmental factors influencing crime; and in the last edition of his work he emphasised these factors much more. Notwithstanding both the latter developments, Lombroso is seen as having instigated the "individual differences" approach to the understanding of crime.

Crime as Normal and Inevitable

An alternative approach to thinking about crime involves a reversal of starting-points. What if the purpose of criminological theory were to explain, not why some individuals break the law but why, much of the time, most do not? The central puzzle may be not that a minority of persons deviate and act criminally, but that the bulk of the time the vast majority conform. This tradition of thought stems initially from the work of the "social contract" theorists of the Enlightenment, such as Rousseau and Voltaire. Other concepts within it are derived from the work of the French sociologist Emil Durkheim towards the end of the nineteenth century. The resultant ideas have been expressed in a variety of forms, collectively known as *control theories*. All have in common a pre-supposition that the needs or wishes of the individual and those of society are often (and from some viewpoints inevitably) in opposition to each other. If allowed to do so, individuals will act primarily in pursuit of their own private ends and without regard for others. Thus conformity to society's expectations cannot be taken for granted; on the contrary, crime is "normal". The process of socialisation is one in which authority figures such as parents and teachers must expend considerable effort trying to ensure that developing children learn to behave in a socially acceptable way. Unfortunately, individuals vary in their ability to abide by society's strictures. Attention is thus focused on those restraining factors that keep crime under control, and on what happens in circumstances in which they break down—for example, in conditions of social disorganisation.

CONTINUITIES IN THEORETICAL CONCEPTS

In summary, one perspective on crime is that it results from individual and personal factors. In the first version of this view crimes are construed as outcomes of deliberate, consciously planned actions; while in another they arise from individuals' inherent make-up, predisposing them to act in anti-social ways. The converse, diametrically opposed view is that crime can only be understood as a consequence of social and environmental conditions. Yet another view is that it is a product of an irreconcilable conflict between individual and social forces. The foregoing concepts have been central in shaping criminological theory for much of its existence (Vold, Bernard & Snipes, 1998). Despite extensive changes, discernible continuities have remained in some of the concepts from criminology's inception until the present day. Most contemporary theories represent permutations, in one form or another, of these same basic ideas, though with considerable elaboration of detail and search for empirical support.

Hence one strand reflecting the classical theory of Beccaria and the utilitarian philosophers can be found in the model of the "reasoning criminal", in which the concept of rational choice has been rejuvenated and attained a new influence in some current models of criminal activity (Clarke & Felson, 1993). This has been conjoined with the advocacy of deterrence and proportionality in sentencing as means of reducing crime (see Tonry, 1996).

A second thread, characterised in the early empirical studies of the cartographic school (Guerry, Quetelet) was later pursued by the founders of the ecological approach to crime at the University of Chicago from the 1920s onwards, and gave rise to a wide spectrum of sociologically oriented theories. These approaches, alongside numerous variants, have in many respects been the dominant influence in criminological thinking for most of the twentieth century.

Finally, though they have undergone considerable revision, the ideas of the nineteenth-century "anthropological school" that there may be constitutional differences between offenders and non-offenders, which are a function of underlying (perhaps genetically determined) biological processes, have remained active in some schools of criminology right up to the present. Approaches from an orientation rooted in biological sciences, and relevant research, are addressed in the books by Buikhuisen and Mednick (1988) and Wilson and Herrnstein (1985).

Crime as a Function of the Operation of Law

Over approximately the last three decades, however, an alternative approach to criminological research and theorising has been formulated which represents a significant departure from all the viewpoints dealt with so far. Characterised by various names including "deviance theory", "critical criminology" or sometimes simply "the new criminology", the focus of study within it is the working of the law itself. To an extent this builds upon some of the insights of the *labelling* perspective, to be considered in more detail later. But its theoretical task is conceptualised more broadly, to encompass all the processes by which law is formulated, its edicts are acted upon, and its consequences felt by everyone involved. In the most radical versions of this approach, there are even those who, on epistemological grounds, reject the project of "explaining" crime. It is argued that merely to employ the word "crime" or discuss how it might be "caused" is to impose categories on the world around us; it is this usage of such discourse itself which should be the subject of our research. Some post-modernist authors thereby repudiate the notion that there is something "out there" to be explained (Henry & Milovanovic, 1991). Others have suggested that this perspective can be combined with a more traditional one, envisioning that causation of crime remains a valid subject of inquiry (Schwartz & Friedrichs, 1994).

THEORETICAL APPROACHES AND LEVELS OF EXPLANATION

There are now numerous forms of criminological theory, reflecting the diverse origins of the field. It has manifold links with other areas, and some theories can be traced to the various academic disciplines (biology, psychology, anthropology, sociology, and politics) which have played a part in its formation. In order to find our way through a field in which such a plethora of theoretical models is available, some superordinate scheme or organising principle is needed. Bernard and Snipes (1996) classify theories into two basic types: "individual-difference" and "structure-process" theories. The approach adopted here is to consider models of crime in terms of their focus and explanatory scope. Criminological theories operate at different *levels of explanation* dependent upon the extensiveness or range of convenience that their respective authors seek to achieve.

To simplify our task, therefore, the field of criminological theory will be surveyed and characterised as providing explanations for criminal behaviour on five discrete but interconnected levels. Broadly speaking, these move from macro-cosm to microcosm. To use the analogy of a compound microscope, they represent attempts to view crime through a series of five progressively more powerful lenses. The relationship between them is depicted in Table 7.1.

Level 1: Macro-level Explanations

On the first level crime can be considered to be an ineluctable by-product of certain aspects or forms of society itself. Taking this as a starting-point, criminological theories have been developed which view both crime, and the social conditions commonly associated with it, as intrinsically bound up with the nature of human social organisation.

For example, *conflict theories* such as those derived from Marxist analysis see crime as inevitable given the nature of the relationship between competing groups within society. Society as a whole is thought to have evolved in a state of conflict. There has been relentless competition not just for limited material resources, but also for institutionalised power. The dominant class in a society formulates and administers its laws; and will be likely to do so in a way that serves

Table 7.1 A schematic representation of levels of explanation in criminological theories

Level	Explanatory focus (unit of analysis)	Objective	Illustrative theories
1	Society	To explain crime as a large-scale social phenomenon	*Conflict theory* *Strain theory* *Sociological control theories* *Feminist theories*
2	Localised areas Communities	To account for geographical variations in crime; such as urban–rural differences, or between neighbourhoods	*Ecological theories* *Differential opportunity theory*
3	Proximate social groups	To understand the roles of socialisation and social influence through family, school or peer-group	*Subcultural delinquency theory* *Differential association theory* *Social learning theory*
4	Individual criminal acts	To analyse and account for patterns and types of crime events	*Routine activity theory* *Rational choice theory*
5	Individual offenders	To examine intra-individual factors such as thoughts, feelings and behaviour	*Neutralisation theory* *Psychological control theories* *Cognitive social learning theory*

its own interests. It will seek to control the members of other classes, and exert efforts to sustain its hegemony. Crime is created by this general condition of society and through the specific rules devised by the dominant group for the maintenance of social order and the continuation of its own power. According to this analysis, crime serves a purpose, in furnishing a justification for the maintenance of control over certain segments of the populace.

Other related viewpoints such as the *strain theory* of the American sociologist Robert Merton are also representative of this type or level of explanation. Merton too saw industrialised society as conflict-ridden: its prescribed goals are primarily material ones and its cardinal virtue personal ambition. Since only a limited proportion of citizens can achieve success as defined in this way, others must somehow adapt to the circumstances of failure and find a means to resolve the dilemma into which they have been placed. In attempting to secure the goals appointed for them by society, some individuals will resort to illegitimate means. Within this framework, Merton delineated several types of *deviant modes of adaptation*. Some crime is a form of *innovation*. Deprived people turn to it as a route to the goals they would otherwise be denied; property crime or racketeering may be the result. By contrast, another group known as *retreatists* conquer the strain by abandoning the effort to achieve socially approved goals; they resolve their strains by escaping through various routes including alcoholism, drug addiction, psychosis, vagrancy or ultimately, suicide. Thus, different forms of strain resolution lead to different types of social pathology.

Control theories, briefly mentioned above, can also be considered as belonging to this level of explanation. Their conceptual focus, on a sociological level, is the occurrence of crime in society as a whole and the nature of structures which maintain order. However, various models within this genre also have implications at the individual, psychological level and will be discussed again below.

Feminist theories are more explicitly concerned with the overall patterning of crime in society and with the development of explanatory links between the observable fact that most crimes are perpetrated by males, on the one hand, and other aspects of the male domination of society, on the other. There are numerous strands of interpretation within feminist approaches: over time, their focus and compass have gradually changed (Daly & Chesney-Lind, 1988). An initial prime concern was with institutionalised sexism in criminal justice systems, evident both in the preponderance of males at all stages of decision-making and in sexist assumptions concerning the role of biology in women's offending. At later stages this inquiry widened to address the question of whether theories developed on the basis of research with male offenders are applicable to female offenders (the *generalisability* problem), and also to the factors which lead to there being a gender differential in criminality in the first place (the *gender ratio* problem) (Daly & Chesney-Lind, 1988).

A related issue addressed within these approaches is that of whether, as a consequence of evolving sex roles and the pursuit of equal opportunities for women, there would be a rise in female crime rates to equate with those of males: this has been called the *convergence hypothesis* (Nettler, 1984). Available data, however, have at best provided only mixed support for this expectation. A more recent focus within feminist criminology has been upon men's abuse of, and violence towards, women, and the factors in society which sustain ". . . the gendered nature of much criminal victimization" (Heidensohn, 1994, p. 1024). This both confronts a series of specific issues concerning the position of women as victims, plaintiffs, defendants or prisoners: ". . . in both criminological and lay explanations, criminal women have always been presented as being "Other": other than real women, other than real criminals" (Carlen, 1985, p. 1). It also, more radically, leads to analysis of those factors which maintain the structure of power relations within society.

Level 2: Locality-based Accounts

The grand sweep of theories of the above kind does not, however, serve to explain another of the most salient features of crime: that it is unevenly dispersed across different geographical locations *within* societies. Other criminological theories therefore operate at a second level in which the spatial and social distribution of crime is a prime focus of study.

The first concerted attempts to examine this were undertaken in Chicago in the 1920s. From the mid-nineteenth century onwards, primarily as a result of European migration, the population of the USA increased enormously. Chicago grew from a small town with a population of only 4000 in 1830 to a city of more than two million by 1910. Drawing on ideas from the science of ecology, sociologists at the University of Chicago developed a model of how expanding cities change over time. Clifford Shaw and his colleagues investigated the relationship between urban structure and growth on the one hand, and social disruption and other consequences on the other. They discovered that crime was consistently highest in *transitional zones*: inner-city slum neighbourhoods in which arriving migrants first settled and which were marked by numerous forms of social pathology. This pattern persisted regardless of which ethnic group lived there. As members of incoming groups later moved to more affluent suburbs, their crime rate decreased commensurately. The neighbourhood dynamics of the transitional zone operated in ways that were conducive to delinquency. Crime was thought to be a function of these processes, which arose independently of any known characteristics of individuals living in the identified locations.

These studies have attained considerable prominence in criminology, though Farrington (1993) has questioned whether the evidence adduced is as convincing as has sometimes been claimed. Nevertheless this work ushered in a new era in criminological research and has had far-reaching influences on its course during the twentieth century. Shaw also undertook more detailed studies of delinquent lifestyles, attitudes, and life histories. From this there emerged two further findings. First, it became clear that one factor in criminal conduct was the influence of individual offenders upon each other; for example, of older delinquents upon younger ones. Second, within some localities it appeared that groups of delinquents were in effect serving to transmit a tradition of delinquency from one generation of juveniles to the next.

On the basis of this pioneering work other criminologists developed more elaborate theories to account for different patterns of crime. They include, for example, *differential opportunity theory* which combines concepts drawn from strain theory with the notion of "opportunity structures" within a local neighbourhood area. The pattern of crime displayed will be a function of types of strain which individuals are under, the modes of adaptation they adopt, and the spectrum of crime-opportunities that are accessible relatively close at hand.

Level 3: Socialisation and Group Influence Processes

Some of the aforementioned findings lead naturally on to a third level of explanation. Here, an attempt is made to understand the mechanisms by which some individuals within certain localities or communities are drawn into crime, while others are not. Variations between smaller "proximate" units such as families or adolescent peer-groups, the social networks which are the context for most behaviour, may be important contributory factors in the genesis of delinquent activities.

There are several theoretical formulations specific to this level of explanation. Some are known as *subcultural delinquency theories*. According to this viewpoint, individuals with certain kinds of problems, notably adolescents having difficulties both at school and at home, seek alternative sources of interpersonal affiliation within which they can acquire standing. Such individuals are at risk of being drawn into delinquent groups where they can recoup lost status and restore their self-esteem. They will thereby be socialised into the acceptance of criminogenic norms.

Other researchers have attempted to explain how such assimilation processes occur. To address this question, sociologist Edwin Sutherland adopted a view of criminal activity as simply one form of normal, learned behaviour. The conditions in which individuals grow up affect the chances of their being presented with opportunities or exposed to pressures to participate in crime. Involvement in criminal activity is a product of a complex set of learning experiences, both in terms of basic life circumstances but more importantly acquired attitudes and behaviours. Crime will mean different things to different individuals depending upon the ways in which they have learned to perceive it through association with significant others. The principle tenet of *differential association theory* is that a person becomes delinquent because of an excess of "definitions favourable to violation of law" over definitions unfavourable to it. According to the theory, processes such as this are at work in all strata of society. While youthful street gangs in run-down neighbourhoods may learn attitudes conducive to theft, burglary, or vandalism, economically better-off individuals working in business environments may be induced into acts of fraud, embezzlement, or tax evasion. The theory thus also provided the initial impetus to the study of "white collar crime".

The concepts employed in this model, though developed within a sociological framework, are in principle very similar to those of psychological learning theories. Akers et al. (1979) subsequently developed an integrative *social-learning theory* of crime, "... a revision of differential association theory in terms of general behavioural reinforcement theory" (p. 637). This will be considered in more detail below.

Level 4: Lifestyle and "Routine Activities"

A fourth level of explanation draws on some new directions taken in criminology over the past two decades. Its starting-point is an examination of crime as a form of action, the patterning of criminal acts in time and place, and their relationship to the lifestyles of those who perpetrate them. The theory attempts to account for a range of data linking types of crimes with the manner in which they are committed, on the one hand, and the availability of opportunities to commit them, on the other. For example, burglaries or vehicle thefts are much more common in certain places or at certain times. Criminal acts exhibit patterns which are indicative of the availability of opportunities to individuals within other cycles of activity they are following in their day-to-day lives. *Routine activity theory*, as this approach to criminology is known, considers the bulk of crime to fit this template and to be explicable through the convergence in space and time of "motivated offenders, suitable targets, and the absence of capable guardians" (Cohen & Felson, 1979, p. 589). Felson (1994) expands on the nature of this approach. Most crime is not dramatic, ingenious, and profitable, as its representation via television, films or novels might lead us to believe. Instead, it is typically characterised by triviality, impulsiveness, minimal gain and often plain failure. This approach explicitly disavows any focus on individuals who become involved in crime, other than to postulate the presence of a "likely offender" as a prerequisite for the occurrence of a crime.

Some researchers have found these concepts to be congruent with the premises of *rational choice theory*, the origins of which can be traced to the classical view of crime as premeditated, purposeful calculation. As propounded in that theory, crime is a result of a calculated balance of pain and pleasure made by rational beings acting in their own perceived best interests. In its revised form however, the approach is applied in a more narrowly circumscribed field, to explain certain types of variation in crime. For example, once an overall decision has been made to commit residential burglary, a range of factors is considered in selecting the best target. The list is likely to include the distance to be travelled to the target area, ease of access to a dwelling, likelihood of interruption or detection, and anticipated gain. While ostensibly the focus of this theory is on cognitive processes in individual offenders, and research has been conducted regarding this, rational choice theorists have devoted much more work to the study of likely targets of crime. Some situational crime prevention strategies, such as "target hardening" (making premises more secure, or introducing video surveillance) are derivatives of the joint application of routine activity and rational choice approaches (Clarke & Felson, 1993).

Level 5: Self-definition, Personal and Cognitive Factors

A fifth level of theory construction in the present conceptual scheme explicitly addresses intra-individual or psychological factors. For a period the dominant focus in this respect was upon differences in personality. This type of theory is illustrated by the work of Hans Eysenck, where it is postulated that constitutional factors (individual differences in the functioning of the nervous system, which may be inherited) influence the effectiveness of socialisation processes. This results in differences in measurable personality traits, some of which (higher extraversion, neuroticism and psychoticism) are held to be associated with greater likelihood of involvement in criminality (see Hollin, 1989, for fuller discussion). In essence, this is a form of control theory, as these differences are held to determine individual capacities to adhere to society's rules. Evidence in support of this theory is, however, fairly weak. Indeed overall, it has proved difficult to isolate any type of personality dimension which can be consistently shown to differentiate between offenders and non-offenders. The best potential candidate in this respect is thought by Vold, Bernard and Snipes (1998) to be *impulsiveness*. Other psychological theories place greater emphasis on the social learning process itself and more recently attention has turned to cognitive factors which are hypothesised to be conducive to recurrent participation in crime.

Psychological factors have been posited as elements of sociologically based theories within criminology for some time. One illustrative viewpoint in this respect arose from attempts to address apparent contradictions on the question of whether or not persistent delinquents reject the moral values of "mainstream" society. Whereas subcultural delinquency theories predict that they should, research studies have more often found that even recidivist offenders tend to endorse conventional sets of values. *Neutralisation theory* (Sykes & Matza, 1957) is an attempt to unify these conflicting positions. It is hypothesised that to enable individuals to tolerate incongruity in their feelings and attitudes regarding crimes, they employ a series of internal mechanisms which serve to resolve the incompatibility of deviant and conformist values. These *techniques of neutralisation* include *denial of responsibility; denial of victim; denial of injury; condemning the condemners*; and *appeal to higher loyalties*. By reacting to their crimes in this way, many offenders can resolve the dissonance between their proclaimed beliefs and their actual behaviour.

As noted above there is also a convergence between differential association theory and ideas drawn from behaviourally based accounts of social learning. Here crime is viewed as having its origins, not in individual predispositions or personality differences, but in group interaction and influence processes. Akers et al. (1979)—and see Nietzel (1979)—have elaborated this model, drawing on extensive findings of research on human learning. These authors posited that crime is learned through processes of imitation and differential reinforcement by which individuals may arrive at evaluative definitions supportive of delinquent action. This occurs in the context of social groupings, notably adolescent peer-groups. The relative balance of influences within the groups to which individuals are exposed, conceptualised in learning-theory terms, instigates and maintains illicit use of alcohol and other drugs. Akers and colleagues tested the theory by conducting a self-report survey of involvement in substance abuse among a large sample of teenagers. Significant correlations were found between independent variables (measures of differential association and opportunities for social learning) and dependent variables (levels of substance misuse). Although this study could not explicate the details of the mechanisms involved, it provides firm support for the importance of social learning in the onset of some kinds of proscribed behaviour.

In recent years a number of studies have examined differences between groups of recidivist offenders and non-offenders on a range of cognitive and social skills. It is held that individuals deficient in such skills will be at risk of involvement in crime as a means of solving everyday problems with which they are faced. Skill deficits of this kind arise mainly as a result of a lack of opportunities for "pro-social" learning. The list of skills identified includes, for example, the ability: to generate alternative solutions to personal problems; to take the perspective of another person; to think flexibly concerning problems; to anticipate consequences of actions; to control impulsiveness. Although evidence concerning this is not uniformly supportive, differences along such lines have repeatedly been found (Ross & Fabiano, 1985; Andrews & Bonta, 1998). The most reliable differences, it must be reiterated, are found not between offenders and non-offenders, but between *persistent* offenders and non-offenders. It is not held that such skill deficits alone are responsible for criminality, but that they interact with features of socialisation and with opportunities in the environment in producing criminal acts. Akhtar and Bradley (1991) have formulated an *information processing* model and reviewed research showing how errors at different points in the process contribute to increased likelihood of aggression. Concepts drawn from social-learning theory and concerning the roles of cognitive processes have been combined in a *cognitive-behavioural* model applicable to many types of offence. As will be seen in Chapter 14, these departures have provided the groundwork for a number of successful intervention programmes designed to reduce rates of recidivism among persistent offenders.

MULTI-LEVEL PERSPECTIVES

The demarcation of criminological theories into five explanatory levels is an expository convenience. Its artificiality must be acknowledged, as most theories have implications at more than one of the levels described. For example, control theories make statements concerning the societal restraints placed on individuals that affect the overall rates and patterning of crime, but they also specify types of differences likely to be found between law-abiding citizens and those who habitually break the law. In the *general theory of crime* put forward by Gottfredson and Hirschi (1990), that difference resides in low capacity for self-control. However, Farrington (1996, p. 79) has pointed to the limited prospect of being able to get very far on the strength of "...only one underlying construct of criminal potential".

Another example spanning more than one level is that of *labelling theory*. Its theoretical starting-point is the observation that there is no type of behaviour that is always and everywhere defined as illegal. Even killing does not invariably constitute an act of crime. There are circumstances in which it is believed to be warranted or is expressly allowed (war, judicial execution). The actions involved may cause harm, but the idea that they are *criminal* is a label that has been added. Many people who indulge in the same behaviour in different circumstances will not be labelled as deviant.

The immediate impact of labelling is the process of *stigmatisation* and the associated separation from society of the individual to whom a label is attached. This has repercussions for how the person is seen by others, which in turn induces changes in self-concept. Society's own reaction to delinquency can even contribute to its recurrence—a process known as *deviance amplification*. In terms of our general explanatory scheme, the impact of labelling reverberates from macro- to micro-levels and back again.

Labelling theory has a number of direct implications for policy and practice in criminal justice. The practical relevance of the theory has been through its advocacy of the principle of *minimal intervention*: the idea that we should attempt to restrict the involvement of legal processes particularly in the lives of juvenile offenders, for example through more extensive use of police cautioning. This is paralleled by an emphasis on *decriminalisation* (changing the law so as to exclude some behaviours presently defined as criminal); *diversion* (the development of systems for dealing with young offenders prior to or instead of their formal processing through courts); and *de-institutionalisation* (attempting to reduce the usage of custodial sentences through the provision of community-based measures as alternatives).

INTEGRATIVE MODELS

Considering the diversity of models and theories to be found within criminology, some authors have called for *rapprochement* and conceptual integration. "Unfortunately, the theoretical insights and empirical findings derived from these different approaches remain largely disconnected. Consequently, deviance and crime are understood only in piecemeal fashion, and the various approaches adopted to study these topics are badly in need of some attempt at unification" (Cohen & Machalek, 1988, p. 466). Similarly, given the marked tendency of researchers to advocate models based on one class of variables only, it has been contended that ". . . criminological theories need to be more wide-ranging and need to include all these different types of variables" (Farrington, 1993, p. 30).

Bernard (1990), reviewing the progress of criminological theory over a 20-year period, expressed dismay concerning its status, and suggested that there had been no meaningful advance as nothing could be subjected to the philosophical principle of falsification. There appeared to be little to choose between so many competing, equally plausible standpoints, but within only a few years, Bernard and Snipes (1996) were able to be more sanguine concerning the prospects. One ingredient in this transformation was the emergence of theories of progressively increasing breadth in terms of explanatory power. Over recent years, a series of genuinely integrative theories of crime causation and maintenance has been published by a number of authors.

Some early integrative work was done drawing on a number of theoretical perspectives by Elliott, Ageton and Cantor (1979). Their model combines elements of strain theory, control theory and social learning theory. Individuals experience strain as a result of being unable to achieve success as defined by the culture to which they belong. In conditions of social disorganisation they will also be subject to relatively weak controls and attachment to conventional norms. Social learning processes operate in such a way that the balance of their attachments shifts towards delinquent attitudes, with criminal behaviour as the result. The authors of this early attempt at conceptual integration were castigated by Hirschi (1979) who urged that exercises of such a kind be abandoned. Despite this rebuke, during the period since then attempts to coalesce theoretical models with one another have continued apace. Arguments for the relative merits of theory integration versus theory elaboration or "oppositional" theory-building are debated in the volume edited by Messner, Krohn and Liska (1989). In what follows, some of the most notable attempts to amalgamate theoretical concepts in criminology will be briefly outlined.

Thornberry (1987) has delineated an *interactional* theory of delinquency which conjoins explanatory concepts from the Elliott, Ageton and Cantor (1979) model with other ideas from control theory and social learning theory respectively. The model seeks to explain the net outcome of two processes: how constraints over behaviour may become progressively weakened, and equally how ". . . the resulting freedom is channeled into delinquent patterns" (ibid., p. 865). The model contains six key interactive variables predictive of delinquency: attachment to parents, to school, and to conventional attitudes; and associations with delinquent peers, adoption of their values, and delinquent behaviour itself. However, these factors are not conceived as somehow taking fixed values such that, for example, the developing child's level of parental bonding becomes a static independent variable. Rather, the central tenet of the theory is that it is patterns of interaction over time that must be understood to give an account of the onset of delinquency. In addition, Thornberry places great emphasis on the inclusion in the model of reciprocal processes, and insists that a reliance on the concept of unidirectional causal effects must be discarded. Thus, just as the young person's detachment from parents may lead to gradual immersion in anti-social values, so the latter will also have consequences for the former. The developmental interplay of factors conducive to criminality can be depicted as occurring in an "amplifying causal loop". Finally, the pattern of interaction of the variables is conceptualised as varying between early, middle and later adolescence. Thornberry (1996) adduces a sizeable volume of evidence in support of birectional causal effects in a review of 17 studies of the interrelationships between a number of variables in the model (parental and school attachment, deviant beliefs and attitudes, delinquent associates) and a variety of offence behaviours (minor and serious "generalist" delinquency, theft, vandalism, shoplifting, drug abuse, and interpersonal violence).

An analogous perspective was adopted by Catalano and Hawkins (1996), whose model synthesises control theory, social learning theory and differential association theory, though in a balance slightly different from Thornberry's. These authors see it as essential to incorporate a developmental dimension and, to do so, construct a general model and four age-specific "sub-models". Developmental processes are "transactional" in the sense that not only is there mutual influence between variables but this generates qualitatively different outcomes at successive stages. Three primary external factors set the context for development in general: the individual's position in the social structure (socio-economic class, gender, race and age); constitutional/temperamental factors; and other external environmental constraints. Four constructs are considered as central in influencing the direction of development: (a) perceived opportunities for involvement in interactions with others, (b) the degree of involvement therein, (c) the skills to participate in these activities, and (d) the anticipated reinforcement from participation. When these factors work cohesively, a social bond develops, which may then have separate, independent influence in producing (or failing to produce) controls on later behaviour. The combination of pro-social and anti-social behaviours so learned and the balance between the two will decide whether children proceed along different "pathways". The causal elements in the model yield a number of indicators for points of intervention which Catalano and Hawkins illustrate.

Laub and Sampson (1993) have reminded criminologists that while there are some continuities in criminal careers, there are also turning-points. Some are due to changes occurring naturally over time, others to the impact of life events. Patterns of crime and potential causal or contributory factors are not necessarily stable across different phases of the lifespan. Hence a model which proves applicable to juvenile delinquency may not explain adult criminality; participation, maintenance, escalation, and desistance may each be a function of separate variables, or of similar variables interacting in different ways. Theorists should accept ". . . the futility of an invariant or deterministic conception of human development" (Laub & Sampson, 1993, p. 310). Even once involved in crime, there is evidence that individuals' motivations for such frequent offences as shop theft and vehicle-taking mutate during the years between early and late adolescence, and adulthood (McGuire, 1996, 2000).

Some theories have offered variants of the theme developed here, in which factors contributing to crime are envisaged as operating on several levels. Martens (1993) merges concepts from a perspective based in studies of child development into an ecological frame of reference. The growing child is located in a complex network of associations on four levels: the *microsystem* (the child and his or her immediate surroundings); the *mesosystem* (significant others at home, school, and play); the *exosystem* (the socio-economic position of the parents, the neighbourhood environment); and the *macrosystem* (wider structural and socio-cultural influences). Martens examines the dynamic interplay between various factors at each of these system levels, introducing the additional dimension of change over time. LeBlanc's (1993) "multilayered" perspective is more complex still and comprises several stages of theory construction. First, a distinction is made between delinquent acts, delinquent actors, and delinquency as a social phenomenon. These are themselves seen as products of several interacting variables and a model presented of principal causal pathways in relation to each. The models are then superimposed to construct a three-layered isomorphic model integrating 18 interdependent variables. In essence, its complexity notwithstanding, LeBlanc's is a form of control theory, as the fundamental orientation is towards understanding factors which affect (strengthen or weaken) the individual's bonding to conventional norms, or provide inducements to engage in delinquency. Thus, entered into the equation are factors which might operate to constrain delinquent acts (e.g. the presence of capable guardians *versus* crime opportunities); to produce internal constraints in would-be offenders (e.g. attachments to others, especially pro-social models *versus* criminal associates); or to moderate the level of crime in the community as a whole (legitimate opportunity structures, law enforcement agencies and criminal sanctions *versus* social disorganisation and anomie).

A novel element was introduced into criminological theorising by Cohen and Machalek (1988) who developed an approach to crime which adopts ideas from evolutionary theory and behavioural ecology, applied to expropriative (mainly property) crime. It is proposed that, in common with other species, human beings have through evolutionary history developed a range of methods for securing first material and later symbolic resources. Expropriation is viewed as simply one type of behaviour strategy for acquisition of resources. Such a strategy is likely to be most efficient in certain circumstances and has specific interrelations with types of strategies employed by other members of the population. Adopting this approach, it proves possible to integrate ideas emanating from a number of criminological theories. The normality of crime; its higher frequency in some subcultures or in disorganised neighbourhoods; differential association, social learning, and control processes; and dimensions of individual differences, can all be subsumed by one coherent theoretical framework. It should be noted that the model presented is not a re-packaged form of sociobiology in which a range of behaviour patterns is attributed to genetically driven tactics for maximising reproductive success. Cohen and Machalek explicitly distance themselves from that orientation.

Possibly the most comprehensive model provided to date is the integrative paradigm forwarded by Vila (1994). This builds upon and extends the evolutionary ecological approach of Cohen and Machalek (1988) in order to make it applicable to a wider range of types of crime. Vila first classifies crimes as falling into four major types, an "... arguably exhaustive categorization" (p. 315). Crimes may be *expropriative* (e.g. theft, fraud, embezzlement), the object of which is to obtain material resources such as property from another person without his or her knowledge or co-operation; *expressive* (sexual assault, illicit drug use), to obtain hedonistic resources that increase pleasurable feelings or decrease unpleasant feelings; *economic* (drug trafficking, prostitution), to obtain monetary resources through profitable illegal co-operative activities; or *political* (terrorism, election-rigging), to obtain political resources by using a wide variety of tactics. In common with some models already outlined, Vila also describes three levels of analysis of multiple connections between contributory factors: *ecological* (interactions between persons and their physical environment), *macro-level* (interactions between social groups), and *micro-level* (factors affecting the motivations of individuals). The three levels in turn are considered to interact synergistically; and the entire system of relationships is placed in a developmental context in which it also evolves dynamically over time.

Integrative theories such as these must have a number of features. Obviously, they must take into account a large number of variables. They must address variables from different levels (e.g. individual, family, community, society) and make statements concerning the interrelations of those levels. They must be dynamic, and take into account developmental and environmental change. Given this degree of complexity, such models are probabilistic rather than deterministic. Factors are interpreted as having causal relations but their interactions may take place in multiple directions, and are context-dependent, such that while the pattern as a whole can be described, the outcome for any one individual cannot be predicted with certainty. To quote Vila (1994, p. 311), the outcome of his attempt at integration is an "... emphatically nondeterministic paradigm".

A second important feature of successful integrative theories is that they should address both *structure* and *process*. For example, statements concerning the varying prevalence of crime across localities, even if firmly supported by data, are unsatisfactory in themselves unless they also explain the sequence of events which bring such differences about. Some of the integrated theories meet both of these demands and identify plausible interconnections between the two categories of variables. However, what is still missing is that none of them incorporates the behaviour of the law itself as an integral dimension. The present chapter too has paid scant attention to this, and while acknowledging it as an independent variable has focused instead on the orthodox position that certain aspects of criminal acts and actors can in themselves be a legitimate subject of inquiry.

Vold, Bernard and Snipes (1998) have proposed a *unified conflict theory* of crime which attempts to meet all of these criteria. Their model is designed to address both structure and process while simultaneously taking into account variations in the operation of the law. Much work remains to be done in refining and validating a model such as this, but it is important to have demonstrated the possibility in principle of constructing a theory of this kind. Given the ambitious nature of the project, it may be unlikely that a consensus will be reached regarding unified criminological theory in the near future; and Bernard and Snipes (1996) point out that the level of generality in such a theory could be so great as to render it untestable.

RISK AND PROTECTIVE FACTORS

An important source of evidence in assisting the development of integrative models has been a series of longitudinal studies of cohorts of developing children, followed in some cases over a period of more than 30 years. Studies of this kind have been carried out at a number of sites around the world: in the UK, Sweden, Finland, the USA, Canada and New Zealand. A repeated finding in these studies (as well as in cross-sectional surveys) is that a relatively small proportion of youths is responsible for a comparatively large proportion of criminal offences. This has led to an emphasis on those variables most regularly found to be associated with the "criminal career", or extended involvement in criminality for a significant proportion of the lifespan.

Farrington (1996) has summarised a series of 12 major factors or categories of variables shown to be important in this respect. They are: (a) prenatal and perinatal factors, (b) hyperactivity and impulsivity, (c) below-average intelligence and attainment, (d) parental supervision, discipline, and attitudes, (e) broken homes, (f) parental criminality, (g) large family size, (h) socio-economic deprivation, (i) peer influences, (j) school influences, (k) community influences, and (l) situational variables.

The type of empirically driven approach endorsed by Farrington (1995, 1996) and many others has led, as with integrative models, to a conceptualisation of crime in which theories are not expressed in terms of direct causal determinants. Instead, crime is viewed as an outcome of an interaction or combination of a range of risk and protective factors. *Risk factors* are individual or environmental variables, such as those just listed, which have been shown to be associated with great likelihood of involvement in criminal activity (Blackburn, 1993). *Protective factors* are those which ". . . enhance the resilience of those exposed to high levels of risk and protect them from undesirable outcomes" (Catalano & Hawkins, 1996, p. 153).

A similar orientation has been compellingly advocated by Andrews and his colleagues (Andrews, 1995; Andrews & Bonta, 1998) who have marshalled considerable quantities of evidence for the validity and usefulness of approaching crime from this perspective. To cite Andrews (1995, p. 36):

... individuals varying in their criminal past (as documented by cross-sectional studies) and their criminal future (as documented in longitudinal studies) may be differentiated at levels well above chance on a number of situational, circumstantial, personal, interpersonal, familial and structural/cultural/economic factors.

Drawing together several hundred studies of variables associated with offending, these authors concluded that the major factors associated with crime were: (a) anti-social or pro-criminal attitudes, beliefs and cognitive-emotional states; (b) association with pro-criminal peers; (c) a number of temperamental and personality factors including impulsivity, restless aggressive energy, egocentricism, and poor problem-solving and self-regulation skills; (d) a varied history of anti-social behaviour; (e) family history of criminality, evidence of poor parental supervision and discipline; and (f) low levels of personal, educational, vocational or financial achievement. By contrast, social class variables, judged in terms of socio-economic background conditions, and indicators of personal distress, manifested for example through low self-esteem or mental health problems, were only weakly linked to criminality.

Broadly speaking, these factors are presumed to interact in a cumulative or additive manner. The larger the number of risk factors recorded concerning an individual, and the farther along a risk continuum he or she is in respect of each, the greater the probability of delinquency and/or adult criminality. Much work remains to be done in developing more precise models of this process.

A useful distinction to be made here is between *static* and *dynamic* risk factors. The former are generally demographic or criminal-history variables which, at the time of making a risk assessment, are "fixed" or already determined: for example, an individual's age when first convicted of an offence; gender; present age; the type of offence committed; and total number of previous convictions. The latter are factors which fluctuate more rapidly over time, and reflect internal states or temporary circumstances of the individual. Research suggests that these play a pivotal role in the occurrence of re-offending (Zamble & Quinsey, 1997). They are additionally important in being factors which, if changed, will alter the likelihood of future re-offending.

With reference to specific types of crime such as assaults, while the risk factors are broadly similar to those found for delinquency in general, there is evidence that they may interact in specific sequences (Patterson & Yoerger, 1993; and see McGuire, 1997). Recent work has shown that the prediction of recidivism among mentally disordered offenders also entails the same variables as can be discerned among non-disordered offender populations (Bonta, Law & Hanson, 1998).

THE PRACTICALITY OF THEORY

It is a frequently cited dictum that "there is nothing so practical as a good theory". From the standpoint of a practitioner engaged daily in the investigation of crimes, or working with persons convicted of crimes, explanatory models of criminal action have immense potential. That potential can be realised if they are regarded as tools capable of guiding practice. They can have applications in assessment, prediction, intervention, and evaluation.

As Laub and Sampson (1993) have pointed out, theoretical models in criminology are typically based on aggregate samples, and fail to take account of the heterogeneity of individuals. Consequently there sometimes appears to be an unbridgeable gap between theoretical concepts, such as those at level 1 in the conceptual scheme offered earlier, and the more routine task of making sense of particular offences or of the people who have committed them. One massive advantage of the "risk factors" approach is that it enables linkages to be made between large-scale theory and single cases. However elusive a unified theory may continue to be, the more modest task of comprehending individual offence patterns may be feasible using ideas currently available.

To accomplish this ideally requires the conduct of a comprehensive in-depth assessment. Theoretical models provide frameworks for areas in which to search for likely contributing factors. Employing the list of major criminogenic categories identified by Farrington (1996), or the sets of risk factors listed by Andrews and Bonta (1998), a systematic examination of the offence pattern of an individual can be conducted. In addition, it is important to carry out a functional analysis of the offence itself, to detect situational factors or momentary internal states that may have played parts in its occurrence.

Risk-needs models have been used to construct a number of assessment instruments which can be employed as predictors of future involvement in crime. If the focus is simply prediction of average re-offence rates among selected offender populations, a reasonably high level of predictive accuracy can be attained on the basis of "static" factors alone (Lloyd, Mair & Hough, 1994). Indeed recent research has suggested that although social variables are closely associated with reconviction, ". . . their effect in improving prediction is only slight" (May, 1999, p. ix). In the UK this has led to development of "actuarial" risk predictors such as the *Offender Group Reconviction Scale* (OGRS; Copas & Marshall, 1998). Several scales now exist for combined risk–needs assessment. They include, for example, the *Level of Service Inventory* (Andrews & Bonta, 1998; Bonta, 1996). Each of these instruments has an empirical grounding in research data concerning criminogenic risks and needs. This type of approach, based on amalgamation of variables, is widely perceived as having more practical value than any single theoretical model, though the contents of such scales may be derived from formal theoretical precepts (Andrews & Bonta, 1998).

A framework for understanding criminal acts might therefore entail an inventory of the following list of factors:

- The sequence of events leading up to, during, and after the crime was committed.
- The circumstances in which the event occurred, as related to opportunity structures and activity routines of the perpetrator.
- The individual's thoughts, feelings and behaviour before, during and after the offence, with particular reference to mood states and self-talk.

- Psychological aspects of the individual's make-up, including levels of cognitive, social and self-management skills, attitudes and beliefs, involvement in substance misuse, and other pertinent risk factors.
- His or her developmental history, socialisation, background and other life-history variables.
- Proximal factors, including criminal associates and situational variables, and taking account of the behaviour of others.
- Socio-cultural factors, including prevailing norms regarding the behaviour in question, and the role of power relationships and imbalances in providing contexts for the behaviour.
- General environmental variables including socio-economic conditions both in the immediate locality and the wider community.

These implements not only yield estimates of future risk, they are also designed to identify targets for intervention with individual offenders which may help to reduce the chances of future anti-social behaviour. This can provide a focus for future work with individual clients, or a rationale for allocating them to specific services or programmes. Good practice in criminal justice, mental health and social services agencies ought to be founded on systematic, integrative assessments. Pre-sentence reports, sentence plans, care programme reports and other documents recommending or stipulating work to be carried out with individuals should contain material assembled in this way. Whether or not we do so formally or self-consciously, in attempting to understand any person's behaviour we are in a sense developing a theory about him or her. These are explicit strategies for carrying this out, collectively known as *case formulation*. The process is greatly facilitated by being able to take advantage of the available conceptual tools, models and evidence.

A BRIEF NOTE ON FURTHER READING

There are many books dealing with criminological theory or aspects of it. The most highly recommended is Vold, Bernard and Snipes (1998). For a shorter outline of key theories, see Hollin (1992). For useful collections of key papers, see the volumes edited by Cordella and Siegel (1996) or Henry and Einstadter (1998).

REFERENCES

Akers, R.L., Krohn, M.D., Lanza-Kaduce, L. & Radosevich, M. (1979) A social learning theory of deviant behavior. *American Sociological Review*, **44**, 635–655.
Akhtar, N. & Bradley, E.J. (1991) Social information processing deficits of aggressive children: Present findings and implications for social skills training. *Clinical Psychology Review*, **11**, 621–644.
Andrews, D.A. (1995) The psychology of criminal conduct and effective treatment. In J. McGuire (Ed.) *What Works: Reducing Re-offending: Guidelines from Research and Practice*. Chichester: John Wiley & Sons.

Andrews, D.A. & Bonta, J. (1998) *The Psychology of Criminal Conduct* (2nd edn). Cincinnati, OH: Anderson.

Bernard, T.J. (1990) Twenty years of testing theories: What have we learned and why? *Journal of Research in Crime and Delinquency*, **27**, 325–347.

Bernard, T.J. & Snipes, J.B. (1996) Theoretical integration in criminology. *Crime and Justice: A Review of Research*, **20**, 301–348.

Blackburn, R. (1993) *The Psychology of Criminal Conduct*. Chichester: John Wiley & Sons.

Bonta, J. (1996) Risk-needs assessment and treatment. In A.T. Harland (Ed.) *Choosing Correctional Options That Work: Defining the Demand and Evaluating the Supply*. Thousand Oaks, CA: Sage Publications.

Bonta, J., Law, M. & Hanson, K. (1998) Prediction of criminal and violent recidivism among mentally disordered offenders: A meta-analysis. *Psychological Bulletin*, **123**, 123–142.

Buikhuisen, W. & Mednick, S.A. (Eds) (1988) *Explaining Criminal Behaviour*. Leiden: E.J. Brill.

Carlen, P. (1985) Introduction. In P. Carlen (Ed.) *Criminal Women*. Cambridge: Polity Press.

Catalano, R.F. & Hawkins, J.D. (1996) The social development model: A theory of antisocial behavior. In J.D. Hawkins (Ed.) *Delinquency and Crime: Current Theories*. Cambridge: Cambridge University Press.

Clarke, R.V. & Felson, M. (Eds) (1993) *Routine Activity and Rational Choice*. Advances in Criminological Theory, Vol. 5. New Brunswick, NJ: Transaction Publishers.

Cohen, L.E. & Felson, M. (1979) Social change and crime rate trends: A routine activity approach. *American Sociological Review*, **44**, 588–608.

Cohen, L.E. & Machalek, R. (1988) A general theory of expropriative crime: An evolutionary ecological approach. *American Journal of Sociology*, **94**, 465–501.

Conklin, J.B. (1992) *Criminology* (4th edn). New York: Macmillan.

Copas, J. & Marshall, P. (1998) The Offender Group Reconviction Scale: A statistical reconviction score for use by probation officers. *Applied Statistics*, **47**, 159–171.

Cordella, P. & Siegel, L. (Eds) (1996) *Readings in Contemporary Criminological Theory*. Boston, MA: Northeastern University Press.

Daly, K. & Chesney-Lind, M. (1988) Feminism and criminology. *Justice Quarterly*, **5**, 497–538.

Elliott, D.S., Ageton, S.S. & Cantor, R.J. (1979) An integrated theoretical perspective on delinquent behavior. *Journal of Research in Crime and Delinquency*, **16**, 3–27.

Farrington, D.P. (1993) Have any individual, family or neighbourhood influences on offending been demonstrated conclusively? In D.P. Farrington, R.J. Sampson & P.H. Wikström (Eds) *Integrating Individual and Ecological Aspects of Crime*. Stockholm: National Council for Crime Prevention.

Farrington, D.P. (1995) The development of offending and antisocial behaviour from childhood: Key findings from the Cambridge Study in Delinquent Development. *Journal of Child Psychology and Psychiatry*, **36**, 929–964.

Farrington, D.P. (1996) The explanation and prevention of youthful offending. In J.D. Hawkins (Ed.) *Delinquency and Crime: Current Theories*. Cambridge: Cambridge University Press.

Felson, M. (1994) *Crime and Everyday Life: Insight and Implications for Society*. Thousand Oaks, CA: Pine Forge Press.

Furnham, A. (1989) *Lay Theories*. Oxford: Pergamon Press.

Glick, L. (1997) *Criminology*. Boston, MA: Allyn & Bacon.

Gottfredson, M.R. & Hirschi, T. (1990) *A General Theory of Crime*. Stanford, CA: Stanford University Press.

Heidensohn, F. (1994) Gender and crime. In M. Maguire, R. Morgan & R. Reiner (Eds) *The Oxford Handbook of Criminology*. Oxford: Clarendon Press.

Henry, S. & Einstadter, W. (Eds) (1998) *The Criminology Theory Reader*. New York, NY: New York University Press.

Henry, S. & Milovanovic, D. (1991) Constitutive criminology: The maturation of critical theory. *Criminology*, **29**, 293–315.

Hirschi, T. (1979) Separate and unequal is better. *Journal of Research in Crime and Delinquency*, **16**, 34–38.

Hollin, C.R. (1989) *Psychology and Crime: An Introduction to Criminological Psychology*. London: Routledge.

Hollin, C.R. (1992) *Criminal Behaviour*. London: Falmer Press.

Laub, J.H. & Sampson, R.J. (1993) Turning points in the life course: Why change matters to the study of crime. *Criminology*, **31**, 301–325.

LeBlanc, M. (1993) Prevention of adolescent delinquency, an integrative multilayered control theory based perspective. In D.P. Farrington, R.J. Sampson & P.H. Wikström (Eds) *Integrating Individual and Ecological Aspects of Crime*. Stockholm: National Council for Crime Prevention.

Lilly, R.J., Cullen, F.T. & Ball, R.A. (1989) *Criminological Theory: Context and Consequences*. Newbury Park, CA: Sage Publications.

Lloyd, C., Mair, G. & Hough, M. (1994) *Explaining Reconviction Rates*. Home Office Research Study No. 136. London: HMSO.

Martens, P.L. (1993) An ecological model of socialisation in explaining offending. In D.P. Farrington, R.J. Sampson & P.H. Wikström (Eds) *Integrating Individual and Ecological Aspects of Crime*. Stockholm: National Council for Crime Prevention.

May, C. (1999) *Explaining Reconviction following a Community Sentence: The Role of Social Factors*. Home Office Research Study No. 192. London: Home Office.

McGuire, J. (1996) "Irrational" shoplifting and models of addiction. In J. Hodge, M. McMurran & C.R. Hollin (Eds) *Addicted to Crime?* Chichester: John Wiley & Sons.

McGuire, J. (1997) Psycho-social approaches to the understanding and reduction of aggression in young people. In V. Varma (Ed.) *Violence in Children and Adolescents*. London: Jessica Kingsley.

McGuire, J. (2000) Property offences. In C.R. Hollin (Ed.) *Handbook of Offender Assessment and Treatment*. Chichester: John Wiley & Sons.

Messner, S.F., Krohn, M.D. & Liska, A.E. (Eds) (1989) *Theoretical Integration in the Study of Deviance and Crime*. Albany, NY: State University of New York Press.

Nettler, G. (1984) *Explaining Crime* (3rd edn). New York, NY: McGraw-Hill.

Nietzel, M.T. (1979) *Crime and its Modification: A Social Learning Perspective*. New York, NY: Pergamon Press.

Patterson, G.R. & Yoerger, K. (1993) Developmental models for delinquent behavior. In S. Hodgins (Ed.) *Mental Disorder and Crime*. London: Sage.

Ross, R.R. & Fabiano, E.A. (1985) *Time to Think: A Cognitive Model of Delinquency Treatment and Offender Rehabilitation*. Johnson City, Tenn.: Institute of Social Sciences and Arts, Inc. (Now available from AIR Training and Publications, Ottawa.)

Schwartz, M.D. & Friedrichs, D.O. (1994) Postmodern thought and criminological discontent: New metaphors for understanding violence. *Criminology*, **32**, 221–246.

Sykes, G.M. & Matza, D. (1957) Techniques of neutralization: A theory of delinquency. *American Sociological Review*, **22**, 664–670.

Thornberry, T.P. (1987) Toward an interactional theory of delinquency. *Criminology*, **25**, 863–891.

Thornberry, T.P. (1996) Empirical support for interactional theory: A review of the literature. In J.D. Hawkins (Ed.) *Delinquency and Crime: Current Theories*. Cambridge: Cambridge University Press.

Tonry, M. (1996) *Sentencing Matters*. New York, NY: Oxford University Press.

Vila, B. (1994) A general paradigm for understanding criminal behaviour: Extending evolutionary ecological theory. *Criminology*, **32**, 311–359.

Vold, G.B., Bernard, T.J. & Snipes, J.B. (1998) *Theoretical Criminology* (4th edn). New York, NY: Oxford University Press.

Walker, M.A. (Ed.) (1995) *Interpreting Crime Statistics*. Oxford: Clarendon Press.

Wilson, J.Q. & Herrnstein, R.J. (1985) *Crime and Human Nature*. New York, NY: Simon & Schuster.

Zamble, E. & Quinsey, V. (1997) *The Criminal Recidivism Process*. Cambridge: Cambridge University Press.

Chapter 8

Psychosis and Offending

Aisling O'Kane
Wirral and West Cheshire Community NHS Trust, UK
and
Richard Bentall
Department of Psychology, University of Manchester, UK

The relationship between psychiatric disorder and offending has stimulated debate, not only among researchers, but also among politicians and members of the general public. Public concerns have focused on the apparent risk of violence by people suffering from severe mental illness and this in turn has strongly influenced the development of our civil commitment laws (Monahan, 1993).

Davis (1991) has suggested that the public tend to view aggression by psychiatric patients as caused by, "The spontaneous manifestation of underlying pathology". Appleby and Wessely (1988) persuaded Gallup pollsters to include a question on the perception of psychiatric patients in a poll of the UK public carried out in May 1987. A third of the sample agreed that mentally ill people are likely to be violent. There is therefore considerable tension between the public perception that the mentally ill person represents a high risk of violence and the reality of statistics that demonstrate relatively low levels of violence among this group. Undoubtedly, this tension reflects the fact that the major source of information on matters relating to people with a mental illness for members of the public is the media. For example, Philo et al. (1994) analysed the content of British television programmes over a one-month period, finding that two-thirds of items about mental health suggested a link between psychiatric disorder and violence.

While public perceptions of those with psychiatric disorders has remained consistently negative, the views of academic researchers have shifted over the years. In a recent editorial in the journal *Archives of General Psychiatry*, Marzuk (1996) has commented that:

Behaviour, Crime and Legal Processes: A Guide for Forensic Practitioners.
Edited by James McGuire, Tom Mason and Aisling O'Kane.
© 2000 John Wiley & Sons Ltd.

Ironically, it is only in recent years that we mental health professionals and advocates for the mentally ill have begun to appreciate the association between violence and mental illness, a link that has been recognized by the general public for centuries. What took us so long? Why were we so blind?

Marzuk lays the blame for the apparent "blindness" of his colleagues on a variety of factors: poorly designed studies which have often been retrospective; unstandardised and vague definitions of violence and mental illness; biases in case records; and a lack of sensitivity to social, demographic and situational variables. This list highlights the difficulties encountered when attempting to tease out the nature of the relationship, if any, between severe mental illness and offending.

In this chapter, we will try to steer our way through these difficulties focusing, in particular, on the most severe "psychotic" disorders, characterised by hallucinations, delusions, and an apparent loss of contact with reality. We will begin by giving a brief historical account of the origins of the current diagnostic system and the difficulties in deciding when people are psychotic and when they are not. We will then focus on the difficulties inherent in identifying causal pathways linking major mental illness to offences, especially violent behaviour and sexual offences.

DEFINING PSYCHOTIC DISORDERS

It is unfortunate that the independent variable employed in most studies of the relationship between psychiatric disorder and violence—a diagnosis of mental illness—itself remains a matter of controversy. This controversy reflects more than a century of unresolved debate about the best way of describing behaviour that is regarded by ordinary people as "insane", "mad" or "crazy".

Modern medical conceptions of psychosis derive from the work of nineteenth-century psychiatrists, mainly Germans, the most important of whom was Emil Kraepelin (Bentall, 1998). Like others of his time, Kraepelin believed that the key to understanding psychiatric disorders would be a workable system of psychiatric classification. He reasoned that each illness should consist of a cluster of symptoms that go together, that have a common prognosis, and that reflect a common underlying pathophysiology (Berrios & Hauser, 1988; Rieder, 1974). After studying the symptoms and histories of his patients, carefully recorded over a number of years, he came to the view that there were three major types of psychosis—"dementia praecox", "manic depression" and "paranoia". The term "dementia praecox", which was later replaced by Bleuler's (1911/1950) term "schizophrenia", implies a degenerative brain disease in young people, a description that accurately characterises Kraepelin's view of the disorder. In addition to intellectual deterioration, Kraepelin observed that patients with this condition frequently complained of hallucinations and delusions. In contrast, patients suffering from manic depression were said to experience extremes of mood, particularly episodes of depression and mania (characterised by euphoria, irritability and panic), but the long-term prognosis was more favourable. The main feature of paranoia was delusions (usually of a persecutory or grandiose nature) but, again, the long-term outcome was generally more favourable than that experienced by dementia praecox patients.

Kraepelin's system has undergone numerous revisions. For example, both Bleuler, (1911/1950) and Schneider (1959) described schizophrenia in ways that differed not only from Kraepelin but also from each other. According to Bleuler, the fundamental symptoms of schizophrenia were subtle phenomena which have been later described as Bleuler's "four A's": disordered associations, emotional ambivalence, inappropriate affect and autistic thinking. Schneider, on the other hand, highlighted hallucinations and delusions as "first rank" symptoms of schizophrenia, and his view has prevailed in more recent definitions of the disorder. In a further revision, Leonhard (1957/1979) made the important distinction between bipolar disorder and unipolar depression, both of which were classified as "manic depression" by Kraepelin. Nonetheless, Kraepelin's general approach remains dominant today. Indeed, the authors of the influential third edition of the American Psychiatric Association's classification system (DSM-III; American Psychiatric Association, 1980) described themselves as "neoKraepelinians" (Klerman, 1978). Within the DSM system, Kraepelin's three main diagnostic concepts of schizophrenia, manic depression and paranoia (now known as "delusional disorder") survive, albeit in modified forms.

DSM-III was published at the end of a long period of scepticism about the value of psychiatric diagnoses, brought about in part by the observation that diagnoses were often highly unreliable (that is, clinicians would often disagree about patients' diagnoses; Spitzer & Fliess, 1974). By including operational definitions of each disorder, it was hoped that the DSM-III system (and its successors DSM-III-R and DSM-IV) would solve the reliability problem, and its authors concluded that it had succeeded in this respect (Hyler, Williams & Spitzer, 1982). A more recent critical review of data on the DSM system has concluded that its reliability is, if anything, slightly poorer than that of some of the diagnostic systems it superseded (Kirk & Kutchins, 1992). This difficulty, alone, would impose limitations about what can be said about the relationship between psychiatric disorders and violence. However, at the heart of the system lies a series of assumptions that are even more problematic.

The DSM system, and indeed most other approaches to psychiatric classification, employ categorical diagnoses, so that mentally ill people are divided into a number of mutually exclusive diagnostic groupings. In addition to being criticised for poor reliability, such systems have been criticised on the grounds that they lack scientific validity. For example, if diagnoses are to be useful, the symptoms of each disorder should cluster together; that is, the presence of one symptom should lead to a high probability that others will be experienced. Factor analytic studies have convincingly shown that schizophrenic symptoms fall into at least three separate clusters: hallucinations and delusions, symptoms of cognitive disorganisation, and negative symptoms (Liddle, 1987). Studies of bipolar symptomatology have revealed a similar degree of complexity (Cassidy et al., 1998) and some investigators have proposed that the factors revealed overlap substantially with those found from schizophrenia patients (Toomey et al., 1998).

Useful diagnostic systems should also have predictive validity: on the basis of a patient's diagnosis it should be possible to predict important outcomes such as the probable course of the disorder and its likely response to treatment. If it is believed that psychosis plays a causal role in offending, this type of validity is required for an adequate assessment of the risk of future offences. Despite Kraepelin's pessimism about the course of schizophrenia, studies have shown that the long-term outcome is highly variable, with some patients remaining constantly ill, some experiencing a full recovery, and some experiencing a mixed or mildly chronic course (Ciompi, 1984). Although bipolar patients, on average, have a better outcome than schizophrenia patients, there is substantial overlap in the relative fates of the two groups (Kendell & Brockington, 1980). Response to drug treatment has proved equally difficult to predict on the basis of diagnosis. A study in which psychotic patients were randomly assigned to a neuroleptic medication (usually employed to treat schizophrenia), or lithium carbonate (usually employed to treat bipolar disorder), or to both, or to neither, found that drug response was unrelated to primary diagnosis but was predictable from symptoms—delusions and hallucinations tended to respond to the neuroleptic whereas mood symptoms tended to respond to lithium carbonate (Johnstone et al., 1988).

In the face of these difficulties, researchers have adopted a number of strategies. Some have advocated the progressive refinement of the categorical approach, resulting in further editions of the DSM system, with an ever-increasing number of disorders (including subdiagnoses, rising from 163 in DSM-III to 201 in DSM-IV (cf. Blashfield, 1996). Others, for example Crow (1991), have returned to the *einheitspsychose* or unitary psychosis concept advocated by some of Kraepelin's rivals (Berrios & Beer, 1995). Still others have argued that a dimensional approach to classification, perhaps based on Liddle's three-factor model, might be a way ahead (the authors of DSM-IV give this option some credence, but note that substantial research will be required before a consensus approach to dimensional classification can be achieved). A more radical approach, advocated mainly by psychologists, advocates the abandonment of classification in favour of focusing on symptoms (Bentall, Jackson & Pilgrim, 1988; Costello, 1992; Persons, 1986). On this view, patients' difficulties are best described by listing their symptoms rather than by assigning them to heterogeneous diagnostic groups. As we will see, such an approach lends itself to the exploration of the complex relationship between psychosis and violence.

PSYCHIATRIC DIAGNOSES AS PREDICTORS OF OFFENDING

Studies of the relationship between psychosis and offending were conducted even as Kraepelin's diagnostic system was being developed. Even to this day, one of the best documented case studies of violent homicide apparently caused by a psychotic illness was that of the German school teacher Ernst Wagner, who was the subject of an insightful analysis by the psychiatrist Robert Gaup (1914/1974, 1938/1974).

> Wagner killed his wife and four children on the night of 3rd/4th September 1913, slitting their throats as they slept. Travelling from his home in the village of Degerloch some distance to the village of Muhlhausen, on the following night he set fire to several houses and fired shots at the fleeing inhabitants, killing eight men before he was overpowered.
>
> Wagner's behaviour appeared to be entirely premeditated. Before embarking on his murderous spree, he had written letters of farewell to his friends, and a postcard to his landlady in Degerloch asking her to forgive him for the deeds he was about to commit. Subsequently discovered notes, poetry and diaries written over a number of years clearly described his intensions. On examination prior to his court hearing, Gaupp (1914/1974) found that Wagner had harboured a complex series of paranoid delusions, fuelled by sexual guilt. As a young man, he had consulted a doctor about his inability to control his masturbation, which he believed to be irreconcilable with his professional standing. Later, after taking up a post at Muhlhausen, and still unable to control the sexual urges which he thought so undesirable, he committed a series of sexual acts with animals. After marrying and moving to Degerloch he gradually came to believe that others knew about this behaviour. Determined to punish his imagined accusors from the village of Muhlhausen, he came to the conclusion that he must also murder his children because they might carry the germ of the sexual perversion that was his own undoing. At his trial, he was found to be not guilty of his crimes by reason of his insanity, and was sent to a psychiatric hospital. Wagner died in 1938, an enthusiastic supporter of the Nazi regime.

Although this kind of evidence appears to point compellingly to a causal link between psychosis and violence, most modern researchers have mistrusted case studies and have preferred to pursue statistical approaches. Unfortunately, statistical data can be as open to multiple interpretations as detailed case studies. In an influential review of research conducted prior to the early 1980s, Monahan and Steadman (1983) suggested that there was little if any relationship between violence and mental disorder. They argued that many studies that had appeared to point to an association between psychosis and offending had failed to pay attention to confounding demographic factors such as poverty and unemployment. According to Monaghan and Steadman, when these kinds of factors were taken into account, the apparent relationship between psychosis and violence disappeared.

Monaghan and Steadman's analysis highlighted methodological weaknesses in existing research, and set new standards for subsequent studies. However, such studies have not generally supported their conclusion that no link exists between psychosis and offending, and Monahan (1993) has since abandoned this position. One research strategy has involved comparing psychiatric and criminal records in the general population. Hodgins et al. (1996) examined psychiatric hospitalisations and violent offences committed prior to the age of 43 years in an unselected Danish birth cohort of over 300,000 people. They found that a history of hospitalisation resulted in a 3–11 times increased probability of having a criminal conviction for violent and non-violent offences. A second strategy has focused on particular types of offences. For example, Eronen, Hakola and Tiihonen (1996) examined 700 Finish homicide offenders who accounted for almost 70% of all known homicides carried out in that country in a seven-year period. They concluded that homicidal violence was substantially higher among men and women with a diagnosis of schizophrenia, anti-social personality disorder and alcoholism.

One limitation of these studies is that they have relied on psychiatric diagnoses and arrest or conviction data. It is known that many people with psychotic symptoms do not seek or receive psychiatric treatment (Tien, 1991; Verdoux et al., 1998). Moreover, arrests and convictions may severely under-represent the frequency with which anti-social or dangerous behaviour actually occurs. An important investigation that attempted to overcome these difficulties was carried out by Swanson et al. (1990) using data from the Epidemiologic Catchment Area (ECA) study (Robins & Locke, 1991). In the ECA, over 18,000 US citizens in five catchment areas were randomly selected for a diagnostic interview, and more than 15,000 were reinterviewed one year later. The participants in the study were also asked to report acts of violence that they had committed. The findings indicated that the incidence of violence among people who met the DSM-III diagnostic criteria for serious mental disorders such as schizophrenia or bipolar disorder was five times higher than the incidence among people without a mental disorder. Interestingly, an even stronger association was noted between substance abuse and violence. The results from this study are particularly important because of the absence of bias in the sample, which was obtained from the general population.

The importance of not relying on criminal records was confirmed by Link, Andrews and Cullen (1992), who compared arrest rates and self-report violence in a number of patient groups and a sample of adults who had no involvement with psychiatric services. They found that there were higher rates of violence among the patient groups. Controlling for potentially confounding factors such as socio-economic status, ethnicity, residential mobility and even local homicide rates did not affect this difference. However, controlling for psychotic symptoms both in the patients and the never-treated community residents eliminated the group differences in rates of violence, suggesting a close association between symptoms and violent behaviour. Despite this observation, Link and Steuve caution that the association may not simply be causal. For example, fearful and mistrustful reactions to psychotic symptoms by ordinary people may in turn trigger the violent acts by the psychotic individual. Moreover, it is possible that people who experience psychotic symptoms are more likely to receive psychiatric treatment if they also have a history of violence.

Whereas epidemiological studies and studies of individuals who have committed particular kinds of offences point to an association between psychosis and violence, studies comparing recidivism rates in mentally ill and mentally well offenders tell a different story. For example, Rice and Harris (1992) compared schizophrenic and non-schizophrenic offenders and observed no evidence that the schizophrenic group was more dangerous. They found that, among their schizophrenic group, those who were seriously disturbed at the time of the offence were no more likely to commit another offence upon release than those who were less disturbed. Their schizophrenic group as a whole were less likely to commit any offence upon release than their non-schizophrenic counterparts. Rice and Harris subsequently developed an actuarial instrument, the Violence Risk Appraisal Guide (VRAG), for assessing both violent offenders and also forensic psychiatric patients (Harris, Rice & Quinsey, 1993; Rice & Harris, 1995). Again, a diagnosis of schizophrenia was found to be negatively correlated with violent recidivism among both groups.

These observations were recently borne out in a meta-analysis carried out by Bonta, Law and Hanson (1998) who attempted to establish the relative importance of criminological and clinical predictors of recidivism. Like Monahan and Steadman (1983) before them, Bonta and colleagues argued that persistent offending in mentally ill offenders might be a product of the same criminogenic social and demographic factors that predict recidivism in non-mentally ill offenders. Data from a total of 64 studies were included in their analysis. Consistent with previous studies of non-mentally ill offenders, Bonta and co-workers found that the biggest predictor of further offending in mentally disordered offenders was a criminal history. Other social and criminological variables, including juvenile delinquency, family problems, poor living arrangements and substance abuse, were also shown to be important predictors of future offending. However, the only clinical variable that strongly predicted re-offending was a diagnosis of anti-social personality disorder; other clinical variables, including a diagnosis of psychosis, were *negatively* associated with future offending.

These findings are not as inconsistent with some of the other research we have considered as they might at first appear because of the different samples studied. For example, Swanson et al. (1990) studied ECA data to determine whether, in a random population sample, psychosis was associated with violence, whereas, as we have seen, the analysis of Bonta and co-workers focused specifically on disordered offenders. The apparent inconsistency is therefore resolved when it is recognised that psychotic patients appear to have a higher rate of offending than the general population, but a lower rate of offending when compared with non-mentally disordered offenders.

In comparison with studies of the relationship between psychosis and violence, far less attention has been paid to possible associations between psychosis and sexual offending, and research in this area has tended to consist of case studies (for example, Criassati & Hodes, 1993; Huckle & Jones, 1993). In an earlier review of the literature, Chiswick (1983) concluded that only a small number of sex offenders suffer from a mental illness. This observation was supported by a study conducted by Henn, Herjac and Vanderpearl (1976), who examined records of 239 individuals charged with sexual offences, and found that serious mental illness was very rare among those who had been charged with rape and those who had offended against children. Noting that sexual factors often play a role in violent offences, Taylor (1985) suggested that researchers may have underestimated the association between psychosis and sexual offending. However, more studies will be required before this supposition can be substantiated.

THE SYMPTOM APPROACH

Although there appears to be a modest association between psychosis and offending that cannot be attributed to social and demographic variables, it is not immediately obvious why psychotic illness leads to violent actions in a minority of patients. In our review of the problems associated with psychiatric diagnoses we noted that many modern researchers have abandoned broad diagnostic categories in favour of research focusing on symptoms. Although the main advantage of this approach is that it avoids disputes about diagnosis, a further advantage is that it is helps to clarify the relationship between psychosis and anti-social behaviour.

Studies that have focused on the association between delusions and violence have yielded evidence that is strikingly consistent with Gaupp's analysis of the Wagner case. In comparing psychotic patients who had committed murder and those without a history of violence, Hafner and Boker (1982) observed that delusions were significantly more prevalent in the homicidal group, even though delusions were a common symptom in the sample as a whole. In an analysis of data collected from patients' case records, Hafner and Boker further found that the delusions of violent offenders were more often systematic (that is, logically organised around a coherent theme) than the delusions of non-offending psychotic patients. Most of the violent patients were described in the records as being in a delusional relationship with their victims, whom they often regarded as enemies. However, violent actions seemed to be directly triggered by delusional interpretations in only a minority of cases.

Taylor (1993) found that passivity delusions, especially those implicating paranormal influences, religion and external factors such as X-rays, were associated with violent "acting out". Buchanan et al. (1993) interviewed 83 psychotic patients within one month of admission to hospital using a schedule for the assessment of delusional beliefs. Informants who had observed the patients' behaviour were also questioned. The majority of the patients reported at least one delusional action, and 20% reported three or more. Persecutory delusions were more likely to be acted on than any other kind of delusional belief. In a further study using the same approach, Taylor et al. (1994) found that patients who had actively sought evidence to support their delusional beliefs were most likely to act on them.

These findings have been broadly supported by more recent studies. For example, Nestor et al. (1995) found that psychotic individuals with organised delusions involving personal and accessible targets were especially likely to commit either lethal or near lethal acts. Estroff et al. (1994) and Grossman et al. (1995) found that paranoid symptoms are associated with violent behaviour. Straznickas, McNiel and Binder (1993) have suggested that patients who have persecutory delusions sometimes resort to violence in order to protect them-selves against perceived threats. Similarly, Junginger (1996) proposed that violent behaviour is often a rational response to patients' irrational beliefs or percep-tions. This hypothesis receives some support from a study by Whittington and Wykes (1996), who examined acts of violence carried out by psychiatric in-patients. They found that violent incidents tended to occur when patients ex-perienced aversive interactions with others.

Other studies have focused on hallucinations, especially command hallucina-tions in which a hallucinated voice or voices tells the patient to carry out some kind of anti-social act. Rogers et al. (1990) observed that the content of command hallucinations often involves aggression, dependency and self-punishment. They found that 43% of all forensic referrals with auditory hallucinations reported experiencing command hallucinations related to their offending. Nonetheless, in a study of cases of legal insanity in the USA, Thompson, Gregory and Holden (1992) found that, although command hallucinations appeared to be over-represented in this population, they were rarely directly implicated in offences. Indeed, those who experienced command hallucinations were significantly less likely to commit violent offences than other individuals who had been found not guilty by reason of insanity. Consistent with this finding, Honig (1991) observed that most patients who experience command hallucinations are able to ignore them, but that repetitive commands that occur over an extended period can increase the likelihood that the patient will comply with them.

Command hallucinations have also been implicated in sexual offences. For example, Jones, Huckle and Tanaghow (1992) have described four case studies in which attacks on adult women were attributed to hallucinated voices. Impor-tantly, they concluded that in the absence of thorough mental state assessments, the sexual assaults might have been attributed to personality factors or sexual deviance.

In an attempt to identify predictors of compliance with command hallucina-tions, Junginger (1990) assessed the most recent command hallucinations of 51 psychiatric in-patients and out-patients. He found that patients who reported hallucination-related delusions and who could assign an identity to their voices were especially likely to respond to a hallucinated command. In a further study, Junginger (1995) asked independent judges to estimate both dangerousness and level of compliance with command hallucinations in a sample of 93 patients. Twenty-seven out of 59 (46%) patients reported partial compliance with com-mands judged to be either somewhat or very dangerous, and 11 out of 47 (23%) reported full compliance with very dangerous commands.

One psychotic symptom that does not appear to be implicated in aggressive behaviour is thought disorder. Hafner and Boker's (1982) observation of sig-nificantly more thought disorder among violent than non-violent subjects diag-nosed with schizophrenia has not been replicated. For example, Gardner et al. (1996) found that the presence of thought disorder was negatively associated with violence.

Some investigators have suggested that associations between symptoms and violence might be clarified by paying more attention to symptom content. Link and Stueve (1994) expounded the principle of "rationality-within-irrationality" according to which the apparent irrationality of psychotic symptoms should be ignored; once it is accepted that symptoms are experienced as real by the patient, violent behaviour can be regarded as a rational consequence of the symptoms. (This principle is similar to the approach advocated by Straznickas, McNiel and Binder, 1993, and Junginger, 1996, described above.) This principle enabled Link and his colleagues to make predictions about violence in the context of particular kinds of psychotic experience. They argued that experiences involving a loss of self-control (for example, thought insertion) would lead to a loss of self-imposed constraints on behaviour and a consequent increase in the probability of violent acts. In contrast, they argued that experiences that do not involve intrusion or threatening forces (for example, positive hallucinations) should be associated with a relatively low probability of violent behaviour. Link and his colleagues therefore divided psychotic symptoms into two groups: threat/control override (TCO) symptoms and others.

On testing this hypothesis, Link and Stueve (1994) discovered that TCO symptoms were not only significantly correlated with violence in a psychiatric group but also in a non-psychiatric control group. In an attempt to clarify the role of TCO symptoms, Swanson (1996) carried out a further analysis of the Epidemiological Catchment Area (ECA) data. Their findings supported those of Link and Stueve. Specifically, they found that individuals who reported that they had felt threatened by others and unable to have control over their own thoughts in the past year were twice as likely to have been violent during that period than those who had reported other psychotic symptoms such as non-TCO hallucinations and delusions.

Overall, these findings are fairly consistent, and suggest that certain types of symptoms, especially delusions and hallucinations with TCO content, should be of particular concern to clinicians assessing the risk of violent offending. However, it is important to note one important limitation of some of these studies: it is possible that some offenders implicate psychotic symptoms, especially command hallucinations, in their offences as a strategy for mitigating their own guilt. Pollock (1998) has recently argued that as many as 33% of prisoners referred to forensic mental health services may be malingering.

SYMPTOMS IN CONTEXT

The study by Swanson et al. (1996) highlighted the importance of considering psychotic symptoms in the context of other factors. They found that a combination of substance abuse and TCO symptoms very strongly predicted future violence. The significance of this observation is indicated by other studies that have shown that substance abuse and psychotic illness often occur together. Abram (1989) found that, among a group of city jail detainees who had a psychotic illness, 84.8% were reported to be alcohol dependent and 57.9% drug dependent.

Other studies by Drake et al. (1993) and Owen et al. (1996) similarly found that substance abuse is common among patients with severe mental illness. Swanson et al. (1996) suggested that psychotic states and drug intoxication may alter the individual's perceptions, impair cognitive processes and perhaps impede impulse control. They also proposed four pathways by which substance abuse may make an indirect contribution to aggressive behaviour in psychotic patients: first, by influencing the development of co-morbid anti-social personality disorder early in life; second, by exacerbating psychotic symptoms; third, by introducing patients to hostile and unsafe social environments; and, finally, by causing non-compliance with drug treatments and services.

The question of co-morbid personality disorder is also important when assessing the relative contribution that psychotic symptoms make to the commission of violence. Research by Mbatia and Tyrer (1988) indicated that 56% of a sample of mentally ill patients in an English special hospital met criteria for personality disorder. Similarly, Rasmussen and Levander (1996) found that a third of schizophrenic offenders in a Norwegian secure hospital met the criteria for a diagnosis of anti-social personality disorder. Given the well-established link between anti-social personality disorder and violence (Hare, McPherson & Forth, 1988; Harris, Rice & Cormier, 1991), such findings have obvious implications for risk assessment with this group.

These analyses suggests that, even when a clear link between psychotic symptoms and offending can be established, the underlying causal relationships may be highly complex. Other researchers have suggested further causal pathways that might be involved. Drawing from work by Kessler and Magee (1994) and Winfield et al. (1990), Hiday (1995) has noted that many people with a mental illness have also been victims of violence. She suggests that these experiences result in feelings of fear and suspicion which, in turn, may have impacted on their mental state and later behaviour. Taylor (1993) observed that psychotic offenders were noticeably lacking in empathy for their victims, and suggested that this deficit may have played a role in their offences.

CONCLUSIONS

Overall, the evidence we have considered suggests that much of the violent behaviour attributed to psychotic persons can be explained by the same factors that determine anti-social behaviour by people who are mentally well. Nonetheless, when these factors are taken into account, there appears to be a small increased risk of violence associated with psychosis. There is relatively good evidence that this small increased risk is in part attributable to paranoid delusions, and suggestive evidence that command hallucinations may also play an occasional role in violent offences. The evidence linking psychosis to sexual offending is less impressive, but this topic has been almost totally ignored by researchers.

The observations have different implications for different interest groups. The research certainly does not support the more extreme fears experienced by some members of the general public and fostered by media reports. On the basis of the evidence, an ordinary member of the public would be safer living next to a psychiatric patient than living next to a mentally well person with a criminal history. Indeed, the evidence suggests that it would be safer to live next to a mentally disordered *offender* than to a mentally well person who had committed similar offences.

With regard to mental health professionals, the evidence suggests that psychiatric diagnoses have little value for assessing the risk that a psychiatric patient will commit offences in the future. Much of the work on risk prediction in the field of forensic mental health has been based primarily on clinical judgement. This approach has been heavily criticised by authors, such as Mossman (1994), who advocate the use of actuarial methods based on criminogenic factors and have illustrated their superiority over clinical methods in a meta-analysis of studies which have focused on the prediction of violence. Similarly, Gendreau, Little and Goggin (1996) found that objective risk assessment was better in terms of predictive validity than clinical risk assessments of dangerousness.

The danger of relying entirely on actuarial assessment methods is highlighted by the Blackburn (1993) comment that "an apparent lack of a relationship at the aggregate level does not preclude significant relationships at the individual level". It is at this individual level that most clinicians are operating and where the difficulty of accurate risk prediction is most acutely felt. However, even when attempting an individual formulation of the events leading to an offence, the astute clinician will not assume that the patient's behaviour can be entirely attributed to illness factors. Indeed, it is important to remember that symptoms usually do not provoke acts of violence and that, when they do, other factors are always involved.

REFERENCES

Abram, K.M. (1989) The effect of co-occurring disorders on criminal careers: Interaction of antisocial personality, alcoholism and drug disorders. *International Journal of Law and Psychiatry*, **12**, 133–148.

American Psychiatric Association (1980) *Diagnostic and Statistical Manual of Mental Disorders* (3rd edn). Washington, DC: American Psychiatric Association.

Appleby, L. & Wessely, S. (1988) The influence of the Hungerford massacre on the public opinion of mental illness. *Medicine, Science and Law*, **28**, 291–295.

Bentall, R.P. (1998) Why there will never be a convincing theory of schizophrenia. In S. Rose (Ed.) *From Brains to Consciousness*. London: Penguin.

Bentall, R.P., Jackson, H.F. & Pilgrim, D. (1988) Abandoning the concept of schizophrenia: Some implications of validity arguments for psychological research into psychotic phenomena. *British Journal of Clinical Psychology*, **27**, 303–324.

Berrios, G. & Hauser, R. (1988) The early development of Kraepelin's ideas on classification: A conceptual history. *Psychological Medicine*, **18**, 813–821.

Berrios, G.E. & Beer, D. (1995) Unitary psychosis concept. In G. Berrios & R. Porter (Eds) *A History of Clinical Psychiatry*. London: Athlone Press.

Blackburn, R. (1993) *The Psychology of Criminal Conduct: Theory, Research and Practice.* Chichester: Wiley.

Blashfield, R.K. (1996) Predicting DSM-V. *Journal of Nervous and Mental Disease,* **184**, 4–7.

Bleuler, E. (1911/1950) *Dementia Praecox or the Group of Schizophrenias* (Trans. E. Zinkin). New York: International Universities Press.

Bonta, J., Law, M. & Hanson, K. (1998) The prediction of criminal and violent recidivism among mentally disordered offenders. *Psychological Bulletin,* **123**, 123–142.

Buchanan, A., Reed, A., Wessely, S., Garety, P., Taylor, P., Grubin, D. & Dunn, G. (1993) Acting on delusions II: The phenomenological correlates of acting on delusions. *British Journal of Psychiatry,* **163**, 77–81.

Cassidy, F., Forest, K., Murry, M. & Carroll, B.J. (1998) A factor analysis of the signs and symptoms of mania. *Archives of General Psychiatry,* **55**, 27–32.

Chiswick, D. (1983) Sex crimes. *British Journal of Psychiatry,* **143**, 236–242.

Ciompi, L. (1984) Is there really a schizophrenia? The long term course of psychotic phenomena. *British Journal of Psychiatry,* **145**, 636–640.

Costello, C.G. (1992) Research on symptoms versus research on syndromes: Arguments in favour of allocating more research time to the study of symptoms. *British Journal of Psychiatry,* **160**, 304–308.

Criassati, J. & Hodes, P. (1993) Mentally ill sex offenders. *British Journal of Psychiatry,* **161**, 846–849.

Crow, T. (1991) The failure of the binary concept and the psychosis gene. In A. Kerr & H. McClelland (Eds) *Concepts of Mental Disorder: A Continuing Debate.* London: Gaskell.

Davis, S. (1991) Violence by psychiatric inpatients: A review. *Hospital and Community Psychiatry,* **42**, 585–590.

Drake, R.E., Bartels, S.J., Teague, G.B., Noordsy, D.L. & Clark, R.E. (1993) Treatment of substance abuse in severely mentally ill patients. *Journal of Nervous and Mental Disease,* **181**, 606–611.

Eronen, M., Hakola, P. & Tiihonen, J. (1996) Mental disorders and homicidal behavior in Finland. *Archives of General Psychiatry,* **53**, 497–501.

Estroff, S., Zimmer, C., Lachicotte, W. & Benoit, J. (1994) The influence of social networks and social support on violence by persons with serious mental illness. *Hospital and Community Psychiatry,* **45**, 669–679.

Gardner, W., Lidz, C.W., Mulvey, E.P. & Shaw, E.C. (1996) Clinical versus actuarial predictions of violence in patients with mental illness. *Journal of Consulting and Clinical Psychology,* **64**, 602–609.

Gaupp, R. (1914/1974) The scientific significance of the case of Ernst Wagner. In S.R. Hirsch & M. Shepherd (Eds) *Themes and Variations in European Psychiatry: An Anthology.* Bristol: Wright.

Gaupp, R. (1938/1974) The illness and death of the paranoid mass murderer, schoolmaster Wagner: A case history. In S.R. Hirsch & M. Shepherd (Eds) *Themes and Variations in European Psychiatry: An Anthology.* Bristol: Wright.

Gendreau, P., Little, T. & Goggin, C. (1996) A meta-analysis of the predictors of adult offender recidivism: What works! *Criminology,* **34**, 575–607.

Grossman, L.S., Haywood, T.W., Cavanaugh, J.L., Davis, J.M. & Lewis, D.A. (1995) State hospital patients with past arrests for violent crime. *Psychiatric Services,* **46**, 790–795.

Hafner, H. & Boker, W. (1982) *Crimes of Violence by Mentally Abnormal Offenders: A Psychiatric and Epidemiological Study in the Federal Republic of Germany* (trans. H. Marshall) Cambridge: Cambridge University Press.

Hare, R.D., McPherson, L.M. & Forth, A.E. (1988) Male psychopaths and their criminal careers. *Journal of Consulting and Clinical Psychology,* **56**, 710–714.

Harris, G.T., Rice, M.E. & Cormier, C.A. (1991) Psychopathy and violent recidivism. *Law and Human Behaviour,* **15**, 625–637.

Harris, G.T., Rice, M.E. & Quinsey, V.L. (1993) Violent recidivism of mentally disordered offenders: The development of a statistical prediction instrument. *Criminal Justice and Behavior*, **20**, 315–335.

Henn, F., Herjac, M. & Vanderpearl, R.H. (1976) Forensic psychiatry: Profiles of two types of sex offenders. *American Journal of Psychiatry*, **133**, 694–696.

Hiday, V.A. (1995) The social context of mental illness and violence. *Journal of Health and Social Behaviour*, **36**, 122–137.

Hodgins, S., Mednick, S.A., Brennan, P.A., Schulsinger, F. & Engberg, M. (1996) Mental disorder and crime: Evidence from a Danish birth cohort. *Archives of General Psychiatry*, **53**, 489–496.

Honig, A. (1991) Psychotherapy with command hallucinations in chronic schizophrenia: The use of action techniques within a surrogate family setting. *Journal of Group Psychotherapy, Psychodrama and Sociometry*, **44**, 3–18.

Huckle, P.L. & Jones, G.H. (1993) Mentally ill sex offenders. *British Journal of Psychiatry*, **162**, 568.

Hyler, S., Williams, J. & Spitzer, R. (1982) Reliability in the DSM-III field trials. *Archives of General Psychiatry*, **39**, 1275–1278.

Johnstone, E.C., Crow, T.J., Frith, C.D. & Owens, D.G.C. (1988) The Northwick Park "functional" psychosis study: Diagnosis and treatment response. *Lancet*, **ii**, 119–125.

Jones, G., Huckle, P. & Tanaghow, A. (1992) Command hallucinations, schizophrenia and sexual assaults. *Irish Journal of Psychological Medicine*, **9**, 47–49.

Junginger, J. (1990) Predicting compliance with command hallucinations. *American Journal of Psychiatry*, **147**, 245–247.

Junginger, J. (1995) Command hallucinations and the prediction of dangerousness. *Psychiatric Services*, **46**, 911–914.

Junginger, J. (1996) Psychosis and violence: The case for a content analysis of psychotic symptoms. *Schizophrenia Bulletin*, **22**, 91–103.

Kendell, R.E. & Brockington, I.F. (1980) The identification of disease entities and the relationship between schizophrenic and affective psychoses. *British Journal of Psychiatry*, **137**, 324–331.

Kesslet, R.C. & Magee, W.J. (1994) Childhood family violence and adult recurrent depression. *Journal of Health and Social Behaviour*, **35**(1), 13–27.

Kirk, S.A. & Kutchins, H. (1992) *The Selling of DSM: The Rhetoric of Science in Psychiatry*. Hawthorne, NY: Aldine de Gruyter.

Klerman, G.L. (1978) The evolution of a scientific nosology. In J.C. Shershow (Ed.) *Schizophrenia: Science and Practice*. Cambridge, MA: Harvard University Press.

Leonhard, K. (1957/1979) *The Classification of Endogenous Psychoses* (trans. R. Berman). New York: Irvington.

Liddle, P.F. (1987) The symptoms of chronic schizophrenia: A reexamination of the positive-negative dichotomy. *British Journal of Psychiatry*, **151**, 145–151.

Link, B.G., Andrews, H.A. & Cullen, F.T. (1992) The violent and illegal behavior of mental patients reconsidered. *American Sociological Review*, **57**, 275–292.

Link, B.G. & Stueve, A. (1994) Psychotic symptoms and the violent/illegal behaviour of mental patients compared to community controls. In J. Monahan & H.J. Steadman (Eds) *Violence and Mental Disorder: Developments in Risk Assessment*. Chicago: Chicago University Press.

Marzuk, P.N. (1996) Violence, crime and mental illness: How strong the link? *Archives of General Psychiatry*, **53**, 481–486.

Mbatia, J. & Tyrer, P. (1988) Personality status of dangerous patients in a special hospital. In P. Tyrer (Ed.) *Personality Disorders: Diagnosis, Management and Course*. London: Wright.

Monahan, J. (1993) Mental disorder and violence: Another look. In S. Hodgins (Ed.) *Mental Disorder and Crime*. Newbury Park, CA: Sage.

Monahan, J. & Steadman, H.J. (1983) Crime and mental disorder: An epidemiological approach. In M. Tonry & N. Morris (Eds) *Crime and Justice: An Annual Review of Research.* Chicago: Chicago University Press.

Mossman, D. (1994) Assessing predictors of violence: Being accurate about accuracy. *Journal of Consulting and Clinical Psychology,* **62**, 783–792.

Nestor, P.G., Haycock, J., Doiron, S., Kelly, J. & Kelly, D. (1995) Lethal violence and psychosis. *Bulletin of the American Academy of Psychiatry and Law,* **23**, 331–341.

Owen, R.O., Fischer, E.P., Booth, B.M. & Cuffel, B.J. (1996) Medication noncompliance and substance abuse among patients with schizophrenia. *Psychiatric Services,* **47**, 853–858.

Persons, J. (1986) The advantages of studying psychological phenomena rather than psychiatric diagnoses. *American Psychologist,* **41**, 1252–1260.

Philo, G., Secker, J., Platt, S., Henderson, L., McLaughlin, G. & Burnside, J. (1994) The impact of the mass media on public images of mental illness: Media content and audience belief. *Health Education Journal,* **53**, 271–282.

Pollock, P. (1998) Feigning auditory hallucinations by offenders. *Journal of Forensic Psychiatry,* **9**, 305–327.

Rasmussen, K. & Levander, S. (1996) Symptoms and personality characteristics of patients in a maximum security unit. *International Journal of Law and Psychiatry,* **19**, 27–37.

Rice, M.E. & Harris, G.T. (1992) A comparison of criminal recidivism among schizophrenic and non-schizophrenic offenders. *International Journal of Law and Psychiatry,* **15**, 387–408.

Rice, M.E. & Harris, G.T. (1995) Violent recidivism: Assessing predictive validity. *Journal of Consulting and Clinical Psychology,* **63**, 737–748.

Rieder, O. (1974) The origin of our confusion about schizophrenia. *Psychiatry,* **37**, 197–208.

Robins, L.N. & Locke, B.Z. (Eds) (1991) *Psychiatric Disorders in America.* New York: Free Press.

Rogers, R., Gillis, J., Turner, E.R. & Frise-Smith, T. (1990) The clinical presentation of command hallucinations in a forensic population. *American Journal of Psychiatry,* **147**, 1304–1307.

Schneider, K. (1959) *Clinical Psychopathology.* New York: Grune & Stratton.

Spitzer, R.L. & Fliess, J.L. (1974) A reanalysis of the reliability of psychiatric diagnosis. *British Journal of Psychiatry,* **123**, 341–347.

Straznickas, K., McNiel, D. & Binder, R. (1993) Violence towards family caregivers by mentally ill relatives. *Hospital and Community Psychiatry,* **44**, 385–387.

Swanson, J.W., Borum, R., Swartz, M.S. & Monahan, J. (1996) Psychotic symptoms and disorders and the risk of violent behaviour. *Criminal Behaviour and Mental Health,* **6**, 309–329.

Swanson, J.W., Holzer, C.E., Ganju, V.K. & Jono, R.T. (1990) Violence and psychiatric disorder in the community: Evidence from the Epidemiological Catchment Area surveys. *Hospital and Community Psychiatry,* **41**, 761–770.

Taylor, P. (1985) Motives for offending among violent and psychotic men. *British Journal of Psychiatry,* **147**, 491–498.

Taylor, P.J. (1993) Schizophrenia and crime: Distinctive patterns in association. In S. Hodgins (Ed.) *Crime and Mental Disorder.* Newbury Park, CA: Sage.

Taylor, P.J., Garety, P., Buchanan, A., Reed, A., Wessely, S., Ray, K., Dunn, G. & Grubin, D. (1994) Delusions and violence. In J. Monahan & H.J. Steadman (Eds) *Violence and Mental Disorder: Developments in Risk Assessment.* Chicago: Chicago University Press.

Thompson, J.S., Gregory, S.L. & Holden, C.E. (1992) Command hallucinations and legal insanity. *Forensic Reports,* **5**, 29–43.

Tien, A.Y. (1991) Distribution of hallucinations in the population. *Social Psychiatry and Psychiatric Epidemiology,* **26**, 287–292.

Toomey, R., Faraone, S.V., Simpson, J.C. & Tsuang, M.T. (1998) Negative, positive and disorganized symptom dimensions in schizophrenia, major depression and bipolar disorder. *Journal of Nervous and Mental Disease*, **186**, 470–476.

Verdoux, H., Maurice-Tison, S., Gay, B., Van Os, J., Salamon, R. & Bourgeois, M.L. (1998) A survey of delusional ideation in primary-care patients. *Psychological Medicine*, **28**, 127–134.

Whittington, R. & Wykes, T. (1996) Aversive stimulation by staff and violence by psychiatric inpatients. *British Journal of Clinical Psychology*, **35**, 11–20.

Winfield, I., George, L.T., Swartz, M. & Blazer, D.G. (1990) Sexual assault and psychiatric disorders among a community sample of women. *American Journal of Psychiatry*, **147**(3), 335–341.

Chapter 9

Risk Assessment and Prediction

Ron Blackburn
Department of Clinical Psychology, University of Liverpool, UK

INTRODUCTION

Appraising risk is universal in human decision-making. Insurers, bankers, medical practitioners and engineers frequently require explicit risk estimates to guide their decisions, but risk evaluation is also implicit in more mundane activities such as buying a car. Risk generally refers to the possibility of loss or costs when an outcome is uncertain, but in clinical and criminal justice settings, it means *the chance of an adverse outcome*. Undesired outcomes of decisions about individuals made by legal bodies or institutional staff can include re-offending, clinical relapse, disruptive behaviour, or suicide. The focus here, however, is on the risk of serious harm to others.

The judgement that a person may harm others influences legal decisions at several points in criminal and civil justice proceedings, such as bail, sentencing, parole, the release of mentally disordered offenders, and child custody hearings (Shah, 1978). Assessment of risk has traditionally been the province of psychiatrists and psychologists, from whom legal bodies require clinical judgements of dangerousness. However, risk assessments are increasingly made by other professionals for purposes of institutional or community management, and are not confined to work with offenders.

The task of assessing potential for serious harm is intrinsically difficult and subject to error, and despite a voluminous literature, there is no agreed set of procedures. Nevertheless, research on the evaluation and prediction of violence has produced a clearer understanding of the risk assessment process and ways of reducing decision errors. This chapter describes how risk assessment

Behaviour, Crime and Legal Processes: A Guide for Forensic Practitioners.
Edited by James McGuire, Tom Mason and Aisling O'Kane.
© 2000 John Wiley & Sons Ltd.

and prediction are studied, summarises research on the prediction of violence, and examines recent attempts to develop more effective and defensible risk assessments.

THE RISK ASSESSMENT TASK

Risk assessment is the process of determining an individual's potential for harmful behaviour. It entails consideration of a broad array of factors related to the person, the situation, and their interaction (Megargee, 1976; Monahan & Steadman, 1994; Mulvey & Lidz, 1984; Pollock, McBain & Webster, 1989). The clinician constructs a tentative model of the person assessed, forms hypotheses, and gathers information to test these. An estimate of risk follows from the identification of past or current risk characteristics, the strength of these tendencies, and known future circumstances.

Recent discussions emphasise that the purpose of risk assessment is not simply to predict future harm, and that the goal is *risk management*, i.e. interventions to reduce or minimise risk (Douglas, Cox & Webster, 1999; Hart, 1998; Monahan & Steadman, 1994; Quinsey & Walker, 1992). The assessor's role, however, is often limited to providing advice to legal bodies who decide future management. Nevertheless, there is agreement that assessors should specify not only the likelihood of harmful behaviour, but also the conditions that may increase or mitigate risk and the time frame for which the estimate is made. Risk evaluations should also be reviewed regularly.

Dangerousness and Violence

The term "risk assessment" is now preferred to the traditional notion of *prediction of dangerousness*. Dangerousness denotes a potential to cause harm and may describe acts, situations, or persons. Because a potential refers to a *current* or ongoing characteristic, not a future predictable event, it is not very meaningful to talk of the *prediction* of dangerousness. "Dangerousness" also attracts the objection that it is a vague dispositional concept not referring to specific behaviour (Monahan, 1981). However, risk assessment cannot avoid reference to dispositions, and problems of vagueness are not entirely overcome by focusing on "serious harm" or "violence".

The appropriate focus of risk assessment is usually seen as the prediction of dangerous or endangering *behaviour*, which is equated with *violence* (Grisso, 1996; Megargee, 1976; Monahan, 1981; Shah, 1978). Shah (1978), for example, defines dangerous behaviour as "... acts characterised by the application of or overt threat of force and that are likely to result in injury to other persons" (p. 224). He notes that this encompasses the events considered to be crimes of violence in law, notably actual or attempted murder, aggravated assault, forcible rape, and robbery, and excludes criminal acts not resulting in injury, such as arson, making threats, or carrying weapons.

Dangerous behaviour and violence are not, however, synonymous (Mulvey & Lidz, 1984). Violent acts are usually considered dangerous, but not all dangerous acts are violent, for example drunken driving. Recent definitions of violence have also been broadened to include verbal threats and "fear-inducing behaviours", such as stalking (Douglas, Cox & Webster, 1999; Otto, 1992; Webster et al., 1997). It is argued that this accords with recent legal concepts of dangerous behaviour. However, broadening the definition of violence to include non-physical harm increases problems of unreliability and vagueness.

Contact between legal concepts of harm and the scientific literature would be better maintained by referring to *aggression*, and by distinguishing harmful behaviours in terms of their form, motivation, type of victim, or level of seriousness. For example, different predictors distinguish physical from verbal aggression (Kay, Wolkenfeld & Murrill, 1988), and victims of psychotic patients in the community are more likely to be family members than strangers (Steadman et al., 1998). Much of the research on the prediction of violence fails to make such distinctions, but it should be clear that the term "violence" is often a global catch-all covering a variety of harmful acts. Clinicians should be aware of the limits to generalising from research findings with populations decribed as "violent" to the individual being assessed.

Dispositions and Prediction

Risk estimates are commonly characterised as predictions, but a prediction of future violence follows from the evaluation of a person's *potential* for such behaviour. Evaluation therefore has two components, the judgement that a person has the potential and the estimate of the behaviour occurring. This raises questions not only about what is being predicted but also about what *can* be predicted.

A potential refers to a disposition or tendency, and dispositional concepts are implicit "if . . . then" predictions. The "if" refers to the conditions under which the potential will be realised as an act. For example, a sex offender may be said to be "likely to assault children" because of past offences when drunk, continuing sexual interests in children, and failure to respond to treatment. The description implies that *if* he experiences stress and has access both to alcohol and children, it is probable that he will commit a sexual assault. But the probability of these conditions occurring is not the same as the probability that the person has a harmful disposition. It is, for example, one thing to identify a substance as having the disposition "soluble in water", but quite another to predict the likelihood of its getting wet.

The "prediction" of future violence may therefore often be no more than an elaboration of a dispositional description. While discussions of the prediction of violence appear to assume that clinicians are forecasting an outcome, they may in practice be judging only the probability or strength of a person's tendencies (Gordon, 1977). As Litwack and Schlesinger (1987, p. 233) observe, ". . . it is . . . a mistake to expect them (clinicians) to prophesize a definite future event rather than merely to describe a behavioural tendency, propensity, or proclivity . . .". Gordon (1977) notes that dispositional concepts are *stochastic*, i.e. they imply an element of chance or randomness in behaviour, and many violent acts are the result of a fortuitous coming together of circumstances which could not have been predicted in advance (Holland, Holt & Beckett, 1982). This does not mean that estimates of future violence are not possible, but it emphasises the inevitability of errors. Gordon argues that it is unrealistic to expect correlations between risk estimates and outcomes higher than 0.5.

If statements of the likelihood of future violence are conditional probabilities derived from knowledge of the person's current potential, clinicians will rarely be able to give a precise estimate for an individual. Although some writers urge that risk estimates should be communicated as probabilistic statements (Grisso & Appelbaum, 1992), precise estimates are feasible only with statistical prediction methods in which probabilities are known for different classes of offender. Estimates using broad categories of "low", "moderate", "high", and "imminent" are more realistic for clinical practice (Douglas, Cox & Webster, 1999).

THE STUDY OF RISK ASSESSMENT AND PREDICTION

A Conceptual Framework

Risk assessment practices need to build on research findings. Some research examines the accuracy of clinical judgements or how decision-makers use information. Other work seeks to identify predictive factors in the background and characteristics of violent people to determine reliable indicators of future violence. Relationships between the variables of interest can be conveniently organised within an adaptation of the "lens model" developed by Brunswik (1956) for the study of human judgement (Grisso, 1996; Monahan & Steadman, 1994).

Figure 9.1 identifies three sets of variables. *Cues* or *risk factors* are the variables that indicate violence. They may be features of the person's history (e.g. violent crimes), current personal characteristics (e.g. psychiatric disorder), or environmental attributes (e.g. domestic arrangements). The *criterion* we aim to predict is the behaviour covered by the term "violence". The third set of variables is the *judgements* made by clinicians or criminal justice decision-makers in estimating an individual's likelihood of violence. Three kinds of relationships can be studied (Figure 9.1). *Criterion–judgement* relationships indicate the accuracy or precision of clinical judgements, while *cue–judgement* relationships reflect the use of information by clinicians in making their judgements. *Criterion–cue* relationships determine which variables predict the criterion, risk factors being *predictors* insofar as their presence is associated with increased likelihood of future

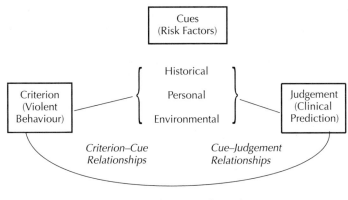

Figure 9.1 Lens model framework for the analysis of risk assessment

violence. The association need not be causal nor does its magnitude need to be large. For example, a correlation of 0.30 between a variable and a measure of recidivism broadly represents a 30% difference in recidivism rates between those showing and not showing the characteristic.

Criterion–judgement relationships are described as *clinical prediction* to indicate a subjective evaluation by the clinician. This contrasts with *statistical* or *actuarial prediction*, in which known risk factors are combined mechanically to produce an objective index of risk (Dawes, Faust & Meehl, 1989; Grove & Meehl, 1996; Meehl, 1954). The distinction oversimplifies decision-making processes, which vary not only in how data are combined, but also in the kinds of information utilised (Sawyer, 1966). Clinical judgements, for example, may be quantified (e.g. by a rating scale) and form part of a statistical predictor, while the latter may be one element in clinical decision-making.

Statistical prediction is defined by the method of combining information, not its source, but actuarial prediction commonly relies on historical personal facts, such as age at first conviction. Such factual information is a *static* or unchanging ("tombstone") feature. Many argue that *dynamic* or changeable factors, such as response to treatment, are more relevant to risk management and have equal significance in risk assessment. Quinsey et al. (1998), however, note problems in the definition and predictive utility of dynamic factors.

Evaluating Predictive Accuracy

Research on judgement–criterion and cue–criterion relationships is concerned with accuracy in predicting future violence. Accuracy, or *validity*, is the extent to which the prediction correctly identifies those who are and are not violent, but validity depends on the *reliability* (consistency of measurement) of both predictor and criterion. Reliability is sometimes limited by reliance on poor quality records. A reliable measure may or may not be valid, but an unreliable measure cannot be valid.

Predictive accuracy is commonly evaluated by means of a 2×2 table in which predictor and criterion are dichotomised (Figure 9.2). As the upper part of the figure shows, accuracy of the prediction is reflected in the proportion of the sample falling in each of the four cells of the table. A *true positive* prediction results when the predictor correctly predicts a violent outcome (a), while a *false positive* or "false alarm" arises when the prediction of violence turns out to be incorrect (b). Similarly, a *true negative* arises when the predictor correctly identifies the non-violent (d), while a *false negative* or "miss" represents those erroneously predicted to be non-violent (c).

		Actual Outcome		
		Violent	Not Violent	Totals
	Violent	True Positives a	False Positives b	$a + b$
Predicted Outcome	Not Violent	False Negatives c	True Negatives d	$c + d$
Totals		$a + c$	$b + d$	$a + b + c + d = N$

Index	Definition	Equation
Sensitivity	Proportion of the actually violent who are correctly predicted	$a/(a + c)$
Specificity	Proportion of the actually nonviolent who are correctly predicted	$d/(b + d)$
Positive Predictive Value	Proportion of the predicted violent who are correctly predicted	$a/(a + b)$
Negative Predictive Value	Proportion of the predicted nonviolent who are correctly predicted	$d/(c + d)$
False Positive Rate	Proportion of the actually nonviolent who are incorrectly predicted	$b/(b + d)$
False Negative Rate	Proportion of the actually violent who are incorrectly predicted	$c/(a + c)$
Overall Correct Prediction	Proportion of the total who are correctly predicted	$(a + d)/N$
Relative Improvement Over Chance	Maximum proportion of the violent correctly predicted	$(ad - bc)/(a + c)(c + d)$

Figure 9.2 Evaluating predictive accuracy

An accurate and desirable predictor is one which maximises the correct "hits" (*a* and *d*) and minimises the errors (*b* and *c*). However, while false positives and false negatives are equally undesirable in scientific terms, they do not have equal social consequences. False negatives are undesirable for society but a high proportion of false positives is undesirable from a civil liberties perspective. Overconcern with either error therefore reflects social value judgements (Monahan, 1981).

The accuracy of prediction can be gauged in several ways, and research is inconsistent in the choice of indices. The lower half of Figure 9.2 shows more commonly used indices (Kessel & Zimmerman, 1993; Mossman, 1994). These represent different perspectives on the utility of the predictor and none provides a complete evaluation. Overall correct prediction, for example, indicates the proportion of the total sample correctly predicted to be dangerous or safe, but it does not indicate whether errors are false negatives or false positives. It may also be influenced by chance agreement between predicted and actual outcome. Relative Improvement Over Chance (RIOC: Loeber & Dishion, 1983) aims to correct for this. Other indices are useful for specific purposes. For example, a predictor with low sensitivity but high specificity may be useful in screening out those who do not merit lengthy risk assessments (Gardner et al., 1996a).

Base Rate, Selection Ratio and the Efficiency of Prediction

The efficiency of a predictor is the extent to which it predicts beyond chance. This depends not only on a positive association with the criterion, but also on the *base rate* and the *selection ratio* (Meehl & Rosen, 1955). The base rate is the frequency of the criterion in the population of interest (i.e. $(a + c)/N$ in Figure 9.2), while the selection ratio is the proportion of the total assigned a positive prediction by the predictive measure (i.e. $(a + b)/N$). Base rates have a significant impact on predictive accuracy because predicting the non-occurrence of an infrequent event has a high probability of being correct by chance alone and low base rate events can generally be predicted only at the expense of many false positive errors.

To illustrate, suppose that a prediction study identifies a risk factor as present in 40 of 50 violent recidivists and absent in 40 of 50 non-recidivists. The base rate of violence in this sample is 50%, and the overall correct prediction is $(40 + 40)/100$, or 80%. The false positive rate is 20% $(10/(40 + 10))$, while the false negative rate is also 20%. The predictor is relatively efficient, since it correctly identifies 30% more of the total sample than would be identified by chance alone, i.e. the base rate of 50%. However, this does not apply with samples having different base rates. If the predictor is applied to a new sample of 1000 with a base rate of violence of only 10%, 80 (80%) of the 100 violent recidivists are correctly identified, but there are now 180 false positives (20% of the 900 non-violent). Moreover, although overall accuracy remains 80%, this actually entails more errors than would be made by relying solely on the base rate, and predicting everyone to be non-violent.

Although the base rate is often unknown, early research suggested a base rate of serious violent recidivism in populations such as released mentally disordered offenders of below 20%, leading to pessimism about the prospects for improving risk predictions. Recent studies using more sophisticated measures or longer term follow-up find much higher rates of 30% or more. Nevertheless, low base rates preclude accurate predictions in many areas of practice.

Prediction errors also depend on the selection ratio, but this can be changed to alter the false positive or false negative errors. For example, when the predictor is a score on a continuous measure, the cutting point may be raised to yield fewer positive predictions overall. While this will reduce the number of false positives, it also reduces the true positives and increases the false negatives.

Because indices of predictive accuracy are misleading when the predictor is applied to populations with different base rates and selection ratios, indices that are not dependent on these two variables are desirable. RIOC has some advantages because it is only partly dependent, but the most satisfactory representation of accuracy comes from an analysis of Receiver Operating Characteristics (ROC: Mossman, 1994; Rice & Harris, 1995). ROC analysis originates in signal detection research, and essentially entails a graphical plot of the true positive detection rates (sensitivity) against the false alarm rates (1 − specificity) at different cut-off points along a graded predictor. This yields an index of accuracy (AUC − area under the curve) which is unaffected by changes in the base rate or selection ratio (Rice & Harris, 1995). The AUC can range from 0.5 (no discrimination) to 1.0, and reflects the likelihood that a randomly selected recidivist would have a higher score on the prediction measure than a randomly selected non-recidivist. For example, an AUC of 0.75 would indicate a probability of 0.75, and relatively good accuracy. This index is increasingly used in prediction research.

THE CLINICAL PREDICTION OF VIOLENCE

Research on criterion–judgement relationships has focused on clinical judgements about the mentally disordered because of assumptions that mental disorder increases the risk of violence and that mental health professionals have a particular expertise in judging risk. However, evidence accumulating during the 1970s suggested that clinical predictions of dangerousness by psychiatrists and psychologists were highly inaccurate (Ennis & Litwack, 1974; Monahan, 1981). More recently, this conclusion has undergone a re-appraisal.

First-Generation Outcome Studies of Predictions of Dangerousness

Early evidence came from naturalistic studies of mentally disordered offenders released from institutions by court orders, contrary to psychiatric judgements that they were dangerous (Monahan, 1981). This "first generation" of research demonstrated consistent over-prediction of dangerousness and high rates of false positives. For example, Kozol, Boucher and Garofalo (1972) reported a five-year follow-up of sex offenders, of whom 386 were released as non-dangerous following treatment, and 49 released against clinical advice. Eight per cent of the former and 35% of the latter committed further serious offences, suggesting some treatment effect in reducing dangerousness. Nevertheless, 65% of those judged dangerous were false positives, highlighting inaccuracies in clinical predictions.

A seminal study followed a ruling by the United States Supreme Court in 1966 that Johnny Baxtrom had been wrongfully detained in a prison hospital for the criminally insane. This resulted in the transfer of 969 patients to civil mental hospitals. A four-year follow-up of a quarter of the "Baxstrom patients" revealed that while 17% had been arrested at some time, only nine individuals had been convicted, mostly for non-violent offences (Steadman & Keveles, 1972). In terms of predicted dangerousness, then, over 80% were false positives. Similar rulings leading to the release of smaller samples in other states had comparable outcomes, only a small minority being subsequently convicted for serious crimes.

Low predictive accuracy was also demonstrated at a Canadian forensic assessment clinic (Sepejak, Webster & Menzies, 1984). Mean correlations of pre-trial ratings of predicted dangerousness with dangerous behaviour during the next two years ranged from 0.20 for psychiatrists to 0.03 for social workers, respectively. However, individual correlations ranged from −0.48 to +0.47, indicating considerable variability in accuracy between clinicians. In a six-year follow-up at the same centre, Menzies and Webster (1995) obtained even less encouraging results, only 13 of 345 correlations of clinical predictions with violent outcome criteria being significantly better than chance.

Monahan (1981) concluded that predictions of dangerousness by clinicians are accurate in no more than one in three cases. However, the early studies were criticised for poor research methodology, notably unrepresentativeness of some of the samples, failure to assess actual predictions, underestimation of actual violence, and questionable generalisability to other clinical settings (Gordon, 1977; Blackburn, 1984; Litwack & Schlesinger, 1987). It was also noted that some studies tested prediction from institutional environments to future community settings, despite large temporal and situational gaps.

Second-Generation Prediction Studies

The "second-generation" approach takes a more cautiously optimistic view, arguing that predictions of more imminent dangerousness may reveal clearer evidence of accuracy (Hall, 1987; Litwack & Schlesinger, 1987; Monahan, 1981, 1984). Later research has therefore focused on short-term predictions within the context in which judgements are made. These studies use a variety of methods and yield mixed findings (Otto, 1992; Wettstein, 1984).

Some studies assume that emergency civil commitments are *de facto* predictions of imminent dangerousness. McNiel and Binder (1987), for example, claim to have demonstrated predictive accuracy of clinical judgements in a comparison of patients involuntarily committed as dangerous to others with involuntary patients admitted for other reasons. They found that 72% of the involuntary patients exhibited at least one assault-related act during the first 72 hours following admission (physical assault, seclusion, use of restraint, verbal threats or abuse) compared with 30% of involuntary patients. However, the differences were due mainly to verbal aggression, and some findings suggest that involuntary admission status and immediate post-admission behaviour are unreliable criteria (Apperson, Mulvey & Lidz, 1993).

Other research employs an analogue approach by examining the predictive accuracy of clinicians provided with standard information. These studies typically find low levels of predictive accuracy. For example, Cooper and Werner (1990) found that when predicting violence in prison from pre-admission criminal and demographic data, only one of 21 psychologists and case managers predicted above chance level.

Some recent naturalistic studies, however, demonstrate better than chance prediction. McNiel and Binder (1991) examined the predictive accuracy of nurses and physicians in a short-term in-patient unit. Staff judged the probability of violence during the next seven days for each of 149 patients, and judgements were divided into low, moderate, and high probability levels. Significant relationships were found between risk estimates and subsequent assault for both groups of clinicians. For example, 10%, 24%, and 40% of patients in the nurses' low, moderate and high categories, respectively, were physically aggressive. However, 60% of patients in the high probability category are false positives.

Lidz, Mulvey and Gardner (1993) attempted to overcome the methodological shortcomings of earlier research by attention to the measurement of clinical predictions and violence. Nurses and psychiatrists in the emergency department of an urban psychiatric hospital rated their concerns about possible violence, and 357 patients with high ratings were matched on demographic variables with a control group given zero ratings. Violent incidents during the following six months were documented from multiple sources, and 53% of the experimental group were found to have behaved violently, compared with 36% of controls. The difference is significant, but held only for male patients. Also, on a criterion of serious, life-threatening violence, only 14% of the experimental group were true positives.

Otto (1992) concludes from second-generation research that one in two of short-term predictions are probably accurate. However, much of the research may underestimate predictive accuracy. Apperson, Mulvey and Lidz (1993), for example, showed that clinicians at a short-term treatment centre successfully distinguished patients who were aggressive during their stay, but the level of accuracy depended on the prediction criterion, the nature of the comparison group, and the time period during which violence was measured. These variables are not consistently defined in the prediction research. Mossman (1994) also argues that studies have relied on inadequate indices of predictive accuracy. Using ROC methods, he re-examined 58 data sets on the prediction of violence, and found that 81% yielded significantly greater than chance results, mean AUC being 0.73. Consistent with recent appraisals, second-generation studies produced better evidence of accuracy (mean AUC of 0.84) than earlier studies (mean AUC of 0.75).

The recent research therefore demonstrates that clinicians *can* judge the potential of patients to behave violently beyond chance levels. However, the level of accuracy demonstrated remains modest, and rates of false positive errors continue to be high. Much of the research also continues to suffer from poor definition of predictors, weak criteria of violence, constricted validation samples, and poorly synchronised research efforts (Monahan & Steadman, 1994).

THE PROCESS OF CLINICAL JUDGEMENT

Clinicians' judgements of risk can draw on a potentially wide array of information. This will clearly be a selective process. Where the outcome research addresses questions of the validity of prediction, cue–judgment studies examine factors in the process of prediction which may attenuate validity, such as low reliability or attention to inappropriate cues.

Evidence on reliability was obtained by Quinsey and Abtman (1979), who presented vignettes of offenders to four forensic psychiatrists and nine school-teachers, and obtained ratings on several predictive scales. Inter-rater agreement on the likelihood of an assaultive offence was generally low, though higher for teachers (0.24 to 0.57) than for psychiatrists (0.19 to 0.48). Multiple regression analyses indicated that both groups combined data in similar ways, suggesting that there was nothing distinctive about the judgement of psychiatrists. Other research confirms that agreement between clinicians is generally low (Cooper & Werner, 1990; Werner, Rose & Yesavage, 1983).

Research on the information considered in predicting violence identifies a few regularly recurring factors, such as clinical state, prior violent history, and childhood aggression (Mulvey & Lidz, 1984). Studies of both long-term and short-term predictions consistently find that offence-related behaviour, particularly prior violence, is strongly weighted (Cooper & Werner, 1990; Menzies & Webster, 1995; Quinsey & Maguire, 1986; Werner, Rose & Yesavage, 1983). Werner and colleagues also found that in short-term predictions, Brief Psychiatric Rating Scale (BPRS) measures of hostility, excitement, suspicion, and uncooperativeness were significantly related to predictions of violence by both psychiatrists and psychologists. This pattern was replicated in a subsequent study of dangerousness judgements made at the time of release (Werner & Meloy, 1992), suggesting that similar psychiatric status factors influence risk appraisals across settings, professions and stages of treatment.

Studies using Brunswik's lens model to examine how cues utilised by clinicians relate to actual outcome generally find that clinicians weight cues that are empirically unrelated to actual violent outcome. Quinsey and Maguire (1986), for example, found that dangerousness ratings were strongly influenced by institutional assaultiveness, but this was unrelated to serious re-offending in discharged patients. Clinicians also emphasised prior homicide, but this correlated with a non-dangerous outcome. However, McNiel and Binder (1995) demonstrated that clinicians may use appropriate cues for some subgroups of patients. Comparing patients correctly or incorrectly predicted by physicians to be violent in the short term, they found that recent violence, diagnosis and psychiatric state (BPRS ratings) distinguished true positives from true negatives, suggesting appropriate use of established risk factors. False negative errors were associated with neglect of known correlates of risk.

Biases in the selection of cues by clinicians may arise from personal characteristics such as cultural background and values (Ennis & Litwack, 1974) or training and education (Monahan, 1981). However, individual variability between clinicians in levels of accuracy (Sepejak, Webster & Menzies, 1984) suggests that limitations of clinical judgement reflect not simply biased selection of cues but also idiosyncratic strategies for combining cues. Accuracy in judging risk is also likely to be attenuated by the cognitive biases inherent in human decision-making, such as simplifying heuristics which ignore basic rules of probability. Biasing phenomena identified include seeking out confirmatory rather than disconfirmatory evidence, ignoring base rates, and reliance on illusory correlations (Faust, 1986). Overall, the findings on clinical risk assessment are consistent with more general evidence that human decision-makers do not behave optimally (Gottfredson, 1987).

RISK FACTORS AND ACTUARIAL PREDICTION

Criterion–cue relationships indicate the predictive utility of specific factors. Many variables have been associated with violence, ranging from firesetting in childhood to phase of the lunar cycle, but only some of these are conclusive predictors (for reviews, see Blackburn, 1993; Klassen & O'Connor, 1994; Mulvey & Lidz, 1984). Violent criminal recidivism is predicted by many of the factors that predict general criminal recidivism, strongest of which are adult criminal history, anti-social personality, anti-social companions, criminogenic needs (i.e. cognitions, values or behaviours facilitating criminal activities), younger age, family rearing practices, interpersonal conflict, and lack of social achievement (Gendreau, Little & Goggin, 1996). Other factors, however, need to be considered for some specific offences. For example, both general and non-sexual violent recidivism among sex offenders are predicted by factors similar to those identified by Gendreau, Little and Goggin (1996), but sexual recidivism is most strongly predicted by measures of sexual deviance, such as phallometric assessment and prior sexual offences (Hanson & Bussière, 1998). Similarly, predictors of recidivist arson differ from those for violent recidivism (Quinsey et al., 1998).

Risk Factors for Violence

Some risk factors are specific for violence, particularly short-term and non-criminal violence. Following Monahan and Steadman (1994), established or promising risk factors are summarised under the headings of historical, dispositional, clinical, and contextual variables.

The most predictive *historical factors* are previous violence, adverse family conditions, and failure to adjust to school or to adult roles in relationships or at work. Previous violence includes childhood aggression and behaviour disorder, such as cruelty to animals (Felthous & Kellert, 1987), although early and repeated violence is more predictive than single criminal acts, particularly among the mentally disordered (e.g. Black & Spinks, 1985). Longitudinal studies typically find higher rates of parental deviance, marital conflict, parental indifference, lack of supervision, and the experience of physical abuse in the family histories of violent offenders (Farrington, 1994).

Demographic characteristics of age, gender, race and social class are predictive in many studies, but may be of greater significance for theory and policy. Although male gender is a well-established correlate of violence and crime in general, it is less clearly predictive in psychiatric samples (Lidz, Mulvey & Gardner, 1993), and is obviously not discriminating in male offender populations. Within such populations, however, younger age at first violent offence and younger current age are risk factors for violence (Harris, Rice & Quinsey, 1993).

Dispositional variables cover cognitive, emotional and social tendencies or traits. Deviant cognitive functioning distinguishes violent from non-violent offenders in several studies. This includes lower intellectual levels and neuropsychological deficits as well as deficient problem-solving skills and anti-social beliefs (see Blackburn, 1993). Although personality tests tend to be relatively weak predictors of violence (Megargee, 1970), some studies find that self-report scales of anger, impulsivity, hostility, and social deviance make a moderate contribution to prediction (Black & Spinks, 1985; Cornell, Peterson & Richards, 1999; Selby, 1984). Observer rating scales of interpersonal style also predict institutional aggression (Cooke, 1996).

Consistent evidence has emerged for the predictive utility of *psychopathy* as measured by the Psychopathy Checklist—Revised (PCL-R: Hare, 1991, 1996). Assessment entails a semi-structured interview and a review of collateral information, from which scores are derived on 20 traits (see Table 9.1). Total score measures a unitary construct, but the scale divides into two correlated factors. Factor 1 measures a callous and remorseless style of relating to others, while Factor 2 measures a socially deviant lifestyle. A 12-item screening version (PCL-SV: Hart, Hare & Forth, 1994) is an effective short form of the full instrument.

Retrospective studies support the association of psychopathy with both violent and non-violent offending (Blackburn, 1999; Hart, Hare & Forth, 1994), but the PCL-R also predicts both violent and non-violent recidivism in released

Table 9.1 The Psychopathy Checklist—Revised (adapted from Hare, 1991)

1. Glibness/superficial charm[1]	11. Promiscuous sexual behaviour
2. Grandiose sense of self worth[1]	12. Early behavioural problems[2]
3. Need for stimulation/proneness to boredom[2]	13. Lack of realistic, long-term goals[2]
4. Pathological lying[1]	14. Impulsivity[2]
5. Conning/manipulative[1]	15. Irresponsibility[2]
6. Lack of remorse or guilt[1]	16. Failure to accept responsibility for own actions[1]
7. Shallow affect[1]	17. Many short-term marital relationships
8. Callous/lack of empathy[1]	18. Juvenile delinquency[2]
9. Parasitic lifestyle[2]	19. Revocation of conditional release[2]
10. Poor behavioural controls[2]	20. Criminal versatility

[1] Contributes to Factor 1;   [2] Contributes to Factor 2.

prisoners and mentally disordered offenders (Hemphill, Hare & Wong, 1998; Salekin, Rogers & Sewell, 1996). Factor 2 correlates more highly with general recidivism than does Factor 1, but both factors contribute equally to the prediction of violence. The PCL-R is comparable to actuarial measures for predicting general recidivism, but superior for violent recidivism. The PCL-SV also predicted both treatment compliance and aggression in the shorter term within a maximum security hospital (Hill, Rogers & Bickford, 1996). Its predictive utility has led to the incorporation of the PCL-R into several recent risk assessment procedures (see below).

The contribution of *clinical factors* to violence continues to be a central concern in risk assessment, and is the focus of a major project, the MacArthur Violence Risk Assessment Study (Monahan & Steadman, 1994; Steadman et al., 1998). Contrary to earlier criminological views, recent evidence indicates that major mental disorders increase the risk of violence (Hodgins et al., 1996; Swanson et al., 1990), although the combination of major mental disorder and substance abuse is a more significant factor in the community violence of psychiatric patients than psychosis alone (Steadman et al., 1998).

Nevertheless, clinical factors are relatively weak predictors of recidivism among offenders compared to gender or prior criminal history (Gendreau, Little & Goggin, 1996; Marzuk, 1996; Monahan, 1997). From a meta-analysis of studies of recidivism among mentally disordered offenders, Bonta, Law and Hanson (1998) concluded that the majority of variables predicting violent recidivism were the same as those predicting general recidivism, and that historical and demographic variables, such as younger age or prior criminal history, were stronger predictors than clinical variables, except for anti-social personality disorder. However, this analysis did not include studies of specific symptoms or of violence in psychiatric hospitals. Specific symptoms are stronger risk factors then diagnostic categories (Marzuk, 1996). For example, state variables such as agitation or hostile thinking, have been related to in-patient violence (e.g. Kay, Wolkenfeld & Murrill, 1988), and delusional misperceptions of imminent threat predict community violence (Swanson et al., 1996). The predictive utility of measures of change following treatment intervention remains to be investigated (Gendreau, Little & Goggin, 1996; Quinsey & Walker, 1992).

Personality disorder is widely considered a significant risk factor. Of the categories recognised in the DSM-III and DSM-IV classifications, anti-social and borderline personality disorder are assumed to be most strongly associated with violence, but the predictive utility of borderline personality disorder is inconclusive (Widiger & Trull, 1994). There is also some evidence that paranoid and passive–aggressive disorders are associated with violence in male offenders (Blackburn, 1999). The predictive significance of anti-social personality disorder is confirmed by recent meta-analyses, which consistently find that this category is a moderately strong predictor of general, violent, and sexual recidivism. However, anti-social personality disorder has been loosely defined in these analyses as synonymous with "criminal lifestyle", thereby confounding the role of personality variables and criminal history.

Situational factors such as the behaviour of others, the presence of a weapon, or the characteristics of the location in which an aggressive incident occurs, are major proximal determinants of violence. Inability to predict these in advance imposes limits on the validity of any risk assessment. Nevertheless, *contextual factors* in the current and future environment are potential risk factors, and are a primary consideration in risk management. These include stressors, social networks, and access to the means for harm, which provide not only triggers and opportunities for violence but also restraints against interpersonal conflict (Monahan, 1997).

Social stressors, such as break up of a relationship, work problems, family bereavement, unemployment, and family disharmony, have been identified as risk factors for violence in several studies (Bonta, Law & Hanson, 1998; Klassen & O'Connor, 1994). Social networks and support have received less attention. Lack of social support as indicated by being single is a significant risk factor for violent recidivism among mentally disordered offenders (Bonta, Law & Hanson, 1998). However, while some social networks, such as a trusting family, may reduce the likelihood of violence, others, such as living with strangers or in a conflictful family may increase the risk (Estroff & Zimmer, 1994).

Actuarial Prediction of Violence

Few risk factors are sufficiently powerful predictors to be used in isolation, and actuarial prediction relies on the statistical combination of several factors. Items included in actuarial measures of recidivism are typically historical variables such as age on first conviction or number of convictions. These are usually combined by a simple addition of unweighted points for each predictor or a linear weighted total based on multi-variate analyses (Gottfredson, 1987). Actuarial measures assign a probability of future criminal behaviour to groups (not individuals) defined by different levels on the predictive index.

The predictive accuracy of general recidivism indices is typically in the 60% to 80% range (Andrews, 1989). However, because the strength of any predictor–criterion relationship depends on sample and setting characteristics, and varies over time, actuarial indices cannot be assumed to generalise beyond local conditions without cross-validation. Indices developed for predicting risk of reconviction of male prisoners, for example, do not predict violent recidivism or recidivism among women or minority ethnic groups (Nuffield, 1989). Similarly, actuarial predictors of violence developed in one setting should not be assumed to be applicable to different populations.

Early attempts to predict future violent offences among prisoners or assaultive behaviour by psychiatric patients met with limited success because of low base rates. Wenk, Robison and Smith (1972), for example, described three unsuccessful attempts to predict violence among parolees in the California Youth Authority, all of which yielded high false positive rates, and concluded that attempts to predict reported violence were futile because of the unreliability of the criterion. Subsequent studies using broader criteria of violence have reported more positive but mixed findings.

Klassen and O'Connor (1989) defined violence as arrest for a violent crime or re-admission to hospital for violence, and examined the prediction of violence in the community by psychiatric patients at a one-year follow-up, using five items (early family quality, intimate relationships, arrest history, hospitalisation history, assault occurring in the presenting problem). When applied to a cross-validation sample with a base rate of violence of 25%, the scale had a correlation of 0.32 with subsequent violence, and an optimal cutting score yielded an overall correct classification of 76%. However, 48% of those predicted to be violent were false positives. Lower levels of accuracy of actuarial prediction were found by Menzies and Webster (1995) in their six-year follow-up of forensic assessment, despite a very high base rate of violence of 62%.

Harris, Rice and Quinsey (1993) developed a more successful actuarial instrument that predicts long-term violent recidivism in serious offenders. Historical and admission data were obtained from the files of 618 men admitted to a maximum security hospital for treatment or pre-trial assessment, who were followed up for an average of seven years following release. The base rate of violent reconviction was 31%, and 12 items consistently discriminated recidivists across subgroups of the sample (see Table 9.2). The strongest single predictor was the PCL-R ($r = 0.34$), and the multiple correlation of all 12 items with recidivism was 0.46. An optimal cut off on the resulting scale, the Violence Risk Appraisal Guide (VRAG) yielded a sensitivity of 0.60, a specificity of 0.78, and 45% false positives. The AUC was 0.76 (Rice & Harris, 1995). Quinsey et al. (1998) describe a similar instrument that predicts recidivism among sex offenders (SORAG: Sex Offender Risk Appraisal Guide). The authors suggest that these scales can *anchor* clinical judgments and be adjusted to take account of dynamic or idiosyncratic case factors ("structured discretion"), and proposed guidelines for doing this (Webster et al., 1994). More recently, however, they question the wisdom of this practice (Quinsey et al., 1998).

Table 9.2 Predictor variables in the Violence Risk Appraisal Guide and their correlations with violent recidivism (adapted from Harris, Rice & Quinsey, 1993)

Variable	Correlation
Psychopathy Checklist	0.34
Separation from parents under age 16	0.25
Victim injury in index offence	−0.16
DSM-III schizophrenia	−0.17
Never married	0.18
Elementary school maladjustment	0.31
Female victim—index offence	−0.11
Failure on prior conditional release	0.24
Property offence history	0.20
Age at index offence	−0.26
Alcohol abuse history	0.13
DSM-III personality disorder	0.26

All correlations are significant ($N = 618$).

Other research has focused on the prediction of assaultive behaviour in the short term, and within hospital environments (Convit et al., 1988; Kay, Wolkenfeld & Murrill, 1988; McNiel & Binder, 1994). These studies show that violence can be predicted successfully by simple actuarial measures, although false positive rates again tend to be high. McNiel and Binder (1994), for example, attempted to predict inpatient aggression with a checklist of five items (history of physical attacks or fear-inducing behaviour within two weeks prior to admission, absence of suicidal behaviour, diagnosis of schizophrenia or mania, male gender, and currently married or cohabiting). A cut-off score above two significantly distinguished patients who displayed physical attacks or fear-inducing behaviour during their stay. For example, 55% of those in the high risk group were physically assaultive. The scale may therefore have potential utility in screening for the violent patient.

Negative findings have, however, been reported. Palmstierna and Wistedt (1990), for example, failed to derive a predictor of in-patient assaults from 12 commonly cited risk factors (e.g. unemployed, alcohol abuse, conviction for a violent crime). Kay, Wolkenfeld and Murrill (1988) also found that different sets of predictors were necessary for immediate and longer term prediction, suggesting that clinical state variables are more important than trait variables in predicting imminent aggression. However, a limitation of hospital based studies is the attempt to predict assaults within environments which aim to minimise violence.

Most actuarial research relies on historical and clinical variables, but personality measures add to actuarial prediction in some studies (e.g. Hooper & Evans, 1984; Shaffer, Waters & Adams, 1994). A few studies have also used a non-linear approach in the form of a decision tree (Monahan, 1981). Gardner et al.

(1996a) demonstrated the potential of this method in predicting community violence by psychiatric patients. For example, a regression tree entailing "yes–no" responses to questions concerning the patient's self-reported hostility, age, number of prior acts of violence, and drug use had low sensitivity but very high specificity, and could hence screen out patients unlikely to be violent. The accuracy of this method was comparable to that of other actuarial methods, and yielded significantly higher AUCs than unaided clinical predictions (Gardner et al., 1996b).

Critical Issues in Actuarial Prediction

Many workers argue that the increased use of actuarial prediction in risk assessment is both desirable and inevitable (Monahan, 1997; Quinsey et al., 1998). Actuarial measures are more reliable than clinical prediction because they rely on standard information and eliminate the variability of human judgement. Recent findings on the prediction of violence also seem consistent with the evidence that actuarial prediction outperforms clinical prediction (Dawes, Faust & Meehl, 1989; Grove & Meehl, 1996). However, clinicians have used predictive devices infrequently, and several concerns continue to be expressed about the limitations of actuarial prediction.

First, levels of accuracy are moderate. Correlations with criterion measures rarely exceed the level of 0.4 found for statistical predictors of recidivism generally (Simon, 1971), and the rate of false positives is generally similar to that found in clinical prediction studies. Second, the range of predictors examined is limited. Despite frequent pleas that the selection of predictors should be guided by theory rather than "shotgun empiricism", predictors examined are predominantly those that are readily accessible in records or hallowed by criminological traditions (Gendreau, Little & Goggin, 1996). Yet historical risk variables associated with violence reflect the conditions that shape stable individual tendencies or are early manifestations of those tendencies, and findings with the PCL-R suggest that it may be more useful to assess these tendencies directly. Klassen and O'Connor (1994) also demonstrated that theoretical order can be imposed on the variety of risk factors by organising them in terms of the origins, instigators, and regulators of aggression proposed by social learning theory. However, only a few risk assessment measures (e.g. Menzies & Webster, 1995) have been theoretically based.

Reliance on static biographical data as predictors is also criticised for being "unforgiving of the past" (Nuffield, 1989) and for neglecting the effects on future behaviour of custody or treatment and the environment to which an offender returns (Andrews, 1989, 1995). Dynamic risk factors are as effective as static factors in predicting general recidivism (Gendreau, Little & Goggin, 1996), and some research suggests that criminogenic needs may be more significant than historical factors in predicting violent recidivism (Taylor, 1998). Composite actuarial risk scales that include both static and dynamic factors may therefore improve prediction. For example, the Level of Supervision Inventory (LSI)—a standard-ised interview schedule that combines biographical data with dynamic vari-ables—was found by Gendreau and colleagues to be the best composite measure predicting general recidivism. Harris, Rice & Quinsey (1993) also found that the LSI significantly predicts violent recidivism.

The most contentious issue is whether actuarial measures should replace clin-ical judgement. Although there is a case for using actuarial measures to anchor clinical assessment (Harris, Rice & Quinsey, 1993), the evidence suggests that when allowed discretion, clinicians identify too many exceptions, thereby reduc-ing accuracy (Dawes, Faust & Meehl, 1989). As Sawyer (1966) demonstrated, the most effective combination of actuarial and clinical methods is not the incorpo-ration of statistical data into clinical judgements, but rather the objective report-ing of clinical judgements which can be used statistically. Quinsey et al. (1998) now accept this, and argue for the complete replacement of existing risk assess-ment practices with actuarial methods. Webster and his colleagues, on the other hand, continue to have reservations about reliance on actuarial methods because of their inflexibility, restricted generalisability, and limited utility for clinical risk management, and argue instead for the use of structured clinical guidelines (Douglas, Cox & Webster, 1999; Hart, 1998; Webster et al., 1997).

IMPROVING CLINICAL RISK ASSESSMENT

A wholesale shift to the use of actuarial methods is currently unlikely, if only because validated indices are unavailable in many settings. Given recent evidence that clinical judgements of risk can be at least moderately accurate, many argue for improving clinical judgement. Reliability, for example, can be increased by averaging over independent clinical judges (Werner, Rose & Yesavage, 1983).

Improved validity is likely to be achieved by attention to empirically validated risk factors. How these are integrated to produce a judgement remains a critical question. As Pollock, McBain & Webster (1989) note, simply conducting a wide-ranging interview or administering many tests in search of possible risk factors is neither sufficient nor scientifically defensible. They emphasise that despite the characterisation of the clinical method as subjective, it is a process of hypothesis formulation and testing guided by a general theory of violence. The aim is to uncover factors that are causally related to dangerous behaviour by identifying predisposing facilitating and inhibiting influences, transient or enduring situa-tional factors, and the conditions under which self-regulatory processes become disorganised.

This depiction of the clinical process has much in common with *functional analysis* employed in applied behaviour analysis. Functional analysis identifies the personal and situational variables of which behaviour is a function and pro-vides a systematic approach to identifying risk factors in the individual case (Owens & Bagshaw, 1985). Despite its common clinical application in behav-ioural and cognitive interventions, functional analysis has received little attention in the risk assessment literature, but its potential is demonstrated by Clark, Fisher and McDougall (1993). They found that offence-related behaviours in prison that are functionally equivalent to those preceding offending (e.g. anger in response to rejection) could be predicted with 65% accuracy from a behavioural analysis of the individual's offence. Monitoring of these behaviours in the prison environment could therefore indicate changes in risk level.

The lack of a universally accepted theoretical framework for understanding violence is the major limitation to theoretically driven clinical assessments. Nevertheless, clinical judgements are defensible when the basis for judgements of risk is made explicit and transparent. The need for accountability has become particularly important in the light of litigation surrounding clinical decisions when released patients have committed acts of violence in the community (Kroll & Mackenzie, 1983; Reed, 1997). A significant direction in risk assessment is therefore the development of clinical guidelines that make the decision-making process more explicit.

Risk Assessment Guidelines

Risk assessment entails decisions first about whether to proceed and second about the conduct of the examination. Procedural decisions are necessary because an assessment may be professionally inappropriate when the referral question is unclear, the clinician's training, knowledge of the literature or of the legal framework is insufficient, or when there is no known history of violence. The conduct of the assessment will depend on which risk factors are considered and how they are elicited.

Monahan (1981) suggested 14 questions that clinicians should answer to provide a defensible structure for estimating the probability of future violence. These cover both procedural issues and risk factors to be identified. Several similar guides have subsequently been proposed (Hall, 1987; Kroll & MacKenzie, 1983; Marra, Konzelman & Giles, 1987; Meloy, 1987). Marra and colleagues, for example, present a flexible hypothesis testing approach for assessing the single case. This entails the use of a "Dangerousness Assessment Sheet" to record high-, medium- or low-risk levels for several risk categories, including history of dangerous behaviour, institutional record, and actuarial scale results.

However, the utility of these guides is unclear because they do not agree on the information to be sought by the clinician. Their virtue lies in requiring the clinician to attend to information which might otherwise be ignored. This may ensure reliability, but may not be sufficient to increase the validity of clinical judgement. There is little indication in the professional literature that these guides have been widely adopted by practitioners.

Evidence has, however, been presented for the utility of the HCR-20 (Webster et al., 1997). This instrument is an exploratory *aide-memoire* or "assessment protocol" for assessing risk in offenders that draws on findings from the risk assessment literature. A checklist of risk factors guides the clinician to evaluate factors

Table 9.3 Items in the HCR-20

Historical (past)		Clinical (present)		Risk management (future)	
H1	Previous violence	C1	Lack of insight	R1	Plans lack feasibility
H2	Young age at first violent incident	C2	Negative attitudes	R2	Exposure to destabilisers
H3	Relationship instability	C3	Active symptoms of major mental illness	R3	Lack of personal support
H4	Employment problems	C4	Impulsivity	R4	Non-compliance with remediation attemps
H5	Substance use problems	C5	Unresponsive to treatment	R5	Stress
H6	Major mental illness				
H7	Psychopathy				
H8	Early maladjustment				
H9	Personality disorder				
H10	Prior supervision failure				

Adapted from Webster et al. (1997).

of known or likely relevance to violence organised around ten past (historical) items, five present (clinical) items, and five future (risk management) items (Table 9.3). Information is derived from interview and files, but supplemented by psychological testing and consultations with staff. Items are coded on a three-point scale (absent, possibly present, definitely present), but the final assessment is a clinical judgement of risk level. For research purposes, however, summary scores may be treated as actuarial scales.

Douglas, Cox & Webster (1999) argue that the HCR-20 provides an empirically validated, structured clinical assessment that overcomes limitations of actuarial prediction and has implications for risk management. They summarise research supporting both the reliability and validity of the HCR-20. For example, in a follow-up of a psychiatric sample released to the community, AUCs ranged from 0.76 for any violent act to 0.80 for arrest for violence. Levels of predictive validity were similar to those of the VRAG. Douglas and coworkers describe three related instruments, the Spousal Assault Risk Assessment (SARA), the Sexual Violence Risk (SVR-20), and the Early Assessment Risk List for Boys (EARL-20B) for which similar validity data have been reported.

Professional and Ethical Issues

Clinical judgements of risk of harm are probably no less accurate than professional judgements in many areas, but inaccuracies in predicting violence have greater implications for both the civil liberties of the offender and the safety of the public. Clinicians therefore need to ensure that risk assessments are fair as well as accurate (Pollock, McBain & Webster, 1989). Although public safety is a primary consideration in risk assessment, the individual assessed also has rights which must be respected.

Codes of professional conduct oblige mental health professionals to give primacy to the welfare of their clients. Risk assessment raises the question of "who is the client?" Because the assessment is undertaken to ensure the safety of others, the client is society, as represented through legal or other decision-makers requesting the assessment, and the normal obligation that clinicians should not disclose information given to them in confidence is suspended (Blackburn, 1996). This raises ethical conflicts for clinicians asked to assess clients receiving their treatment services which have been offered on the understanding of confidentiality. Appelbaum (1997) argues that the clinical and forensic roles are incompatible and that mental health professionals should decline risk assessments for the courts on their clients. This is a contentious view, but individuals assessed for risk have the right to be informed in advance of the limits of confidentiality.

Ensuring fairness to the individual and the public requires that risk assessments are conducted competently. As noted earlier, several guidelines propose that clinicians should routinely ask questions regarding the purpose of the assessment and their competence to undertake it. It is sometimes argued that the levels of accuracy of clinical prediction are insufficient to justify claims to competence and the involvement of practitioners in legal decisions about violent people. However, Grisso and Appelbaum (1992) suggest that this objection is met when risk assessment is empirically grounded.

Although clinicians have expressed concerns about possible legal consequences of inaccurate risk assessments, liability in law is related not to the inaccuracy of a decision but rather to whether that decision followed from established procedure (Kroll & Mackenzie, 1983; Shapiro, 1990). The relevant standard is appropriate assessment and consultation. While explicit national professional standards for risk assessment and management have yet to emerge, general guidelines on risk assessment have been issued by the Department of Health in Britain (Reed, 1997), and "best practice" recommendations on risk management have been published by the Royal College of Psychiatrists (1998) and the British Psychological Society (Centre for Outcomes, Research and Effectiveness, 1998). Borum (1996) argues that recent developments in knowledge of risk assessment are sufficient to derive practice guidelines for assessing and managing people at risk for violence, and that risk assessment should be defined as a proficiency area.

CONCLUSIONS

Recent research challenges the view prevalent a decade ago that violence cannot be accurately predicted. Not only has it been established that clinicians can identify the potentially violent individual with better than chance accuracy, it has also been shown that similar levels of accuracy can be achieved by the statistical combination of a few risk cues. As Hart (1998) notes, the levels of accuracy of predictions of violence achieved in recent studies equal the predictive accuracy of many intervention decisions in psychological treatment, medicine and education.

Despite continuing debates about the relative merits of clinical and actuarial approaches to risk assessment, there is now a general consensus that unguided clinical judgement is unreliable, and that improved risk assessment depends on better assessment technology. In turn, this requires better use of theory in defining harmful behaviour and in identifying facilitating and inhibiting factors. While perfect predictive accuracy is not attainable, current developments indicate that better informed judgements can be achieved.

REFERENCES

Andrews, D.A. (1989) Recidivism is predictable and can be influenced: Using risk assessments to reduce recidivism. *Forum on Corrections Research*, **1**, 11–18.

Andrews, D.A. (1995) The psychology of criminal conduct and effective treatment. In J. McGuire (Ed.) *What Works: Reducing offending: Guidelines from Research and Practice* (pp. 35–62). Chichester: Wiley.

Appelbaum, P.S. (1997) Ethics in evolution: The incompatibility of clinical and forensic functions. *American Journal of Psychiatry*, **154**, 445–446.

Apperson, L.J., Mulvey, E. & Lidz, C. (1993) Short term clinical prediction of assaultive behavior: Artefacts of research methods. *American Journal of Psychiatry*, **150**, 1374–1379.

Black, D.A. & Spinks, P. (1985) Predicting outcomes of mentally disordered and dangerous offenders. In D.P. Farrington & R. Tarling (Eds) *Prediction in Criminology* (pp. 35–58). Albany: State University of New York Press.

Blackburn, R. (1984) The person and dangerousness. In D.J. Müller, D.E. Blackman & A.J. Chapman (Eds) *Psychology and Law* (pp. 102–111). Chichester: Wiley.

Blackburn, R. (1993) *The Psychology of Criminal Conduct: Theory, Research and Practice*. Chichester: Wiley.

Blackburn, R. (1996) What *is* forensic psychology? *Legal and Criminological Psychology*, **1**, 3–16.

Blackburn, R. (2000) Psychopathy and personality disorder in relation to violence. In C.R. Hollin (Ed.) *Clinical Approaches to Violence* (2nd edn). Chichester: Wiley.

Bonta, J., Law, M. & Hanson, K. (1998) The prediction of criminal and violent recidivism among mentally disordered offenders: A meta-analysis. *Psychological Bulletin*, **123**, 123–142.

Borum, R. (1996) Improving the clinical practice of violence risk assessment: Technology, guidelines, and training. *American Psychologist*, **51**, 945–956.

Brunswik, E. (1956) *Perception and the Representative Design of Psychological Experiments*. Berkeley: University of California Press.

Centre for Outcomes, Research and Effectiveness. (1998) *Assessment and management of patients presenting risk to others. CORE Miniguide Series, No. 2*. Leicester: British Psychological Society.

Clark, D.A., Fisher, M.J. & McDougall, C. (1993) A new methodology for assessing the level of risk in incarcerated offenders. *British Journal of Criminology*, **33**, 436–448.

Convit, A., Jaeger, J., Lin, S.P., Meisner, M., Brizer, D. & Volavka, J. (1988) Prediction of violence in psychiatric patients. In T.E. Moffitt & S.A. Mednick (Eds) *Biological Contributions to Crime Causation* (pp. 223–245). Dordrecht: Martinus Nijhoff.

Cooke, D.J. (1996) Predicting offending in prison: The predictive validity of the Prison Behaviour Rating Scales. *Legal and Criminological Psychology*, **1**, 65–82.

Cooper, R.P. & Werner, P.D. (1990) Predicting violence in newly admitted inmates: A lens model analysis of staff decision making. *Criminal Justice and Behavior*, **17**, 431–447.

Cornell, D.G., Peterson, C.S. & Richards, H. (1999) Anger as a predictor of aggression among incarcerated adolescents. *Journal of Consulting and Clinical Psychology*, **67**, 108–115.

Dawes, R.M., Faust, D. & Meehl, P.E. (1989) Clinical versus actuarial judgment. *Science*, **243**, 1668–1674.

Douglas, K.S., Cox, D.N. & Webster, C.D. (1999) Violence risk assessment: Science and practice. *Legal and Criminological Psychology*, **4**, 149–184.

Ennis, B.J. & Litwack, T.R. (1974) Psychiatry and the presumption of expertise: Flipping coins in the courtroom. *California Law Review*, **62**, 694–753.

Estroff, S.E. & Zimmer, C. (1994) Social networks, social support, and violence among persons with severe, persistent mental illness. In J. Monahan & H.J. Steadman (Eds) *Violence and Mental Disorder: Developments in Risk Assessment* (pp. 259–295). Chicago: University of Chicago Press.

Farrington, D.P. (1994) Childhood, adolescent and adult features of violent males. In L.R. Huesmann (Ed.) *Aggressive Behavior: Current Perspectives* (pp. 215–240). New York: Plenum.

Faust, D. (1986) Research on human judgment and its application to clinical practice. *Professional Psychology: Research and Practice*, **17**, 420–430.

Felthous, A.R. & Kellert, S.R. (1987) Childhood cruelty to animals and later aggression against people: A review. *American Journal of Psychiatry*, **144**, 710–717.

Gardner, W., Lidz, C.W., Mulvey, E.P. & Shaw, E.C. (1996a) A comparison of actuarial methods of identifying repetitively violent patients with mental illness. *Law and Human Behavior*, **20**, 35–48.

Gardner, W., Lidz, C.W., Mulvey, E.P. & Shaw, E.C. (1996b) Clinical versus actuarial predictions of violence in patients with mental illness. *Journal of Consulting and Clinical Psychology*, **64**, 602–609.

Gendreau, P., Little, T. & Goggin, C. (1996) A meta-analysis of the predictors of adult offender recidivism: What works! *Criminology*, **34**, 575–607.

Gordon, R.A. (1977) A critique of the evaluation of Patuxent Institution, with particular attention to the issues of dangerousness and recidivism. *Bulletin of the American Academy of Psychiatry and the Law*, **5**, 210–255.

Gottfredson, S.D. (1987) Prediction: An overview of selected methodological issues. In D.M. Gottfredson & M. Tonry (Eds) *Prediction and Classification: Criminal Justice Decision Making* (pp. 21–51). Chicago: University of Chicago Press.

Grisso, T. (1996) Clinical assessment for legal decision-making in criminal cases: Research recommendations. In B. Sales & S. Shah (Eds) *Mental Health and Law: Research, Policy and Services* (pp. 109–140). Durham, NC: Carolina Academic Press.

Grisso, T. & Appelbaum, P.S. (1992) Is it unethical to offer predictions of future violence? *Law and Human Behavior*, **16**, 621–633.

Grove, W.M. & Meehl, P.E. (1996) Comparative efficiency of informal (subjective, impressionistic) and formal (mechanical, algorithmic) prediction procedures: The clinical-statistical controversy. *Psychology, Public Policy, and Law*, **2**, 293–323.

Hall, H.V. (1987) *Violence Prediction: Guidelines for the Forensic Practitioner*. Springfield, Ill.: Charles C. Thomas.

Hanson, R.K. & Bussière, M.T. (1998) Predicting relapse: A meta-analysis of sexual offender recidivism studies. *Journal of Consulting and Clinical Psychology*, **66**, 348–362.

Hare, R.D. (1991) *The Hare Psychopathy Checklist—Revised*. Toronto: Multi-Health Systems.

Hare, R.D. (1996) Psychopathy: A clinical construct whose time has come. *Criminal Justice and Behavior*, **23**, 25–54.

Harris, G.T., Rice, M.E. & Quinsey, V.L. (1993) Violent recidivism of mentally disordered offenders: The development of a statistical prediction instrument. *Criminal Justice and Behavior*, **20**, 315–335.

Hart, S.D. (1998) The role of psychopathy in assessing risk for violence: Conceptual and methodological issues. *Legal and Criminological Psychology*, **3**, 121–137.

Hart, S.D., Hare, R.D. & Forth, A.E. (1994) Psychopathy as a risk marker for violence: Development and validation of a screening version of the revised Psychopathy Checklist. In J. Monahan & H.J. Steadman (Eds) *Violence and Mental Disorder: Developments in Risk Assessment* (pp. 81–99). Chicago: University of Chicago Press.

Hemphill, J.F., Hare, R.D. & Wong, S. (1998) Psychopathy and recidivism: A review. *Legal and Criminological Psychology*, **3**, 139–170.

Hill, C.D., Rogers, R. & Bickford, M.E. (1996) Predicting aggressive and socially disruptive behavior in a maximum security forensic hospital. *Journal of Forensic Sciences*, **41**, 56–59.

Hodgins, S., Mednick, S.A., Brennan, P.A., Schulsinger, F. & Engberg, M. (1996) Mental disorder and crime: Evidence from a Danish birth cohort. *Archives of General Psychiatry*, **53**, 489–496.

Holland, T.R., Holt, N. & Beckett, G.E. (1982) Prediction of violent versus nonviolent recidivism from prior violent and nonviolent criminality. *Journal of Abnormal Psychology*, **91**, 178–182.

Hooper, F.A. & Evans, R.G. (1984) Screening for disruptive behavior of institutionalised juvenile offenders. *Journal of Personality Assessment*, **48**, 159–161.

Kay, S.R., Wolkenfeld, F. & Murrill, L.M. (1988) Profiles of aggression among psychiatric inpatients: II. Covariates and predictors. *Journal of Nervous and Mental Disease*, **176**, 547–557.

Kessel, J.B. & Zimmerman, M. (1993) Reporting errors in studies of the diagnostic performance of self-administered questionnaires: Extent of the problem, recommendations for standardised presentation of results, and implications for the peer review process. *Psychological Assessment*, **5**, 393–399.

Klassen, D. & O'Connor, W.A. (1989) Assessing the risk of violence in released mental patients: A cross-validation study. *Psychological Assessment*, **1**, 75–81.

Klassen, D. & O'Connor, W.A. (1994) Demographic and case history variables in risk assessment. In J. Monahan & H.J. Steadman (Eds) *Violence and Mental Disorder: Developments in Risk Assessment* (pp. 229–257). Chicago: University of Chicago Press.

Kozol, H., Boucher, R. & Garofalo, R. (1972) The diagnosis and treatment of dangerousness. *Crime and Delinquency*, **18**, 371–392.

Kroll, J. & Mackenzie, T.B. (1983) When psychiatrists are liable: Risk management and violent patients. *Hospital and Community Psychiatry*, **34**, 29–37.

Lidz, C.W., Mulvey, E.P. & Gardner, W. (1993) The accuracy of predictions of violence to others. *Journal of the American Medical Association*, **269**, 1007–1011.

Litwack, T.R. & Schlesinger, L.B. (1987) Assessing and predicting violence: Research, law, and applications. In I.B. Weiner & A.K. Hess (Eds) *Handbook of Forensic Psychology* (pp. 205–257). New York: Wiley.

Loeber, R. & Dishion, T.J. (1983) Early predictors of male delinquency: A review. *Psychological Bulletin*, **94**, 68–99.

Marra, A.M., Konzelman, G.E. & Giles, P.G. (1987) A clinical strategy for the assessment of dangerousness. *International Journal of Offender Therapy and Comparative Criminology*, **31**, 291–299.

Marzuk, P.M. (1996) Violence, crime and mental illness: How strong a link? *Archives of General Psychiatry*, **53**, 481–486.

McNiel, D.E. & Binder, R.L. (1987) Predictive validity of judgments of dangerousness in emergency civil commitment. *American Journal of Psychiatry*, **144**, 197–200.

McNiel, D.E. & Binder, R.L. (1991) Clinical assessment of the risk of violence among psychiatric inpatients. *American Journal of Psychiatry*, **148**, 1317–1321.

McNiel, D.E. & Binder, R.L. (1994) Screening for inpatient violence: Validation of an actuarial tool. *Law and Human Behavior*, **18**, 579–586.

McNiel, D.E. & Binder, R.L. (1995) Correlates of accuracy in the assessment of psychiatric inpatients' risk of violence. *American Journal of Psychiatry*, **152**, 901–906.

Meehl, P.E. (1954) *Clinical versus Statistical Prediction*. Minneapolis: University of Minnesota Press.

Meehl, P.E. & Rosen, A. (1955) Antecedent probability and the efficiency of psychometric signs, patterns, or cutting scores. *Psychological Bulletin*, **52**, 194–216.

Megargee, E.I. (1970) The prediction of violence with psychological tests. In C.D. Spielberger (Ed.) *Current Topics in Clinical and Community Psychology*, Volume 2 (pp. 109–146). New York: Academic Press.

Megargee, E.I. (1976) The prediction of dangerous behavior. *Criminal Justice and Behavior*, **3**, 1–22.

Meloy, J.R. (1987) The prediction of violence in outpatient psychotherapy. *American Journal of Psychotherapy*, **41**, 38–45.

Menzies, R.J. & Webster, C.D. (1995) Construction and validation of risk assessments in a six-year follow-up of forensic patients: A tridimensional analysis. *Journal of Consulting and Clinical Psychology*, **63**, 766–768.

Monahan, J. (1981) *Predicting Violent Behavior: An Assessment of Clinical Techniques*. Beverly Hills, CA: Sage.

Monahan, J. (1984) The prediction of violent behavior: Toward a second generation of theory and policy. *American Journal of Psychiatry*, **141**, 10–15.

Monahan, J. (1997) Clinical and actuarial predictions of violence. In D. Faigman, D. Kaye, M. Saks & J. Sanders (Eds) *Modern Scientific Evidence: The Law and Science of Expert Testimony*, Volume 1 (pp. 300–318). St Paul, MN: West Publishing Company.

Monahan, J. & Steadman, H.J. (1994) Toward a rejuvenation of risk assessment research. In J. Monahan & H.J. Steadman (Eds) *Violence and Mental Disorder: Developments in Risk Assessment* (pp. 1–17). Chicago: University of Chicago Press.

Mossman, D. (1994) Assessing predictions of violence: Being accurate about accuracy. *Journal of Consulting and Clinical Psychology*, **62**, 783–792.

Mulvey, E.P. & Lidz, C.W. (1984) Clinical considerations in the prediction of dangerousness in mental patients. *Clinical Psychology Review*, **4**, 379–401.

Nuffield, J. (1989) The "SIR scale": Some reflections on its application. *Forum on Corrections Research*, **1**, 19–22.

Otto, R.K. (1992) Prediction of dangerous behavior: A review and analysis of "second generation" research. *Forensic Reports*, **5**, 103–133.

Owens, R.G. & Bagshaw, M. (1985) First steps in the functional analysis of aggression. In E. Karas (Ed.) *Current Issues in Clinical Psychology*, Volume 2 (pp. 285–307). New York: Plenum.

Palmstierna, T. & Wistedt, B. (1990) Risk factors for aggressive behaviour are of limited value for predicting the violent behaviour of acute involuntarily admitted patients. *Acta Psychiatrica Scandinavica*, **81**, 152–155.

Pollock, N., McBain, I. & Webster, C.D. (1989) Clinical decision making and the assessment of dangerousness. In K. Howells & C.R. Hollin (Eds) *Clinical Approaches to Violence* (pp. 89–115). Chichester: Wiley.

Quinsey, V.L. & Abtman, R. (1979) Variables affecting psychiatrists' and teachers' assessments of the dangerousness of mentally ill offenders. *Journal of Consulting and Clinical Psychology*, **47**, 353–362.

Quinsey, V.L. & Maguire, A. (1986) Maximum security psychiatric patients: Actuarial and clinical prediction of dangerousness. *Journal of Interpersonal Violence*, **1**, 143–171.

Quinsey, V.L. & Walker, W.D. (1992) Dealing with dangerousness: Community risk management strategies with violent offenders. In R.D. Peters, R.J. McMahon & V.L. Quinsey (Eds) *Aggression and Violence Throughout the Lifespan* (pp. 244–262). Newbury Park, CA: Sage.

Quinsey, V.L., Harris, G.T., Rice, M.E. & Cormier, C.A. (1998) *Violent Offenders: Appraising and Managing Risk*. Washington, DC: American Psychological Association.

Reed, J. (1997) Risk assessment and clinical risk management: The lessons from recent enquiries. *British Journal of Psychiatry*, **170** (Suppl. 32), 4–7.

Rice, M.E. & Harris, G.T. (1995) Violent recidivism: Assessing predictive validity. *Journal of Consulting and Clinical Psychology*, **63**, 737–748.

Royal College of Psychiatrists (1998) *Management of Imminent Violence: Clinical Practice Guidelines to Support Mental Health Services*. London: Royal College of Psychiatrists.

Salekin, R.T., Rogers, R. & Sewell, K.W. (1996) A review and meta-analysis of the Psychopathy Checklist—Revised: Predictive validity of dangerousness. *Clinical Psychology: Science and Practice*, **3**, 203–213.

Sawyer, J. (1966) Measurement and prediction, clinical and statistical. *Psychological Bulletin*, **66**, 178–200.

Selby, M.J. (1984) Assessment of violence potential using measures of anger, hostility, and social desirability. *Journal of Personality Assessment*, **48**, 531–544.

Sepejak, D.S., Webster, C.D. & Menzies, R.J. (1984) The clinical prediction of dangerousness: Getting beyond the basic questions. In D.J. Müller, D.E. Blackman & A.J. Chapman (Eds) *Psychology and Law* (pp. 113–123). Chichester: Wiley.

Shaffer, C.E., Waters, W.F. & Adams, S.G. (1994) Dangerousness: Assessing the risk of violent behavior. *Journal of Consulting and Clinical Psychology*, **62**, 1064–1068.

Shah, S.A. (1978) Dangerousness: A paradigm for exploring some issues in law and psychology. *American Psychologist*, **33**, 224–238.

Shapiro, D.L. (1990) Standard of care in the prediction of violent behavior. *Psychotherapy in Private Practice*, **8**, 43–53.

Simon, F.H. (1971) *Prediction Methods in Criminology*. London: HMSO.

Steadman, H.J. & Keveles, G. (1972) The community adjustment and criminal activity of the Baxstrom patients: 1966–1970. *American Journal of Psychiatry*, **129**, 304–310.

Steadman, H.J., Mulvey, E.P., Monahan, J., Robbins, P.C., Appelbaum, P.S., Grisso, T., Roth, L.H. & Silver, E. (1998) Violence by people discharged from acute psychiatric inpatient facilities and by others in the same neighbourhoods. *Archives of General Psychiatry*, **55**, 393–401.

Swanson, J., Holzer, C., Ganju, V. & Jono, R. (1990) Violence and psychiatric disorder in the community: Evidence from the Epidemiological Catchment Area surveys. *Hospital and Community Psychiatry*, **41**, 761–770.

Swanson, J., Borum, R., Swartz, M.S. & Monohan, J. (1996) Psychotic symptoms and disorders in the risk of violent behaviour in the community. *Criminal Behaviour and Mental Health*, **6**, 309–329.

Taylor, G. (1998) Offender needs—providing the focus for our correctional interventions. *Forum on Corrections Research*, **10**, 3–8.

Webster, C.D., Douglas, K.S., Eaves, D. & Hart, S.D. (1997) *HCR-20: Assessing Risk for Violence—Version 2*. Vancouver: Mental Health, Law, and Policy Institute, Simon Fraser University.

Webster, C.D., Harris, G.T., Rice, M.E., Cormier, C. & Quinsey, V.L. (1994) *The Violence Prediction Scheme: Assessing Dangerousness in High Risk Men*. Toronto: Centre for Criminology.

Wenk, E.A., Robison, J.O. & Smith, G.B. (1972) Can violence be predicted? *Crime and Delinquency*, **18**, 393–402.

Werner, P.D., Rose, T.L. & Yesavage, J.A. (1983) Reliability, accuracy and decision-making strategy in clinical predictions of imminent dangerousness. *Journal of Consulting and Clinical Psychology*, **51**, 815–825.

Werner, P.D. & Meloy, J.R. (1992) Decision making about dangerousness in releasing patients from long-term psychiatric hospitalisation. *Journal of Psychiatry and Law*, **12**, 35–47.

Wettstein, R.M. (1984) The prediction of violent behavior and the duty to protect third parties. *Behavioral Science and the Law*, **2**, 291–316.

Widiger, T.A. & Trull, T.J. (1994) Personality disorders and violence. In J. Monahan & H.J. Steadman (Eds) *Violence and Mental Disorder: Developments in Risk Assessment* (pp. 203–226). Chicago: University of Chicago Press.

Chapter 10

Systems of Services

David Heywood
Stockton Hall Psychiatric Hospital,
Stockton-on-the-Forest, York, UK

Forensic psychiatry covers a range of secure in-patient facilities including high security and both public sector and private sector medium security. It also includes the provision of court reports, advice and consultancy services to mainstream agencies, and after-care in the community. In addition, Consultant Forensic Psychiatrists occasionally have access to less secure facilities in High Dependency Units. These are tertiary services with various referral sources both within the Criminal Justice System and general psychiatry. Multi-disciplinary working is central to the function of forensic psychiatry with an integrated approach to assessment, treatment, rehabilitation and after-care of patients who are often considered to be a high risk and present with complex multi-faceted needs. Accurately assessing need, however, is complicated by a number of factors outside the immediate sphere of influence of clinical staff (Cohen & Eastman, 1997).

In recent years there have been a number of important developments, which have significantly influenced the delivery of forensic psychiatry services. Owing to the recommendations of reports and inquiries, including the Reed Report (1991), Ashworth Inquiry Report (Blom-Cooper, 1992), the number of Special Hospital beds has been gradually reduced but conversely the number of medium secure beds has significantly increased towards meeting the level of need anticipated in the mid 1970s (Glancy Report, 1974; Butler Report, 1975). It is likely that the impact of the Fallon Report (1999) will be to add to this momentum. In this context the number of independent sector medium secure facilities has become proportionately greater, creating challenges in terms of co-ordinating systems of care and enabling carers and relatives to remain actively involved. In addition commissioning arrangements for high and medium secure services are adopting a more strategic and integrated approach (Health

Behaviour, Crime and Legal Processes: A Guide for Forensic Practitioners.
Edited by James McGuire, Tom Mason and Aisling O'Kane.
© 2000 John Wiley & Sons Ltd.

Service Circular, 1999) which it is anticipated will have a major impact on future developments.

This review of services will focus on case examples which illustrate and emphasise various key aspects of managerial and clinical issues associated with forensic psychiatry and how it interacts with other agencies including the prisons, general psychiatry, the probation service, social services and the independent sector. I have primarily focused on in-patient facilities because of the inclusion of a chapter in this volume on "Care and Management in the Community" (see Chapter 11). Owing to the functional analysis of the role of forensic psychiatry services it is often the interrelationship with the external environment and the statutory framework which are the defining elements. The specific methods of accessing forensic psychiatry services will inevitably vary from area to area due to local conditions, and this is a gradually evolving set of circumstances. The pre-existing relationship between the agencies involved, the range of secure and non-secure facilities available within the locality, strategic planning initiatives and the demand/need for services or a combination of these factors will have a crucial effect upon decision-making options. The other key components at the point of referral and discharge include the seriousness of an offence, perceived risk factors based on information available at the time, management difficulties, the section of the Mental Health Act 1983 under which the patient is compulsorily detained, and public perceptions which can have "political" implications.

ROUTES INTO FORENSIC PSYCHIATRY SYSTEMS

How a referral is made and to whom, what is being requested and the availability of resources are important considerations. The proportion of "forensic" offender patients in a particular facility may be governed by the view of senior clinicians and managers but is also dependent on whether there are sufficient facilities within the locality offering lower security or semi-secure options. The freedom of clinicians to make a judgement based on an accurate assessment may be influenced by objective systemic factors as much as clinical skill. However, there are common referral routes which all forensic services, from lower security to maximum security, will access. These ways by which patients enter the system have a significant bearing on how they are managed within the services provided and also the options available to exit from the system. Whether a patient has been convicted of a criminal offence, the nature of the offence, the section under which he or she has been admitted and is being assessed or treated, diagnostic criteria, purchasing issues and associated costs, and the reputation the patient has acquired have a potential to create blocks and resistances to other agencies maintaining an involvement or becoming involved in this process. This is as significant for the independent sector as it is for the public sector even though there may appear to be potential financial incentives for commissioning bodies to facilitate more rapid transfers to conditions of lesser security.

Detention in Police Custody

The earliest stage at which forensic psychiatry services are able to intervene is a detention in a police station of a person who is alleged to have committed a criminal offence. Diversion from custody and inter agency working to achieve it have been well established throughout the UK (Joseph & Potter, 1993), but the actual provision of this service is variable. Where there are deficits in this regard there are inevitable consequences both individually and systemically. The local schemes that have been established in specific localities are usually operated and managed by mainstream psychiatric services. The function of diversion is to avoid inappropriate detention in the Criminal Justice System rather than necessarily discontinuing the judicial process. Consequently, before or at the initial court appearance, a mental health professional—usually a community psychiatric nurse although occasionally a social worker—will have assessed the person involved. Recommendations are made on the basis of current mental health, taking into account past psychiatric history. The seriousness of the alleged offence and the associated requirement of a particular level of security are also significant factors influencing decision-making at all stages of the process. The majority of individuals in this situation are "diverted" to general psychiatry services either as in-patients or out-patients. This can be achieved by the charges being dropped; a use of cautioning; application of a "bind-over"; or by conditions of bail being imposed. The option of a "civil section" under the Mental Health Act 1983 can be considered which could run parallel with due legal process or be a substitute for further detention within the Criminal Justice System.

It has been hypothesised that the reduction of psychiatric hospital beds throughout the country over the last 40 years has led to psychiatric patients committing offences in the community because of precipitive discharges, inadequate after-care and unsuitable placements. The offences involved, contrary to press coverage and public perception, are invariably of a relatively minor nature, such as criminal damage and breach of the peace. The person involved is often detained in police cells not because of the nature of the offence but due to his or her need for psychiatric assessment. At this stage there may also be substance abuse issues and/or personality factors, which influence the presentation and behaviour of the individual, and the options available for psychiatric intervention.

How do forensic psychiatry services become involved? In the event of a more serious offence or where there has been past or current service involvement, a fuller psychiatric assessment may be requested. The process followed would usually involve the custody sergeant at the police station where the alleged offender has been detained requesting the involvement of the Forensic Medical Examiner (FME), also known as the Police Surgeon. The FME is responsible for assessing persons detained in the cells who are considered to be presenting with psychiatric as well as physical health problems. The FME will then refer to the psychiatrist in accordance with the assessment and perceived need.

Local forensic psychiatry services based at Medium Secure Units (MSUs) offer an "on call" system and a psychiatrist may be able to respond to a request for an assessment in the cells at fairly short notice. Usually at this stage other members of the clinical team will not be involved but the custody sergeant or the FME will probably have contacted an Approved Social Worker from the local Social Services Department if a compulsory admission is being actively considered. The forensic psychiatrist must conclude that the alleged offender fulfils the criteria for a "civil section" under the Mental Health Act 1983 in accordance with statutory considerations. Recommendations by two doctors and an application by an Approved Social Worker would be necessitated for this option to become viable.

Additionally, a number of factors are crucial at this stage, including: (a) the need for a particular level of security which is based on past as well as current behaviour; (b) the attitude of the person to a psychiatric admission; (c) risk factors which are related to the nature of the offence; (d) the need to ensure public protection; (e) the availability of a bed in the identified facility; (f) the views of carers and relatives will require to be taken into account, with specific relevance to the powers of the nearest relative under a "civil section". Any one or more of these factors may assume particular prominence, depending on the circumstances. The Approved Social Worker is responsible for assessing the need for admission, assisting in identifying a bed and conveying the person to hospital. It is important to note that the psychiatric and judicial processes are separate where a "civil section" is completed for a person who continues to be subject to criminal proceedings. Whether the person is charged with an offence may depend on whereas the FME and/or the psychiatrist considers that he or she is fit for police interview. If criminal charges are pursued, the involvement of an Appropriate Adult under the Police and Criminal Evidence Act 1984 will be required. The following case illustrates some of the dilemmas caused as a consequence of an arrest and detention in a Police Station.

Case 1
Charlie is an 18-year-old African-Caribbean man living in a predominantly white community. He has been living with his two younger siblings and has not been in employment since leaving school. There is no known psychiatric history and Charlie has not been convicted of a criminal offence previously or been aggressive until recently. His relationship with his mother has deteriorated in the past few weeks, with Charlie accusing her of spreading rumours about him thus preventing him from leaving the house. His personal hygiene has become a problem, which is out of character; he has refused to answer the door and has begun to talk of his mother as the devil. His mother has heard him talking to himself in his bedroom which he has barricaded to prevent other members of the family from entering. Religious symbols have been placed on the door. When his mother returns from the local shops he locks her in the kitchen and sets fire to the furniture in the lounge. He leaves the house, and when he is arrested in the locality an hour later he asks whether the devil has been destroyed. His mother has been able to escape from the house through the back door but the house is severely damaged. Charlie is detained at the local police station and the custody sergeant is anticipating charging him with arson with intent to endanger a life. A forensic psychiatry assessment results in him being trans-

ferred to a local Medium Secure Unit under Section 2 of the Mental Health Act 1983 for assessment and treatment. This would probably not have been possible in many areas due to problems associated with bed availability.

The decision-making options available with regard to this case were either to have Charlie remanded in custody perhaps pending further psychiatric assessment, refer for a Special Hospital opinion, admit to a local catchment area MSU or seek an admission to conditions of lesser security in a High Dependency Unit or a locked ward. The psychiatrist's ability to make an MSU bed available and the seriousness of the offence, coupled with his lack of psychiatric or offending history, created the preconditions for an admission to this level of security, initially for assessment. However, if there had not been a bed available a less suitable placement would have had to have been considered. The advantage of a "civil section" in this case was that it allowed flexibility in clinical management, although the possibility of discharge by a Mental Health Review Tribunal was a potentially complicating factor. For Charlie to be admitted via a "remand section" he would have had to have been remanded in custody, thus complicating the assessment by delaying multi-disciplinary involvement and the provision of potential treatment options.

Prisoners on Remand

Subsequent to a remand in custody forensic psychiatry services can be accessed by a request from the Crown Prosecution Service or the defence solicitor for a psychiatric report or a referral from the Prison Medical Service for an assessment. Medium Secure Unit (MSU) psychiatrists may provide regular sessions at local prisons within their catchment area which facilitates effective networking and monitoring of difficult cases. Consequently, the need for psychiatric intervention can be identified and appropriate action taken. Medication can only be administered in the Criminal Justice System with the consent of the prisoner. Transfer to a health care centre in the prison may be necessitated in order to provide a treatment regime and monitor the prisoner more closely. Qualified psychiatric nurses employed by the Prison Service are increasingly being made available to assist in this process. However, a prison environment is not equivalent to a hospital facility and there are structural and interpersonal aspects which are likely to be counter-therapeutic in this context. Additionally, many prisoners on remand are not willing to accept medication and do not co-operate with the albeit limited support available. Inevitably, this often leads to mental health deterioration which increases the urgency of a transfer to hospital. The ability of a forensic psychiatrist to offer suitable in-patient facilities is also dependent on the resources being available, taking into account the other demands, which commonly lead to waiting lists being established.

An in-patient forensic psychiatry assessment is also advantageous because it facilitates the involvement of the multi-disciplinary team with the Consultant

Psychiatrist fulfilling the lead role as Responsible Medical Officer. Forensic social workers are unlikely to become actively involved until an admission has occurred and therefore relatives and carers may not have been adequately consulted or actively involved in the process. The role of relatives and carers is an important aspect of the assessment process and the support systems made available by forensic psychiatry services. The expertise of nursing staff to manage what are invariably very difficult behavioural problems, often involving assaultative behaviour and on occasion self harm, is also invaluable. Notwithstanding the recent improvement in the availability of trained nurses within the Criminal Justice System only a minority of prisons have appropriately staffed health care centres and there are usually great difficulties in significantly ameliorating the milieu of a prison regime. This factor influences the decision-making process when, for example, a remand prisoner, who may or may not have a psychiatric history, presents with serious management problems but does not respond to the usual strategies employed by prison staff. Therefore a referral is made to psychiatric services and an assessment by a forensic psychiatrist for a transfer to hospital under a "remand section" is necessary.

The availability of a visiting forensic psychiatrist for advice and support to prison staff provides accessibility, and a relatively speedy response. MSU psychiatrists have direct access to beds whereas Special Hospital psychiatrists are required to present cases to the Admissions Panel at the hospital, which has jurisdiction over admissions. Waiting lists can make even an urgent request for transfer difficult to facilitate without causing delays leading to further mental health deterioration. It needs to be borne in mind that there are resource implications which are relatively more profound in certain regions of the country where the supply of MSU in-patient beds is far exceeded by the actual need or demand, particularly in inner city socially deprived areas (Coid, 1998). This has created the circumstances whereby patients are required to be transferred to independent sector facilities, which are frequently located away from the local community.

At the point of referral a remand prisoner has usually begun to display serious behavioural problems which are considered by the prison staff to be associated with their mental health. If the individual involved has a psychiatric history, it is possible that forensic psychiatry services will already be aware of his or her detention; otherwise an episode or series of episodes may create the need for an urgent referral for admission.

Case 2
Jack is a 28-year-old Caucasian man who is the youngest of six siblings. His father died while he was an infant and his mother who was the central person within the family brought him up. All Jack's siblings had left home to start their own families. He had a poor school record including frequent truancy. Since leaving school he has not worked. He established a serious drinking problem in his late teens which he financed by stealing or borrowing money from his mother and the occasional property offence for which he received non-custodial sentences when he was convicted. Over the past 12 months Jack's behaviour has changed. He has become increasingly irritable and verbally aggressive. His few social contacts have ceased altogether and

members of the family have expressed concern about his behaviour. There are increasingly frequent arguments with his mother which she does not divulge to other members of the family because of her tendency to protect Jack. He has one brief informal admission to a local District General Hospital Psychiatric Unit when it is considered his problems were primarily alcohol related. However, he does not accept out-patient treatment from the alcoholism service. A very serious altercation occurs between Jack and his mother at home during which he accuses her of not being his real mother. He shouts at her that she was an alien life force and proceeds to stab her a number of times using a bread knife which he has taken from the kitchen. He is subsequently charged with attempted murder and remanded in custody. In prison he is described as being uncontrollably disturbed, shouting and crying. He is not sleeping and refuses to eat because he is convinced his food is being poisoned. The situation becomes critical when he assaults a prisoner whom he attempts to strangle. Jack is admitted to an MSU for urgent assessment and treatment.

There are a number of common factors involved in referrals from the Criminal Justice System of which Jack's case is illustrative. He created management difficulties because he did not respond to attempts at controlling his behaviour within the prison. He would not access medication and his mental health was deteriorating. The forensic psychiatrist considered that, due to the long-standing alcohol and personality problems, the treatment of his psychiatric disorder would of necessity be multi-faceted and he had potentially longer-term needs. It was considered that the assault on his mother had been potentially life threatening. There were also complicated family dynamics which influenced the way the case was managed.

Attempts at managing Jack on remand proved unsuccessful and the assault on the prison officer created an urgent need for admission. Despite concerns about longer stay needs and risk factors indicating a need for sufficiently high levels of security, Jack was admitted to the MSU initially for assessment. Many of the intra-familial conflicts came to light after his admission which added a further dimension to his case. There were tensions within the family between those members who considered him to have been personally responsible for his actions and therefore favoured punishment rather than treatment and those who held the view that he had been developing mental health problems for a number of years and his drinking was symptomatic of an illness process. This dichotomy was reflected in discussions in the multi disciplinary clinical team about accountability and responsibility for his actions.

There are additional issues which may arise for forensic psychiatry staff with regard to referrals of remand prisoners. Considerable scepticism and uncertainty is often expressed where there is only an indirect relationship between the nature of the offence and presenting behaviour in prison. For instance, when a person charged with serious sexual offences exhibits symptoms of clinical depression while on remand, and is threatening serious self harm, there may be little alternative but to facilitate an admission as a consequence of the current risk factors. The individual's presentation may be due to environmental factors pertaining to prison culture and personality problems but in the event of an admission there may be more wide-ranging expectations. Subsequent exploration of a non-custodial sentence in consultation with the Probation Service, perhaps utilising a Probation Order with a condition of psychiatric treatment, may become an option but assessing psychological needs in the context of an admission to an MSU is fraught with dangers. The role of the clinical psychologist in this process is likely to be pivotal. It is often difficult to differentiate between the immediate psychological aspects of a case and the nature of an offence which may be the consequence of cultural and/or developmental factors which militate against therapeutic progress. Where there is a vested interest for a patient to co-operate with in-patient management to avoid a custodial sentence these circumstances are likely to change significantly after a case has come to trial. The attitudes of the patient towards treatment may become less positive as a consequence.

Forensic psychiatry, at all levels of security, has the tendency to "inherit" cases for which clinical responsibility is assumed, creating dilemmas in terms of future management. Of course, re-offending may well also influence public perception of forensic psychiatry services. Mainstream services and agencies are, perhaps understandably, extremely reluctant to become involved in following up high-risk cases who may be considered not to be suffering from "severe and enduring mental health problems". Consequently, decision-making from the beginning of the process often has a major impact on later options. Careful and judicious "gate-keeping" is an essential element in forensic psychiatry fulfilling its primary functions. In these circumstances it is not surprising that MSUs in particular admit a high proportion of patients suffering from psychiatric conditions whose treatment needs may be considered to be clearer and who are significantly less likely to re-offend (Bailey & MacCulloch, 1992) although by what extent is questionable (Buchanan, 1998).

The treatment of personality disorders is particularly contentious, raising issues about whether they should be dealt with within the mental health system, in the Criminal Justice System or by a "third way" (Home Office & Deptartment of Health, 1999). It is interesting that these has been an under-utilisations of the Crime Sentences Act 1997, which was intended to provide the option of a protracted period of assessments of treatability in hospital during which the patient can be returned to prison.

Sentenced Prisoners

In recent the years the number of admissions of sentenced prisoners to forensic psychiatry units has significantly increased while there has been a steady growth in the prison population. The Reed Report (1991) and also Gunn, Maden and Swinton (1991) identified the unmet needs of this client group, recommending the transfer to hospital of prisoners requiring assessment and treatment. Evidence of psychiatric and psychological problems experienced by both sentenced and remand prisoners has also been demonstrated in a more major recent study (Singleton et al., 1998). There have been consequences both for the prisoners involved and the units to which they have been referred.

Prisoners serving longer sentences who are transferred to hospital face the prospect of being returned to prison after the stabilisation of their mental disorder. Medication can only be given compulsorily in a hospital setting. Therefore the potential exists for the patient or prisoner to be transferred back to prison because he or she no longer requires to be detained in hospital, only to relapse and be re-referred. This can create a "revolving door" problem, involving multiple transfers between hospital and prison, thus causing inevitable further deterioration of mental functioning. It is questionable whether this is an effective use of resources but the practitioners involved have a duty to provide beds for people requiring in-patient services and therefore a pragmatic view is often taken. Conflicting demands on forensic beds and resource problems can cause difficulties in managing these cases effectively.

A further consequence of the increase in the proportion of sentenced prisoners on forensic psychiatry units is the cultural effect of introducing criminal attitudes and behaviour into essentially treatment-orientated regimes. The balance between containment and therapeutic roles has certainly changed a great deal in recent years. Nursing morale can be adversely affected in the process of managing unresponsive and unco-operative patients. Leave outside hospital is often unrealistic for transferred prisoners, which leads to frustration and disillusionment for both staff and patients. There is a sense of the patient having little or nothing to lose, which may impact on behaviour and attitude towards treatment. Substance abuse also has potentially negative affects for the mental health of individual patients and the milieu in which they are being treated. This has become a more significant factor in the management of secure facilities as well as mainstream services in recent years and is clearly strongly associated with risk the of violence (Ward & Applin, 1998).

Case 3
Steve is 45 years of age and is of mixed heritage. His father was Nigerian and his mother was Caucasian. He is the middle child of three but he does not retain close involvement with his family. At the age of 27 years, after a number of convictions for relatively minor criminal offences, he receives a life sentence for the murder of an acquaintance over a drug-related conflict. In prison he is generally co-operative during the first ten years of his sentence but he is considered to be socially isolated. His behaviour changes and he becomes increasingly hostile to both fellow prisoners and prison officers. He is observed to be talking to himself, particularly when he is by himself in his cell. After a number of relatively less serious incidents Steve attacks his cell mate, causing him extensive injuries. He is referred to a visiting forensic psychiatrist who strongly recommends a Special Hospital admission on the basis of his lack of insight, his strong antipathy towards psychiatric treatment and his perceived dangerousness based on past and current behaviour. After a Special Hospital assessment the Consultant Forensic Psychiatrist recommends an urgent admission. The Admissions Panel at the Special Hospital considers his case and he is transferred under Section 47/49 of the Mental Health Act 1983.

Steve's referral caused the Admissions Panel at the Special Hospital concern in a number of areas. It was considered that the combination of his mental health and personality difficulties would conspire against therapeutic optimism. The risk assessment report indicated that he was a prickly, rigid individual who was hostile to authority figures. He had little insight into his condition and therefore was unlikely to voluntarily co-operate with treatment. Additionally, the fact that he was under the jurisdiction of both penal and mental health systems, created concerns about delays in moving him on.

Referrals from NHS facilities

In all forensic psychiatry facilities there are patients who are subject to "civil" rather than "forensic" sections. The proportion of patients transferred from NHS facilities varies between units, which is partly based on the availability of a spectrum of care at lower levels of security. This patient population also includes a proportion who are re-admitted forensic psychiatry service patients previously discharged to live in the community but who have relapsed or are in the process of relapsing, as well as referrals from general psychiatry services of patients who are presenting with problematic behaviour. The needs of this latter group were identified by the Glancy Report (1974) as requiring similar levels of security to the mentally disordered offender population. In reality these patients often cause serious management problems because of the inter-agency and "boundary" problems they bring with them in addition to their presenting behaviour.

Patients who are referred from NHS facilities to forensic psychiatry units often have committed anti-social acts, sometimes of a serious nature, for which they have not been prosecuted. The police and the Crown Prosecution Service may not pursue criminal convictions against psychiatric patients because they are often already detained under the Mental Health Act, and therefore there is no immediate public protection issue, and their behaviour is perceived to be a consequence of psychiatric symptoms. In any case witnesses, perhaps including victims, may also be suffering from mental health problems, and be considered incapable of providing admissible evidence in court. The willingness and ability of professionals to intervene to have a patient charged with an offence presents with complicated ethical dilemmas. Perhaps understandably, due to conflict of interests, convictions are rarely pursued with vigour. Offences for which psychiatric patients have not been prosecuted have included arson, serious assaults and sexual offences. This latter category may concentrate minds in the light of the Sex Offenders (Registration) Act 1997. The consequences of patients not being convicted are numerous and include: difficulties in them taking responsibility for their actions; the details of the "offence" are not being recorded in depositions (typescript witness statements to the police) and therefore becoming blurred or distorted over a period of time; and victims are denied the right to be protected. This course of action also excludes the possibility of a Hospital Order (perhaps with restrictions) being brought into force, with all the implications for after-care under Psychiatric and Social Supervision.

Concerns are frequently expressed by staff working in forensic psychiatry units about referrers not remaining involved during the admission, and an associated unwillingness to transfer the patient back to low or non-secure facilities after stabilisation of his or her condition and behaviour. The relationship between the professionals involved in general psychiatry services and forensic psychiatry services is an important factor in this regard. These agencies have a mutually dependent relationship and for the system to work satisfactorily a high degree of flexibility and trust is required. Furthermore, for as long as a patient remains in a Special Hospital, an MSU or an independent sector secure unit/hospital beyond the time that he or she is benefiting from the respective level of security, this means that a bed is not available for another patient who may have greater need for these scarce resources. Once again inter-agency co-operation is crucial. However, it needs to be borne in mind that these patients have often created major management difficulties previously causing morale to suffer, particularly among the nursing staff. Therefore it is not altogether surprising that there is a hesitancy to transfer a patient back to conditions of lesser security. Relatives and carers may also express anxiety about a family member being treated alongside serious offenders in forensic psychiatry facilities without appreciating that the patient may require similar levels of security due to his or her behaviour, albeit that this has not resulted in a criminal prosecution.

Case 4
Sally is a 28-year-old Caucasian woman who has had a number of admissions to a psychiatric unit at the local District General Hospital diagnosed at different times as manic depressive, schizo-affective disorder and personality disorder. She is a single mother with a daughter of 6 years old who is cared for by her grandparents when Sally is in hospital. Sally has spoken about having been sexually abused by a neighbour while she was a child but this has not been investigated by the police. Her parents are aware of this disclosure and tend to view it with scepticism because Sally has made other allegations in the past which have proved groundless. During her current admission, under Section 3, Sally has become enraged by her situation and she has made repeated telephone calls to the police demanding action is taken against the alleged perpetrator. She experiences conflict with nursing staff whom she accuses of being provocative and not taking her disclosures seriously. Her mood becomes labile and a decision is made by the clinical team to discontinue visits from her daughter until she has settled because of potential risks to the child of an emotional rather than physical nature. This rapidly leads to an escalation in Sally's antisocial behaviour and she assaults nursing staff, sometimes impulsively but often involving a degree of planning. She is also increasingly becoming sexually disinhibited. A referral to the MSU follows an attempt to stab a member of nursing staff who has been specialing Sally. An admission is necessitated due to unpredictable behaviour and her increased propensity to be violent. In the meantime the Social Services Children and Families Team have become involved due to concerns expressed by the school about her daughter's aggressive behaviour towards other children.

Sally was admitted to a predominantly male ward. Although she had not been convicted of a criminal offence she was considered to be the most disturbed and challenging patient on the ward at the MSU. She continued to be aggressive but with careful management the frequency and severity of the assaults were reduced. Within the multi-disciplinary team concerns were expressed about the nature and extent of Sally's mental health problems, the difficulties in addressing the sexual abuse disclosures and her vulnerability due to her sexually disinhibited provocative behaviour. In addition, Sally's family voiced negative views about her placement, stating that she had never committed a criminal offence and there were men on the ward who were known to have exhibited sexually dysfunctional behaviour.

It is not uncommon for forensic psychiatry services to become actively involved in child protection issues, thus requiring liaison with Social Services departments. For instance, the need to protect children visiting patients in secure units has been the subject of a major debate within forensic psychiatry recently (Fallon Report, 1999; Mental Health Act 1983 *Code of Practice*, 1999). Difficulties can be experienced between agencies whose primary focus and responsibilities are for different members of the same family. Although it is considered to be good practice to be "transparent" and share information in the interests of both parties, there may be matters which ought to remain confidential to one particular agency because of limited relevance to the wider family. Family members often have a major impact by advocating on behalf of a particular course of action.

In Sally's case the family was strongly supportive of her "right" to see her daughter and rejected the view that there was potential harm due to the disinhibited nature of Sally's behaviour. The Social Services Children and Families Team were concerned about her daughter's emotional development. When Sally's behaviour began to stabilise she was assessed by the clinical psychologist on the team who recommended a referral to the local psychology service and a transfer back to the District General Hospital Psychiatric Unit at the earliest opportunity. In the meantime contact with her daughter required to be carefully evaluated, taking full account of the child's best interest, which potentially conflicted with Sally's views. The establishment of child-visiting policies within forensic units requires the involvement of local Social Services Departments (Health Service Circular/LA Circular, 1999), which has further stressed the importance of inter-agency working.

RELATIONSHIPS BETWEEN FORENSIC PSYCHIATRY SYSTEMS

Forensic psychiatry, as already indicated, comprises three interwoven systems. These are the Special Hospitals which constitute high security and have been shrinking in terms of bed numbers in recent years; public sector MSUs covering a specific catchment area; and independent sector secure units/hospitals which take referrals on a national basis. The "downsizing" of the Special Hospitals, coupled with the greater emphasis on public safety, has significantly increased demand for medium and lower securing beds. The interrelationships among these systems have changed due to the way they have each been managed, and to clinical/purchasing systems imposed by the *Care Programme Approach* (Department of Health, 1995) and *Care Management* (NHS & Community Care Act 1990). The involvement of the Probation Service and Social Services is essential to the functioning of forensic psychiatry less directly but no less importantly in terms of decision-making at crucial stages of the process.

A number of pilot schemes and initiatives have been established in recent years to explore the options for relieving pressure on existing services in providing more suitable facilities for patients presenting with more intractable and treatment-resistant conditions. A proportion of patients currently involved in high- and medium-security services require such facilities. However, estimating the level of need is an extremely complicated process (Cohen & Eastman, 1997). It is influenced by factors such as the patient's mental state, where he or she is currently being detained, the options and resources available, perceived risk to self and others and how the process is managed in a particular area. Waiting lists and pressure from other referral sources can significantly affect the short-term and longer-term options available.

Steve (Case 3), who had been admitted to a Special Hospital as a sentenced prisoner, was required to remain in this environment for more than two and a half years despite responding fairly quickly to treatment and not presenting management problems within this setting. Informal liaison with his catchment area MSU was followed by a referral for rehabilitation in conditions of lesser security, thus facilitating opportunities for escorted and unescorted leave which are not available to the same extent at a Special Hospital. The assessment process identified potential difficulties for Steve's eventual discharge because of his status as a transferred prisoner. There would be the need for his case to be dealt with simultaneously by both penal and mental health systems which have often divergent decision-making procedures and functions. Consequently, his progress was governed by his status as a life sentence prisoner in addition to his clinical presentation and behaviour.

There are often non-clinical issues which must be addressed and overcome to facilitate transfer within the sub-systems of forensic psychiatry. Public attitudes can form a potential obstacle in this process. Eventual discharge options and the systemic problems which may arise often create a disincentive in arranging for a transfer to conditions of lesser security. Once again, "gate-keeping" factors may play a predominant role in the optimum use of scarce resources which are high in cost and low in density. The Probation Service, in consultation with the multidisciplinary team, is likely to be involved in mapping out pre-discharge planning for a sentenced prisoner in accordance with clinical progress and needs. Further areas of concern regarding a transfer to conditions of lesser security may include: (a) the need for further offence-related work; (b) the effect of a changed environment on behaviour; (c) the attitude of the patient towards the proposed move; (d) contingency planning in the event of problems arising; and (e) the timescale involved in arranging for eventual discharge under the NHS and Community Care Act 1990. Each of these factors requires to be considered prior to the transfer, usually under the initial conditions of six months' "trial leave" enabling the patient to be transferred back to higher security should the need arise.

The role of the Home Office Mental Health Unit is important to the management of patients under Restriction Orders (Section 37-41) or Restriction Directions (Section 47-49) The Home Office retains responsibility for patients throughout this process by monitoring, reviewing and processing the movement of mentally disordered offenders as they are transferred between the criminal justice system and psychiatric services. Its jurisdiction includes remand prisoners/patients, sentenced prisoners transferred to hospital and patients on Restriction Orders both in hospital and on Conditional Discharge. The Home Office can offer valuable assistance in cases where careful planning and decision-making are necessary. However, tensions can develop over cases where the Home Office is considered to be unresponsive to requests for increased leave arrangements, thereby slowing down the process. It is not unusual for clinicians to feel frustrated because the Home Office establishes expectations to be fulfilled prior to agreeing a particular course of action (such as a successful completion of a number of periods of escorted leave). Nevertheless the Mental Health Unit should be considered as a useful source of guidance and assistance, because it can offer an impartial and objective view. Clinical autonomy, however, is invariably modified as a consequence.

Transfers between Medium Security and High Security

In the case of Steve (Case 3) a pre-transfer case conference was arranged at the Special Hospital, to which the Home Office were invited in order to discuss clinical and systemic aspects prior to a decision being made about further assessment and rehabilitation at the MSU. Due to the length of Steve's imprisonment, which was beyond the tariff originally established, it was unlikely that the Home Office would agree to a transfer back to prison. Being returned to prison would have had the effect of jeopardising his mental health which had originally deteriorated within a penal setting. His willingness to co-operate with treatment was also questionable, thus posing potential difficulties in pre-discharge planning and after-care. The other option which was taken into account was a referral to an independent sector secure unit/hospital which would have had to be purchased by his local Health Authority.

The environment and working practices of MSUs differ greatly from high-security Special Hospitals (Snowden, 1990, 1995; Murray, 1996). These facilities are usually far smaller, of mixed gender, there is a more rapid turnover of patients and they are usually located within the locality from which the patient originates. Smaller sized MSU's provide opportunities to establish a collaborative culture between members of the multi-disciplinary team, thus creating a commonality of purpose. In addition, by providing a service within a defined catchment area, MSUs are able to fulfil the expectations of the Butler Report about local services and accessibility. However, training and research options may be limited relative to the Special Hospitals which enjoy the advantages of economies of scale. Most MSUs have a policy restricting admissions to two years, which is not always achievable but reflects the relatively high demand for beds. The need for longer stay medium secure facilities is highlighted by the blocking of beds in MSUs, which has only been partially addressed by the expansion of the independent sector.

MSUs are also able to provide a seamless (parallel) service by facilitating after-care which has a significant impact on decision-making functions because of the high level of accountability and professional responsibility this imposes (Higgins, 1981). Perhaps more than any other characteristic this distinguishes MSUs from both the Special Hospitals and independent sector units. In recent years MSUs have tended to become "stand-alone" facilities rather than being attached to large psychiatric hospitals, due to the generalised hospital closure programme. This has led to changes to the provision of non-clinical services, it has reduced opportunities for leave within the hospital grounds which have inevitably shrunk in size and brought MSUs closer to their communities. To develop this latter point further, there has been a tendency for communities to express their feelings of vulnerability in an increasingly assertive and at times hostile way, particularly when things go wrong. The development of new initiatives both in the community and in hospital settings entails taking this factor into account.

A transfer of a patient from medium security to high security usually occurs following a period of sustained aggressive and assaultative behaviour, occasionally involving self-harm, of a degree which warrants continuous observation and the frequent need for crisis management. The milieu of an MSU can thus be significantly damaged, thus impacting on the treatment and safety of other patients. Substance abuse, which has become as endemic in psychiatric facilities as in the Criminal Justice System, creates complications. Hostility to staff and other patients, resistance to treatment and the creation of an anti-therapeutic culture commonly occur as a consequence of various forms of substance abuse interacting with mental health problems. Advice and support may be sought from specialist drug, alcohol and public protection organisations, further emphasising the need for effective multi-agency working.

Another dilemma, which is regularly debated in forensic psychiatric services, is the relationship between a psychiatric condition such as schizophrenia, which is the most common diagnosis in forensic psychiatry facilities, and personality factors. The level of risk and dependency is often related to underlying emotional/psychological factors which may have occurred prior to the onset of mental health problems. This is likely to become more evident at the point of movement away from an institutional setting such as an MSU. Debates about diagnosis are perhaps less important than acknowledging that personality components inevitably influence the management of these highly complex cases in forensic psychiatry. This tends to militate against a single-track medical model or psychosocial model and creates the need for a multi-axial approach incorporating a number of different disciplines and perspectives. However, the manner in which this is co-ordinated between and within the systems involved can be exceptionally problematic, as the next case illustrates.

Case 5
Lynn is a 32-year-old Caucasian woman. She is the youngest of four children, with
two sisters and a brother. Her childhood was disrupted due to her parents' separation when she was 2 years of age. Her father left the family and her mother was subsequently admitted to psychiatric hospitals over a ten-year period suffering from
clinical depression. This resulted in Lynn and her siblings being received into the
care of the local authority on a number of occasions. Lynn had foster and residential placements which usually resulted in conflict with authority figures. Attempts to
rehabilitate her back home proved unsuccessful. While her siblings appeared to
adapt reasonably well to this lifestyle Lynn's behaviour became increasingly uncon-
trollable. She was admitted to an assessment centre for girls presenting with challenging behaviour and remained in care until she was 17 years old. Thereafter she
was unable to establish a stable lifestyle in the community and drifted into petty
crime which eventually resulted in custodial sentences. Her first psychiatric admission occurred when she was 21 years of age. She is diagnosed to be suffering from
schizophrenia. She is eventually referred to forensic psychiatry services when she is
on remand for an assault on a stranger in the street at the age of 27 years. She is
admitted to the catchment area MSU after assaulting a number of female prison
officers and attempting to barricade herself in her cell.

This case caused dilemmas because of Lynn's history of anti-social behaviour and
emotional instability which had been prevalent prior to the onset of her major
health problems. The pattern of anti-social behaviour appeared to replicate her
interpersonal difficulties while she was in care. Although her psychiatric symptoms appeared to improve, her management was complicated by increasingly
problematic periods of aggressive behaviour towards nursing staff. She was convicted of malicious wounding, for which she was made subject to a Hospital Order
with Restrictions. A Restriction Order was required due to the seriousness of the
offence and persistent risk factors including her continued aggressive behaviour
after an apparent improvement in the symptoms of her psychiatric illness.
The Probation Officer, the author of a Pre-Sentence Report, was concerned about
the prospect of supervising Lynn in the community on the grounds of her unpre-
dictability. The family presented information to the forensic social worker about
Lynn having exhibited impulsively aggressive behaviour from early childhood.
    All forensic psychiatry units experience difficulties with patients who present
with management problems as a consequence of limited responsiveness to treatment due to the effect of personality difficulties and substance abuse problems.
When patients demonstrate a negative attitude towards discharge back to the
community, this may be conditioned by unresolved developmental issues such as
insecure attachment. The level of dependency can be masked by an apparent
enthusiasm to be out of hospital and, in Lynn's case, high levels of life skills. This
creates a paradoxical situation for the forensic staff involved. Lynn also involved
her solicitor in a number of allegations about staff acting unprofessionally, and
concerning which she made complaints. This scenario is often enacted at Mental
Health Review Tribunal hearings when the issue of discharge is being considered
and the implications for the patient become increasingly apparent.
    The treatment of female patients in forensic psychiatry units has been the
subject of much controversy. Female patients invariably form a relatively small

proportion within the patient group. Due to the sexual pathology of many of the male patients in forensic psychiatry settings, and the environmental factors associated with living in a communal unit, there have been strong arguments in support of single gender facilities in recent years (Henderson & Reveley, 1996; Barlow & Wolfson, 1997; Warner & Ford, 1998). The treatment needs of female patients tend to be different from male patients because of the relatively greater significance of personality factors, including a history of abuse and self-harm which leads to particular vulnerability. They also have fewer convictions for violence (Women in Secure Hospitals Report, 1999). Both the public sector and the independent sector have begun to develop initiatives nationally in order to protect female patients. Lynn was referred to an independent sector secure unit offering a female only ward. However, following a series of increasingly serious premeditated assaults on staff a referral was made for her to be transferred to conditions of high security at a Special Hospital.

The clinical management arrangements of the three Secial Hospitals vary significantly from MSUs. The Special Hospitals are in the process of becoming more managerially autonomous and clinically accountable (Higgins, 1996) as a consequence of the establishment of the three Special Health Authorities leading to integration into NHS Trusts, although there has been the perceived need to retain a degree of external influence on issues such as professional development and training. The purchasing of high security services is being devolved to regionally based commissioning bodies (Health Service Circular, 1999), which will adopt a more integrated strategic approach to financial management and service development.

Clinical services in the Special Hospitals are divided into units to address the needs of specialist groups such as women, learning-disabled and personality disorder, taking into account levels of dependency, risk and geographical factors. Patients classified as mentally ill still form the largest group, although dual diagnosis is common. The management and treatment of patients with a primary diagnosis of personality disorder in the Special Hospitals, has attracted particular controversy. The Fallon Report (1999) emphasised the difficulties inherent in boundary-setting, establishing a balance between therapy and security and evaluating the efficacy of treatment for serious violent and sexual offenders with personality disorders.

The policy of the Special Hospitals to admit and treat patients who are presenting with behaviours which are considered to be a "grave and immediate danger to the public" is central to the decision-making process with regard to referrals. This invariably causes a dilemma when a patient is referred from another secure unit where he/she can be managed, albeit with increasingly problematic consequences. The treatment of other patients within an MSU may be significantly undermined by the deployment of nurses in managing a single problematic individual who is presenting with a particularly high level of aggressive behaviour. For instance, the premeditated nature of much of Lynn's behaviour created a great deal of anxiety among staff and discharge was an unrealistic expectation because each attempt to consider the options was met with a further escalation in anti-social behaviour. This created a vicious circle for her as it does for other patients for similar reasons.

When Lynn's case was presented to the Admissions Panel of the Special Hospital, concern was expressed about her lack of co-operation, her dependency on the MSU and the probability that she would adapt to the culture of the ward to which she was being referred by copying the behaviour of other patients. A problem associated with this and other referrals to Special Hospitals is that dependency needs may be exacerbated in the process, thus further militating against the prospect of eventual discharge. The establishment of units to address the needs of patients requiring longer stay medium security would plug a gap which is becoming increasingly apparent in all forensic psychiatric facilities. However, there are inevitable human resource and financial issues to be resolved both locally and nationally before longer stay medium security becomes a viable option in the public sector.

Inter-agency Issues Involving the Independent Sector

In the meantime, and probably for the foreseeable future, the independent sector offers facilities for the transfer of cases who cannot be accommodated in their local catchment area MSU because the demand for beds far exceeds the supply in certain areas of the country, or patients require particular forms of treatment not available elsewhere. Logistical problems, dislocation from local community and the potential for isolation from outside agencies create challenges in terms of multi-agency working and the provision of support to patients and their families.

The Care Programme Approach, essentially a Health Service led system, and Care Management, which has been primarily the responsibility of Social Services Departments under the NHS and Community Care Act 1990, both aim to ensure that multi-agency working is effective at key stages of the process. There has been a greater co-ordination between these functions and a drive towards amalgamation partly due to the development of Community Mental Health Teams (Social Services Inspectorate, 1999). Forensic psychiatry also requires to take account of the need for clinical audit, performance indicators/standards, organisational targets and evidence-based practice (Department of Health, 1999). In this context agencies will be required to work more closely together, which has the potential to facilitate appropriate treatment and avoid patients blocking beds. The movement towards commissioning agencies actively collaborating with service providers may also lead to a more systematic use of resources in forensic psychiatry in the coming years. These clinical and managerial changes would be expected to create the environment in which the public and independent sectors could work in partnership towards establishing mutually agreed objectives based on the assessment of need for this particularly vulnerable and problematic client group.

Case 6
Alan is a 23-year-old African-Caribbean man who has a five-year history of contact with psychiatric services. He comes from a large family with whom he has maintained close relationships. He has had three admissions to a catchment area District General Hospital Psychiatric Unit but has failed to co-operate with after care which has resulted in relapse in his mental health problem. He is diagnosed as suffering from schizophrenia. His current admission, under Section 3 of the Mental Health Act, has involved a brief transfer to a Medium Secure Unit due to assaultative behaviour. Alan has not got a criminal history but the open ward report a great deal of concern about his behaviour after he attacked a member of staff with a chair which was considered to be potentially extremely dangerous. His behaviour at the MSU was reported to be unproblematic but after the transfer back to the open ward his behaviour deteriorated once again. It was considered that he would require longer term treatment in conditions of medium security and a recommendation was made to the District Health Authority that a bed was sought in the private sector on the grounds of risk to staff and others and the associated need for continued detention. By this time he was being specially observed by two nurses on a 24-hour basis and the psychiatric unit reported difficulties with staff morale which was adversely affecting the treatment of other patients on the ward. The MSU was adamantly opposed to re-admission on the grounds that there were other patients on the waiting list who were in greater need of these facilities.

This case encompasses some of the dilemmas encountered in transferring clinical responsibilities between the public and independent sectors. Alan was moved to a hospital geographically distant from his local community but was considered to be the most suitable placement available for him. Attempts to facilitate family visits and liaise with local services, necessary as they are, may not be an adequate substitute for accessibility that can be most satisfactorily achieved within the local community (Butler Report, 1975). Nevertheless, there may on occasions be positive virtues for patients to be removed from their local area. Frequent incidents of absconding, though not a criteria for admission to a secure unit, is often a contributory factor to support the need for a higher level of security, and moving away from the area of origin may present certain advantages in this regard. There may be other stress factors that would make an out-of-area placement less problematic and potentially helpful such as intra-familial difficulties and availability of illicit drugs.

Specialist treatment is a further option available in the independent sector. There requires to be an explicit understanding that continuity of care is a central factor and that purchasing decisions and the provision of services should flow from an accurate and realistic assessment of need. A problem may be created by the lack of incentives for local services to consider transferring patients back to their area of origin due to perceived longer stay needs, risk factors, and the pressures experienced from other referral sources. Once again a co-ordinated multi-agency approach is required.

Additionally, in Alan's case, ethnicity is a significant issue. Black patients, particularly from the African-Caribbean community, represent a disproportionately large group within psychiatry generally (Koffman et al., 1997) and forensic units in particular (Maden et al., 1999). The reasons for this are complicated and contentious (Boast & Chesterman, 1995; Fernando, 1991; Fernando, Ndegwa & Wilson, 1998), but the reality is that there are insufficient staff of a similar ethnic origin and a number of reports and inquiries have focused on the need for units to take a more explicit and proactive view of cultural needs (see, for example, Ritchie, 1994; Woodley, 1995). A range of voluntary sector black mental health organisations and agencies have been established in the larger urban areas during the past decade. This has been an important development in order to ensure advocacy is provided on behalf of patients and their families. The potential also exists for direct involvement in service development in forensic psychiatry to address the unmet needs of patients from minority ethnic groups. (Webbe, 1998).

MSUs often experience a high level of demand from a number of sources which lead to the establishment of waiting lists, particularly in socially deprived areas. Therefore a judicious use of the resources available may necessitate the "least bad" option being employed. Professional development and training does not always reflect the need for public and independent sector professional groups to work in a collaborative way. The Mental Health Act Commission and Mental Health Review Tribunals frequently recommend that patients should be transferred to more suitable facilities because the original purpose of their placement is no longer justifiable. The Reed Report (1991) continues to be relevant in terms of the need for flexibility and creativity from those managing and resourcing the systems involved in forensic psychiatry.

ROUTES OUT OF FORENSIC PSYCHIATRY SYSTEMS

It is often within the context of discharge planning that dilemmas and tensions involved in inter-agency working are demonstrated most clearly. The process of discharge is by necessity influenced by the following factors: (a) past patterns of behaviour; (b) clinical progress and presentation; (c) risk assessment and management; (d) the need for effective liaison with a variety of community agencies which often have widely differing priorities and functions; (e) the attitudes of relatives and carers; (f) public attitudes and perceptions; (g) financial/purchasing issues; and (h) the complications often experienced in settling patients into facilities outside of their catchment area. Although it is usually the forensic social worker who has primary responsibility for liasing with social care agencies about pre-discharge and after-care issues this is a multi-disciplinary function.

Most cases in forensic psychiatry require a longitudinal approach with decisions about discharge and disposal at the court having a profound influence on options available for eventual discharge. For instance, Charlie (Case 1) had responded well to treatment and presented with few management problems at the MSU. The clinical team at the MSU considered that the offence he committed was a direct consequence of his mental health problems although his condition was also exacerbated by the use of illicit drugs. He was eventually convicted of arson and there was considered not to have been intent to endanger life due to the lack of premeditation or a direct threat to his mother whose attitude was consistently supportive towards him. The fact that the offence-related behaviour was atypical for Charlie also contributed to the view that he should receive a psychiatric disposal at court. Due to his compliance with treatment and the relatively less serious conviction, a Hospital Order with Restrictions was considered to be unnecessarily rigid both because of the implications it would have had for a more protracted admission and the need for Conditional Discharge under the auspices of the Home Office. A Hospital Order, Section 37, was therefore recommended with the key discharge issues focusing on whether he should receive after-care from the Forensic Psychiatry Service or local general psychiatry services based on his need for supervision and structure in the community. Neither a Supervised Discharge Order under the Mental Health (Patients in the Community) Act 1995 nor the Supervision Register were considered necessary because of his co-operation with treatment and his satisfactory progress. Therefore, when he was discharged from the MSU his after-care was managed by mainstream psychiatric services.

Jack (Case 2) received a Hospital Order with Restrictions because his offence was considered to be directly attributable to a mental disorder and it led to a conviction for malicious wounding with intent to endanger life, a high tariff offence. In addition his in-patient and his out-patient treatment was likely to be complicated by substance abuse and personality difficulties. A Restriction Order is imposed by the court as a recognition of the need for public protection in preventing similar behaviour from occurring in the future by imposing rigorous management both while the patient remains in hospital and under the terms of Conditonal Discharge, with the option of a recall to hospital in the event of mental health deterioration and/or the re-emergence of risk factors. Jack's admission was protracted because his dependency needs became more apparent during periods of change. During the course of his admission it was discovered that he had additional problems due to a mild learning disability. He had considerable difficulty in accepting that his progress was relatively slow, with each stage of his leave outside of hospital being carefully evaluated by the clinical team in consultation with the Home Office.

Involvement with Relatives and Carers

As already indicated, a major obstacle experienced in Jack's case was the attitude of his family who continued to be split. This problem became further exacerbated during his admission, thus causing dilemmas for the clinical team in relation to the confidentiality of information about his discharge, the need to address victim issues and the assessment and management of risk. Relatives and carers, as well as other victims of serious offences committed by mentally disordered offenders who have been made subject to psychiatric disposal at court, do not automatically receive information and support in accordance with the

Victim's Charter although a number of local protocols have been established through the involvement of the Probation Service. The Victim's Charter was established in 1990 to address the needs of victims of criminal offences. The Probation Service has a clear responsibility to ensure that victims are consulted in cases of serious offending but there is lack of this provision for victims of offences perpetrated by mentally disordered offenders. This is often perceived as a major deficit which is only partially ameliorated by the ad hoc interventions of probation officers and Victim Support, a voluntary sector agency.

Research shows that the majority of victims of very serious offences committed by mentally disordered offenders are well known to the perpetrator (Boyd, 1996; Estroff et al., 1994). Relatives form a significant proportion of this group which presents specific difficulties with regard to consulting victims. This can create dilemmas for clinicians because a central aspect of the Care Programme Approach necessitates that relatives and carers under the jurisdiction of psychiatric and social care agencies are incorporated into the decision-making process. Where there are victims who have strong sympathy for or antipathy towards an offender, this can pose significant difficulties for the clinical team, often reflecting what has been known about the potentially negative effects of high expressed emotion for many years (Vaughn & Leff, 1976). This goes some way towards explaining the complications in making the flow of information more transparent.

Hostile relatives who are also victims are perceived to have the potential to disrupt progress towards discharge. Adverse press coverage and public relations should not be underestimated as factors involved in the success or failure of a discharge plan. For instance, in Jack's case there were members of his family who were prepared to divulge information to the press in order to stall his planned discharge. There are few national guidelines to assist clinicians working in forensic psychiatry about how to manage conflicting and often counterpoised feelings and rights, even though carers now have the right to request an assessment under the Carers (Recognition and Services) Act 1995. When and how to consult with relatives presents legal and ethical dilemmas which require the clinical team in forensic psychiatry to take a wider view of their responsibilities and duties. Mental Health Review Tribunals may become the forum for debates about rights issues which are likely to be further complicated by European Court judgements and the Human Rights Act 1998.

Out-of-area Placements

There are a variety of reasons why out-of-area placements may be required for forensic psychiatry patients. This may be the consequence of the nature of the index offence and the inadvisability of a return to the area where it was committed. Additionally, there may be a need for a specialist service, often involving high levels of staffing in private or independent sector facilities. The attitude of the patient, the views of his or her relatives and the problems associated with setting up a placement for a patient who has committed a serious offence and presents with multi-faceted needs require to be addressed. Out-of-area residential placements, often involving joint funding arrangements and logistical and inter-agency complexities require to be strategically managed by the RMO and the multi-disciplinary team.

In Jack's case the placement away from his area of origin was indicated because of the potential threat he would experience from some of his relatives, his own feelings of anxiety and his need for a highly structured, well-staffed residential facility does to the potential risks. The first issue to be addressed was the mechanism by which discharge was to be facilitated. Patients subject to a Hospital Order with Restrictions can be granted a Conditional or an Absolute Discharge either directly by the Home Office or by a Mental Health Review Tribunal. Absolute Discharge is rarely viable during an admission and for a considerable period, perhaps two or three years, afterwards because of the need for tangible evidence of sustained co-operation and progress. Complex discharge arrangements involving a variety of agencies require to be carefully co-ordinated. The development of trust and clear understanding of responsibilities and functions of all the agencies involved is a prerequisite for successful multi-agency working to be achieved at this pivotal stage.

The management of leave from hospital where a patient continues to be subject to Hospital Order with Restrictions presents potential administrative difficulties. Residential facilities are rarely registered for taking patients who are currently detained under the Mental Health Act. Purchasing and commissioning arrangements can create obstacles because of the need for high levels of funding for specialised residential facilities. Given the multi-faceted needs of many forensic psychiatry patients and strategic inter-agency considerations, the usual mechanisms and systems employed by Local Authority care managers/social workers to assess need and to facilitate discharge arrangements tend to be limited by being rather short term and relatively narrow. Adequate exchange of information and liaison between forensic psychiatry agencies and mainstream agencies must be effective in order to support the patient and ensure public protection. Management of risk is a key component of the process when the patient is being moved from a relatively more controlled and structured environment to one where the boundaries are more negotiable and less predictable.

Supervision in the Community

A further issue to address under Conditional Discharge is psychiatric and social supervision. The psychiatric supervisor will focus on clinical factors and the need for contingency planning in the event of the patient requiring to be recalled to hospital as a result of deterioration in his or her condition and exacerbation of the risk factors. There are inevitable resource implications should this occur with particular regard to the provision of a required level of security. Whether a patient remains within the forensic psychiatry service or is transferred to mainstream psychiatric services for after-care purposes is a key decision. For the more serious offenders it is likely that the forensic psychiatry service will be required to remain involved, at least for a period of time until there is evidence of demonstrable psychiatric and social stability.

The style and level of supervision has to be considered by psychiatric and social supervisors with effective liaison being a key factor. The CPA Review system requires to be explicitly planned from the outset, with professional responsibilities clearly allocated and effectively monitored. In Jack's case his ambivalence, which was partly a consequence of his high level of dependency and anxiety, necessitated a lengthy hand-over between in-patient and community agencies. Personality factors and substance abuse issues became more apparent within the context of discharge planning with Jack demonstrating predictable hesitancy and resistance to change.

Social supervision can be provided either by a Social Worker or a Probation Officer although the former is more common. Social supervision by a Probation Officer may be considered for a patient who has a significant offending history prior to the onset of mental health problems. For instance, Steve (Case 3), whose psychiatric condition became apparent during his prison sentence, could only be discharged through his case being considered by both a Mental Health Review Tribunal and the Parole Board which took a long time to co-ordinate. He eventually served twice the average life sentence for murder due to the complications associated with his mental health problems, delays in facilitating transfer down the spectrum of security and the medico-legal aspects of his case. It is a common fallacy that transfer to psychiatric facilities from the penal system is "a soft option" because a prisoner/patient may be detained for a longer period of time as a consequence. Transferred prisoners who have reached their earliest date of release and would be automatically released to the community from prison require to remain in hospital unless their psychiatric disorder is sufficiently well treated for them to be discharged. This can lead to frustration and resentment towards forensic psychiatry services. Steve was eventually supervised by the Probation Officer who in effect fulfilled the role of Social Supervisor.

Sally (Case 4) posed further difficulties in two areas. Firstly, the involvement of child protection services in assessing the emotional and psychological needs of her daughter required a high level of careful multi-disciplinary liaison between the MSU and the Social Services Department. The focus of responsibility, and whether, when and how to share information needed to be resolved within this process. A patient's own experience of abuse can sometimes lead to problems in carrying out enquiries into their parenting skills. This can have the effect of creating tensions between agencies with different and at time divergent responsibilities.

Furthermore, Sally had originally been transferred from a general psychiatric unit. It was as a consequence of local psychiatric services being resistant to accepting her back and her own preference for follow up from the forensic psychiatry service that after-care was provided by the MSU community psychiatric nurses. The need for effective "gate-keeping" had to be counter-balanced by the attitudes of general psychiatry services and the patient. It is perhaps ironic that the system which is intrinsically involved in offering secure treatment can exercise a great deal of control over its client group but is not able to gain anything like this degree of influence over agencies within the external environment. It is undoubtedly in the interest of the forensic psychiatry service for "non-offenders" to be transferred to local services at the earliest opportunity because of the professional and resource consequences of not doing so, but this is not always achievable or clinically desirable. There is also the common misconception that "non-offender" patients represent a lower risk, which is not always borne out in practice.

The other two cases described here also possess features which are indicative of dilemmas which occur for forensic psychiatry services over discharge planning. Lynn (Case 5), who was transferred from an MSU to a Special Hospital as a consequence of a pattern of persistent and assaultative behaviour, may stabilise over a period of time due to the relatively slower pace of change and the implementation of clear boundaries in conditions of high security. In this event, a transfer back to the MSU for rehabilitation and eventual discharge to the community, given that she remains subject to a Restriction Order, may not be practical or realistic due to her previous behaviour in this setting which will have the potential to create a negative response both from her and the staff involved. Consequently, alternative referral routes may be considered, including a independent sector unit or a discharge from Special Hospital directly into community care.

Should a request be made to the Home Office for a problematic patient to be discharged where the risk factors have not or cannot be tested out satisfactorily, the Secretary of State has the option of referring the case to the *Aavold Committee*, the Advisory Board on Restriction Order patients. Consequently, an independent assessment will be submitted to the Secretary of State, taking into account all relevant information. The Secretary of State is then able to make a judgement about whether to act on the advice provided. This is an important safety valve for the political decision-makers regarding particularly complex cases that potentially present a high risk.

Discharge from the Independent Sector

Alan (Case 6) is a patient in an independent sector secure unit. Effective inter-agency working requires a collaborative approach, often involving liaison across relatively long distances. This complicates discharge/transfer planning. A strong commitment from the independent sector and the public sector agencies is required in order to address clinical need and facilitate movement back to his area of origin at the optimum time. This process would normally be co-ordinated through CPA Reviews, which is becoming more formalised through the development of inter-agency commissioning arrangements for each locality (Health Service Circular, 1999).

The purchasing District Health Authority may be motivated by financial incentives whereas provider units may have been rather more concerned with the prospect of re-admitting a patient who has been disruptive and may block a bed. Patients placed in the independent sector are more likely to be transferred to other in-patient facilities rather than discharged directly to the community. The complications involved in discharging Alan directly to the community, perhaps as a consequence of a Mental Health Review Tribunal judgement, present characteristically tricky, strategic, logistical problems. Assessing need and evaluating risk in this context is fraught with potential problems if there is not sufficient trust between agencies. This emphasises the need to develop more satisfactory liaison and partnerships between the independent sector and the public sector at both clinical and managerial levels. Otherwise the independent sector may become as organisationally and professionally isolated as the Special Hospitals have been criticised for being (Fallon report, 1999).

CONCLUSION

The three discrete but interrelated and interdependent systems within which forensic psychiatry must operate can only fulfil their functions efficiently and effectively by developing and maintaining positive relationships with the other agencies who are responsible for the care and management of mentally disordered offenders and others requiring similar services. The precise dynamics involved in these systems vary in relation to management arrangements, market forces and the resources available in a particular area, geographical factors, purchasing/commissioning aspects and the pre-existing relationship between clinicians and managers making often extremely complicated decisions in the wider environment.

There are a number of developments occurring nationally which have the potential to create opportunities to further improve the provision of forensic psychiatry services. We await the new Mental Health Act which will have a profound effect on service delivery in forensic psychiatry (Department of Health, 1999a), 1999). The specialised commissioning arrangements for high and medium security which is being established on a regional basis are designed to co-ordinate and systematise the planning and delivery of services using a multi-agency perspective (Health Service Circular, 1999). The future of the Special Hospitals has been the subject of much debate with the reduction in their size, the change towards greater managerial autonomy through trust status, and an emphasis on accountability. The relationship between public sector and independent sector forensic psychiatry units is undergoing inevitable change partly due to the disproportionate increase in the size of the latter. There has been a movement towards purchasing and commissioning decisions being made in a more strategic way, with contracts identifying specific outcomes, and being clearer about responsibility and accountability (Department of Health, 1999b). The development of longer stay medium secure units has the potential to reduce pressure from within the system, thus increasing the options available to address clinical need more accurately. The treatment of people suffering from personality disorders is undergoing re-appraisal with the Government being keen to actively consider the legal and clinical options available. There is also the influence of the European judicial system and the Human Rights Act 1998 to be taken into account, specifically with regard to civil liberties.

Opportunities for multi-agency/multi-disciplinary training, and the establishment of joint posts and protocols governing the expectations between agencies have the potential to improve communication between and within forensic psychiatry systems. Targeting high-cost resources more accurately to benefit this highly problematic but also vulnerable client group is a major challenge. This is particularly important given the emphasis at a national political level to stress community safety as a primary responsibility of professionals involved in managing potentially high-risk offenders.

It is noteworthy that some of the current debates reflect the dynamics which have existed throughout the history of forensic psychiatry, particularly with regard to the benefits or otherwise of developing highly specialist services with the danger of becoming isolated from other key agencies. There is clearly a need for careful and systematic co-ordination with the other agencies without whose co-operation and support forensic psychiatry would become considerably less effective. The relationship between forensic psychiatry and external systems can engender mutual benefit by the establishment of flexible working through initiatives to create partnership, greater transparency and strategic planning at both clinical and managerial levels.

REFERENCES

Barlow, F. & Wolfson, P. (1997) Safety and security: a survey of female psychiatric in-patients. *Psychiatric Bulletin*, **21**, 270–272.

Boyd, W.D. (1996) *Report of the Confidential Inquiry into Homicides and Suicides by Mentally Ill People*. London: Royal College of Psychiatrists.

Bailey, J. & MacCulloch, M.J. (1992) The characteristics of 112 cases discharged directly to the community from a new Special Hospital and some comparisons of performance. *Journal of Forensic Psychiatry*, **3**, 91–112.

Boast, N. & Chesterman, P. (1995) Black people and secure psychiatric facilities: Patterns of processing and the role of stereotypes. *British Journal of Criminology*, **35**(2), 218–235.

Blom-Cooper, L., Chair (1992) *Report of the Committee of Inquiry into Complaints about Ashworth Hospital*. London: HMSO.

Butler Report (1975) *Report of the Committee on Mentally Abnormal Offenders*. London: HMSO.

Buchanan, A. (1998) Criminal conviction after discharge from Special (High Security) Hospital. Incidence in first 10 years. *British Journal of Psychiatry*, **172**, 472–477.

Cohen, A. & Eastman, N. (1997) Needs assessment for mentally disordered offenders and others requiring similar services. Theoretical issues and methodological framework. *British Journal of Psychiatry*, **171**, 412–416.

Coid, J.W. (1998) Socio-economic deprivation and admission rates to secure forensic psychiatry services. *Psychiatric Bulletin*, **22**(5), 294–297.

Estroff, S.E., Zimmer, C., Lachiotte, W.S. & Benoit, J. (1994) The influence of social networks and social support on violence by persons with serious mental illness. *Hospital and Community Psychiatry*, **15**(4), 669–679.

Department of Health (1995) *Building Bridges. A Guide to Arrangements for Inter-agency Working for the Care and Protection of Severely Mentally Ill People.* London: HMSO.

Department of Health (1999) *Reform of the Mental Health Act 1983—Proposals for Consultation.* London: The Stationery Office.

Department of Health (1999) *National Service Framework for Mental Health—Modern Standards and Service Models.* London: Department of Health.

Fallon Report (1999) *Report of the Committee of Inquiry into the Personality Disorder Unit, Ashworth Hospital, Volume I.* London: The Stationery Office.

Fernando, S. (1991) *Mental Health, Race and Culture.* London: MIND.

Fernando, S., Ndegwa, D. & Wilson, M. (1998) *Forensic Psychiatry, Race and Culture.* London and New York: Routledge.

Glancy Report (1974) *Revised Report of the Working Party on Security in NHS Psychiatric Hospitals.* London: Department of Health and Social Security.

Gunn, J., Maden, A. & Swinton, M. (1991) Treatment needs of prisoners with psychiatric disorders. *British Medical Journal*, **363**, 338–341.

Health Service Circular (1999) *The New NHS–Specialised Commissioning, High and Medium Security Psychiatric Services.* NHS Executive (HSC 1999/141), Department of Health.

Health Service Circular/LA Circular (1999) *Guidance on the Visiting of Psychiatric Patients by Children—Mental Health Act 1983 Code of Practice* (HSC 1999/222: LA (99) 32).

Henderson, C. & Reveley, A. (1996) Is there a case for single sex wards? *Psychiatric Bulletin*, **20**, 513–515.

Higgins, J. (1981) Four years experience of an interim secure unit. *British Medical Journal*, **282**, 889–893.

Higgins, J. (1996) Future of the Special Hospitals. *Criminal Behaviour and Mental Health*, 65–72.

Home Office & Department of Health (1999) *Managing Dangerous People with Severe Personality Disorder—Proposals for Policy Development.* London: HMSO.

Joseph, P. & Potter, M. (1993) Diversion from Custody. *British Journal of Psychiatry*, **162**, 325–334.

Koffman, J., Naomi, J., Fulop. Pashley. D. & Coleman, K. (1997) Ethnicity and use of acute psychiatric beds: One-day survey in north and south Thames regions. *British Journal of Psychiatry*, **171**, 238–241.

Maden, A., Friendship, C., McClintock, T. & Rutter, S. (1999) Outcome of admission to a medium secure psychiatric unit. Role of ethnic origin. *British Journal of Psychiatry*, **175**, 317–321.

Mental Health Act 1983 *Code of Practice* (1999) London: The Stationary Office.

Murray, K. (1996) The use of beds in NHS medium secure units in England. *The Journal of Forensic Psychiatry*, **1**(3), 504–524.

Reed Report (1991) *Review of Health and Social Services for Mentally Disordered Offenders and others Requiring Similar Services.* London: HMSO.

Ritchie, J., Chair (1994) *The report of the Inquiry into the Care and Treatment of Christopher Clunis.* London: HMSO.

Singleton, N., Meltzer, H. & Gatward, R. (with Coid, J. & Deasy, D.) (1998) *Psychiatric Morbidity among Prisoners in England and Wales.* London: The Stationary Office.

Social Services Inspectorate (1999) *Still Building Bridges.* Report of a national inspection of arrangements of the interaction of Care Programme Approach with Care Management. London: Social Services Inspectorate.

Snowden, P. (1990) Regional secure units and forensic services in England. In R. Bluglass

& P. Bowden (Eds) *Principles and Practice in Forensic Psychiatry* (pp. 1375–1386). Edinburgh: Churchill Livingstone.

Snowden, P. (1995) Facilities and treatment. In D. Chiswick & R. Cope (Eds) *Seminars in Practical Forensic Psychiatry* (pp. 164–209). London: Gaskell.

Vaughn, C. & Leff, J. (1976) The influence of family and social factors on the cause of psychiatric illness. A comparison of schizophrenic and depressed neurotic patients. *British Journal of Psychiatry*, **129**, 125–137.

Ward, M. & Applin, C. (1998) *The Unlearned Lesson: The role of alcohol and drug misuse in homicides perpetrated by people with mental health problems.* Wynne Howard Books.

Warner, L. & Ford, R. (1998) Conditions for women in in-patient psychiatric units: The Mental Health Act Commission 1996 National Visit. *Mental Health Care*, **1**(7), 225–228.

Webbe, A. (1998) Ethnicity and mental health. *Psychiatric Care* **5**(1), 12–16.

Women in Secure Hospitals Report (1999) *Defining Gender Issues Redefining Women's Services*. London: WISH.

Woodley, L., Chair (1995) *Report of the Independent Review Panel to East London and the City Health Authority and Newham Council, following a Homicide in July 1994 by a Person Suffering with a Severe Mental Illness.* East London and the City Health Authority.

Legislation Referred to:

Carers (Recognition and Services) Act 1995
Crime Sentences Act 1997
Human Rights Act 1998
Mental Health Act 1983
Mental Health (Patients in the Community) Act 1995
NHS and Community Care Act 1990
Police and Criminal Evidence Act 1984
Sex Offenders (Registration) Act 1999

Chapter 11

Care and Management in the Community

Tom Mason
Caswell Clinic, Glanryhd Hospital, Bridgend, UK

The move to decant considerable numbers of individuals experiencing mental illness or with learning disabilities from large institutions to a more localised support framework, based in what is termed the "community", involves a shift in ideology which purports that these primary care sites are deemed to be a more appropriate location for the management of the majority of people with such problems. This always assumes, of course, that services and resources within the community settings are available to provide the necessary structure to furnish the required support. In relation to mentally disordered offenders this focus has led to both the development of new initiatives and the expansion of extant services within the community. However, these are very much at an inchoate stage in their evolution, and require careful nurturing to enable them to develop their professional practice. Despite growing public concern regarding the release of mentally disordered persons into community settings, the political and professional will to establish locally based services for this group of patients has continued. This is also evidenced with the parallel growth in small-scale medium secure units throughout England and Wales. Furthermore, this community service development has persevered despite a number of sensational cases of homicide by mentally disordered persons who were, to one degree or another, already in contact with the mental health system. While not diminishing the tragedy to victims and survivors, the ensuing public inquiries and official reports repeatedly highlighted a lack of cohesive planning between services, fuelling the impetus for a more systematic approach to service delivery. The often hurried government response has been to instigate legislation which aims to ensure a closer supervision in the community of mentally disordered persons who are considered a

Behaviour, Crime and Legal Processes: A Guide for Forensic Practitioners.
Edited by James McGuire, Tom Mason and Aisling O'Kane.
© 2000 John Wiley & Sons Ltd.

danger to others or to themselves, emphasising once again the need for public safety.

One difficulty to arise from such a community development concerns the disparity between those who consider that this social setting is the most appropriate placement for such persons and the extent of public outrage when offenders are placed within their vicinity; particularly sex offenders. "Community" is an ill-defined concept which is difficult to delineate but has a populist interpretation of being "anywhere/everywhere outside of a hospital" (Bachrach & Lamb, 1989; Beale et al., 1993). However, there is a philosophical discord, as well as a practical difficulty, between the political and professional thrust towards a community care programme when, in reality, the care of the community for this population is somewhat curtailed, as evidenced by the "Not In My Back Yard" (NIMBY) movement (Bhugra, 1989; Glasgow University Media Group, 1993). Although society's conscience may well be pricked by scenes of homeless mentally ill persons sheltering in cardboard boxes, or when they are seen to be at risk as in the case of Ben Silcock climbing into the lions' enclosure at London Zoo, their concern turns towards a more self-protectionist and defensive position in the case of disordered offenders, as recently witnessed with the released Sidney Cook, a convicted paedophile in the south-west of England. Without doubt it is when a mentally disordered person in the community is perceived as a danger to members of society that the greatest public (and thus political) outcry is felt (Harris & Bergman, 1988; Goodwin, 1989).

When the placement of mentally disordered offenders in the community leads to re-offending, the resultant public remonstrance is usually levelled at the lack of adequate services to maintain the protection of the public, the lack of skill within professional groups to manage such patients, and the level of blame that can be attached to an identified individual (Mueller & Hopp, 1987). Yet, just as general psychiatric patients who are discharged home may well relapse for whatever reason (Cutler, Tatum & Shore, 1987), mentally disordered offenders too may regress (Cooke et al., 1994). Unfortunately, in the case of the latter group a corollary of their condition may well involve criminal activity with the tragic result of creating further victims. Without follow-up services making time and effort to locate non-contact patients, they are unlikely to come to the attention of mental health professionals until their behaviour is such that they transgress the law or disturb the community in which they are purportedly being cared for. Thus, it is a point of irony that they then need to be removed from the environment that is deemed the most appropriate for them (Goldfinger, Hopkins & Surber, 1984; Marcos & Cohen, 1986; Heilbrun & Griffin, 1998).

Because of the foregoing serious consequences, the care and management of mentally disordered offenders in the community requires a more systematic structure, which deals with the questions revolving around societal concerns of safety, but which are undertaken in a more professional manner (Andrews & Teeson, 1994). These involve issues regarding the management of resources, the appropriateness of the systems in place, the skill levels of the staff operating such systems, the adequacy of the knowledge base, the suitability of training, and the efficacy of practice (Intagliata, Barry & Egri, 1988). In dealing with these issues this chapter will outline the policy development relating to mentally disordered offenders in the community and survey what are considered the most appropriate methods of supervision, and systems of maintenance. Amid these concerns there are issues of skills, assessments, training, education and research regarding such matters as case management, outreach services, and desistance (Lynn-McHale, Fitzpatrick & Shaffer, 1993).

POLICY DEVELOPMENT

For several hundred years the main thrust of legislation regarding the mentally disordered has been concerned with removing them from the community towards incarceration in asylums. The Vagrancy Act of 1714 allowed for the removal of "furiously mad and dangerous persons" authorised by two justices of the peace, in chains if needed. The Criminal Lunatics Act 1800 was the result of the well-known events involving James Hadfield who, following his pistol shots at George III, was then considered too dangerous to be released back to the community. Although the County Asylums Act 1808 and the Lunatics Act 1845 made provision for the building of special places for all lunatics, including criminal lunatics, it was not until the Criminal Lunatics Act 1913 that provision of housing for mental defectives were established at Rampton and Moss Side. Two other acts are worthy of note: the Mental Treatment Act 1930, which introduced the idea of voluntary treatment, and the Mental Health Act 1959, which emphasised a move away from institutional care towards a community orientation. However, it was not this Act alone which provided the impetus for this policy shift, as political and economic considerations emerged in the post-war era to influence ideology in relation to asylum care.

The general trend in hospital services in the late 1950s and early 1960s was geared towards an "open-door" ethos with many initiatives and policy changes based on the libertarian spirit of this period, coupled to a growing concern with the economics of the NHS. Furthermore, the dismantling of institutional provision, with the resultant move to community-based services, can also be said to have its roots in this period with the pivotal speech in 1961 by the MP Enoch Powell, who called for a closure of large asylums with a relocation back into the community of the mentally ill population. However, this move towards the "open-door" also had its drawbacks, which included an increase in the psychiatric population in prisons and a stagnating, and overcrowded, special hospital system. This was recognised as early as 1961 with the Ministry of Health welcoming the "open-door" philosophy but cautioning that, in the government's view, secure psychiatric provision would still be required. Unfortunately, we had to await the Glancy Report (Department of Health and Social Security, 1974) for a recommendation that each of the Regional Health Authorities should provide a secure unit for mentally disordered offenders. Alongside this, the Butler Committee—sitting since 1972 to review secure provision in England and Wales—recognised in its interim report the yawning gap between the high security special hospitals and the "open-door" of the National Health Service (Home Office & Department of Health and Social Security, 1974). The final report (Home Office & Department of Health and Social Security, 1975) served to pump-prime money for the development of a mid-range secure psychiatric service between these extreme poles. Unfortunately, few Regional Health Authorities took this opportunity to develop this type of service—although they took the money—and it was not until 1980 that the first Regional Secure Unit eventually opened. Although there are now over 30 such facilities in England and Wales these units have not solved the problem they were designed to alleviate (Vaughan & Badger, 1995).

A number of policy developments and related legislation in the 1990s need also to be mentioned as contributing factors in the move towards a community care focus for mentally disordered offenders. The Home Office circular No. 66/90 in September 1990 was concerned with emphasising that it was government policy for mentally disordered offenders to receive treatment from Health and Social Services rather than face prosecution, wherever feasible. Thus, it was argued that a close co-operation between health authorities, social services, and criminal justice professionals was needed, which ought to focus attention on the use of caution and support in the community for such minor offenders. In April 1991 the Care Programme Approach (CPA) was initiated in which all in-patients who are about to be discharged should have drawn up an individual care plan suited to their specific needs (Department of Health, 1990). This will be discussed in more detail later. The Reed Committee (Department of Health & Home Office, 1992) undertook an extensive review of health and social services for mentally disordered offenders and has been very influential in forming policy since then. The main principles were that (a) quality care needs to be developed on an individual basis, (b) care in the community ought to be prioritised where possible, (c) the security surrounding patients should be no more than that required, (d) rehabilitation and independent living are main objectives, and (e) they should be located as near as possible to their own homes and families. Without doubt, this report will have far-reaching consequences for services for mentally disordered offenders if the 276 recommendations are ever implemented. Two years later the NHS Management Executive (1994) required health service providers of mental health care to set up registers of psychiatric patients who are liable to be at risk. This will be expanded upon later in the chapter.

Finally, we ought to mention three further parliamentary Acts which have helped shape, to one degree or another, the community care policy. The first is the Police and Criminal Evidence Act 1984 (revised in 1991) which protects mentally disordered, or handicapped, persons when being interviewed by the police. Special care is now needed and the involvement of an Appropriate Adult (AA) is sought in these cases. The National Health Service Community Care Act 1990 was implemented in April 1993 and was concerned to emphasise that it is the main objective for people to live as normal a life as possible in their own homes, or in a homely environment, in community settings. Service development, it was argued, should revolve around (a) flexibility and sensitivity to individual needs, (b) an encouragement for independence based on minimum intervention, (c) a range of options being available, and (d) a focus on greatest need. Finally, the Criminal Procedures Insanity Act 1991 was implemented in January 1992 and is based on several principles: (a) a trial of the facts pertaining to each case; (b) a verdict of "not guilty by reason of insanity" can only be returned on the evidence of two or more medical practitioners; (c) there should be a range of disposal options; (d) a Hospital Order with Restrictions can be applied; (e) a supervision and treatment order can be made; and (f) in the case of trivial offences, the offender can be given an absolute discharge.

What draws all these foregoing themes together is the fact that in caring for mentally disordered offenders in the community—either those who have been successfully treated or those whose offences are deemed of a trivial nature not warranting secure provision—the overarching consideration is the level of supervision required. If serious offenders are to be helped in maintaining a state of mental health and to avoid re-offending, and if those mentally disordered persons whose offences are minor are to be assisted in not going on to more serious offences, then the nature of the psychiatric supervision is crucial. Supervision of mentally disordered offenders in the community can take many forms and the remainder of this chapter will review some of these.

EXPANSION OF COMMUNITY INITIATIVES

Currently there is a wide number of differing professions that contribute at one level or another to the management of this group of patients. However, as each different discipline tends towards a particular philosophy, conceptual framework, and/or body of knowledge, then a differing focus of attention ensues. For example, in developing risk assessment procedures and risk management strategies, psychiatrists in out-patient departments may base their judgements on the manifestation of clinical psychopathology, whereas probation officers may undertake their evaluation based on criminal history variables or an analysis of social networks and circumstances. These perspectives, however pertinent and relevant to each other, will often tend to overlook their counterparts. There are many professional groups whose perspective and decisions play parts in this elaborate process.

- *Crown Prosecution Service.* This profession has access to expert advice on the appropriateness of mentally disordered offenders going to trial and for decision-making purposes will find it necessary to establish whether the alleged offender is fit to plead.

- *Solicitors.* Some solicitors specialise in, and receive specialist training in, provisions for mentally disordered offenders.

- *General Practitioners.* This group of professionals are often the first point of contact for those clients who may require specialist referrals to forensic psychiatry services.

- *Judiciary.* Judges make decisions, to some degree based on expert advice, regarding the disposal of offenders either to the mental health system or to the criminal justice system.

- *Prison Medical Service.* That there is a significant number of mentally disordered persons in prison is well documented, and prison hospital wings play a large part in assessing offenders' appropriateness for referral to Special Hospitals and Secure Units.

- *Community Psychiatric Nurses* (CPNs). These are community nurses who may have on their case load patients who have a history of criminal or anti-social behaviour, but the nurses do not receive any specialist training or may not have any experience with mentally disordered offenders.

- *Forensic Community Psychiatric Nurses* (FCPNs). These nurses usually have experience with the forensic services and the group of patients allocated to these services. They may also have specialist training in this field, and will usually be attached to a Regional Secure Unit.

- *Social Services Departments.* Approved Social Workers play a pivotal role in the operation of the Mental Health Act and liaise with colleagues concerning provision of other community and residential care services.

- *Probation Services.* Probation Officers and Bail Officers are often involved with mentally disordered offenders not only at the throughcare and follow-up stages but also with court diversion schemes (see below).

- *Specialist clinics.* There are a number of specialist clinics that cater for forensic patients, with their treatment usually part of the court's ruling. To date, these have been developed mainly for work with individuals found guilty of sexual offences.

- *Voluntary agencies.* These bodies can become involved with service users as part of visiting schemes and ex-user groups.

In recent years a number of new departures have been taken in attempts to foster closer working between some of these diverse groups, to identify individuals in need of assistance at an earlier stage and to provide access to systems of service and support. These initiatives include *Court Diversion Schemes*, of which there are now approximately 100 in the United Kingdom. They vary considerably in their approach, training, and personnel (Kennedy & Ward, 1992; Home Office, 1990). Depending on the specific function many such initiatives prefer the term "court liaison" to indicate that they actually work with the courts in undertaking assessments and preparing evidence.

Other initiatives taken by the police include a variety of schemes dealing with mentally disordered offenders which facilitate the making of referrals as early as possible to mental health professional services. These include the training of Custody Sergeants in basic assessments in mental health, and the attendance of Forensic Psychiatric Nurses in police stations.

We can see from this list that any discipline dealing with mentally disordered offenders is, in the first instance, likely to draw upon the knowledge and experience relevant to their parent profession. In terms of the management of mentally disordered offenders, it would appear that a distinctive role needs to be developed which would incorporate the germane material pertinent to the forensic patient as the focus of case management in the community but drawing on relevant knowledge from a number of disciplines. With such a diverse number of professions becoming involved in, or having an invested interest in, the management of mentally disordered offenders in the community it is not surprising that a number of approaches have evolved.

CARE MANAGEMENT

The concept of care management has developed with the decreasing use of prisons being employed as *de facto* accommodation for the homeless "vagrant", along with the corresponding need to develop community-based initiatives as an alternative to such institutional provision. Furthermore, as court diversion, and liaison, schemes are expanded it is clear that there needs to be some to place to which the mentally disordered offender can be diverted. Unfortunately, it is often the case that the lack of resources do not allow for the adequate provision of such services and "anecdotal evidence seems to suggest that many vulnerable individuals placed in the 'community' find themselves in quite unsupportive, even desperate, circumstances" (Watson, 1993, cited in Vaughan & Badger, 1995, p. 125). The care manager concept has emerged in response to the requirement that there be someone who has an overall impression of the needs of the patient in the community, and the level and type of services that he or she requires. Care managers can be from any profession but generally come from social services or the mental health services, and within their role they can adopt any number of models, some of which are outlined below.

Probation Order

Another mechanism for managing the person in the community is the probation order. This facility allows the courts to make a probation order usually with a condition that the person receives some form of psychiatric treatment. Vaughan and Badger (1995) point out that although this mechanism appears as an ideal route for those offenders with mild forms of mental disorder, it does not appear to be a popular disposal route employed by the courts. This order lasts between six months and three years for any offence except murder, and requires that the person receives supervision from a probation officer, but can also have certain other conditions attached to it, such as a limited curfew. If treatment is a condition of the order then this is voluntary, unless emergency conditions apply, and the role of the probation officer is that for any other offender under supervision.

Supervision and Treatment Order

This order arises from the Criminal Procedure (Insanity and Unfitness to Plead) Act (HMSO, 1991). It is a relatively new community disposal option and is used in cases where the person is considered unfit to be tried but it allows for a "trial of the facts" surrounding the offence to be undertaken. If the person is known to have committed the offence or is found to be suffering from a mental disorder the court has the option of making a supervision and treatment order. The order usually requires supervision from a social worker, or probation officer, and is issued where it is believed that the mental disorder is susceptible to treatment without admission to hospital. The court needs to be satisfied that the offender does not pose a serious risk to society.

Guardianship Orders

Guardianship orders can arise from the Mental Health Act (HMSO, 1983) under Section 7 for civil patients and under Section 37 for mentally disordered offenders, or they can arise from the Criminal Proceedings (Insanity and Unfitness to Plead) Act 1991. They are designed to enable patients to receive care in the community without compulsory powers, which allows them to live as normal a life as possible, within an authoritative framework, but with a minimum of constraint. The guardian can be an overall local authority or an identified responsible person who will (Vaughan & Badger, 1995):

- decide where the patient will be accommodated;
- assist in formulating a structured approach to occupation, education, treatment or training;
- ensure that the person is accessible to professionals such as medical practitioners and social workers when required.

SUPERVISION REGISTERS

In December 1993 the Secretary of State for Health announced a requirement for all health authorities to ensure that those "mental health service providers establish and maintain supervision registers" (NHS Management Executive, 1994). These registers were initially to be operationalised on 1 April 1994 but it was quickly realised that this was an unrealistic target and full implementation was delayed until October 1994 (HSG[94]5). The registers were to ensure that:

- they identify and provide information on patients who are, or are liable to be, at risk of committing serious violence or suicide, or of serious self neglect, whether existing patients or newly accepted by the secondary psychiatric services;
- all initial assessments and follow up reviews of patients under the Care Programme Approach consider the question of whether the patient should be registered;
- all provider units incorporate the supervision register in the development of mental health information systems to support the full implementation of the Care Programme Approach (NHS Management Executive, 1984).

Following this announcement a debate ensued between the Royal College of Psychiatrists and the Department of Health regarding several main concerns over the registers. Caldicott (1994), the then president of the Royal College of Psychiatrists, outlined the profession's main worries as follows:

1. Inclusion criteria were too broad
2. There would be significant financial implications
3. There would be an increased risk of litigation when things went wrong
4. Risk assessment was not an exact science
5. Key workers who would be responsible would be difficult to find
6. The broad inclusion of personality disordered would absorb scarce resources
7. There are ethical concerns regarding the use of such registers
8. Placement on the register may damage the therapeutic relationship
9. Confidentiality would be difficult to guarantee
10. Those on the register may have difficulty obtaining primary health care.

Also, Harrison and Bartlett (1994) pointed out that the register may well extend both the legal responsibility for the patient and the role of psychiatrists as agents of social control. They further argued that the supervision registers put both the psychiatrist and key worker in the unenviable position of being responsible for a patient who would probably no longer wish to see them and who may actively try to evade them. However, the Department of Health countered these criticisms by arguing that the criteria for inclusion on the register were such that only those most at risk ought to be placed on it. Thus, they did not see large numbers of patients on the register but only those most in need (Glover, McCulloch & Jenkins, 1994). If this were the case, they rationalised, the remaining concerns were very much lessened.

In defence of the register Glover and colleagues felt that the inclusion criteria were sufficiently stringent to ensure that, if reviewed appropriately by the multi-disciplinary team, only those at serious risk would be registered. They argued that inclusion on the register was appropriate under the following conditions:

- if the patient is under the care of the specialist psychiatric services,
- if a multi-disciplinary review concludes that it is required,
- if the patient is suffering from a severe mental illness,
- if there is a risk of one of the three adverse outcomes,
- if there are some foreseeable circumstances which should be set out, and
- if the circumstances are likely to arise in the particular case being reviewed.

The thrust of their argument being that if a person does not fulfil all the above criteria then that person ought not to be placed on the register, and although accepting that many patients *could* be included, unless all the criteria are met, they should be managed by other means.

The responsibility for the implementation and maintenance of the registers lies with the health authorities who should work closely with provider units. The operational practice of inclusion on, and removal from, the registers should be undertaken within a team review as part of the Care Programme Approach (discussed in more detail below). Without this close collaboration between services and multi-disciplinary staff, it is unlikely that the register will function adequately to target resources at those most in need. Thus, the individual suffers, as does the society as a whole. The importance of this is recognised in the overall case management of mentally disordered offenders in the community.

CASE MANAGEMENT

Case management has become an internationally recognised term within a relatively short period of time (Bergen, 1992; Petryshen & Petryshen, 1993). This wide acceptance of the general concept is probably indicative of the similarities of the problems which case management has emerged to counteract (Onyett, 1992). The historical roots of case management appear to be linked into North American social casework which developed throughout the 1970s and 1980s in response to the problems encountered in that country with the transition of many mentally ill persons from institutional care to the community (Chamberlin, Rogers & Sneed, 1989; Muijen, 1994). This ethos was accompanied by an impetus to maintain mentally ill persons in the community at the initial point of contact rather than give them what was perceived as the negative experience of total institutional care. The major theme that runs through the notion of case management is that it represents an attempt to manage what is seen as a fragmented service (Brunton & Hawthorne, 1989; Onyett, 1991).

The literature on case management is both diffuse and diverse. However, there are several themes that emerge from both the American and British publications. Firstly, it has been developed as a response to deinstitutionalisation and the need for cost-effective community service provision (Richardson & Higgins, 1990; Sherman & Johnson, 1994). Secondly, there was a dissatisfaction with services which were delivered in a paternalistic manner based more on the needs of the providers than the users (Brown & Smith, 1989). Thirdly, there was a political will to drive services which are community based and to locate an identifiable and responsible structure of accountability (Franklin et al., 1987). Fourthly, the politico-economic stimulus has increased public awareness of the potential problems of community care for the mentally ill and catalysed professional liability in this area (Dill, 1987; Bergen, 1992).

Within these four broad themes there are further unifying ideas that constitute case management. These can be broken down into various model approaches. One is the "service brokerage" model in which the case manager acts as a patient advocate linking services to needs but is usually not a budget holder. A second is the "social entrepreneurship" model; here, the case managers are budget holders within an agency, usually social services, and can purchase services for the patient. A third option is the "extended co-ordinator" model which is based on a multi-disciplinary team approach with a key worker attempting to co-ordinate services (Beardshaw & Towell, 1990). A further constituent part of case management is the operationalisation of the theory, whichever model is adapted. This is usually depicted as occurring in phases, which typically include (a) case identification, (b) assessment, (c) need analysis, (d) service design, (e) implementation, (f) monitoring/observing, (g) evaluation, and (h) re-assessment. Another integral part is the form of practice of case management underpinning the conceptual framework. This component entails unravelling the diverse practices of the case management approach by identifying the constructs involved in the role itself (Holloway, 1991). However, the diversity involved makes a summary very difficult, given the limitation of space. Finally, there is an urgency to establish the effectiveness of the case management approach usually by various research strategies providing evidence of outcomes (Anthony & Blanch, 1989).

Forensic case management, or more accurately, case management of forensic (actual or potential) psychiatry patients, is equally as diffuse as its counterpart in the wider field of general psychiatry. Furthermore, the problems of forensic case management are broadened, in that (a) it carries specific problems relating to offending behaviour, (b) there is an increased liability in the event of relapse/recidivism, and (c) there are extended responsibilities that fall outside the usual client–therapist relationship. These three major facets are premised on assumptions pertaining to the relationship between mental disorder and offending behaviour. Although no direct causal link between these two central aspects of forensic psychiatry has been conclusively established, there is an axiomatic understanding that they are related *a priori*. Therefore, case management of forensic patients is fraught with the inherent problems of this added dimension.

OUTREACH: ASSERTIVE AND PASSIVE

Outreach is concerned with the marrying of patients' needs with community support services. Although this is neither new nor innovative in relation to community care, its contemporary version is envisaged in terms of a recognition of the complex developments in social administration, bureaucratic structures, public welfare and entitlements. Couple to this an increased stress in living, and competing, in modern society, and it is no surprise that mental illness referrals in many countries are on the increase (Nordentoft et al., 1997; Balon, 1997; Sammut, 1997; Sheperd et al., 1998). The section on case management above outlined the pressures to maintain patients in the community and to limit hospitalisation as far as is possible. Moreover, with the burgeoning pressures to reduce costs there is a further impetus to maintain patients in a state of "wellness". This means ensuring that patients in the community receive enough support to sustain a healthy stress-free lifestyle (or as much as is possible) which may also involve community treatment programmes (Tzirides, 1988).

Outreach has been categorised into *passive* and *assertive* forms. In the former it is a question of ensuring the maximum provision of services and offering encouragement, support and treatments designed to motivate the patient to take up the services provided. This may entail waiting for patients who fail to attend appointments to "surface" in the system at a later stage, but who will, unfortunately, probably have deteriorated and have ended up in clinics, hospitals, or police stations. Although proponents of passive outreach argue that this is based in the liberty of the patients to accept or reject services, it can be a more expensive method of maintaining the "revolving door" scenario and can be seen as immoral in allowing patients to regress. In *assertive* outreach a more determined approach to the provision of resources, and the take-up of services, is advocated. This not only involves searching for and locating patients who have failed to attend appointments, but also involves ensuring that follow-up contacts are maintained. Services are more aggressively sought for patients which may involve the outreacher applying pressure to housing departments for appropriate accommodation, or pursuing social security agencies to ensure that financial assistance (social security payments) is forthcoming for the patient.

Assertive outreach programmes would appear to have been developed from three main incentives. The first concerns the identification of vulnerable patients in the community. This views those patients who, for whatever reason, tend not to be able to defend themselves in society, are not able to navigate the labyrinth of expectations, and are unable to seek appropriate redress of their grievances against individuals or groups which, accidentally or purposefully, cause them harm. Vulnerable groups may include: some children who are neglected or abused; some elderly people who are mistreated; some mentally or physically disabled who are left without help or support; some terminally ill persons who are left alone and in pain; or some mentally ill people who are feared, shunned and outcast.

The second motivation for outreach approaches is based on the assumption that those targeted would, if our reasoned thought is a yardstick, prefer the services and treatments which are provided rather than remaining in a neglected and all too frequently impoverished state. This, of course, assumes that, in some cases, compulsory treatment is a necessary and appropriate strategy, i.e. in the case of mentally ill persons who may harm themselves or others.

The third motivation for outreach developments for the mentally disordered is based on another assumption; that is, the assumed link between the provision of services, the stress-reduced lifestyle, the applied treatment programmes and their positive effects on the person's mental health. Although many would feel comfortable with this proposition, others may well point out that despite this level of service provision some patients continue to deteriorate mentally and require hospitalisation.

Although there is a paucity of literature on outreach services specifically referring to mentally disordered offenders, the foregoing section is equally pertinent to this latter patient population. Moreover, the importance of assertive outreach is clearly emphasised with this patient group as the consequences of allowing such patients to come under increased stress by poor service provision may result in the tragedy of re-offending. The possible creation of victims who otherwise may not have been harmed, with the probable further incarceration of the offender, are clear grounds for an assertive outreach programme.

Offenders with serious mental disorders would tend to have experienced long periods of institutionalised care either in prison or hospital, when leaving such structured environments for some form of community living must be supported by a wide array of services (Hosty, Cope & Derham, 1994). If, on release, they have few of life's necessities and have lost some of the skills for legitimately acquiring them, they are more likely to become stressed and, thus, have little motivation for not re-offending. With adequate support and some personal investment in society they are more likely to survive the everyday pressures of community living. This was pointed out by Cooke et al. (1994) who argued that: "it seems vital to target services at developing 'something to lose' for clients who commit offences. In this way the client also becomes more amenable to interventions aimed at improving mental health." Although their study was a small-scale project it highlighted three fundamental points which it would be wise to be aware of when managing mentally disordered offenders in the community. The first is that service provision for forensic patients must integrate health and social care to such an extent that they have "something to lose". Second, for some, an intensive crisis management service should be provided which requires an assertive outreacher to closely monitor their patients' attendances at appointments. Thirdly, for a few, no amount of provision or assertive outreach is sufficient to guarantee that they will not re-offend.

There is a small, but growing, body of specialist forensic community mental health workers who are beginning to focus attention on their role in caring for mentally disordered offenders. Pederson (1988) highlighted the fact that this group of patients had always been in existence but that services and specialist professional staff were only recently deemed important enough to receive resources to maintain patients in the community. Moon (1993) expands the Forensic Community Psychiatric Nurse (FCPN) role to include such aspects as the assessment of risk relating to violence and criminal offending, assessing exhibited criminal or other anti-social behaviour, and liaison with solicitors, police, probationary services and forensic resources. Although these are early forays into the role of FCPNs they are important in setting the scene for developing assertive outreach programmes for forensic patients in the community.

CARE PROGRAMME APPROACH

The Department of Health produced a local authority circular (LAC[89]7) in February 1989 drawing attention to the responsibilities of health authorities for discharging patients from hospital, and requesting them to review procedures to ensure that patients who are discharged have adequate resources. Although the earlier health circular (H[89]5), to which it was referring, was concerned with all in-patients in general (physical/medical) hospital settings, it specifically mentioned certain vulnerable categories who may require special attention which included patients suffering from psychiatric illnesses. The importance of this circular was that it recognised a difficulty of communication between the many different disciplines involved in the discharge and subsequent support of patients. Furthermore, it represents an early reference point stressing the importance of adequate planning in any discharge process. The following year saw the publication of the joint health/social services circular dealing specifically with patients with a mental illness referred to specialist psychiatric services (Department of Health, 1990). This circular concerned itself with the Care Programme Approach (CPA) and it was requested that it be implemented by 1 April 1991.

The Care Programme Approach could be developed locally with discussions between relevant parties and could be flexible enough to respond to specific requirements. However, the Department of Health (1990) circular stated that there were key elements which all CPA plans should incorporate:

1. Systematic arrangements for assessing the health care needs of patients who could, potentially, be treated in the community, and for regularly reviewing the health care needs of those being treated in the community.
2. Systematic arrangements, agreed with appropriate social services authorities, for assessing and regularly reviewing what social care such patients need to give them the opportunity of benefiting from treatment in the community.
3. Effective systems for ensuring that agreed health and, where necessary, social care services are provided to those patients who can be treated in the community.

In operationalising this it would be necessary for psychiatrists, nurses, social workers, psychologists, other professional staff, and social services authorities to address issues relating to (a) inter-professional collaborative working, (b) involving patients and carers in care plan construction, (c) maintaining contact with patients and ensuring the provision of agreed services, and (d) delineating the role of key workers. The thrust of the CPA is to provide a systematic analysis of the needs of the patient, through multi-professional and multi-agency discussion, with the identification of a key worker. The key worker has overall responsibility for ensuring the effective management of the patient in the community through the establishment of an appropriate care plan, which is to be regularly reviewed. This approach, it was argued, ought to ensure that the patient is relatively closely monitored and the system should provide the mechanism for quick interventions should the need arise.

In relation to mentally disordered offenders it would seem extremely important for the establishment, and operation, of CPA with specific development in relation to collaborative working between professionals and services including those from the Criminal Justice System. Vaughan and Badger (1995) point out that the National Association for the Care and Resettlement of Offenders ". . . makes provision for extending the CPA to include prisoners identified as being mentally ill, so that no such prisoners are released without appropriate plans and arrangements for their care in the community" (p. 135). If mentally disordered offenders released under supervision in the community are to be helped in not re-offending, then the CPA would seem a potentially effective mechanism for furthering this.

DESISTANCE

Desistance refers to those factors that contribute to an offender ceasing offending behaviour. This has been the focus of many studies in penology and criminology but little work has been carried out with mentally disordered offenders. Knight and West (1975) studied temporary and continuing delinquency and identified several factors that they considered important in distinguishing between the two. These factors included seriousness of the juvenile record, motives for juvenile offences, offending in company, involvement with adolescent peer groups and psychological variables. The thrust of their paper focused on the reasons why temporary delinquents desist and continuing delinquents do not. They reported that: ". . . among the reasons for giving up delinquency volunteered by the temporary delinquents themselves the most prominent were the consequences of being caught" (Knight & West, 1975, p. 47). Continuing delinquents, however, were more casual about their conviction experiences and found penal experience neither beneficial nor a deterrent.

In a later study, Osborne (1980) suggested that home environment was a major determinant of delinquent behaviour. This was a complex factor which was difficult to unravel but, for Osborne, was a central issue in future offending behaviour. The study focused on background factors relevant to future offending and the rate of moving home. Osborne (1980, p. 59) suggested that:

> . . . delinquents moved home more frequently than non-delinquents but not because they more often left the parental home. It seems likely that delinquency is associated with a relatively unstable home situation and that frequent changes of address by the family as a whole reflect that instability.

Taking a different perspective, Shover (1983) focused on changes within the delinquents over time as major determinants of desistance. This study identified four areas of interest, as follows:

- The temporal contingencies included an identity shift in middle age, incommodious time (time as a diminishing entity), and aspirations and goals that develop later in life.
- The interpersonal contingencies, such as ties to another person and ties to a job.
- Interdependence contingencies in which the former two sets did not occur in a fixed sequence.
- Negative cases in which offenders felt it was "too late" for them to change.

West (1982) contrasted delinquents and non-delinquents and identified several measurable features on which the former scored higher. These included being tattooed, an unstable job record, leisure described as "hanging about", an admission of drinking and driving, heavy gambling, and an anti-establishment attitude. In trying to establish what factors contribute towards delinquents desisting from offending, West outlined four groups of contrasting careers. These were (a) juvenile, one-time offenders, (b) latecomers to crime, (c) temporary recidivists, and (d) persisting delinquents. The distinguishing features between them were the extent to which a range of factors could be detected, such as being poorly socialised, aggressive, impulsive, hedonistic, exhibiting low frustration to tolerance, self-centredness, and manifesting hatred of authority. More recently Tarling (1993) found that careers of offenders changed with the age of the offender, when they no longer associated with delinquent friends, with marriage, when they developed a critical and detached perspective of criminal youth, and when they had a change in aspirations.

What the foregoing studies show is the diversity of perspectives used by researchers in an attempt to understand offending behaviour and its desistance. However, it is fair to say that this complex question, as yet, remains largely unanswered. Whether it be home environmental upbringing, personality factors, social structures, psychopathology, or a combination of them all, it is clear that the causes of offending and desistance from it remains a difficult and complex issue.

FORENSIC PSYCHIATRIC PATIENTS AND DESISTANCE

Although there is little literature referring to explanations regarding why mentally disordered offenders desist from re-offending, the follow-up studies of released and discharged patients give us some indication as to the rates of recidivism. Probably the best example of a study of desistance of forensic patients is the case of Baxström in America.

On 23 February 1966, the Supreme Court of the United States held that Johnnie K. Baxström had been denied equal protection of the laws by the statutory procedure under which he was held at the Dannemora State Hospital (*Baxström v. Herold* 383 U.S. 107). Baxström had been certified as insane and transferred to Dannemora in June 1961 while serving a sentence in a state prison. When his maximum sentence expired in December 1961, Baxström was civilly committed to Dannemora under the provisions of section 384 of the Correction Law, which gave procedures for retaining persons found to be still mentally ill on expiration of sentence.

The Supreme Court in effect held section 384 to be in violation of the equal protection clause of the Fourteenth Amendment on two counts. Firstly, it had failed to grant the right to "the jury review available to all other persons civilly committed in New York". Secondly, it had enacted civil commitment to an institution beyond the expiration of his prison term, without a judicial determination that he was dangerously mentally ill such as that afforded to others so committed. Compliance with the Supreme Court decision required immediate administrative moves. Baxström was one of approximately 400 patients held at Dannemora under section 384 and an additional 250 patients at the Matteawan State Hospital of the Department of Correction were in a similar situation.

The Correction Department hospitals were readied to move the patients as fast as the receiving civil hospitals could take them. Meanwhile the civil hospitals had been notified of the impending influx and of the approximate numbers they could expect. The guiding principle was to send each patient to the hospital serving his or her district of residence, but this was not always so simple. The transportation of the patients began in the middle of March and by the end of the month 388 had been moved, with 323 transferred during April. Thereafter the flow was less. The total reached 969 by the end of August 1962. The receiving hospitals were reminded that the patients they were about to receive were now civil cases with nothing in their legal status requiring special security measures. By the end of May all the patients had been absorbed into the hospital populations and scattered throughout the various wards. At least one fourth were known to reside on open wards.

There were staff anxieties at all levels when the Baxström operation was announced. Officials of the Unions objected and demanded special training and pay for employees. In the neighbourhoods there was a flurry of anxiety. Serious public concern occurred in one town as a reactivation of panic from an event that had occurred some eight years previously.

By the end of the first year, however, none of the hospitals had anything untoward to report and Directors used similar terms in conveying information regarding Baxström patients as any other patient. Staff no longer thought of them in any special way and no references were heard regarding this group. One ward actually requested their share of Baxström patients because they had turned out to be such "good patients". At the end of February 1967, 702 of the 969 Baxström patients were in civil hospitals with 176 discharged; 147 were in the community, the remainder into other type of hospitals. There were 24 deaths and a "a few were on escape, leave or family care" (Hunt & Wiley, 1968).

Prior to their discharge it was anticipated that a fourth of all Baxström patients might prove too dangerous for civil hospitals. As it worked out only seven had been found difficult enough to warrant commitment to a Correctional Institution. Of those released there is a record of one subsequent arrest for petty larceny. The corollary of this case was that 99% of Baxström patients did well in civil hospitals. Therefore, the anticipated outbreak of crime and violence did not materialise.

The Baxström case had repercussions that are still felt today. Bridgewater is a State Hospital of the Massachusetts Correctional Institution restricted to male patients only. Following Baxström the Massachusetts Attorney-General was of the opinion that the decision applied equally to Massachusetts procedures for commitment to Bridgewater. Two hundred and sixty-six men were identified as "Baxström patients" by examination from Bridgewater psychiatric staff and psychiatrists from the Department of Legal Medicine (DLM). The Department of Mental Health (DMH) challenged only 22 of the DLH referrals of which only nine were recommitted to Bridgewater (Steadman, 1973). Fifteen men made court appearances in Massachusetts (all misdemeanours except one; the most prevalent offence being drunkenness; others included motor vehicle charges, procuring liquor for a minor, being idle and disorderly). One was charged with a felony (receiving stolen goods, armed robbery, attempted escape, and assault and battery on an officer of the jail).

Other studies have emanated from the landmark case of Baxström. Tennent and Way (1984), studying the English Special Hospitals over a 12- to 17-year follow-up period, made an examination of the subsequent careers of the male ex-patients who were at liberty, seeking to compare those who did not offend with those who offended violently and those who did so non-violently. Between 1961 and 1965 there were 1046 male admissions to the English Special Hospitals comprising 1001 different individuals (45 men had more than one admission). Case notes were examined for circumstances of admission, current and past social status, past and present psychiatric diagnosis, and treatment and criminal behaviour. Follow up information was obtained in 1970 and again in 1979 for discharge and source, from the criminal record office regarding subsequent offending, from the mental health enquiry regarding subsequent mental hospitalisation, and from the National Health Service Register regarding deaths. Information was also checked with the Special Hospitals' Case Register in case of re-admission to a Special Hospital.

Comparing the three high-security hospitals from which patients had been discharged, violent re-offending was found among 18% of Moss Side patients, 19% of Broadmoor patients, and 25% of Rampton patients. Non-offenders were reported as 27% Moss Side, 36% Rampton, and 61% Broadmoor. Of the violent patients 129 were responsible for 5 murders (one a double murder), 6 attempts or threats to murder, 2 manslaughters, 31 GBH, 86 other assaults, 27 robberies, and 6 rapes.

Black (1982) in a five-year follow-up study of male patients discharged from Broadmoor Hospital, sampled 128 male discharged patients to the community between 1960 and 1965. This author posed three basic questions: (a) Did these individuals "survive"? (b) Did they stay in the community for the next five years? (c) Did they commit further offences? The outcome data produced 101 cases of "no re-admissions" to any psychiatric hospital; 97 had no imprisonments; 76 had no further court appearances; and only 13 out of 125 committed assaults of a dangerous kind.

The most recent study of this type was that of Bailey and MacCulloch (1992a) who followed-up patients discharged to the community from the newer Park Lane Special Hospitals. This study examined the differences between groups of patients diagnosed as mentally ill and those categorised as psychopathically disordered. Clear and consistent differences were noted with more patients in the latter group having greater re-conviction rates than those diagnosed as mentally ill. When re-convicted, the psychopathically disordered group were given sentences almost twice as long as the mentally ill group (Bailey & MacCulloch, 1992b).

From all these foregoing studies it is apparent that a good proportion of mentally disordered offenders do not re-offend on release to the community.

However, what is also quite clear is that we do not necessarily know, prior to discharge (a) which patients will re-offend, and (b) the factors that have contributed to the desistance of non-offenders.

CONCLUSIONS

This chapter has provided an overview of some of the many community initiatives for the care and management of mentally disordered offenders in community settings. It is without doubt an expanding area of professional interest which is both rewarding and challenging. If forensic mental health work is to prove its worth it must successfully rehabilitate patients back into the community from whence they came, and unless there is evidence that this can be achieved it is unlikely that it will continue as a therapeutic enterprise. There are many issues involved in making this endeavour successful, not least of all in protecting members of the public who may well become victims if the professional services are not effective.

REFERENCES

Andrews, G. & Teeson, M. (1994) Smart versus dumb treatments: Services for mental disorders. *Current Opinion in Psychiatry*, **7**, 181–185.

Anthony, W.A. & Blanch, A. (1989) Research on community support services—what have we learned? *Psychosocial Rehabilitation Journal*, **12**(3), 55–81.

Bachrach, L.L. & Lamb, H.R. (1989) What have we learned from deinstitutionalisation? *Psychiatric Annals*, **89**, 12–21.

Bacher-Holst, T. (1994) A new window of opportunity: The implications of the Reed Report for psychiatric care. *Psychiatric Care*, March/April, 15–18.

Bailey, J. & MacCulloch, M.J. (1992a) Characteristics of 112 cases discharged directly to the community from a new special hospital and some comparisons of performance. *Journal of Forensic Psychiatry*, **3**, 91–112.

Bailey, J. & MacCulloch, M.J. (1992b) Patterns of reconviction in patients discharged directly to the community from a special hospital: Implications for after-care. *Journal of Forensic Psychiatry*, **3**, 445–461.

Balon, R. (1997) Italian psychiatric reform. *American Journal of Psychiatry*, **154**(10), 1485.

Beale, A., Davies, J., Nixon, J. & Smith, D. (1993) Rising to the challenge. *Nursing Times*, **89**(24), 44–46.

Beardshaw, V. & Towell, D. (1990) *Assessment and case management: Implications for the implementation of "Caring for People"*. King's Fund Institute Briefing Paper 10.

Bergen, A. (1992) Case management in community care: Concepts, practices and implications for nursing. *Journal of Advanced Nursing*, **17**, 1106–1113.

Bhugra, D. (1989) Attitudes towards mental illness. *Acta Psychiatrica Scandinavica*, **80**, 1–12.

Black, D.A. (1982) A 5-year follow-up study of male patients discharged from Broadmoor hospital. In J. Gunn & D. Farrington (Eds) *Abnormal Offenders, Delinquency, and the Criminal Justice System*. Chichester: John Wiley & Sons.

Brown, H. & Smith, H. (1989) Whose ordinary life is it anyway? *Disability, Handicap and Society*, **4**, 105–119.

Brunton, J. & Hawthorne, H. (1989) The acute non-hospital: A Californian model. *The Psychiatric Hospital*, **20**(2), 95–99.

Caldicott, F. (1994) Supervision registers: The college's response. *Psychiatric Bulletin*, **18**, 385–386.

Carr, P., Butterworth, C.A. & Hodges, B. (1980) *Community Psychiatric Nursing.* Edinburgh: Churchill Livingstone.

Chamberlin, J., Rogers, J.A. & Sneed, C.C. (1989) Consumers, families and community support systems. *Psychosocial Rehabilitation Journal*, **12**(3), 91–106.

Cooke, A., Ford, R., Thompson, T., Wharne, S. & Haines, P. (1994) "Something to lose": Case management for mentally disordered offenders. *Journal of Mental Health*, **3**, 59–67.

Cutler, D.L., Tatum, E. & Shore, J.H. (1987) A comparison of schizophrenic patients in different community support treatment approaches. *Community Mental Health Journal*, **23**, 103–113.

Department of Health and Social Security (1974) *Revised Report of the Working Party on Security in NHS Psychiatric Hospitals.* London: DHSS.

Department of Health (1990) *The Care Programme Approach for People with a Mental Illness Referred to the Specialist Psychiatric Services*, HC (90) 23, LASSL (90), II. London: DOH.

Department of Health & Home Office (1992) *Review of Health and Social Services for Mentally Disordered Offenders and Others Requiring Similar Services.* Final Summary Report, Cm. 2088. London: HMSO.

Dill, A.E.P. (1987) Issues in case management for chronically mentally ill. *New Directions for Mental Health Services*, **36**, 61–70.

Franklin, J.L., Solovitz, B., Mason, M., Clemens, J.R. & Miller, G.E. (1987) An evaluation of case management. *American Journal of Public Health*, **77**, 674–678.

Glasgow University Media Group (1993) *Mass Media Representation of Mental Health/Illness—Report for Health Education Board for Scotland.* Glasgow University Media Group, Glasgow University.

Glover, G.R., McCulloch, A.W. & Jenkins, R. (1994) Supervision registers for mentally ill people. *British Medical Journal*, **309**, 809–810.

Goldfinger, S.M., Hopkins, J.T. & Surber, R.W. (1984) Treatment resisters or system resisters? Towards a better service system for acute care recidivists. *New Directions for Mental Health* Services, **21**, 17–27.

Goodwin, S. (1989) Community care for the mentally ill in England and Wales: Myths, assumptions and reality. *Journal of Social Policy*, **18**(1), 27–52.

Harris, M. & Bergman, H. (1988) Clinical case management for chronically mentally ill: A conceptual analysis. *New Directions for Mental Health Services*, **40**, 5–13.

Harrison, G. & Bartlett, P. (1994) Supervision registers for mentally ill people. *British Medical Journal*, **309**, 551–552.

Heilbrun, K. & Griffin, P.A. (1998) *Community Based Forensic Treatment.* New York: The Guilford Press.

Her Majesty's Stationery Office (1983) *The Mental Health Act.* London: HMSO.

Her Majesty's Stationery Office (1984) *Police and Criminal Evidence Act.* London: HMSO.

Her Majesty's Stationery Office (1990) *National Health Service and Community Care Act.* London: HMSO.

Her Majesty's Stationery Office (1991) *The Criminal Procedures (Insanity and Unfitness to Plead) Act.* London: HMSO.

Holloway, F. (1991) Case management for the mentally ill: Looking at the evidence. *International Journal of Social Psychiatry*, **37**(1), 2–13.

Home Office & Department of Health and Social Security (1974) *Interim Report of the Committee on Mentally Abnormal Offenders.* Cm. 5698. London: HMSO.

Home Office & Department of Health and Social Security (1975) *Report of the Committee on Mentally Abnormal Offenders.* Cm. 6244 (the Butler Report). London: HMSO.

Home Office (1990) *Provision for mentally disordered offenders (Circular 66/90).* London: Home Office.

Hosty, G., Cope, R. & Derham, C. (1994) 1000 forensic outpatients: A descriptive study. *Journal of Medicine, Science and the Law*, **34**(3), 243–246.

Hunt, R.C. & Wiley, E.D. (1968) Operation Baxström after one year. *American Journal of Psychiatry*, **124**(7), 134–138.

Intagliata, J., Barry, W. & Egri, G. (1988) The role of the family in delivering case management services. *New Directions for Mental Health Services*, **40**, 39–50.

James, D.V. & Hamilton, L.W. (1992) Setting up psychiatric liaison schemes to magistrates' courts: problems and practicalities. *Journal of Medicine, Science and the Law*, **32**(2), 167–176.

Kennedy, N.M. & Ward, M. (1992) Training aspects of the Birmingham court diversion scheme. *Psychiatric Bulletin*, **16**, 630–631.

Knight, B.J. & West, D.J. (1975) Temporary and continuing delinquency. *British Journal of Criminology*, **15**, 43–50.

Lynn-McHale, D.J., Fitzpatrick, E.R. & Shaffer, R.B. (1993) Case management: development of a model. *Clinical Nurse Specialist*, **7**(6), 299–307.

Marcos, L.R. & Cohen, N.L. (1986) Taking the suspected mentally ill off the streets to public General Hospitals. *New England Journal* of Medicine, **315**, 1158–1161.

Moon, W. (1993) The expanding role of the forensic community psychiatric nurse. *The Journal for Nurses and Other Professionals in Forensic Psychiatry*, **3**, 12–13.

Mueller, B.J. & Hopp, M. (1987) Attitudinal, administrative, legal and fiscal barriers to case management in social rehabilitation of the mentally ill. *International Journal of Mental Health*, **15**(4), 44–58.

Muijen, M. (1994) Rehabilitation and care of the mentally ill. *Current Opinion in Psychiatry*, **7**, 202–206.

NHS Management Executive (1994) *Introduction of Supervision Registers for Mentally Ill People from 1 April 1994*: HSG(94)5. London: NHSME.

Nordentoft, M., Knudsen, H.C., Jessen-Petersen, B., Krasnik, A., Saelan, H., Brodersen, A.M., Treufeldt, P., Loppenthin, P. & Sahl, I. (1997) *Social Psychiatry and Psychiatric Epidemiology*, **32**(7), 369–378.

Onyett, S.R. (1991) An agenda for care programming and care management. *Health Services Management*, **87**(4), 180–183.

Onyett, S.R. (1992) *Case Management in Mental Health*. London: Chapman & Hall.

Osborne, S.G. (1980) Moving home, leaving London and delinquent trends. *British Journal of Criminology*, **20**, 54–61.

Pederson, P. (1988) The role of community psychiatric nurses in forensic psychiatry. *Community Psychiatric Nursing Journal*, **8**(3), 12–17.

Petryshen, P.R. & Petryshen, P.M. (1993) The case management model: an innovative approach to the delivery of patient care. *Journal of Advanced Nursing*, **17**, 1188–1194.

Reed, J. (1992) *Review of Health and Social Services for Mentally Disordered Offenders and Others Requiring Similar Services: Final Summary 1*. London: HMSO.

Richardson, A. & Higgins, R. (1990) *Case Management in Practice: Reflections on the Wakefield Case Management Project*. Nuffield Institute/University of Leeds, Working Paper 1, Leeds.

Sammut, R.G. (1997) TAPS project 34: Out of hours referrals, before and after psychiatric admission bed changes. *Journal of Mental Health*, **6**(4), 389–398.

Sheperd, M., Gunnell, D., Maxwell, B. & Mumford, D. (1998) Development and evaluation of an inner city mental health team. *Social Psychiatry and Psychiatric Epidemiology*, **33**(3), 129–135.

Sherman, J.J. & Johnson, P.K. (1994) CNS as unit-based case manager. *Clinical Nurse Specialist*, **8**(2), 76–80.

Shover, N. (1983) The later stages of ordinary property offender careers. *Social Problems*, **31**, 208–218.

Steadman, H.J. (1973) Follow-up on Baxström patients returned to hospitals for the criminally insane. *American Journal of Psychiatry*, **130**(3), 317–319.

Steadman, H.J. & Halfon, A. (1971) The Baxström patients: Backgrounds and outcomes. *Seminars in Psychiatry*, **3**(3), 376–385.

Tarling, R. (1993) *Analysing Offending: Data, Models and Interpretations.* London: HMSO.

Tennent, G. & Way, C. (1984) The English special hospital—a 12–17 year follow-up study: A comparison of violent and non-violent re-offenders and non-offenders. *The Journal of Medicine, Science and the Law*, **24**(2), 81–91.

Tzirides, E. (1988) Health outreach program: Marketing the "health way". *Nursing Management*, **19**(4), 55–57.

Vaughan, P.J. & Badger, D. (1995) *Working with the Mentally Disordered Offender in the Community.* London: Chapman & Hall.

Watson, W. (1993) Future directions for research. In W. Watson & A. Grounds (Eds) *The Mentally Disordered Offender in an Era of Community Care: New Directions in Provision.* Cambridge: Cambridge University Press.

West, D.J. (1982) *Delinquency: Its Roots, Careers and Prospects.* London: Heinemann.

Chapter 12

Treatment of Sexual Deviation and Aggression

Julie Hird
Mental Health Services of Salford, Manchester, UK

OVERVIEW

Public and professional concern about sexual abuse and assault has increased markedly in the past two decades, due to consciousness-raising and pressure from the feminist movement regarding the extent and seriousness of the problems (e.g. Sanday, 1981; Russell, 1984). This heightened interest has led to a proliferation of research articles about sexual aggression, focusing upon the characteristics and behaviours of sex offenders and more latterly on treatment, outcome and risk management.

As a consequence, the present-day response to a sexual offence has become both sophisticated and complex, involving many different agencies. The introduction of a supervision register for sex offenders (Sex Offenders Act 1997) and legal cases concerning the right of a community to be informed about such an individual living among them (Conway & Butler, 1997) demonstrate the level of concern.

The present chapter will be of interest to all those whose professional practice brings them into contact with sex offenders, whether they are working in the probation service, the health service, social services, prisons, the police or other agencies. Beginning with a brief consideration of the extent of sexually abusive behaviour, it then examines the major theories that have been put forward to account for the occurrence of this kind of behaviour. This section concludes with a description of multi-factorial models of causation, which underpin the cognitive-behavioural treatments currently employed in the majority of intervention programmes. Since treatment initiatives and facilities have expanded at a great

Behaviour, Crime and Legal Processes: A Guide for Forensic Practitioners.
Edited by James McGuire, Tom Mason and Aisling O'Kane.
© 2000 John Wiley & Sons Ltd.

rate during the 1990s, I will then focus on effects on recidivism rates and the growth of treatment–outcome studies over recent years. Finally, a description will be given of the programmatic approaches to treatment in prisons; in probation and community-based services; and in secure psychiatric hospitals. Features of treatments that have been found to be effective or, by contrast, unhelpful will also be described.

This review covers available information about adult male sex offenders. Although there is overlap in many of the issues that arise, adolescent, female and learning-disabled sex offenders will unfortunately be excluded, due to lack of space. The reader is advised to consult other texts which specifically address the needs of these groups of sexual abusers.

THE EXTENT OF THE PROBLEM

The amount of sexually abusive behaviour in society is difficult to quantify accurately and therefore there have been several different approaches to this task. Obtaining official crime statistics, asking adults about sexual victimisation histories and asking sexual offenders about their histories of sexually abusive behaviour are the methods considered here.

Official Home Office statistics revealed that the number of reported sexual offences rose by 40% between 1979 and 1988 (although this was also the case for most other categories of crime). In 1988 sexual offences totalled 26 529, but accounted for less than 1% of all crimes. Sex offenders comprised only 3% of males on probation orders and only 8% of the prison population (Home Office, 1989). Russell (1984), however, highlighted the problem with these figures due to the general under-reporting of sexual offences by victims. She compared victim surveys with official figures and estimated that only about 10% of sexual crimes are reported to the police and less than 1% result in a criminal conviction. Since such a small percentage of sexual assaulters end up in the criminal justice system, one must ask how representative they are of the total sample.

There have been many prevalence studies in which attempts have been made to estimate the rates of child sexual abuse by asking adults about their own experiences as children. These studies contain many methodological problems such as using different definitions of sexual abuse, different methods of obtaining the information and different sample characteristics and so, perhaps unsurprisingly, their reported rates of abuse vary enormously.

North American studies report child abuse rates of between 7% (Fritz, Stoll & Wagner, 1981) and 62% (Wyatt, 1985) and rape or attempted rape rates of between 9% (Kilpatrick et al., 1985) and 44% (Russell, 1984). Two British researchers (Nash & West, 1985) estimated that 42% of a sample of female GP patients and 54% of a sample of female students reported either contact or non-contact sexual abuse. Other studies have also included prevalence figures for males sexually abused as children, and although the rates are generally lower (7–27%), they indicate that sexual abuse affects a significant proportion of all the normal population (Kelly, 1991). In addition, several studies have concentrated upon clinical populations and report high rates of childhood sexual abuse, which are often associated with many psychological difficulties (e.g. Briere & Runtz, 1993).

As already noted, sexual abusive behaviour is often neither disclosed nor reported, so when a sexual offender is brought to court, there is a good likelihood that he may have previously engaged in abusive acts. In general, asking offenders about past, unreported offences is unlikely to yield reliable information, partly due to their tendency to deny and minimise their behaviour, but largely due to their concerns about further prosecution.

Several studies are notable exceptions. Groth, Longo and McFadin (1982) carried out an anonymous survey of imprisoned rapists and child abusers and they admitted up to five times more sexual assaults than were on their criminal record. Abel et al. (1987) guaranteed anonymity to 567 sexual-offenders who were questioned about their sexual-offending histories, prior to being offered voluntary treatment. The numbers of unreported prior sexual offences in each offender group were staggeringly high. For example, they interviewed 224 men who had sexually assaulted a female child outside the family and they disclosed 4435 victims, an average of 19.8 for each perpetrator. The authors also reported significant cross-over rates between type of offence, gender of victims and whether the assault took place inside or outside the family. While such data are striking it is also necessary to be cautious, since group data can easily be skewed due to a small number of very high rate offenders. Also, the sample of offenders (those seeking voluntary treatment) may not be representative of all sexual offenders. Nonetheless, the evidence does seem to indicate that sexually assaultive behaviour is rarely an isolated, one-off occurrence and this is an assumption generally made by professionals working with this group of offenders.

Although it is possible that for some individuals, their first contact with the criminal justice system might significantly reduce the likelihood of their re-offending in the future, despite their history, there is clearly a need for treatment programmes which will target high-risk offenders in particular, address the problem of deviant sexual interest and hopefully reduce future victimisation rates.

Community treatment programmes began to appear in Britain in the late 1980s, and just a decade later, major statutory agencies such as the probation service and the prison service are now significantly involved in treating and managing the risk presented by the sexually offending population.

THEORIES OF SEXUAL AGGRESSION

Following the occurrence of a high-profile sexual assault, professionals, the media and the general public engage in considerable speculation about why sex offenders do what they do. Also, many sexual abusers attending for treatment will state that their main motivation is to uncover the reason why they did what they did, which they present as being a complete mystery. Relatives of offenders are often shocked and disbelieving that someone that they knew so well had the capacity to commit a sexual crime. In a recent interview conducted by the author with parents of an 18-year-old man who had admitted attempted rape and was imprisoned on remand, they offered their view that many things in the case simply did not add up (despite an accurate description of their son by the victim) and they wondered if he was covering up for someone else.

The majority of sexual offenders appear to be completely normal individuals and there is no psychiatric interview or psychological test that can identify them as potential offenders. Nonetheless, an understanding of why they offended has obvious implications for effective treatment. Various theories have been postulated to account for the occurrence of sexual aggression and form an important aspect of the knowledge-base needed when working with sex offenders.

It has been proposed that genetic make-up and levels of sex hormones are implicated (biological theories), that early development and unconscious wishes and feelings are responsible (psychodynamic theories), that particular sexual experiences shape an individual's future behaviour (learning theories) and that the position of men and women in society make sexual aggression the norm (sociological theories). These single-factor theories will be described in more detail below, followed by a consideration of multi-factorial models, which propose that sexual aggression is caused by more than one of these factors.

Biological/Physiological Theories

Quinsey (1984) postulated that in human evolutionary history sexual aggressiveness in males may have ensured their survival. Various writers have also pointed out that aggression and sex are physiologically closely linked (e.g. MacLean, 1962; Marshall & Barbaree, 1990a), since both are activated by the sex steroids in the endocrine system.

At puberty there is a huge increase in the production of testosterone, which is correlated with the beginning of sexual development and interest. Perhaps not surprisingly, several studies have shown that there is a relationship between sex hormone levels and sexual drive. For example, Urdy, Billy and Morris (1984) measured sex hormone levels in 102 adolescent boys and asked them about their sexual behaviour. They reported that 70% of those with high testosterone levels were engaging in sexual activity, compared to 16% of those with low testosterone levels.

However, a search for endocrinological abnormalities in sexual assaulters has been less successful. A review of those studies can be found in Hucker and Bain (1990), who conclude that results obtained are conflicting and the evidence for an abnormality is not well supported. In another review, Bradford (1990) claims that several studies have established that there is a relationship between testosterone levels and sexual aggression and that this indicates the usefulness of hormonal treatment in sexual offenders.

Marshall and Barbaree (1990a) present an multi-factorial model which suggests that ". . . biological factors present the growing male with the task of learning to appropriately separate sex and aggression and to inhibit aggression in a sexual context", but they add that environmental factors nonetheless play the most important role in sexually assaultive behaviour.

While the above seems most appropriate in the explanation of the behaviour of rapists, physiology has also been implicated in the aetiology of child abusers, since it has been established that many such offenders are exclusively sexually aroused by children (e.g. Abel et al., 1981; Freund & Blanchard, 1989). Indeed paedophilia is described by some researchers as a "disease" (Abel et al., 1994). Treatment programmes which support this theory of causation concentrate on the modification of sexual preferences using behavioural techniques, but Quinsey and Earls (1990) warn that any reported changes in sexual preference have to be interpreted conservatively due to the possibility of dissimulation. Hall and Hirschman (1992) also point out that a theory of child sexual abuse based solely upon the presence of deviant arousal to children is inadequate, since many men who abuse children do not show phallometrically measured sexual arousal to children and some normal non-offending males do show such a presentation.

Psychodynamic Theories

The psychodynamic approach emphasises early childhood experiences, typically ascribing parental relationships as the root of sexual deviations in later life. The sexual aspect of the offender's behaviour is usually minimised and offending is seen as being motivated by attempts to meet other psychological needs. Sexual fantasies are viewed as rewarding, due to their non-sexual aspects of control and mastery.

Howells (1981) suggested that men who have a sexual interest in children are attempting to avoid anxiety-laden heterosexuality, often due to unresolved oedipal conflicts. Alternatively, others have suggested that childhood is idealised and men who abuse boys seek out those that they see like themselves and treat them as they wish they had been treated by their mothers (Kline, 1987).

Sexual abuse within the family is regarded differently by psychoanalysts since it involves intense family dynamics (Glasser, 1988). Bentovim (1996) views such sexual abuse in families as either conflict-avoiding or conflict-regulating and, as such, is often used to stabilise family life. Rape is seen as a displacement of hostility due to ambivalent feelings towards the mother (Rada, 1978).

There are few treatment centres which offer psychodynamic therapy to sexual offenders; however, there is a fair amount of scepticism about its usefulness in promoting change. The Portman Clinic in London offers long-term group psychodynamic psychotherapy for offenders, although the exclusion criteria usually rule out most sex offenders, due to their high levels of denial (Craissati, 1998). Nonetheless, the notion of unconscious motivations in sex offending (for example, displaced anger, sexual inadequacy) are found in other explanatory models, most notably in Knight and Prentky's (1990) rapist typology.

Learning Theories

The notion that deviant sexual behaviour is learned via classical and operant conditioning mechanisms has been proposed many times in the literature (e.g. Sidman, 1960). Laws and Marshall (1990) consider both the acquisition and maintenance of deviant sexual interest in their theory. Acquisition can occur quickly, as a result of one association or more between a stimulus and a response, since some stimuli are "prepared" to be paired with a sexual response due to evolutionary history. This association is then strengthened and maintained via the pairing of a cognitive event (a fantasy) and masturbation. They also refer to the central role played by social learning processes, such as observational learning and self-statements (Bandura, 1973) and propose that both of these could account for how victims sometimes become victimisers in later life.

Learning theories have the advantage of being orderly and simple to operationalise, both in research studies and in therapeutic interventions. They have underpinned decades of work which has attempted to modify sexual preferences using masturbatory reconditioning techniques. However, they do not explain why some offenders, particularly rapists and incest offenders, commit sexual crimes, but do not apparently have sexual fantasies about their victims. In fact Marshall (1996) estimated that less than 10% of sex offenders appear to have been solely motivated by strong sexual fantasies about their victims. Equally, it is known that many individuals with deviant sexual fantasies do not act upon them. Briere and Runtz (1989) reported that 21% of 193 male undergraduates reported some sexual attraction to small children. Thus, deviant sexual fantasises are apparently neither necessary nor sufficient for a sexual assault to occur.

Sociological Theories

With the rise of the feminist movement, many writers have argued that rape functions as a mechanism of social control (Brownmiller, 1975).

Herman (1990) proposes that since men have power and control over women in society, sexual assaults are seen as normal and the inquiry should focus upon why all men do not engage in this behaviour rather than why some of them do.

Other areas of research lend support to this argument. The finding that the vast majority of perpetrators are male and most victims are female is a starting point. Furthermore, the presence of pro-rape myths and attitudes in non-offending males has been well documented (Burt, 1980; Lonsway & Fitzgerald, 1994). Moreover, Malamuth (1981) found that 35% of male college students admitted some likelihood of raping, if they were assured they would not be caught.

Further support comes from phallometric studies of rapists which have often found little difference between the sexual preference patterns of rapists and non-rapists (Baxter et al., 1984; Marshall et al., 1986; Murphy et al., 1984). In fact, Marshall and Eccles (1991) conclude that the usefulness of phallometric assessments in rapists is quite limited. However, a subsequent meta-analysis of all phallometric studies involving rapists (Lalumiere & Quinsey, 1994) claimed that there is a difference between rapists and normals in their interest in coercive sex.

Several writers have emphasised that rape is often motivated by non-sexual drives such as anger and power (e.g. Groth, Burgess & Holstrom, 1977) and indeed sexual or anger motivation is considered to be the first subdivision in assigning a rapist to a typological classification (Knight & Prentky, 1990).

The usefulness of this sociological model in relation to understanding rape is probably uncontroversial, but it is less clear whether it has any bearing upon the occurrence of child sexual assault. However, a study which examined the attitudes of 50 incest offenders (Hanson, Gizzarelli & Scott, 1994) discovered that sex role beliefs seemed to play an important role, in that the men significantly more strongly endorsed attitudes supportive of male sexual entitlement compared to the other groups.

Multi-factorial Models

Owing to the heterogeneous nature of sexual offenders and the diverse nature of sexual offences, it is not surprising that many writers, particularly those involved in treating this population, have combined aspects of the single-factor theories to explain the occurrence of sexual aggression.

Marshall and Barbaree (1990a) describe three factors in their integrated model—biological influences, learning experiences and sociocultural attitudes—and their model is briefly described here. They propose that all men are endowed with the ability to use aggression to obtain sexual goals and that the crucial time period is adolescence. Learning experiences as a child will either help or hinder the young male to separate sex and aggression at this time, and if this is not successful then cultural beliefs about the domination of women by men are also likely to contribute to the possibility that they will commit a sexual assault when a particular situation presents itself to them. Despite their claim that their theory is able to account for many kinds of sexual offences, it does appear to relate to most rape offenders.

Hall and Hirschman (1992) propose a multi-factorial model to explain sexual aggression against children, involving (1) physiological sexual arousal, (2) cognitions that justify sexual aggression against children, (3) negative mood states and (4) personality problems. They further suggest that the relative prominence of these four factors may be useful in differentiating the different subtypes of child abuser. They argue that the majority of men who sexually assault children exhibit sexual arousal to children. Such sexual arousal is not sufficient, however, to explain the offending. They must then engage in justifying their sexual contact with a child and they develop cognitive distortions, e.g. the child is willing. Thirdly, a sexual act with a child is often seen to be an attempt to cope with a depressed mood state. Finally, personality precursors which are usually due to negative childhood experiences and appear as adjustment problems, are also going to make a sexual offence more likely.

Both of the models described above contain flexibility between factors, acknowledging the heterogeneous nature of sexual offenders, and are very useful in the assessment of an individual sex offender. The next section will describe a further two multi-factorial models (Wolf, 1985; Finkelhor, 1984) that attempt to explain both the cause and the process of sexual offending against children. These models have been very influential and are used in the majority of group treatment programmes. Their description of the process towards offending is easily understood by the majority of offenders and enables them to acknowledge that they can control their deviant sexual behaviour in the future, even if they do not feel they have an explanation of why it happened in the first place.

The idea of a sexual assault cycle was developed initially by Wolf (1985) and subsequently by Ryan and colleagues (1987) in their work with adolescent sex offenders. Wolf suggests that child victimisation of any kind leads to the development of a personality characterised by egocentricity, a distorted self-image, social isolation and sexual preoccupation. They will also have developed beliefs that men are powerful and can do as they please, and that sex is a useful form of escapism. So they will masturbate about deviant sexual experiences (in which they are powerful) when feeling vulnerable and, over time, their inhibition against offending will decrease and their desire to act on their fantasies will increase.

The sexual assault cycle begins with a poor self-image, an expectation of rejection from others and a subsequent withdrawal from them. The offender then engages in sexual fantasies that enable him to escape from the isolation and feel more in control. Distorted thinking then allows him to start planning the offence, including setting up a situation and grooming the victim. The abuse takes place, reinforced by orgasm either at the time or later during masturbation, and there then follows a short period of guilt, in which he decides not to offend again. But the knowledge that he is a sex offender increases his negative self-image even further and brings him back to the start of the cycle, with the potential for subsequent assaults. Although the aetiological aspect of this model is not supported by many of the research findings described in this chapter, the sexual assault cycle retains a strong popularity among treatment providers.

Finkelhor's (1984) four-factor framework also attempted to explain both the cause and process of sexual offending against children. *Factor 1* relates to the kind of relationship that abusers tend to have with children, which he described as emotionally congruent. Howells (1979) suggested that this is because children are weak and non-threatening objects for abusers. *Factor 2* describes the development of sexual attraction to children and Finkelhor states that this is largely learned from early childhood sexual experiences. As already stated above, the research evidence does not support the notion that sexual arousal to children is necessary for a sexual assault to take place. Also, more than half of sexual offenders do not report having been sexually abused as a child (Abel et al., 1984).

Factor 3, "blockage", concerns the reasons why consenting adult relationships do not meet the needs of abusers and proposes that they are either developmentally "blocked" and do not relate to their peer group, or are "blocked" from having sexual activity in a particular relationship. Social skills deficits in child abusers have been documented (e.g. Freund, 1990; Segal & Marshall, 1985). *Factor 4* is "disinhibition" and refers to the way in which abusers overcome their normal levels of self-restraint. Alcohol has often been cited as a disinhibiting factor although the evidence for this is mixed (Williams & Finkelhor, 1990).

Alongside this causal framework is another four-stage model which describes the pre-conditions for a sexual assault. The first is the motivation to sexually abuse, which refers to deviant sexual arousal and has been described above. The second is overcoming internal inhibitions. Finkelhor suggests that all offenders know that their behaviour is wrong, but they make a decision that it is okay for them and this is often a cognitive distortion concerning the victim's "consent" or agreement. Thirdly, they have to overcome external inhibitions, which basically refers to the setting up of an appropriate and secret opportunity to carry out the abuse. This could be accomplished by offering to baby-sit, or encouraging a mother to take up a regular evening activity. Fourthly and finally, the offender must overcome the resistance of the child. This can be fairly minimal if the child has been "groomed" into sexual contact over some time, or it may include threats, bribes and, more rarely, physical force. There are obvious similarities and overlap between the Wolf and the Finkelhor models, since they both highlight the sequential nature of offending. Although they are not rigorously based upon research evidence, they have both proved useful for a majority of offenders in treatment. Their danger, however, lies in the fact that some practitioners over-invest in these models and view them as being applicable to every sex offender referred to them. So, an offender who does not acknowledge pre-offence fantasy and planning might be wrongly assessed as minimising or in denial. This is particularly relevant with respect to some rape offenders, who do not seem to move through the same sequence of thoughts and behaviours.

TREATMENT PROGRAMMES FOR SEXUAL OFFENDERS

Behavioural treatments for deviant sexual interests have been reported in the literature since the 1960s and this kind of intervention reached the height of its popularity about a decade later. However, as with all psychological treatments based solely upon behavioural principles, there was a growing acknowledgement that, in addition to whatever individuals did, what they said to themselves also played a significant role in the generation or maintenance of their problems. Hence, there was a gradual merging of behavioural treatments, with cognitive approaches, and in the late 1980s cognitive behaviour therapy (CBT) emerged (for a history of this development see Rachman, 1997). As opposed to other forms of psychotherapy, claims have often been made that CBT is more scientific, since everything, despite difficulties in accessing cognitive processes, can theoretically be measured and modified (Gelder, 1997).

CBT interventions for sex offenders, particularly in a group format, have flourished, firstly in the USA and more recently in the UK. In this country the first CBT group treatment programmes started as a result of "the good will of motivated staff" (Morrison, 1994). Several interested practitioners usually from probation and mental health agencies got together and set up a group treatment service, although managerial support was lacking.

Since then various statutory agencies have taken on responsibility by providing both a mandate and a clear infrastructure for this kind of work to occur. In 1990 the Home Secretary announced that sex offenders in prison would soon be able to obtain treatment, and a year later the Probation Service recognised the importance of working with such offenders and approved local level initiatives, including the appointment of specialised staff (Home Office, 1991). Different agency approaches will be further described later in this chapter.

Using CBT as a treatment mode, the interventions usually focus upon identifying offence precursors or sexual assault cycles, correcting distorted thinking patterns, controlling deviant fantasies, increasing victim empathy, increasing social competence and devising relapse prevention skills. Most of these areas are immediately recognised in relation to the models of Finkelhor and Wolf, described earlier in the chapter. Relapse prevention is, as the name implies, a method of avoiding future assaults and is an individualised set of self-management skills (Pithers et al., 1983). For a fuller description of CBT treatment for sex offenders the reader is referred to Salter (1988) or Beckett (1994).

Group formats have become the preferred mode of treatment, because of their clear therapeutic advantages. The group setting provides a forum for both confrontation and support and allows for the development of group processes, or curative factors (Yalom, 1975), including cohesiveness, universality and instillation of hope. Although Yalom describes these factors as operating within a psychodynamic group, Belfer and Levendusky (1985) propose that they are equally applicable in a cognitive behavioural group setting in which "... the goal is accomplished through a combination of members learning to identify problem areas, applying relevant behavioural (and cognitive) interventions and increasing the probability of compliance to these interventions by fostering a group process that holds each member accountable".

The powerful dynamics operating in a group treatment programme is further illustrated by Hossack (1999) who describes the therapeutic role of a treated sex offender co-facilitating in community-based 12-week introductory groups for previously untreated sex offenders. The role is effectively that of a paraprofessional, by offering non-collusive support to the new members, who are likely to be defensive and unmotivated. Hossack has described three stages in the group members' attitudes towards the paraprofessional. At first they see him as an ally, then they see him as a threat, but this is usually followed by ". . . acceptance of the paraprofessional as evidence of rehabilitation and possible hope for the future".

Recidivism

The main rationale for treating sex offenders is to reduce the likelihood of future offending. The research literature on this issue is beset with many methodological problems, such as varying definitions of recidivism and different lengths of follow-up periods; but cumulatively it suggests that many sex offenders will commit further sexual offences (with rates varying between 4% and 71%). Individual risk, however, depends upon many factors, including type of offence, prior offence frequency and other subject characteristics. The contentious issue of whether treatment has an effect upon recidivism rates will also be considered.

Meyer and Romero (1980) divided sex offenders into two groups on the basis of their prior arrest rate. Only 7.9% of those who had previously offended at a rate of 0–0.3 times per year re-offended; considerably less than re-offence rate of 26.2% among those who had previously offended at a rate of 0.31–1.39 per year.

Incest offenders have been shown to re-offend at rates of between 4 and 10% (Gibbens, Soothill & Way, 1981; Frisbie and Dondis, 1965). Estimated rates for extra-familial girl abusers are 10–29% and for extra-familial boy abusers are 13–40% (Furby, Weinrott & Blackshaw, 1989). Rapist recidivism rates have ranged from 7 to 35%. Rice, Harris and Quinsey (1990) followed up 54 rapists released from a high-security hospital for 46 months and obtained a sexual re-cidivism rate of 28% and a violent recidivism rate of 43%. All of the rapists had been assessed with penile plethysmography and the Hare *Psychopathy Checklist*. Arousal to coercive sex or high scores on the Checklist both predicted sexual and violent recidivism.

Those sexual offenders with the highest recidivism rates are exhibitionists. Cox (1980) reported that between 41 and 71% were found to re-offend.

Treatment Outcomes

Since most treatment programmes are run with an explicit child protection remit, the possibility that a few future victims are spared, is often regarded as a sufficient reason for intervention. Evidence that treatment does work and is an effective way of reducing risk is now slowly accumulating in the literature, but unfortunately well-designed outcome studies are few and this issue tends to be overlooked.

There are numerous methodological difficulties in designing a good treatment outcome study. First of all, the sample of sex offenders in treatment needs to be carefully described, not just with demographic variables, but in terms of their level of risk, who is excluded and whether they attend voluntarily. This allows for any sample bias to be detected and noted. After treatment there has to be a considerable follow-up period to enable recording of future sexual offences. This rate of re-offending then has to be compared with a comparison control group, one which is similar in all key respects except that it did not receive treatment. Such control groups rarely exist and Marshall and Barbaree (1990b) argue that allocating offenders to either a treatment or no-treatment group is not ethically acceptable. On the other hand, Quinsey et al. (1993) propose that treatment providers have an ethical obligation to prove that their programme is effective and therefore can justify setting up no-treatment control groups in this way.

The proliferation of CBT treatment programmes for sex offenders in the past decade has largely been based on faith, since the evaluation studies are still underway and the fairly low base rates for sexual recidivism necessitate follow up periods of many years (Marshall et al., 1998). Speedier, more immediate evaluations of programme effectiveness have been demanded and this has led to several studies reporting differences on psychological tests administered before and after treatment (for example, in the STEP research—Beckett et al., 1994—see below for further discussion).

The first attempt to review comprehensively all sex offender treatment outcome studies dating from 1960 onwards was undertaken by Furby, Weinrott and Blackshaw (1989). These authors reached the gloomy conclusion that treatment did not reduce sex offender recidivism. However, they did note that many of the treatment models they considered were obsolete and Marshall and Pithers (1994) pointed out that few of the programmes contained any elements of the CBT approach, which is currently so prevalent and favoured. A subsequent meta-analysis (Hall, 1995) of a larger number of recent treatment studies showed a small effect size for treatment (19% re-offence rate) versus comparison conditions (27% re-offence rate).

There are still, however, a few outcome studies in the literature and those that do exist mainly relate to North American sex offenders and treatment programmes. Rice, Quinsey and Harris (1991) failed to find treatment effects for extra-familial child abusers in a high-security mental health institution. They reported on their own treatment programme, which essentially aimed to reduce deviant arousal and increase arousal to adults. Only half of their sample achieved this goal and these were matched with untreated subjects, insofar as was possible, and subsequent recidivism rates were noted to be the same. Marshall and Pithers (1994) criticised this study and pointed out that the intervention was brief, behaviourally based, had no aftercare or follow-up and may have taken place many years before the offender's release from hospital.

Marshall and Barbaree (1990b) reported treatment effects in their Canadian study of men convicted of child sexual abuse, compared with an untreated group who were motivated, but unable to attend for other reasons. They used not only official arrest records, but also files held by police and child protection agencies. At two years post-treatment, 5.5% had re-offended, compared to 12.5%

of untreated offenders, but the rates rose sharply after four years to 25% of the treated group and 64.3% of the untreated group. They recommended that follow-up periods of less than two years should not be relied upon in outcome studies.

Marques and her colleagues (1994) reported on the initial findings of an ongoing outcome study which has incorporated the most methodologically sound comparison group to date and which will track criminal records for 14 years. All offenders came from the California Department of Corrections, where they were serving sentences for child sexual assault or rape. Among those assessed as suitable for treatment, three groups were formed: a treatment group of men who volunteered for treatment, a no-treatment group of men who volunteered for treatment and a third group of men who did not wish to participate. The treatment group members were transferred to the Atascadero State Hospital, where they remained for an average of two years, until their parole date. The treatment programme used a comprehensive CBT approach, incorporating a significant relapse prevention component. They considered recidivism rates after a mean time of 34.2 months and reported one significant result: the treatment group had lower recidivism rates for sexual offences (8.2%) than the group who did not wish to participate in treatment. Also a markedly high re-offence rate for treatment drop-outs was noted and Marques and her colleagues suggest that this group may represent the most impulsive sex offenders. They concluded that their study was showing promising trends, which they hope will become significant as time passes.

Marshall and his associates (1998) view the outcome studies of the 1990s as "promising", but accept that the multitude of methodological difficulties is such as to "preclude definite conclusions". They nonetheless note that clinicians in many countries world-wide are now engaged in treating sex offenders and believe that efforts must also be made to identify what aspects of the treatment programmes are linked to therapeutic effectiveness.

In Britain the evaluation research is still very much in its infancy, but is firmly on the agenda. The STEP study (Beckett et al., 1994), funded by the Home Office, was the first British systematic short-term evaluation of community treatment programmes for child abusers; six were probation led and one was a specialist residential centre, the Gracewell Clinic, now known as the Lucy Faithfull Foundation (Eldridge & Wyre, 1998). The study investigated the impact of treatment using pre- and post-psychological measures, attempted to identify the effective elements of treatment programmes and collected data for a long-term recidivism study. The psychological tests included several validity scales and the others addressed offence-specific problems and personality functioning. Those that were compiled by the research team were standardised on a sample of 81 non-offending British males.

In all, 52 sex offenders completed the STEP evaluation and were classified either as high-deviancy or low-deviancy. High-deviancy participants typically had previous offences, male or mate and female victims, offences both inside and outside the family and a high risk of re-offending based upon Fisher and

Thornton's (1993) risk algorithm. After treatment 54% of child abusers had profiles which fell largely within the non-offending range, 65% of the low-deviancy group and 42% of the high-deviancy group. The results also showed a relationship between change and length of time in treatment. The authors concluded that treatment success depended upon the degree of clients' deviancy before starting treatment; the length of the treatment programme; and the therapeutic nature of the treatment group. They warned that high-deviancy clients require longer in treatment to achieve change and that cohesive groups performed best.

The STEP team went on to evaluate the Sex Offender Treatment Programme (SOTP) in the British prisons. Using a similar design to the community study, a sample of 77 child abusers, from six prisons, completed pre- and post-tests. The recently published report (Beech, Fisher & Beckett, 1999) found that over two-thirds of these men were successfully treated with regard to pro-offending attitudes and one-third of men show an overall treatment effect (a psychological testing profile largely indistinguishable from that of a non-sex offender). High-deviancy men were the least successful: 43% of this group showed a reduction in pro-offending attitudes and only 14% showed an overall treatment effect. Longer programmes (160 hours) were more effective than shorter ones (80 hours) for all except the low-deviancy males. They also considered the effects of group climate on change and discovered that cohesiveness was clearly linked to treatment success.

The prison-based groups were not exclusively designed for men convicted of sexual assaults on children; however, only three men convicted of rape took up the offer of a treatment place. Whether both types of sex offenders can be treated in the same group is debatable. Maletsky (1991) suggests that rapists are more difficult to treat and Beckett (1998) describes them as less motivated and also voiced a suspicion that practitioners feel less confident in treating them.

The STEP team has identified psychological changes after treatment in sex offender groups run in both community and prison settings. Whether there is a relationship between these short-term changes and future recidivism rates has yet to be seen.

A two-year follow-up study was conducted on 133 sex offenders referred to one of the seven community programmes studied by the STEP team (Hedderman & Sugg, 1996) and they were compared with 191 sex offenders who were given probation orders, but no specific treatment. After two years only 4.5% of offenders of the treatment group had re-offended, compared with 9% of the probation-supervised group. Also, members of the probation-supervised group were five times more likely to have been reconvicted of a non-sexual offence. Beckett (1998) also reports that none of the sexual re-offenders in the treatment group had been identified as "successfully treated" by the STEP psychological measures and he pointed to their potential usefulness in predicting sexual reconviction.

Another British study (Proctor, 1996) evaluated recidivism rates for 54 sexual offenders (including rapists and exhibitionists) over five years, following their involvement in a community probation-run treatment programme. He employed a matched control group using a retrospective sample of untreated offenders. The cognitive-behavioural treatment consisted of ten sessions, each lasting for six hours, over a fortnight, followed by 14 supervision sessions during the six month period immediately after the end of the group. The results indicated promising trends although they did not show a statistically significant treatment effect. Untreated offenders were convicted of a further sexual offence at three times the rate of the treated offenders.

WORKING WITH SEX OFFENDERS IN DIFFERENT SETTINGS

Since 1990 there have been various national initiatives that have greatly extended the treatment services available for sex offenders. Whereas previous facilities were isolated and had no consensus on treatment style or philosophy of intervention, the developments over the past decade have established a cognitive-behavioural treatment orientation and have focused upon self-management of future risk, rather than cure. Three main settings will be covered in this article, the prison service, the probation service and forensic mental health services.

The Prison Service

In 1990 the Home Secretary announced that the Prison Service would introduce a national strategy for the treatment of imprisoned sex offenders. Since then the *Sex Offender Treatment Programme* (SOTP) has been implemented in 25 penal establishments throughout England and Wales (Mann & Thornton, 1998). Eligibility for the treatment programmes was initially restricted to those sex offenders serving a sentence of at least four years, which represented just 29% of all those imprisoned for sexual offences (Grubin & Thornton, 1994). The programme has since been extended so that those serving a sentence of two years or more now have the chance of receiving treatment. Mann and Thornton (1998) reported that about half of the 1400 eligible prisoners offered a place accepted it, but in reality there is still a shortfall in treatment places. In 1996–97, a total of 565 prisoners completed the programme.

The SOTP, as described by Mann and Thornton (1998), consists of an extensive assessment process and several group treatment modules. Assessment involves clinical interviews, extensive psychometric testing and, in some prisons, penile plethysmography. The measures are then repeated on completion of the core programme.

The core programme, which when originally implemented was 60 hours long, now has a duration of 180 hours. It addresses denial and minimisation, victim empathy and relapse prevention. There are three additional modules: the cognitive skills programme lasts 50 hours and is designed to improve decision-making. The extended programme addresses the management of negative emotions, relationships and deviant fantasies, lasts between 40 and 50 hours and can be supplemented with individual sessions. The third module is the "booster" programme, of 50–70 hours' duration which focuses on relapse prevention for those offenders who are about to be released.

The SOTP programme is cognitive behavioural in orientation and delivered by prison officers who receive special training. It is committed to constant evaluation of programme effectiveness and improvements are rapidly put into place.

Mann and Thornton (1998) state that owing to the large numbers of sex offenders involved in the programme there will be considerable data for a recidivism study. However, locating a matched control group is problematic since those not undertaking treatment either did not want it or were assigned a lower risk status.

The Probation Service and Community Treatment Programmes

Although historically involved in this field in an unco-ordinated fashion, the probation service some time ago affirmed the need for sex offender treatment and the specialisation of some officers for conducting this work (Home Office, 1991). In a survey undertaken in the same year, Barker and Morgan (1993) reported that most of the 55 probation services in England and Wales offered specialist interventions for sex offenders on probation. Just over a third (37%) of interventions had been running for two years or less but a further 31% had been running for three to five years. The probation service is now probably the main organiser and provider of community treatment programmes.

Although the treatment style is predominantly cognitive-behavioural groupwork, there are various different models of delivery. Some programmes run intensively over a short period of time, e.g. a fortnight, others are fixed in length and some are rolling programmes, running on a weekly or fortnightly basis. The majority of programmes are aimed at those convicted of child abuse.

By 1995 the probation service's commitment to work with clients found guilty of sexual offences was evident in the level of activity recorded. A survey conducted by the Association of Chief Officers of Probation found that no fewer than 109 community programmes were being run, compared to 63 in 1991. A substantial proportion (82%) of probation service areas had issued a policy statement in relation to the supervision of sex offenders, 55% had created specialist posts and 44% of treatment programmes included other professionals, such as psychologists and social workers.

The majority of community projects are organised on a multi-agency basis, with a strong probation presence, but reflecting the need for a wide range of professionals to be involved in the treatment and management of sex offenders. Service delivery has also become more creative and flexible, acknowledging the need to assess and treat large numbers of sex offenders, rather than offer a luxury long-term service to a small number of highly selected offenders. The most comprehensive and stable programmes also have management commitment and financial support from the different agencies involved and this ensures that the service does not rely on one or two committed practitioners.

The *Thames Valley Project* offers a comprehensive service of this type, as described by Beckett (1998). It has four full-time members of staff, a senior probation officer, a clinical forensic psychologist, a probation officer and an administrator. This team is supported by a management group consisting of probation managers, a consultant clinical forensic psychologist, a consultant child psychiatrist and child protection co-ordinators. Referrals are taken from probation officers, social workers and the health profession. It assesses over 140 sex offenders a year (using the STEP assessment battery) and runs six two-week group treatment programmes, providing 45 hours of treatment for up to eight offenders who have assaulted children, adults or who have exposed themselves. This core programme is then followed by six two-hour groups focusing on relapse prevention. A rolling long-term treatment group is available for high-risk offenders, predominantly child abusers, and they leave only when their psychological profile, as measured by the STEP battery, shows a "treated" psychological profile (Beech, Fisher & Beckett, 1999). There is also a partner's group, aimed at enhancing the protective abilities of the non-abusing parent (Smith, 1994), in circumstances where family re-unification is being considered.

Another example of a multi-agency community programme for child abusers, is the *Challenge Project* in south-east London (Craissati, 1998). It provides both individual and group treatment and uses a cognitive-behavioural approach, but also relies upon psychodynamic understandings of group process. The core programme meets weekly, for one and a half hours, over the course of a year and comprises several treatment modules. This is a "slow/open" group and new members can be admitted at the beginning of a module. The therapists are probation officers and a clinical psychologist. There is also a relapse prevention group which runs twice a year, for ten weeks and complements the core programme.

SECURE MENTAL HEALTH ESTABLISHMENTS

The National Health Service offers a spectrum of secure facilities for mentally abnormal offenders, ranging from Special Hospitals which provide high security through to Medium Secure Units (MSUs), offering medium security. Some offenders will also be found in low-security settings, such as locked wards.

Sexual offenders will be dealt with by these forensic mental health establishments if they are regarded as being mentally disordered, as defined by the Mental Health Act of 1983. Hence they will be either suffering from mental illness, psychopathic disorder, mental impairment, or severe mental impairment and some may have a dual diagnosis.

Individuals with convictions for sexual crimes account for approximately one-third of the Special Hospital population (Briggs, 1994), whereas the number of sex offenders in RSUs tends to be relatively low (Fisher, Grubin & Perkins, 1998). All RSUs also offer out-patient treatment and a large number of sex offenders not deemed to be mentally disordered are seen by the clinical psychologists and forensic psychiatrists. Houston, Thompson and Wragg (1994) found that all RSU psychologists took on a large number of sex offending out-patients and almost a quarter of them were involved in running community treatment groups, usually of a multi-agency nature, as described earlier.

Treatment for sexual offenders in Special Hospitals has been unspectacular until recently. Many were offered behavioural treatment for deviant sexual interest, involving penile plethysmograph assessments. Also, individual psychotherapy with a psychodynamic orientation was usually available, with a focus upon increasing insight into traumatic personal histories, rather than upon the sexual offending. Reiss, Grubin and Meux (1996) conducted a small treatment outcome study of 25 personality disordered patients in Broadmoor Special Hospital, half of whom had a sexual motivation associated with their offending. They had all been treated on a ward specially designed for personality problems that offered a range of psychotherapeutic treatments, but the sex offenders received only psychotherapy or sex education. Twenty per cent re-offended and all new offences were sexual in nature: two sexual killings, two serious sexual offences and one less serious sexual offence. The authors concluded that a cognitive-behavioural treatment programme should be introduced into the ward regime.

Briggs (1994) has described the difficulties in working with sex offenders in Rampton Hospital, one of the three Special Hospitals in England and Wales. He referred to problems in agreeing on treatment needs and approaches by clinical teams, lack of staff training, derogatory attitudes among staff towards this patient group and numerous organisational problems associated with working in a large institutional setting.

The present author was involved in setting up three cognitive-behavioural treatment groups in Ashworth Hospital, for patients convicted of sexual offences respectively classified as suffering from psychopathic disorder, mental illness and mental impairment (in terms of the Mental Health Act 1983). The offence-focused nature of the intervention and the benefits of the group setting enabled the patients to be more open and honest about their sexual offending behaviour and appraisal of future risk. Most of the patients had been in a Special Hospital for many years and progress in treatment rested upon being accepted for transfer by their local MSU or discharge by a Mental Health Tribunal, the former being the most likely outcome. However, there was often a reluctance on the part of MSUs to accept sex offenders, particularly those with a diagnosis of psychopathic disorder. They were often viewed as difficult if not impossible to treat and the few re-offences committed in MSUs have usually been perpetrated by this group of patients (Fisher, Grubin & Perkins, 1998). The difficulty rests upon whether psychopaths can be treated or not, which is a constant debate among professionals. Currently there are far fewer sexual offenders labelled as being "psychopathically disordered" by the psychiatric profession, so that they tend more frequently to go to prison.

Clearly, the indeterminate length of stay in a Special Hospital, often due to factors completely outside the patient's control, does not engender high levels of treatment motivation.

Although this treatment approach did succeed in placing personal responsibility for future risk at the top of many of the patients' agenda, numerous other difficulties that were encountered in running the groups ranged from occasional, but destructive breaks of group confidentiality, to the lack of management interest or support.

Owing to the fact that there are only ever a few sex offenders within an MSU at any one time, and that the majority of them will be suffering from a psychotic illness, there is rarely an opportunity to run a group. Most of the work is therefore individually based, and several treatment/management examples are described by Fisher, Grubin and Perkins (1998). They also highlight the problems of low motivation and apathy, which often preclude any form of assessment or intervention, which then makes it more difficult to move them back into the community due to their unknown level of risk.

PROFESSIONAL SUPPORT

Owing to the rapid expansion of work undertaken with people who sexually assault others, the collaboration between different agencies and the public concern about risk issues, many professionals often find themselves unsure, in conflict, or unhappy about the treatment and management of a particular individual.

It was against this background that a group of multi-disciplinary practitioners formed a North West support group which aimed to offer advice and consultation to themselves and others in their work with sex offenders. In September 1991 this group began operating as a national organisation and took the name NOTA (*The National Association for the Development of Work with Sex Offenders*). In addition to its original function it keeps professionals in touch with others involved in work with all kinds of sex offenders and ensures that they are informed about current research and practice. A national conference is organised annually and numerous training events take place throughout the year. It also produces publications offering guidance on such issues as consulting to others about working with a sex offender (Morrison, 1998) and the ethical use of sexual material (NOTA, 1993), and it also publishes the *Journal of Sexual Aggression*. Its success as an organisation is largely due to the ongoing need for information, advice and support, which reflects the challenges and the difficulties posed by treating and managing sexually abusive individuals.

REFERENCES

Abel, G., Becker, J., Cunningham-Rathner, J., Rouleau, J., Kaplan, M. & Reld, J. (1984) *The Treatment of Child Molesters*. Available from SBCTM, 722 West 168th Street, Box 17, New York, NY 10032.

Abel, G., Becker, J., Cunningham-Rathner, J. & Rouleau, J. (1987) Self reported sex crimes of 561 non-incarcerated paraphiliacs. *Journal of Interpersonal Violence*, **2**, 3–25.

Abel, G., Becker, J., Murphy, W. & Flanagan, B. (1981) Identifying dangerous child molesters. In R.B. Stuart (Ed.) *Violent Behaviour*. New York, NY: Brunner/Mazel.

Abel, G., Lawry, S.S., Karlstrom, E., Osborn, C.A. & Gilliespie, C.F. (1994) Screening tests for paedophilia. *Criminal Justice and Behaviour*, **2**(1), 115–131.

Bandura, A. (1973) *Aggression: A Social Learning Analysis*. Englewood Cliffs, NJ: Prentice-Hall.

Barker, M. & Morgan, R. (1993) *Sex offenders: A Framework for the Evaluation of Community-based Treatment*. London: Home Office.

Baxter, D J., Marshall, W.L., Barbaree, H.L., Davidson, P.R. & Malcolm, B.R (1984) Deviant sexual behaviour: Differentiation of sex offenders by criminal and personal history, psychometric assessment and sexual response. *Criminal Justice and Behaviour*, **11**, 477–501.

Beckett, R. (1994) Cognitive-behavioural treatment of sex offenders. In T. Morrison, M. Erode & R. Beckett (Eds) *Sexual Offending Against Children*. London: Routledge.

Beckett, R. (1998) Community treatment in the United Kingdom. In W.L. Marshall, Y.M. Fernandez, S.M. Hudson & T. Ward (Eds) *Sourcebook of Treatment Programmes for Sexual Offenders*. New York, NY: Plenum Press.

Beckett, R., Beech, A., Fisher, D. & Fordham, A.S. (1994) *Community-based Treatment for Sex Offenders: An Evaluation of Seven Treatment Programmes*. London: Home Office Publishers.

Beech, A., Fisher, D. & Beckett, R. (1999) *An Evaluation of the Prison Sex Offender Treatment Programme*. London: Home Office Publishers.

Belfer, P.L. & Levendusky, P. (1985) Long-term behavioural group psychotherapy. In D. Upper & S. Ross (Eds) *Handbook of Behavioural Group Therapy*. New York, NY: Plenum Press.

Bentovim, A. (1996) Systems theory. In C. Cordess & M. Cox (Eds) *Forensic Psychotherapy*. London: Jessica Kingsley.

Bradford, J.M.W. (1990) The antiandrogen and hormonal treatment of sex offenders. In W.L. Marshall, H.E. Barbaree & D.R. Laws (Eds) *Handbook of Sexual Assault*. New York, NY: Plenum.

Briere, J. & Runtz, M. (1989) University males sexual interest in children: Predicting potential indices of "paedophilia" in a non-forensic sample. *Child Abuse and Neglect*, **13**, 65–75.

Briere, J. & Runtz, M. (1993) Childhood sexual abuse: Long term sequelae and implications for psychological assessment. *Journal of Interpersonal Violence*, **8**, 312–330.

Briggs, D. (1994) The management of sex offenders in institutions. In T. Morrison, M. Erooga & R. Beckett (Eds) *Sexual Offending Against Children*. London: Routledge.

Brownmiller, S. (1975) *Against Our Will: Men, Women and Rape*. New York: Bantam.

Burt, M. (1980) Cultural myths and support for rape. *Journal of Personality and Social Psychology*, **38**, 217–230.

Conway, H. & Butler, J.C. (1997) Not in my backyard—banishing paedophiles. *New Law Journal*, **147**, 1075–1076.

Cox, D.J. (1980) Exhibitionism: An overview. In D.J. Cox & R.J. Daitzinan (Eds) *Exhibitionism: Description, Assessment and Treatment*. New York, NY: Garland STPM Press.

Craissati, J. (1998) *Child Sexual Abusers*. Hove, East Sussex: Psychology Press.

Eldridge, H. & Wyre, R. (1998) The Lucy Faithfull Foundation residential program for sexual offenders. In W.L. Marshall, Y.M. Fernandez, S.M. Hudson & T. Ward (Eds) *Sourcebook of Treatment Programmes for Sexual Offenders*. New York, NY: Plenum Press.

Finkelhor, D. (1984) *Child Sexual Abuse: New Theory and Research*. New York, NY: Free Press.

Fisher, D. & Thornton, D. (1993) Assessing risk of re-offending in sexual offenders. *Journal of Mental Health*, **2**, 105–117.

Fisher, D., Grubin, D. & Perkins, D. (1998) Working with sexual offenders in psychiatric settings in England and Wales. In W.L. Marshall, Y.M. Fernandez, S.M. Hudson & T. Ward (Eds) *Sourcebook of Treatment Programmes for Sexual Offenders*. New York, NY: Plenum Press.

Freund, K. (1990) Courtship Disorder. In W.L. Marshall, H.E. Barbaree & D.R. Laws (Eds) *Handbook of Sexual Assault*. New York, NY: Plenum.

Freund, K. & Blanchard, R. (1989) Phallometric diagnosis of pedophilia. *Journal of Consulting and Clinical Psychology*, **57**, 100–105.

Frisbie, L.V. & Dondis, E.H. (1965) *Recidivism Among Treated Sex Offenders*. (Research monograph #5.) Sacramento, CA: California Department of Mental Hygiene.

Fritz, G.S., Stoll, K. & Wagner, N. (1981) A comparison of males and females who were molested as children. *Journal of Sex and Marital Therapy*, **7**, 54–59.

Furby, L., Weinrott, M.R. & Blackshaw, L. (1989) Sex offender recidivism: A review. *Psychological Bulletin*, **105**, 3–30.

Gelder, M. (1997) The scientific foundations of cognitive behaviour therapy. In D.M. Clark & C.G. Fairburn (Eds) *Science and Practice of Cognitive Behaviour Therapy*. Oxford: Oxford University Press.

Gibbens, T.C.N., Soothill, K.L. & Way, C.K. (1981) Sex offences against young girls: A long term record study. *Psychological Medicine*, **11**, 351–357.

Glasser, M. (1988) Psychodynamic aspects of paedophilia. *Psychoanalytic Psychotherapy*, **3**, 121–135.

Groth, A.N., Burgess, A.M. & Holstrom, L.L. (1977) Rape: Power, anger and sexuality. *American Journal of Psychiatry*, **134**, 1239–1243.

Groth, A.N., Longo, R.E. & McFadin, J.B. (1982) Undetected recidivism amongst rapists and child molesters. *Crime and Delinquency*, **281**, 450–458.

Grubin, D. & Thornton, D. (1994) A national programme for the assessment and treatment of sex offenders in the English prison system. *Criminal Justice and Behaviour*, **21**, 55–71.

Hall, G.C. (1995) Sex offender recidivism revisited: A meta-analysis of recent treatment studies. *Journal of Consulting and Clinical Psychology*, **63**, 802–809.

Hall, G.C. & Hirschman, R. (1992) Sexual aggression against children: A conceptual perspective of etiology. *Criminal Justice and Behaviour*, **19**, 8–23.

Hanson, R.K., Gizzarelli, R. & Scott, H. (1994) The attitudes of incest offenders. *Criminal Justice and Behaviour*, **21**, 187–202.

Hedderman, C. & Sugg, D. (1996) *Does Treating Sex Offenders Reduce Re-offending?* Home Office Research Findings, No 45. London: Home Office.

Herman, J.L. (1990) Sex offenders: A feminist perspective. In W.L. Marshall, H.E. Barbaree & D.R. Laws (Eds) *Handbook of Sexual Assault*. New York, NY: Plenum.

Home Office (1989) *Criminal Statistics England and Wales 1988*. London: HMSO.

Home Office (1991) *The Work of the Probation Service with Sex Offenders: Report of a Thematic Inspection*. London: HMSO.

Hossack, A. (1999) The professional, the paraprofessional and the perpetrator. *Journal of Sexual Aggression*, **4**, 15–21.

Houston, J., Thompson, P. & Wragg, J. (1994) A survey of forensic psychologists' work with sex offenders in England and Wales. *Criminal Behaviour and Mental Health*, **4**, 118–129.

Howells, K. (1979) Some meanings of children for paedophiles. In M. Cook & G. Wilson (Eds) *Love and Attraction*. Oxford: Pergamon.

Howells, K. (1981) Adult sexual interest in children: Considerations relevant to theories of etiology. In M. Cook & K. Howells (Eds) *Adult Sexual Interest in Children*. London: Academic Press.

Hucker, S.J. & Bain, J. (1990) Androgenic hormones and sexual assault. In W.L. Marshall,

H.E. Barbaree & D.R. Laws (Eds) *Handbook of Sexual Assault*. New York, NY: Plenum.

Kelly, L. (1991) *Surviving Sexual Violence*. Cambridge: Polity Press.

Kilpatrick, D.G., Best, C.L., Veronen, L.J., Amick, A.E., Villeponteaux, L.A. & Ruff, G.A. (1985) Mental health correlates of criminal victimisation: A random community survey. *Journal of Consulting and Clinical Psychology*, **53**, 866–873.

Kline, P. (1987) Psychoanalysis and crime. In B.J. McGurk, D.M. Thornton & M. Williams (Eds) *Applying Psychology to Imprisonment: Theory and Practice*. London: HMSO.

Knight, R.A. & Prentky, R.A. (1990) Classifying sexual offenders: The development and corroboration of taxonomic models. In W.L. Marshall, H.E. Barbaree & D.R. Laws (Eds) *Handbook of Sexual Assault*. New York, NY: Plenum.

Lalumiere, M.L. & Quinsey. V.L. (1994) The discriminability of rapists from non-sex offenders with phallometric measures: A meta analysis. *Criminal Justice and Behaviour*, **21**, 150–175.

Laws, D.R. & Marshall, W.L. (1990) A conditioning theory of the etiology and maintenance of deviant sexual preference and behaviour. In W.L. Marshall, H.E. Barbaree & D.R. Laws (Eds) *Handbook of Sexual Assault*. New York, NY: Plenum.

Lonsway, K.A. & Fitzgerald, L.F. (1994) Rape myths: A review. *Psychology of Women Quarterly*, **18**, 133–164.

MacLean, P.D. (1962) New findings relevant to the evolution of psychosexual functions of the brain. *Journal of Nervous and Mental Disease*, **135**, 289–301.

Malamuth, N.M. (1981) Rape proclivity among males. *Journal of Social Issues*, **37**, 138–157.

Maletsky, B.M. (1991) *Treating the Sexual Offender*. Newbury Park, CA: Sage.

Mann, R.E. & Thornton, D. (1998) The evolution of a multisite sexual offender treatment program. In W.L. Marshall, Y.M. Fernandez, S.M. Hudson & T. Ward (Eds) *Sourcebook of Treatment Programmes for Sexual Offenders*. New York, NY: Plenum Press.

Marques, J.K., Day, D.M., Nelson, C. & West, M. (1994) Effects of cognitive-behavioural treatment on sex offender recidivism. Preliminary results of a longitudinal study. *Criminal Justice and Behaviour*, **21**, 28–54.

Marshall, W.L. (1996) Assessment, treatment and theorising about sex offenders: Developments during the past twenty years and future directions. *Criminal Justice and Behaviour*, **21**, 162–199.

Marshall, W.L. & Barbaree, H.E. (1990a) An integrated theory of the etiology of sexual offending. In W.L. Marshall, H.E. Barbaree & D.R. Laws (Eds) *Handbook of Sexual Assault*. New York, NY: Plenum.

Marshall, W.L. & Barbaree, H.E. (1990b) Outcome of comprehensive cognitive-behavioural treatment programmes. In W.L. Marshall, H.E. Barbaree & D.R. Laws (Eds) *Handbook of Sexual Assault*. New York, NY: Plenum.

Marshall, W.L. & Eccles, A. (1991) Issues in clinical practice with sex offenders. *Journal of Interpersonal Violence*, **6**, 68–93.

Marshall, W.L. & Pithers, W.D. (1994) A reconsideration of treatment outcome with sex offenders. *Criminal Justice and Behaviour*, **21**, 10–27.

Marshall, W.L., Barbaree, H.E., Laws, D.R. & Baxter, D. (1986) *Rapists do not have deviant sexual preferences: Large scale studies from Canada and California*. Paper presented at the Twelfth Annual Meeting of the International Academy of Sex Research, Amsterdam.

Marshall, W.L., Fernandez, Y.M., Hudson, S.M. & Ward, T. (1998) *Sourcebook of Treatment Programmes for Sexual Offenders*. New York, NY: Plenum Press.

Meyer, L. & Romero, J. (1980) *A Ten-Year Follow-up of Sex Offender Recidivism*. Philadelphia: Joseph J. Peters Institute.

Morrison, T. (1994) Context, constraints and considerations for practice. In T. Morrison, M. Erooga & R. Beckett (Eds) *Sexual Offending Against Children*. London: Routledge.

Morrison, T. (1998) *Casework Consultation*. London: Whiting & Birch.

Murphy, W.D., Krisak, J., Stalgaitis, S.J. & Anderson, K. (1984) The use of penile tumescence measures with incarcerated rapists: Further validity issues. *Archives of Sexual Behaviour*, **13**, 545–554.

Nash, C.L. & West, D.J. (1985) Sexual molestation of young girls: A retrospective study. In West, D.J. (Ed.) *Sexual Victimisation*. Aldershot: Gower.

NOTA (1993) *Good Practice in the Multi-agency Management of Sex Offenders who Assault Children*. Joint publication of the National Association for the Development of Work with Sex Offenders and National Society for the Prevention of Cruelty to Children.

Pithers, W.D., Marques, J.K., Gibat, C.C. & Marlatt, G.A. (1983) Relapse prevention with sexual aggressives: A self-control model of treatment and maintenance of change. In J.G. Greer & I.R. Stuart (Eds) *The Sexual Aggressor: Current Perspectives on Treatment*. New York, NY: Van Nostrand Reinhold.

Proctor, E. (1996) A five-year outcome evaluation of a community-based treatment programme for convicted sexual offenders run by the Probation Service. *Journal of Sexual Aggression*, **2**, 3–16.

Quinsey, V.L. (1984) Sexual aggression: Studies of offenders against women. In D. Weisstub (Ed.) *Law and Mental Health: International Perspectives*, Volume 1. New York, NY: Pergamon.

Quinsey, V.L. & Earls, C.M. (1990) The modification of sexual preferences. In W.L. Marshall, H.E. Barbaree & D.R. Laws (Eds) *Handbook of Sexual Assault*. New York, NY: Plenum.

Quinsey, V.L., Harris, G.T., Rice, M.E. & Lalumiere, M.L. (1993) Assessing treatment efficacy in outcome studies of sex offenders. *Journal of Interpersonal Violence*, **8**, 512–523.

Rachman, S. (1997) The evolution of cognitive behaviour therapy. In D.M. Clark & C.G. Fairburn (Eds) *Science and Practice of Cognitive Behaviour Therapy*. Oxford: Oxford University Press.

Rada, R.T. (1978) *Clinical Aspects of the Rapist*. New York, NY: Grune & Stratton.

Reiss, D., Grubin, D. & Meux, C. (1996) Young "psychopaths" in special hospital: Treatment and outcome. *British Journal of Psychiatry*, **168**, 99–104.

Rice, M.E., Harris, G.T. & Quinsey. V.L. (1990) A follow-up of rapists assessed in a maximum-security psychiatric facility. *Journal of Interpersonal Violence*, **5**, 435–448.

Rice, M.E., Quinsey, V.L. & Harris, G.T. (1991) Sexual recidivism among child molesters released from a maximum security psychiatric institution. *Journal of Consulting and Clinical Psychology*, **59**, 381–386.

Russell, D.E.H. (1984) *The Secret Trauma: Incest in the Lives of Girls and Women*. New York, NY: Basic Books.

Ryan, G., Lane, S.K., Davis, J.M. & Isaac, C.B. (1987) Juvenile sex offenders: Development and Correction. *Child Abuse and Neglect*, **2**, 385–395.

Salter, A. (1988) *Treating Child Sex Offenders and Victims: A Practical Guide*. Newbury Park, CA: Sage.

Segal, Z.V. & Marshall, W.L. (1985) Heterosocial skills in a population of rapists and child molesters. *Journal of Consulting and Clinical Psychology*, **53**, 55–63.

Sidman, M. (1960) Normal sources of pathological behaviour. *Science*, **132**, 61–68.

Smith, G. (1994) Parent, partner, protector: Conflicting role demands for mothers of sexually abused children. In T. Morrison, M. Erooga & R. Beckett (Eds) *Sexual Offending Against Children*. London: Routledge.

Sanday, P. (1981) *Female Power and Male Dominance: On the Origins of Sexual Inequality*. Cambridge: Cambridge University Press.

Urdy, J.R., Billy, J.O.G. & Morris, N.M. (1984) Serum androgenic hormones motivate sexual behaviour in adolescent boys. *Fertility and Sterility*, **42**, 683–685.

Williams, L.M. & Finkelhor, D. (1990) The characteristics of incestuous fathers: A review of recent studies. In W.L. Marshall, H.E. Barbaree & D.R. Laws (Eds) *Handbook of Sexual Assault*. New York, NY: Plenum.

Wolf, S.C. (1985) A multifactor model of deviant sexuality. *Victimology: An International Journal*, **10**, 359–374.

Wyatt, G. (1985) The sexual abuse of Afro-American and white American women in childhood. *Child Abuse and Neglect*, **9**, 507–519.

Yalom, I. (1975) *The Theory and Practice of Group Psychotherapy*. New York: Basic Books.

Chapter 13

Treatment Approaches with Mentally Disordered Offenders

Adrian Grounds

Institute of Criminology, University of Cambridge, UK

This chapter aims to give an overview of clinical treatment approaches for mentally disordered offenders. Detailed descriptions and evaluations of specific forms of treatment are beyond the scope of this brief review, and the discussion will be confined mainly to issues of general principle. Some aspects of treatment effects and outcomes will be covered in Chapter 14.

To begin, a framework of aims will be outlined. There will then be brief consideration of models of serious mental disorder and multi-disciplinary team working, followed by a discussion of treatment approaches in different institutional and community settings, and finally a note about current policy and service constraints.

PHILOSOPHY OF CARE

The philosophy of care and treatment for mentally disordered offenders should combine models of best practice drawn from general mental health services, an eclectic and broad approach, longitudinal and long-term perspectives, and constant appraisal of issues of risk and public safety.

The elements of this summary need to be sketched out in a little more detail. Firstly, mentally disordered offenders suffer from the same range of conditions as other mentally disordered people, and are entitled to the same standards of treatment and good clinical practice. Forensic patients are particularly likely to

Behaviour, Crime and Legal Processes: A Guide for Forensic Practitioners.
Edited by James McGuire, Tom Mason and Aisling O'Kane.
© 2000 John Wiley & Sons Ltd.

be feared, stigmatised, excluded from mainstream services and held in custodial settings, and so there need to be strong countervailing safeguards to ensure that the quality of care they receive is not compromised. In addition, while the growth of the distinctive clinical specialty of forensic mental health, with its own modes of training and service organisation, is to be welcomed, one of the potential problems that can result from such development is that its practitioners become divided from colleagues in general psychiatric services. This makes it more difficult to remain aware of the most progressive developments in general mental health services, particularly for patients with chronic, long-term and co-morbid mental disorders. Specialists in forensic mental health services need to maintain strong professional and educational links with colleagues in other services in order to ensure that treatment approaches for mentally disordered offenders are continually based on up-to-date models of best practice that apply more generally in hospital and community psychiatry, with due regard to evidence of proven effectiveness and standards of excellence.

Secondly, an eclectic approach is needed. Mentally disordered offenders have a wide range of clinical conditions, and of personal and social problems. Many have complex histories, in psychiatric terms suffer from co-morbid disorders, and their offences may be difficult to understand. It is usually necessary to bring together a variety of clinical perspectives in order to reach a comprehensive understanding of the patient and his or her problems.

Thirdly, a longitudinal and long-term perspective is needed. Many patients in forensic psychiatry services suffer from personality disorders, and the individual's personal and developmental history and formative early experiences need to be elicited and comprehended in detail. Serious criminal offences need to be understood in the context of the individual's life history. A detailed grasp of his or her past history is also essential for making assessments of prognosis and future risk.

Fourthly, our obligations to try to manage patients safely and with proper regard to public safety mean that questions of risk and dangerousness need constantly to be borne in mind and re-appraised over time, especially as patients move from one treatment setting or personal context to another.

MODELS OF MENTAL DISORDER AND MULTI-DISCIPLINARY TEAM WORKING

It follows from the above that no one model of mental disorder and abnormal psychological functioning should narrowly dominate the general approach to the treatment of forensic patients. Perspectives from a range of clinical and theoretical models may be needed in the assessment and management of an individual case. In clinical referrals, a particular presenting problem, such as episodic violence, for example, could arise from a wide range of causative factors. Occasionally, neurological, endocrine or other organic conditions may underlie the problem and need to be detected and diagnosed. In many cases the problem will need to be conceptualised in psychological terms, with the emphasis being on developmental disabilities, abnormalities of cognition or impulse control, other specific features of mental illness, or in terms of psychodynamic theories and concepts. In some cases particular attention will need to be paid to understanding the presenting behaviour in social terms, with reference to the social context, social pressures and social functioning. Furthermore, none of these perspectives is mutually exclusive, and they will often have to be combined to achieve a satisfactory formulation of the presenting behaviour. Medical, psychological and social factors may all contribute to a particular clinical picture or presenting problem. Thus mentally disordered offenders need access to a range of assessment and diagnostic approaches, brought together from different clinical disciplines.

The same approach applies to treatment and management. For most patients under the care of forensic psychiatric services in hospital or in the community, the cornerstone of management is multi-disciplinary team working. Input should be available from psychologists, psychiatrists, social workers, nursing staff, occupational therapists and others. In community settings the patient's family and friends may also have a particularly important role in the provision of ongoing support and care, and may form an indispensable part of the multi-disciplinary care team.

PATIENTS WITH MENTAL ILLNESS

Approaches to the treatment of patients with major psychotic illness should be based on the best standards and protocols that apply in other settings. The majority of patients in medium and high-security hospitals suffer from major mental illness, most commonly schizophrenia. Appropriate regimes of anti-psychotic medication will be central in their clinical management, and in recent years there has been increasing use of newer anti-psychotic drugs which can have a more advantageous balance of efficacy and side-effects.

People with schizophrenia who have committed grave offences have often done so relatively late in the natural history of the illness; their conditions may be chronic and severe. Rehabilitative approaches with the aim of helping individuals achieve their best possible level of psychological and social functioning will be particularly important in these cases. Additional, more innovative, approaches in the management of the chronically mentally ill also merit wider usage in forensic settings, including cognitive approaches to symptom management, psycho-educational work in relation to treatment compliance and early warning signs of psychotic breakdown, and family support and education, where appropriate.

Other specific considerations apply to serious offenders with major mental illness because they may need considerably longer durations of hospital stay than would be the case for non-offenders. Some mentally ill offenders have very chronic and refractory illnesses which respond particularly slowly to treatment. In addition, where serious offences have been committed a high threshold of confidence will be needed before discharge to lower security or to the community can be contemplated. In the case of patients subject to restriction orders, the Home Office or the Mental Health Review Tribunal will need to be satisfied about the issue of risk, and about the practical arrangements for continuing care and supervision before discharge is agreed.

PATIENTS WITH PERSONALITY DISORDERS

The treatment of patients with personality disorders continues to be a topic of controversy and debate. From a clinical perspective the starting point should be a recognition that disorders of personality are mental disorders that can be very severe, associated with high levels of morbidity and psychological distress, and they can be severely disabling. Generally, patients with personality disorders are no more responsible for the fact that they have these conditions, than are patients with major mental illnesses, and they should not be seen as less deserving of clinical care and attention than the mentally ill.

However, with personality disorders, as with other developmental disorders, it may not be a realistic aim of treatment to change the fundamental underlying constitutional psychopathology. Instead treatment is more realistically targeted at functional impairments, social handicaps, secondary symptoms, the promotion of psychological insight, and implementation of cognitive-behavioural strategies for managing problematic behaviour.

Generally, psychotropic medication has a very limited role to play in the treatment of personality disorder, except in the management of secondary symptoms, and co-morbid mental illnesses. Treatment approaches with personality disordered patients will predominantly involve psychological therapies, which may be individual or group-based. The review by Dolan and Coid (1993) of the research evidence on the efficacy of treatment approaches for people with anti-social personality disorders suggested that evidence for therapeutic community treatment was the most promising. Other specific forms of psychological treatment for particular variants of personality disorder which have shown promising results include Linehan's "dialectical behaviour therapy" for patients with borderline personality disorders (Linehan, Hubert & Suarez, 1991). Cognitive behavioural therapy and cognitive analytic therapy (Ryle, 1989) may also be employed in the treatment of personality disordered patients. The clinical management of patients with personality disorder includes not only these specific forms of treatment and intervention: the chronic and disabling nature of the disorders often entails the provision of long-term support in which rehabilitation services have a primary role.

As yet, there is limited evidence in relation to the efficacy of psychiatric and psychological treatment for primary personality disorder. It has to be recognised, however, that the methodological difficulties of carrying out good evaluative research are particularly challenging in this field, as is indicated by some of the evidence reviewed and discussed in the next chapter.

PSYCHODYNAMIC ISSUES

The clinical management of mentally disordered offenders should be well informed by an awareness of psychodynamic issues. Relatively few patients are likely to receive, or be accepted for, formal psychodynamic psychotherapy, but psychodynamic concepts may play a much more general and important role in contributing to an understanding of patients' life histories and their offences (particularly where these have involved grave interpersonal violence). Psychodynamic concepts are also important in clinical management. In the long-term care of forensic patients, the medium through which the clinician works is the relationship established with the patient, and constant attention needs to be paid to maintaining the therapeutic relationship, dealing with misperceptions and misattributions that arise, and understanding conflicts and emotional difficulties in terms of the patient's life experiences and early history.

Among staff teams similar considerations apply. There needs to be an awareness of the risk of becoming drawn in to pathological modes of relating, particularly of a punitive or rejecting character, which re-enact earlier forms of pathological relationship in the patient's life. There also needs to be awareness of the splitting and other adverse phenomena that can arise within staff responses to patients (Main, 1957). Thus, in both hospital and community settings, it is particularly useful to have available advice and input from an experienced psychodynamically trained clinician.

In all contexts, particular attention needs to be paid to the earliest stage of contact with the patient, with a view to establishing a successful rapport and continuing contact. Commonly, patients have had adverse experiences of other services before contact with specialist forensic teams. From the outset the manner in which first interviews are conducted should leave the patient feeling that he or she has been understood and listened to.

TREATMENT IN SECURE HOSPITAL SETTINGS

The high security hospitals predominantly provide care for those mentally disordered offenders who are judged to pose the greatest degree of risk to others, and who could not be safely looked after in conditions of lesser security. The majority of those detained in these settings have committed serious criminal offences, but a minority are detained under civil treatment orders and are in high-security hospitals because of the exceptional difficulties of in-patient management that they pose. Durations of stay in high-security hospitals are often considerably longer than in less secure settings. The longer-term time perspective provides both opportunities and risks. On the positive side it is possible to provide extended courses of medical or psychological treatment in a stable context to help patients who can only progress slowly. Different treatment approaches can be phased in appropriate order, and patients who may appear "untreatable" in services geared to short-term interventions, can be recognised as eminently treatable when they can be held over a much longer term time scale. However, the longer time scale also has attendant risks of patients becoming neglected, and momentum in treatment not being maintained; in some cases, there may be a concomitant risk of institutionalisation. Good frameworks of regular case reviews with rigorous assessment of progress to date and objective setting for the future become particularly important in this context.

In high-security hospital environments in which patients may stay for some years, the quality and size of the environment and the range of non-clinical facilities available to patients assume greater importance than in the small units geared to short-stay admissions. Environmental amenities such as sports areas, gardens and outside work areas are needed, together with good-quality educational and work training opportunities.

TREATMENT IN PRISON SETTINGS

The provision of good-quality clinical treatment for mentally disordered offenders in the prison system is more problematic. Hospitals, by definition, are organised around the delivery of programmes of treatment and care needed by patients. The primary purpose of prisons, however, is to hold in custody those sentenced by the courts for whom the appropriate punishment is deprivation of liberty. While good-quality health care must be provided in prisons, prison establishments and prison regimes are not forms of hospital care, and cannot be organised on that basis.

The consistent and shared intention of Home Office and Department of Health policy is that mentally disordered offenders who need treatment should receive it from health and social services, and offenders most in need of psychiatric hospital care should be transferred out of the prison system to receive it. Historically, however, there have been, and continue to be, major difficulties in achieving this aim. There is a need for stronger partnerships between the National Health Service and the Prison Health Care Service, and continuing effort to ensure that standards of prison health care match those that apply in the NHS (HM Prison Service & NHS Executive, 1999).

Within the prison system, specific treatment approaches for offenders are largely led by psychologists, who have developed sex offender and other treatment programmes. The sex offender treatment programmes have a cognitive-behavioural orientation and are designed to modify distorted attitudes to sexual offending, increase victim awareness, and teach preventive strategies for avoiding relapse (see Chapter 12 by Hird in the present volume). While such structured programmes are helpful and appropriate for many imprisoned offenders, there is much less scope and capacity in the prison service, compared with hospitals, to provide individual psychotherapeutic treatment, or to cater for the small groups of prisoners with the most complex and abnormal forms of character pathology. There is scope for considerably greater collaboration and liaison between high-security hospitals and prison special units in the assessment and management of this particularly difficult group.

TREATMENT IN COMMUNITY SETTINGS

Local and community-based services for mentally disordered offenders remain relatively poorly developed compared with secure hospital services which are longer established. The history of the maximum security hospitals in England dates back to the opening of Broadmoor in 1863. The report of the Butler Committee in the mid-1970s initiated the development of the medium secure unit programme. However, specialist local and community services for mentally disordered offenders are a more recent concept and the specifications of model community forensic psychiatry services have yet to be delineated.

In recent years there has been a growth of court and police-based diversion schemes, together with the development of additional low-security hospital provision and local forensic psychiatric teams. The aim of local forensic psychiatry services should be to provide assessment, treatment, long-term support and supervision for mentally disordered offenders who do not currently require treatment in conditions of maximum or medium security. Given the priority of good risk management, the community-based management of mentally disordered offenders will need to include components of rapid assessment, crisis intervention, assertive outreach and good liaison with criminal justice and other agencies.

Long-term community support of mentally disordered offenders is likely to form a central part of the work of a local service, and the contribution of forensic community psychiatric nurses and social workers is especially vital. Forensic patients in the community may have multiple social problems and their behaviour can make them feared and unpopular. Considerable effort may need to be invested in liaising with other agencies and in advocacy to ensure that patients' social needs (housing and social security benefits, for example) are properly met. Forensic patients can also have histories of poor engagement with services, social isolation and antagonism towards statutory agencies. Innovative work is needed to try to tackle these problems. An example of such a project in Cambridge has been established by *Turning Point*, a charitable agency which provides a small team, led by an experienced ex-probation officer, whose role is to provide practical befriending to mentally disordered offenders and similar patients in the community. This can involve a variety of contacts from daily visits to providing transport, or shared social activities (going out for a drink or to the cinema). Such forms of engagement tend to fall outside the boundaries of conventional clinical professional roles, but may be critically important in enhancing the patient's quality of life, facilitating contact with statutory services, and overcoming the individual's practical difficulties of daily living and functioning.

CURRENT SERVICE PRESSURES

At the present time treatment services for mentally disordered offenders are subject to conflicting pressures. The contemporary structure of general mental health services has arisen from a policy background since the 1960s, which has emphasised the development of community care and contraction of the hospital estate. The ethos of clinical practice has been to maximise the autonomy and independence of patients, providing care in domestic rather than custodial environments, using the least restrictive alternative setting, and minimising the use of compulsory powers. The ideological reforms of the mid-twentieth century entailed basing psychiatric care on therapeutic rather than custodial aims.

However, in more recent years mental health policy has increasingly emphasised the need for more protective measures and better risk management in respect of the minority of patients who pose a serious risk to themselves or others. Public protection has now become an explicit expectation of mental health services (Department of Health, 1999) although the structure and ideology of general mental health services are now poorly equipped to meet that objective. Specialist forensic psychiatric services continue to develop because of the recognition by health authorities and central government that offender patients and others posing a risk to the public need to be more effectively cared for. However, the relationships between forensic and general mental health services can be difficult because of pressures to move troublesome patients out of general services, and there can be reluctance and lack of capacity to take back patients who no longer need specialist forensic care. These tensions and conflicts need to be better understood and resolved if we are to achieve properly integrated mental health services.

REFERENCES

Department of Health (1999) *Modernising Mental Health Services: Safe, Sound and Supportive.* London: Department of Health.

Dolan, B. & Coid, J. (1993) *Psychopathic and Antisocial Personality Disorders: Treatment and Research Issues.* London: Gaskell.

HM Prison Service & NHS Executive (1999) *The Future Organisation of Prison Health Care.* London: Home Office.

Linehan, M.M., Hubert, A.E. & Suarez, A. (1991) Cognitive-behavioural treatment of chronically parasuicidal borderline patients. *Archives of General Psychiatry*, **48**, 1060–1064.

Main, T.F. (1957) The ailment. *British Journal of Medical Psychology*, **30**, 129–145.

Ryle, A. (1989) *Cognitive-Analytic Therapy: Active Participation in Change.* Chichester: John Wiley & Sons.

Chapter 14

Effective Interventions, Service and Policy Implications

James McGuire
Department of Clinical Psychology, University of Liverpool, UK
Tom Mason
Caswell Clinic, Glanryhd Hospital, Bridgend, UK
and
Aisling O'Kane
Wirral and West Cheshire Community NHS Trust

A central issue for many contemporary public services is the provision of evidence concerning the effectiveness of what they provide. The origins of, and rationale for, this concern could be debated at length. In the United Kingdom a focus upon it has commonly been attributed to the massive shift of balance which occurred within government policies during the 1980s. At the political and macroeconomic level, that change was expressed as a drive towards greater accountability in public services. One specific emphasis, which has had an enduring impact, was upon the notion of obtaining "value for money". In many respects this was ideologically driven. It was also seen in some quarters as a disguise for an underlying motive of justifying increased centralisation of power over many services, conjoined with efforts to reduce recurrent costs and overall investment in public welfare. Its net result was lowered levels, and in several cases abolition, of some forms of provision.

It may be that governments at any point on the political spectrum would have pursued similar policies. Parallel trends were observable in many European countries with administrations of diverse allegiances. Whatever its exact roots, the legacy now appears in some respects a permanent fixture. It is not necessary to

Behaviour, Crime and Legal Processes: A Guide for Forensic Practitioners.
Edited by James McGuire, Tom Mason and Aisling O'Kane.
© 2000 John Wiley & Sons Ltd.

endorse an ideological stance essentially hostile to public expenditure in order to become convinced of the necessity of scrutinising the outcomes of intervention efforts, whether in education, health, criminal justice, or other activities that are funded through national or local taxation. Few individuals of any political persuasion now dispute the importance of insisting that statutorily provided services should be accountable, in that they should both monitor and be able to demonstrate their achievement of publicly appointed objectives. Controversies continue about the means by which those outcomes are assessed, and the factors to be taken into consideration when measuring effectiveness; and there is no doubt that some indicators are too crude and simplistic. But the fundamental principle that there should be evaluation in some form is now more or less unanimously accepted. At the present juncture, one route through which this is expressed is in the concept of *clinical governance*, which has been made central in new health care policies. This includes the implementation of evidence-based practice, supporting infrastructure, and the dissemination of evaluated good practice throughout an organisation (Department of Health, 1999).

THE RISE OF SYSTEMATIC EVALUATION

On another level, the emphasis on furnishing an "evidence base" for interventions, particularly in the field of health care, came from within the medical profession. In a highly influential paper, Cochrane (1979), an epidemiologist, raised the question of whether medicine and related health research fields could genuinely claim to have sound empirical foundations, as there was no systematic record of the outcomes of their interventions. "It is surely a great criticism of our profession that we have not organised a critical summary, by specialty or sub-specialty, adapted periodically, of all relevant randomized controlled trials" (Cochrane, 1979). At a later stage Mulrow (1987) examined a set of 50 review articles published in medical journals in a single year (June 1985 to June 1986). She found major shortcomings in the manner in which reviews were conducted and reported. For example, only one review clearly specified the source of information on which it was based; only three reviews employed quantitative methods of synthesising the information obtained from the original articles they had surveyed. Mulrow concluded that there was a need for sizeable improvement in the manner in which reviews, which play such an essential part in the advancement of knowledge, were carried out.

Concerns such as these gave rise to the ensuing inauguration, in 1993, of the *Cochrane Collaboration*, an international network of researchers and reviewers co-ordinated through 15 separate sites in Europe, North and South America, Australia, and South Africa. Over recent years, this has led to a considerable degree of activity in attempting to remedy the deficits identified. Between 1994 and 1999 more than 50 *Review Groups* were established through the Collaboration, each covering a specific field or branch of inquiry. Their task in each case was to locate, evaluate and integrate the results of well-designed intervention studies, usually randomised controlled trials (RCTs). By 1999 the available set of outcome studies, assembled as the *Cochrane Database of Systematic Reviews*, and derived from detailed searches of over 1100 research journals, contained more than 250000 entries. These have been made accessible to researchers and other users through the *Cochrane Library*, which for ease and speed of access is located on the Internet, and is updated on a quarterly basis. In addition, the Collaboration also sponsored a number of *Method Working Groups*, to examine the types of methodology employed in outcome research, and the impact of method itself as a variable in outcome studies.

The pursuit of a more systematic basis on which to draw conclusions concerning outcomes has not been restricted to the field of health. Within education, pioneering work was done in attempting, for example, to clarify the relationship between class size and educational achievement (Glass, McGaw & Smith, 1981). There is currently a high level of interest in the compilation of outcome studies on the effects of numerous variables such as the effects of different teaching methods (Davies, 1999). In respect of social work, despite early reviews questioning aspects of its effectiveness (Fischer, 1973, 1978), later overviews reported more encouraging findings (MacDonald, Sheldon & Gillespie, 1992; Russell, 1990). There is presently a significant drive to establish it on a firmer and more extensive empirical basis (MacDonald, 1999).

In the area of criminal justice, the issue of effective interventions began to be intensely debated from approximately the mid-1970s onwards when, almost simultaneously, research reviews were conducted on both sides of the Atlantic. The objective of most intervention research in this field is to discover methods of reducing offender recidivism. In the United Kingdom, Brody (1976) reviewed 100 studies of the impact of different types of court sentences and other interventions which attempted to evaluate this outcome. The drawing of clear conclusions was hampered by the poor quality of much of the research that had been undertaken, but the available findings appeared to point towards very little if any discernible impact in terms of reduced rates of re-offending. Perhaps more famously, in the USA, a review was published of 231 treatment studies by Lipton, Martinson and Wilks (1976). The significance of these findings was increased prior to their full publication, however, by the extensive publicity arising from the appearance of a paper by Martinson (1974). In that paper Martinson too pointed first to the relatively poor design quality of many criminal justice experiments, rendering it difficult to draw any firm conclusions. Yet his general summary was that "treatment"—by which was meant any added ingredient in criminal justice agencies such as provision of counselling, education, vocational training or psychological therapy—could not be shown to reduce ". . . the powerful tendency for offenders to continue in criminal behavior" (Martinson, 1974, p. 49). Martinson believed that such factors added nothing to the available network of criminal justice sentences, sanctions, or other formalised legal procedures.

These conclusions were questioned by several critics, mainly on the grounds that more positive evidence had been ignored (e.g. Palmer, 1975; Ross & Gendreau, 1980). The latter publication was an edited book containing reports on effective services in which there was evidence of reductions in recidivism. Ironically, in a subsequent publication, the thrust of the initially reported negative findings was reversed by Martinson himself (1979). Current evidence has certainly invalidated the claim that "nothing works" in respect of reducing offender recidivism, as we will see below.

Recently, proposals have been made to launch a new initiative (the *Campbell Collaboration*) as a parallel to *Cochrane*, with its primary centre of activity at the University of Pennsylvania (Boruch, Petrosino & Chalmers, 1999). The focus of its work will be upon social and educational as opposed to medical and health-related interventions. It appears feasible that this collaboration may also bridge the gap between the work of Cochrane Review Groups and of the large-scale reviews undertaken by specialists in the field of "offender treatment" (Petrosino et al., 1999). An initial database of studies, known as the *Social, Psychological and Criminological Trials Register* (*SPECTR*) is in the process of compilation, and included 10 000 entries by July 1999.

The present volume has been concerned with those client groups who frequently fall at (or between) the meeting-points of the mental health, criminal justice and social services agencies. The focus of the present chapter is on evidence concerning the effectiveness of services offered in this complex but somewhat amorphous domain. Whereas a search for such literature in any of these adjacent major sectors of activity would be likely to discover hundreds, if not thousands, of individual studies, investigation of interventions likely to prove beneficial with groups such as mentally disordered offenders will, by comparison, yield relatively few results. The question of which, if any, types of work might prove effective with this group must then be approached by a process of "triangulation", by mapping available evidence from related fields. In conjunction with the small amount of direct evidence available, tentative suggestions concerning possible ways forward can then be offered.

In this chapter, consideration will be given first to the methodology for conducting large-scale systematic review of interventions in any applied field. Next, existing reviews of the efficacy of interventions in the fields of mental health and criminal justice will be briefly reviewed. Following this, the current practical and policy impact of findings in these areas will be briefly examined and discussed.

THE METHODOLOGY OF REVIEWS

In attempting to systematise what has been learned in any field of inquiry, it is essential that periodic reviews are undertaken of the available research literature and the findings reported within it. "Good review articles are precious commodities" (Mulrow, 1987, p. 485). An indispensable tool for this purpose has been the usage of *meta-analysis* or statistical review. This is differentiated from the traditional form of "narrative review" which was the dominant mode of integrating research findings for many decades. In the standard approach, reviewers first find and collect as many as possible of the outcome studies relevant to a specific question. They read the available documents and attempt to make sense of trends within the findings. Dependent on the level of research activity in a given field, that can be a daunting task. The proliferation of research studies in many fields of social science has been such that, for example, even by 1980, it was estimated that there were already more than 5000 studies of gender differences. A simple listing of these papers would in itself constitute a book-length document. Thus, the sheer scale of the task involved in surveying and making sense of a large quantity of information presents a formidable problem for reviewers. A second difficulty was the risk of bias or stereotyping when interpreting the findings of studies. For example, Miller (1977; cited in Glass, McGaw & Smith, 1981) examined the literature on whether psychotherapy plus drug treatment was superior to drug treatment alone. Despite considering the same basic research papers, different narrative reviewers had drawn conclusions from them that were in complete contradiction to each other.

Meta-analytic review is a collection of methods of aggregating the results of studies in order to detect trends within them in a way that will reduce the biases likely to arise when this is done by means of narrative review. A procedure of this type was first used by the eminent statistician Karl Pearson as long ago as 1904, but it was not until the late 1970s that the methodology came to be more extensively employed, originally in education and subsequently in many other fields (Glass, McGaw & Smith, 1981).

Glass (1976) described a useful distinction between three levels of analysis of research results. The first consists of *primary studies*, the original research projects and reports which generate data in a field. Dissection or summary of these data, carried out by the researchers themselves, is called *primary analysis*. As is well known, research studies vary considerably in the quality of their design. Randomised controlled trials, which meet certain widely endorsed criteria for good research design, are perceived as providing the most robust form of evidence, particularly in intervention or "treatment-outcome" studies. Given the difficulty of implementing this in many applied settings, much work of this kind employs non-random or "quasi-experimental" designs (Cook & Campbell, 1979).

Secondary analysis occurs when research data are re-analysed for any purpose, for example to check on their accuracy (if this has been questioned by other researchers). Alternatively, the data may be used for some other purpose than that originally intended. This might occur if the study included variables which were not the prime focus of its authors but were thought to be of interest to researchers studying other questions or hypotheses.

Meta-analysis is a further level of investigation in which the results of several studies are aggregated and statistically combined. Even within a single field, research studies vary in many respects. As already mentioned, some will be better designed or reported in fuller detail than others. They may also vary in sample size, or employ different methods of measuring the outcome variable. They may be published in different languages and conducted in differing contexts. In meta-analysis these differences can be extracted and "coded" as variables. The process thus allows information to be integrated from a series of experiments in which trends might be otherwise difficult to discern, because of the large number of separate studies involved, or of differences between them in the types of factors just listed. Cooper and Rosenthal (1980) undertook a direct comparison of traditional, narrative review and systematic review employing meta-analysis. They allocated the same set of seven primary studies to two different groups of reviewers with instructions to adopt "narrative" or "meta-analytic" approaches respectively. They found the latter consistently out-performed the former in terms of its capacity accurately to reflect the information contained in the primary research.

The process and mechanics of conducting a meta-analysis have been usefully outlined by Durlak and Lipsey (1991). The process comprises the following six stages.

- The first, essential, step is to formulate the research question and state it in precise terms; similarly the subject matter and scope of the literature to be reviewed are defined as clearly as possible (for example, from which sources, in which languages and between which dates).
- Next, the relevant studies must be located. Several methods of search should be used, including electronic databases, hand-search where applicable, and, if possible, direct contact with the known researchers in the field to request copies of both published and unpublished studies. Particular efforts must be made to reduce publication bias by obtaining as many unpublished reports as possible.
- In step three, the variables of interest in the review are *coded*. Information is extracted from the primary studies and converted into a format in which it can be statistically analysed. This applies both to independent and dependent variables. The former may include features of the sample, such as its distribution in terms of age, gender, ethnic group membership; details of the study design; and aspects of "treatment modality" or other criteria for differentiating between groups. The latter are the outcome variables used in each study, which may vary considerably: for example, were the focus of the review the treatment of anxiety, primary studies may have employed a wide range of indicators, including self-report scales of psychological states, interview ratings, behavioural observations, psychophysiological measures, achievement of personal goals, and so on.
- Fourth, effect sizes are computed (see below). This should be done employing more than one statistical method, to check on results and reduce the possibility of biases of various kinds. This also allows estimation of what is known as the *file-drawer n*: the number of unpublished studies with nil effects that would be necessary to undermine an observed effect of a given size.
- In step five, detailed statistical analyses are conducted examining specified inter-relationships amongst the data. Obviously, the larger the number of studies included in the review, the more elaborate the analysis that can be done at this point.
- Finally, the results are prepared in a written report and conclusions and inter-

pretations offered as appropriate. The emphasis throughout, in well-conducted analyses, is upon full and clear reporting to allow scrutiny by external assessors and the possibility that the analysis may be replicated by others as a means of corroborating (or otherwise) the findings obtained.

The end-product of meta-analysis and the key variable of interest is known as the *effect size*. This is a measure of the extent to which, across all the studies subsumed in the analysis, there are discernible differences between experimental and control groups in terms of the outcome variable. There are two main "families" of statistical measures that are utilised for this purpose (Rosenthal, 1994). These are correlations (various coefficients are employed) and d coefficients (expressed as the percent change in experimental sample relative to control, as a function of "pooled" variance of the two samples combined). The effect size may of course be zero, indicating no overall differences between experimental and control conditions (no effect of intervention). Positive and negative effect sizes respectively indicate superiority of treatment over control conditions and vice versa.

The advent and widespread application of meta-analysis has not in itself been problem-free; nor has it been without its critics. A number of these were made in the wake of a wide-ranging review by Lipsey and Wilson (1993) of 301 meta-analyses of psychological, behavioural and educational interventions, across a very broad spectrum of social problems and client groups, with a cumulative sample size in excess of one million participants, including school and college students, employees, mental health service users, and offenders. Sohn (1995), commenting on this paper and on literature review in general, alleged that it was somehow being claimed that new knowledge was being "discovered" through a meta-analytic review that was not available in the original studies themselves. Another criticism is that meta-analysts will rarely be able to locate all the unpublished studies in an area, which are assumed to be more likely to have negative or zero effect sizes. Published studies are thus intrinsically prone to overestimate likely effectiveness of interventions.

Some other reservations that have been expressed concerning meta-analytic review stem from dissatisfaction with the randomised controlled trial itself as a prime means of studying the efficacy of interventions. With reference to psychological therapies, Persons (1991) argued cogently that outcome studies do not accurately reflect the real nature of therapies as actually applied in mental health settings. In the typical case, therapy sessions are more carefully fashioned to meet the needs of the individual client than can be allowed within the necessarily standardised format of a clinical trial. In any case, Persons asserted, the results of aggregate and controlled-trial research are of no value to practitioners dealing with individual cases, as the latter almost always depart from the average profiles which must inevitably be the basis for published reports of large-scale group-based studies. Hayes and Follette (1992), however, dismissed these arguments, responding that many therapeutic interventions are at least partly "manualised" (i.e. procedures within sessions are prescribed in advance), hence comparisons between them are meaningful, and clinical trials of psychological therapies remain valid.

Recently Persons and Silbersatz (1998) debated the arguments for and against the usefulness of controlled trials for informing clinical practice. Despite sharp, probably irreconcilable disagreement concerning their value, these authors agreed that research should be conducted which more closely reflects the way therapies are delivered in health care settings. They also advocated more extensive usage of alternative strategies, such as single-case experimental designs.

IMPACT OF THERAPY: MENTAL HEALTH PROBLEMS

Taking all of these adverse comments into account, meta-analysis has nevertheless come to be used as a central method of inquiry across any field in which questions are being asked about the effectiveness of intervention. In the applied areas of mental health and treatment of offenders, meta-analytic approaches to review of the effectiveness of psychological therapies were reported initially by Smith, Glass and Miller (1980) and more recently by other authors (Lambert & Bergin 1994; Roth & Fonagy 1996; Dobson & Craig 1998).

A first question that may be asked concerning this issue is whether psychological therapy works at all: does it represent any "added value" over and above the effects of spontaneous remission, or of placebo, as Eysenck (1952) argued many years ago it did not? The volume of research evidence supporting the efficacy of psychological therapies for a wide range of mental health problems is now very substantial. Recent reviews in the period 1994–98 have furnished ample evidence for this contention. Looking more broadly still, in the panoramic review previously cited by Lipsey and Wilson (1993) evidence was marshalled from a total of 302 meta-analyses which demonstrated the effects of behavioural and other psychologically based interventions across a very wide spectrum of health and other problems. In the light of their survey the verdict of these authors was that ". . . a strongly favourable conclusion about the efficacy of well-developed psychological treatments is justified by the results of meta-analytic investigation" (ibid., p. 1200).

A second question frequently asked is whether some forms of psychotherapy—of which it has been stated there are more than 400 identifiable types (Mahoney, 1991)—"work better" than others. For some time it was argued that while all forms of psychotherapy are of value to some clients, in terms of outcome there were no real differences between them (Luborsky, Singer & Luborsky, 1975). This led to promulgation of the so-called verdict of the Dodo Bird (a mythical creature in *Alice in Wonderland* who, at the end of a makeshift race, announces that "everyone has won and all must have prizes"). It was adduced that the same verdict held for the outcomes of psychotherapeutic interventions. This conclusion has been echoed in more recent overviews of psychological therapy, for example by Garfield (1995). Subsequently, however, both the reviews by Roth and Fonagy (1996) and Nathan and Gorman (1998) have indicated that there is evidence for the superiority of some therapies over others. One difficulty noted in these reviews and in many others to date is the extreme unevenness with which different types of interventions have been systematically researched and evaluated. There is simply more evaluative research, for example, on cognitive-behavioural and allied interventions than on psychoanalytic and other "dynamic" therapies. There are ongoing debates as to what constitute criteria for therapeutic improvement when viewed from different perspectives.

In 1995, reports were published based on the work of two Task Forces appointed by the American Psychological Association. One was concerned with *Psychological Intervention Guidelines*, while the second addressed the issue of *Promotion and Dissemination of Psychological Procedures*. The report (Task Force, 1995) asserted the possibility of specifying certain "validated" psychological interventions that would be "treatments of choice" for given clinical problems. Controversy arose over the use of the term "validated", as it was held that it could be interpreted as signifying some end-state had been arrived at, with no further work needing to be done. In subsequent revised versions of the report, an alternative term, *empirically supported treatments*, was used instead (Chambless & Hollon, 1998).

Some of the debates in this area set up false and misleading polarities. For a comprehensive picture to be assembled, all types of data are required. There must continue to be RCTs which maximise inferential power; these are of inestimable value for hypothesis-testing purposes, but they have limitations in other respects. In some settings where controlled experimentation is not feasible, for contextual or ethical reasons, quasi-experiments (non-random allocation to groups) can nevertheless provide invaluable indicators concerning the impact of some interventions. Simultaneously, single-case studies can be used to examine both treatment type and process in individual cases, especially where the problems present are unusual, or more complex than in the typical controlled trial. There is a need to synthesise information gained from all of these types of studies both in answering fundamental scientific questions and in designing more effective forms of practice and service delivery.

Nathan and Gorman (1998) have collated a series of reviews of "treatments that work", incorporating studies of both pharmacological and psychological therapies. Some illustrative findings are presented in Table 14.1. The definition of the syndrome in each case is that contained in DSM-IV (American Psychiatric Association, 1994). The quality of the research supporting each intervention is classified adjacent to each treatment according to criteria for judging research designs. "Type 1" refers to randomised controlled trials with all recognised features of the most rigorous research; "Type 2" designs lack one or other of those features; while "Type 3" refers to "open" or pre- and post-test one-sample trials. The table shows only a selection from a very wide range of psychological disorders for which empirically supported treatments have been recognised; a similar list is provided by Crits-Cristoph (1998).

Concentrating more narrowly on therapies for problems that have been linked to anti-social acts, several reviews have found promising outcomes. Tafrate (1995)

Table 14.1   Examples of empirically supported treatments

DSM category	Psychological therapies		Pharmacotherapies	
	Treatment type	Research base	Treatment type	Research base
Schizophrenia	Behaviour therapy	*Five Type 1 RCTs*	"Atypical" anti-psychotic drugs, e.g. clozapine	*Several Type 1 RCTs with both placebo and active drug comparisons*
	Family-based interventions	*Several Type 1 RCTs*		
	Social skills training	*40+ Type 1 or Type 2 RCTs*		
Post-traumatic Stress Disorder	Exposure-based therapies	*Substantial number of Type 1 and Type 2 RCTs*	Selective serotonin re-uptake inhibitors	*One Type 1 RCT and six open trials*
	Anxiety management			

has reviewed studies of anger management through primarily cognitive-behavioural methods; Edmondson and Conger (1996) subsequently extended this set of findings. Novaco (1997) has taken these authors to task for their neglect of research on clinical and offender populations and has reviewed evidence that will be of greater relevance in forensic psychiatry and related fields. There are now preliminary findings, though on a limited scale, illustrating the utility of this type of intervention with a British secure hospital population (Renwick et al., 1997). The general applicability of this approach with offender populations has been discussed by Howells et al. (1997). However, one recent study by these authors found this intervention to be ineffective with violent adult men (Watt & Howells, 1999).

Though originating in the field of mental health, these findings have import for work with individuals at risk of committing serious offences. For example, Zamble and Quinsey (1997) have reported on a follow-up study of 311 discharged prisoners who re-offended and compared them with a much smaller sample (*n* = 36) who did not. Recidivists reported more problems in the period after release, but had fewer or less effective skills for coping with them. Recidivists more often experienced, and had poorer strategies for managing, negative emotional states such as anger, anxiety and depression. They also thought more frequently about substance abuse and possible crimes, and less about employment and about the future in an optimistic light. They experienced greater fluctuation in emotional states in the 48 hours preceding a re-offence.

More severe disturbances of mental state, notably delusions, have been linked through psychiatric research to the risk of violent offending (see O'Kane & Bentall, Chapter 8 in this volume). Though based on comparatively small samples, a modicum of evidence has been obtained concerning the treatment of delusions. Several studies have indicated the possibility of reduction of these very severe symptoms through psychologically based methods (Chadwick & Lowe, 1990; Fowler & Morley, 1989; Garety et al., 1994; Hartman & Cashman, 1983; Lelliott & Marks, 1987; Milton, Patwa & Hafner, 1978; Tarrier et al., 1993; Watts, Powell & Austin, 1973). The methods employed in these studies have included cognitive therapy, cognitive restructuring, belief modification, reality testing, and distraction, among other techniques.

EVIDENCE CONCERNING TREATMENT OF OFFENDERS

In the field of criminal justice the findings of meta-analysis offer an opportunity for some important comparisons to be made which were not previously feasible. Perhaps the most telling is that between the effects of added interventions and the effects of sentencing by itself on the subsequent behaviour of offenders.

The use of punitive sentencing is based on a number of justificatory arguments drawn from different schools of philosophy and penology. Some writers argue from a *retributivist* standpoint, contending that offenders should be punished for committing a crime, and that this is sufficiently justified on grounds of moral principle alone. One variation on this is what is known as the principle of "just deserts". This does not appeal to evidence and cannot be confirmed or disconfirmed by adducing information about outcomes. By contrast, other penologists advocate a *utilitarian* approach, in other words that the value of a sentencing process or decision must be judged partly in terms of its effects. In respect of this approach, empirical evidence is relevant and is in abundant supply.

For a lengthy period, a fundamental debate in criminal justice policy in the United Kingdom was between the use of imprisonment or "custodial sentences" and community alternatives such as probation supervision. Proponents of each side argued that prison or community respectively were more effective, and used official statistics to support their arguments in each case. More recently, it has been possible to examine the impact of different sentences in terms of the changes that can be observed between predicted and actual rates of offending for large samples of re-convicted offenders. The Home Office Research and Statistic Directorate has developed a prediction instrument known as the *Offender Group Reconviction Scale* (Copas & Marshall, 1998). This is derived from a large database of criminal history information which shows that the probability of re-offending in a sample of offenders can be predicted with quite high accuracy using seven pieces of information about individuals. These are: gender; present age; age at first offence; present offence; number of previous convictions; number of previous custodial sentences; and number (if any) of sentences of youth custody.

Using this scale, it can now be shown that when the major types of sentence used for more serious offences are compared, there is no significant difference between the predicted and actual outcomes (in terms of subsequent rates of re-offending) over a two-year period. Whether individuals go to prison or are dealt with in the community, their two-year follow-up recidivism rate can be predicted from their past criminal histories and is not noticeably influenced by the sentences made by the court. Indeed, we could go so far as to say that the sentence is virtually irrelevant as far as later criminality is concerned. Could it be that the legal framework we have established for attempting to protect the community by altering the propensity of offenders to re-offend, simply does not appear to accomplish this purpose? These findings have been obtained twice, with two very large samples (Lloyd, Mair & Hough, 1994; Home Office, 1996).

However, the systematic study of criminal sentencing and of the treatment of offenders has been transformed over recent years by the appearance of review studies based on meta-analysis. Since 1985, when it was initially used in the field of corrections, meta-analysis has been employed in a number of reviews of treatment-outcome studies with offenders (Lösel, 1995). A series of 14 such meta-analyses of offender treatment has recently been reviewed by McGuire (2000). Some basic information concerning these reviews is given in Table 14.2.

It should be noted that the majority of published meta-analyses to date have been of intervention studies with juvenile offenders, and have focused for example on diversion or family intervention programmes. Other reviews have included studies of young adults in the 18–21 age range, and some have focused on studies of adults in prison or on probation. The reviews that have included young adult and adult samples are those by Andrews et al. (1990); Lipsey (1992, 1995); Lipton et al. (1997); Lösel and Koferl (1989), and Redondo, Garrido, and Sánchez-Meca (1999).

On the basis of findings such as those shown in Table 14.2, there is now a consensus that the view that "nothing works" to reduce re-offending is not supported by available evidence and must be rejected. For example, in the largest published meta-analysis to date, reported by Lipsey (1992, 1995), approximately two-thirds of interventions that were studied yielded reductions in recidivism. Most of the available reviews, not to mention the primary studies on which they are founded,

Table 14.2 Meta-analytic reviews of offender treatment

Source	No. of outcomes	Effect size
Garrett (1985)	121	0.18
Gensheimer et al. (1986)	51	0.09
Mayer et al. (1986)	39	0.36
Gottschalk et al. (1987a)	101	0.12
Gottschalk et al. (1987b)	30	0.20
Lösel and Koferl (1989)	18	0.11
Whitehead and Lab (1989)	50	0.13
Andrews et al. (1990)	154	0.10
Izzo and Ross (1990)	46	cog>non-cog, 2.5:1
Roberts and Camasso (1991)	46	0.06–0.81
Lipsey (1992)	397	0.10
Lipton et al. (1997)	822	NA
Lipsey and Wilson (1998)	200	0.22/0.12
Redondo et al. (1999)	57	0.15

originate from North America. However, there are also European counterparts, such as the analysis by Lösel and Koferl (1989) of the impact of Germany's "sociotherapeutic" prison regimes. More recently Redondo, Garrido, and Sánchez-Meca (1999) have analysed 57 intervention studies conducted in Europe. In all of the reviews reported to date, similar trends have been obtained. The same trends are also emerging in the largest study of this kind so far carried out (though not yet published in full) which at the time of writing is still in progress at the National Development and Research Institutes in New York (Lipton et al., 1997). A preliminary analysis of these data also indicates that effect sizes for adult populations tend to be lower than those obtained with juvenile offender samples (Cleland et al., 1997).

Overall, it has been estimated by Lösel (1995) that, on a very large scale, the net effect of treatment as compared with control groups or "business-as-usual" is to reduce the recidivism rate by 10%. While this may appear fairly modest in statistical terms, even this level of reduction would be regarded by many as worth securing. However, when set alongside other meta-analytic effect sizes and judged in terms of practical significance, it compares acceptably well. For example, it is larger than the effect size obtained for the outcomes of some medical interventions, such as the use of aspirin to reduce the risk of a myocardial infarction. It is not far below the effect size for heart bypass surgery to reduce the risk of coronary disease, on which considerable sums are invested (Rosenthal, 1994; and see McGuire, in press).

We should also remember that within the meta-analytic findings there are some "treatments" which do not reduce recidivism at all: indeed they may *increase* it. This is the case for those which employ intensified criminal sanctioning (Andrews et al., 1990) or "deterrence" (Lipsey, 1992, 1995). Contrary to the expectations of many people, punishment does not effectively deter criminal acts among adjudicated offenders: its effect, as judged by large-scale reviews, is neutral and may even be negative. As a measure designed to protect the public and increase community safety, punishment may, paradoxically be counter-productive.

At the other end of the scale, there are more constructive types of interventions which have a correspondingly significant effect in *reducing* rates of re-offending. Some skill-oriented programmes which employ cognitive-behavioural training methods have been found to reduce recidivism by on average between 25 and 30%. On the basis of these studies, several reviewers have argued that it is possible to identify features of programmes which make them more "likely to succeed" (Andrews, 1995; Gendreau, 1996; Hollin, 1999). They include the following elements.

- Those programmes and services which work best are founded on an explicit and well-articulated model of the causes of crime and criminal acts. This should be conceptually clear and be founded on sound empirical evidence.
- A recognition of the importance of assessment of risk of re-offending, based on criminal history and other variables, and allocation to different levels of supervision or service in accordance with this information.

- The need for assessment of *criminogenic needs* or dynamic risk factors, such as attitudes; the influence of criminal companions; skills deficits; substance dependency; or self-control problems; which are known to be linked to offending behaviour and which change over time.
- The application of methods which correspond to the active, focused and participatory learning and change styles encountered in many offenders, alongside an acknowledged need to adapt services to individual differences in this regard. This aspect of programme implementation is known as the principle of responsivity.
- The use of methods characterised by clear objectives, and which require skilled and structured engagement by staff in tasks which are readily accepted as relevant to individual offenders' needs.
- The application of a *cognitive-behavioural* approach, comprising a collection of theoretically interrelated methods which focus on the dynamic interactions between individuals' thoughts, feelings and behaviour at the time of an offence.
- The need for services to be delivered by personnel who have appropriate training and adequate resources; who adhere to their appointed objectives, adopt suitable methods and undertake systematic evaluation of individuals' progress and of the outcomes of their services overall.

When these features are present in combination, the impact on future recidivism may be very impressive. Andrews and his colleagues (1990) have presented evidence that incorporating these ingredients in an offender programme can lead to reductions in recidivism greater than 50% (see McGuire, in press). For a number of published primary studies, yet more substantial outcomes than this have occasionally been obtained among young offender groups (e.g. Borduin et al., 1995).

The group of offenders who not uncommonly cause the greatest concern, however, are those concomitantly diagnosed as suffering from personality disorders, and especially anti-social personality disorder or psychopathy. While there continues to be disagreement over these labels and on the nature of any underlying clinical entity, a sizeable volume of evidence links the proposed features of such a syndrome to greater risk of recidivism. Lösel (1998) has reviewed available evidence concerning the possibility of effective treatment of this group. As so often occurs across this entire field, very few controlled evaluations could be found on which to base firm conclusions.

While there were tentative suggestions that some behavioural, cognitive-behavioural, and therapeutic community programmes were successful in reducing anti-social behaviour among personality-disordered individuals, little evidence was found of treatment effects with "primary psychopaths". Lösel recommended, first, that much more and much better research is needed if the treatment issues in this area are to be clarified and advanced. Second, rather than identifying any preferred treatment approaches, he advocated instead the application of a set of principles based more broadly on the large-scale research findings outlined above.

MENTALLY DISORDERED OFFENDERS:
SPECIAL HOSPITAL FOLLOW-UP STUDIES

The objective of the "triangulation" process adumbrated earlier was to explore adjacent sets of findings in mental health and criminal justice with a view to extracting any evidence relevant to work with mentally disordered offenders. However, there is a small proportion of direct evidence concerning the impact of interventions with this group, but it remains extremely difficult to interpret.

One element of this is information concerning the long-term recidivism or re-admission rates of patients discharged from high-security "special" hospitals. Eight follow-up studies of this kind (see Table 14.3) have been carried out in the United Kingdom. As the table shows, the re-admission or re-offending rates among the samples studied appear comparatively low, given what may be assumed to be the seriousness of offences which warranted incarceration, and the likely severity of other problems (including marked mental disorders) among the populations studied. When compared with criminological data concerning recidivism among non-mentally disordered samples—for example, released prisoners—the criminal recidivism rates could be viewed as reassuring.

However, several aspects of these studies detract from the confidence that might otherwise be felt regarding them. First, these published reports were based

Table 14.3 UK follow-up studies of mentally disordered offenders

Source	Rates of return or re-conviction (%)	
Tong and Mackay (1958)	Re-admitted	14.0
	Imprisoned	14.0
Gathercole et al. (1968)	Re-convicted	8.0
	Returned	22.0
Dell (1980)	Re-admitted	6.6
	Imprisoned	2.8
Black (1982)	Re-admitted	19.2
	Further assault	10.0
Tennent and Way (1984)	All offences	55.0
	Further assault	21.0
Bailey and MacCulloch (1992a, 1992b)	Whole sample	36.6
	Mental illness	21.0
	PD	54.9
Brewster (1998)	Re-offended	12.5
	Re-admitted	17.2
Buchanan (1998)	Any offence	34.0
	Serious offence	15.0

on data collected over a lengthy span of time between the 1950s and the 1990s. Second, it is difficult to make valid comparisons, given the probable dissimilarities in the types of patient detained in secure hospitals between these successive decades. Third, there are no appropriate control groups with which a genuinely meaningful comparison can be made, nor are there any predictor scales (as have been developed for general offending populations) with which the impact of hospitalisation and treatment could be properly evaluated. Finally, the notably higher recidivism rates among those classified as suffering from psychopathic disorder in the studies by Bailey and MacCulloch (1992a, 1992b), and the differences between members of this group given conditional and absolute discharges provides some indications concerning better and poorer risk categories for release and follow-up. The latter findings accord with others reviewed by Lösel (1998) concerning this category of clients.

The absence of well-controlled studies in this area does not in itself mean that there is no evidence that might indicate the usefulness of interventions. Heilbrun and Griffin (1998) reviewed a series of 15 evaluative studies of (a) community-based psychiatric treatment with mentally disordered offenders (patients found *Not Guilty by Reason of Insanity*), together with (b) supervision of clients with mental disorders placed on probation or parole. The methodology in several of these studies consisted of post-hoc analyses of factors which appeared predictive of differential outcomes for patients. The principal criteria employed were re-arrest for new offences or re-admission to hospital, though other indicators were sometimes utilised, such as symptom reduction, clinical progress, community adjustment, and rates of revocation of parole conditions. Eight of the studies included comparison groups. Heilbrun and Peters (2000) reported an extension and updating of this review. In these reviews, only one study was located that approximated the methodology of a controlled trial, so precluding the use of meta-analysis.

Some follow-up studies have allowed comparisons to be made between discharged patients allocated to different forms or levels of intensity of community supervision; however, the findings so obtained are often very difficult to interpret. One reason is that, in many evaluations, comparisons are made between different jurisdictions in which it is not known whether staff practices regarding case management and recall were equivalent. Another is that, in some instances in which patients are allocated to an *Assertive Case Management* service, there has been evidence that the case managers are more likely to re-incarcerate clients for less serious violations of their release conditions. From other, less well-controlled or single-sample studies, some indications emerged that intensive case management has beneficial effects. Generally, re-arrest rates on conditional release were found to be comparatively low (ranging from 2% to 16%). Where clients were made subject to parole revocations (recalled to hospital), an average of 3.9 reasons was given: ". . . the respective frequencies of each reason suggesting an overlapping pattern involving deterioration in mental condition in conjunction with other reasons, such as noncompliance with supervision and treatment or troublesome behaviour" (Heilbrun & Griffin, 1998, p. 179).

Heilbrun and Griffin (1998) and Heilbrun and Peters (1999) have forwarded a set of principles for effective community-based forensic services, combining guidelines for sound ethical practice with such recommendations as can be extracted from the limited evidence base. They include:

- an emphasis on the importance of communications between agencies;
- an explicit balance between individual rights, the need for treatment, and public safety;
- an awareness of the range of treatment needs of clients;
- the usage of a demonstration model in assessing risk of harm and treatability;
- clarification of legal requirements such as confidentiality and duty to protect;
- application of sound risk management procedures; and
- the practice of principles for promoting health care adherence.

Principles such as these are valuable in providing a framework for service delivery within agencies, and as such they are also resonant of guidelines for risk management proposed earlier by Monahan (1993). It is unfortunate that the research base is not yet available to furnish more specific directions in which to develop or arrange provision of treatment and support.

However in this latter respect, findings of some importance have been reported by Bonta, Law and Hanson (1998). These authors conducted a meta-analytic review of long-term follow-up studies, in order to establish which factors were the best predictors of criminal and violent recidivism among mentally disordered offenders. The set of studies identified incorporated 68 independent samples and predictors were classed into four groups: *demographic*; *criminal history*; *deviant lifestyle* and *clinical* factors (including psychiatric diagnosis). The general finding was that the most accurate predictors were criminal history variables: indeed the overall pattern obtained was a close parallel to that customarily found with non-mentally disordered offender populations. Bonta and his associates also found that the poorest predictors of recidivism were clinical variables. Most notably, although a DSM diagnosis of anti-social personality disorder was associated with a greater risk of future criminality, no other diagnostic category, including that of psychosis, emerged as significant: the latter was in fact negatively correlated with future recidivism. If these findings are correct, the intervention approaches adopted in work with offenders in general may be equally applicable to clients with mental disorders. It is highly likely that such clients would also require further services, including both therapies for other mental health problems, and, potentially, additional treatments focused upon mental health symptoms associated with risk of relapse (see O'Kane & Bentall, Chapter 8 in this volume).

It is disappointing that Bonta, Law and Hanson (1998) found only 14 studies that included treatment as an independent variable. There was no overall positive evidence of treatment effects within these studies, but problems of design and methodology—for example, the absence of appropriate comparison groups—once again made the findings difficult to interpret in this respect.

The search for empirically supported treatments for work with mentally disordered offender clients is evidently fraught with difficulty. It may seem of questionable relevance from one standpoint, if it were assumed that the key to rehabilitation or community maintenance resides not in individualised interventions, but elsewhere, in the assembly and delivery of co-ordinated support services. Regrettably, this alone does not appear to be conducive to effectiveness in the absence of clinical intervention. Morrissey (1999) has reviewed some exceptionally well-documented studies of demonstration projects in which considerable extra resources were invested in services for clients with long-term mental health problems. Despite clear evidence of significant changes in the targeted service systems, controlled comparisons failed to discover measurable "client-level improvements". Enhanced case management and allied service improvements, it was held, were ". . . a necessary but not sufficient condition for positive outcome effects for clients" (Morrissey, 1999, p. 462). While services clearly cannot meet clients' requirements where resources are inadequate (see Heywood, Chapter 10 in this volume), it appears that reorganisation of services alone may be insufficient unless it also contains high-quality clinical input.

RECENT DEVELOPMENTS AND THE IMPACT OF RESEARCH FINDINGS

The new sets of findings on reduction of offender recidivism outlined earlier have begun to have an impact on the direction of both practice and policy with offenders in the United Kingdom and elsewhere. The trends within these findings and their potential implications in these respects have been discussed in a number of recently published volumes (Harland, 1996; McGuire, 1995a; Nuttall, Goldblatt & Lewis, 1998; Sherman et al., 1997; Vennard, Sugg & Hedderman, 1997). At the time of writing, developments along such lines are being implemented at a steadily accelerating pace. To conclude this chapter, two examples of such developments will be given.

Developments in the Prison Service

The prison service (England and Wales) has recently embarked on a major initiative to increase the number of prison establishments that provide programmes and activities designed to reduce rates of recidivism following release. As with many other agencies, the process of management in the prison service has been linked to the use of *Key Performance Indicators* (*KPIs*) which are measures of the achievement of core objectives of the service. In 1996, the provision of programmes designed to reduce recidivism was established as an indicator of this kind (*KPI-7*). A specialist panel was appointed for accrediting the programmes to be provided, and it has published a set of criteria for evaluating the design and delivery of programmes (HM Prison Service, 1998):

- Programmes and services should be based on an explicit, empirically-based model of change.
- Programme contents should focus on criminogenic needs.
- They should be designed to take account of the responsivity principle.
- They should employ methods which can be clearly defined and have demonstrated effects on the selected outcome variables.
- There should be an emphasis on the acquisition of skills by participants.
- As criminal acts are multi-factorial in origin, there should be a range of targets of change.
- The intensity, duration and other aspects of "dosage" should be appropriate to the risk level of the participants.
- Throughcare arrangements with regard to community follow-up should be in place and properly managed.
- There should be ongoing monitoring of programme delivery.
- There should be ongoing evaluation of outcomes and impact.

Programmes designed to meet these criteria, and which have been accredited as doing so by independent consultative panels, are now in use in more than 50 of the 150 penal institutions in England and Wales. Similar developments have occurred in the Scottish prison services and it may be that such initiatives will also be pursued by prison services in other countries also.

To sustain an initiative of this kind is a substantial undertaking, and has involved the deployment of significant additional resources. It has entailed an extensive programme of staff training events; creation of a system of monitoring and audit; and associated mechanisms for administration and information management, both within individual prisons and on a service-wide scale. All sessions of cognitive-skills programmes are videotaped for scrutiny (on a sampling basis) by external assessors. Procedures have been put in place for the systematic evaluation of programmes on both a short- and a long-term basis.

Probation Services

The research findings outlined earlier have also had a marked impact on community services for offenders, principally the probation service (and more recently, youth justice services also). During 1997–98, the Probation Inspectorate, which monitors the working standards of probation nationally, conducted a focused or "thematic" inspection to examine the extent to which probation staff employ practices based on research evidence. The main report on this work (Underdown, 1998) proposed a series of new initiatives to extend the usage of evidence-based practice in probation work. This subsequently led to the selection of a number of programmes designated as *Pathfinder* projects which were earmarked for further development. In late 1999, a new accreditation process to operate jointly for prison and probation services was established. It is envisaged that programmes satisfactorily meeting accreditation criteria will be delivered at a large number of sites and that, by the end of 2001, more than 10 000 probation clients will have attended such programmes.

These developments also hold out the added prospect of more effective co-operation between prison and probation settings. It is a stipulation of the prison service programmes that they identify any needs of prisoners that may require further support following their release from prison. An expected outcome of this is that there should be improved links between institutions and community services in this respect.

Many of the programmes which are currently being developed both in prison and probation settings employ methods of "cognitive training", initially piloted in Canada (Robinson, 1995; and see McGuire, 1995b). However, there are several potential approaches to working with offenders which may be "likely-to-succeed", but much more needs to be known about these approaches and, in any case, researchers are still at an early stage in evaluating what the real impact of the current initiatives may be. Existing studies should be replicated but, in addition, many other research questions remain unanswered.

For example, the process of risk–needs assessment must be informed by longer-term validation research and far more needs to be known that might guide practitioners toward better-informed selection of individuals for the most appropriate forms of intervention. In addition, research work with offender groups has been focused almost exclusively on white males. While some studies that have been conducted in the USA have included African-American samples (e.g. Goldstein et al., 1994), still comparatively little is published that would enable us to extrapolate conclusions of existing studies to work with members of other ethnic groups, or with women offenders. More needs to be known also about some key aspects of service delivery, including the most appropriate time to offer participation in programmes to individuals in institutional settings. Finally, with the exception of programmes for sex offenders (see Hird, Chapter 12 in this volume), there are few examples of interventions specially devised for work on specific types of offence.

CONCLUSIONS

Given the beleaguered condition of some services, it may seem to be a retreat from reality to assert that there are at present some grounds for optimism. Given the low morale of some practitioners, it may even appear insensitive to do so. However, research findings, allowing for the numerous gaps within them, do indicate that concerted efforts of specific kinds have the capacity to reduce the distress and disturbance, harm and violence experienced and caused by some individuals. Systematic reviews of research have enabled us to identify trends and patterns that indicate the ways in which gains may be maximised and the areas in which much additional work is required.

Furthermore, the practical and policy impact of these findings is beginning to be significant. With the initiatives being made in "evidence-based medicine" and other allied health fields, professionals and managers are aware as possibly never before of the importance of setting practice on a firm empirical base. In parallel, criminal justice agencies too have at least begun to proceed, in a progressive and systematically monitored way, with large-scale implementation of research-based initiatives. As Carson (Chapter 2 in this volume) has amply shown, the law itself has begun to absorb some of these messages and indeed to generate its own perspectives upon them. The boundaries between the traditional study and application of law as statute and procedure, and the appreciation of its human impact, have at least begun to be breached. It appears possible to integrate human values of co-operation, provision of assistance and social service with the applied scientific study of such work on a systematic and properly validated basis. There are grounds for expecting that it may be feasible to integrate the ethical principles of helping relationships with the usage of applied science to further their aims.

REFERENCES

American Psychiatric Association (1994) *Diagnostic and Statistical Manual of Mental Disorders*. (4th edn). Washington, DC: American Psychiatric Association.

Andrews, D.A. (1995) The psychology of criminal conduct and effective treatment. In J. McGuire (Ed.) *What Works: Reducing Re-offending: Guidelines from Research and Practice*. Chichester: John Wiley & Sons.

Andrews, D.A., Zinger, I., Hoge, R.D., Bonta, J., Gendreau, P. & Cullen, F.T. (1990) Does correctional treatment work? A clinically relevant and psychologically informed meta-analysis. *Criminology*, **28**, 369–404.

Bailey, J. & MacCulloch, M.J. (1992a) Characteristics of 112 cases discharged directly to the community from a new Special Hospital and some comparisons of performance. *Journal of Forensic Psychiatry*, **3**, 91–112.

Bailey, J. & MacCulloch, M.J. (1992b) Patterns of re-offending in patients discharged directly to the community from a Special Hospital: Implications for after-care. *Journal of Forensic Psychiatry*, **3**, 445–461.

Black, D.A. (1982) A 5-year follow-up study of male patients discharged from Broadmoor Hospital. In J. Gunn & D.P. Farrington (Eds) *Abnormal Offenders, Delinquency, and the Criminal Justice System*. Chichester: Wiley.

Bonta, J., Law, M. & Hanson, K. (1998) The prediction of criminal and violent recidivism amongst mentally disordered offenders: A meta-analysis. *Psychological Bulletin*, **123**, 123–142.

Borduin, C.M., Mann, B.J., Cone, L.T. & Hengeller, S.W. (1995) Multi-systemic treatment of serious juvenile offenders: Long-term prevention of criminality and violence. *Journal of Consulting and Clinical Psychology*, **63**, 569–578.

Boruch, R.F., Petrosino, A.J. & Chalmers, I. (1999) *The Campbell Collaboration: A proposal for systematic, multi-national and continuous reviews of evidence*. Background paper for the Cochrane Collaboration meeting, School of Public Policy, University College London, July.

Brewster, S. (1998) *A follow-up study of all patients who left Ashworth Hospital in 1992 with a discussion of Special Hospital "populations" and a view of PD patients*. Unpublished report, Ashworth Hospital.

Brody, S. (1976) *The Effectiveness of Sentencing*. Home Office Research Study No. 35. London: HMSO.

Buchanan, A. (1998) Criminal conviction after discharge from special (high security) hospital: Incidence in the first 10 years. *British Journal of Psychiatry*, **172**, 472–476.

Chadwick, P.D.J. & Lowe, F. (1990) *The Measurement and Modification of Delusional Beliefs*. Research report, Department of Psychology, University of North Wales.

Chambless, D.L. & Hollon, S.D. (1998) Defining empirically supported therapies. *Journal of Consulting and Clinical Psychology*, **66**, 7–18.

Cleland, C.M., Pearson, F.S., Lipton, D.S. & Yee, D. (1997) *Does age make a difference? A meta-analytic approach to reductions in criminal offending for juveniles and adults*. Paper presented at the Annual Meeting of the American Society of Criminology, San Diego, November.

Cochrane, A.L. (1979) 1931–1971: A critical review, with particular reference to the medical profession. In *Medicines for the Year 2000*. London: Office of Health Economics.

Cook, T.D. & Campbell, D.T. (1979) *Quasi-Experimentation: Design and Analysis Issues for Field Settings*. Chicago, Ill.: Rand-McNally.

Cooper, H.M. & Rosenthal, R. (1980) Statistical versus traditional procedures for summarizing research findings. *Psychological Bulletin*, **87**, 442–449.

Copas, J. & Marshall, P. (1998) The Offender Group Reconviction Scale: a statistical reconviction score for use by probation officers. *Applied Statistics*, **47**, 159–171.

Crits-Cristoph, P. (1998) Training in empirically validated treatments: The Division 12 APA Task Force recommendations. In K.S. Dobson & K.D. Craig (Eds) *Empirically Supported Therapies: Best Practice in Professional Psychology*. Thousand Oaks, CA: Sage Publications.

Davies, P. (1999) What is evidence-based education? *British Journal of Educational Studies*, **47**, 108–121.

Dell, S. (1980) Transfer of Special Hospital patients to the NHS. *British Journal of Psychiatry*, **136**, 222–234.

Department of Health (1999) *A First Class Service: Quality in the New NHS*. London: The Stationery Office.

Dobson, K.S. & Craig, K.D. (Eds) (1998) *Empirically Supported Therapies: Best Practice in Professional Psychology*. Thousand Oaks, CA: Sage Publications.

Durlak J.A. & Lipsey, M.W. (1991) A practitioner's guide to meta-analysis. *American Journal of Community Psychology*, **19**, 291–333.

Edmondson, C.B. & Conger, J.C. (1996) A review of treatment efficacy for individuals with anger problems: Conceptual, assessment, and methodological issues. *Clinical Psychology Review*, **16**, 251–275.

Eysenck, H.J. (1952) The effects of psychotherapy: An evaluation. *Journal of Consulting Psychology*, **16**, 319–324.

Fischer, J. (1973) Is casework effective? A review. *Social Work*, **18**, 5–20.

Fischer, J. (1978) Does anything work? *Journal of Social Service Research*, **3**, 213–243.

Fowler, D. & Morley, S. (1989) The cognitive-behavioural treatment of hallucinations and delusions: A preliminary study. *Behavioural Psychotherapy*, **17**, 267–282.

Garfield, S.L. (1995) *Psychotherapy: An Integrative Approach*. New York, NY: John Wiley & Sons.

Garrett, C.G. (1985) Effects of residential treatment on adjudicated delinquents: A meta-analysis. *Journal of Research in Crime and Delinquency*, **22**, 287–308.

Garety, P.A., Kuipers, L., Fowler, D. & Chamberlain, F. (1994) Cognitive behavioural therapy for drug-resistant psychosis. *British Journal of Medical Psychology*, **67**, 259–271.

Gathercole, C., Craft, M., McDougall, J., Barnes, H. & Peck, D. (1968) A review of 100 discharges from a Special Hospital. *British Journal of Criminology*, **8**, 419–424.

Gendreau, P. (1996) Offender rehabilitation: What we know and what needs to be done. *Criminal Justice and Behavior*, **23**, 144–161.

Gensheimer, L.K., Mayer, J.P., Gottschalk, R. & Davidson, W.S. (1986) Diverting youth from the juvenile justice system: A meta-analysis of intervention efficacy. In S.A. Apter & A.P. Goldstein (Eds) *Youth Violence: Programs and Prospects*. Elmsford: Pergamon Press.

Glass, G.V. (1976) Primary, secondary, and meta-analysis of research. *Educational Researcher*, **5**, 3–8.

Glass, G.V., McGaw, B. & Smith, M.L. (1981) *Meta-analysis in Social Research*. Newbury Park, NJ: Sage Publications.

Goldstein, A.P., Glick, B., Carthan, W. & Blancero, D.A. (1994) *The Prosocial Gang: Implementing Aggression Replacement Training*. Thousand Oaks, CA: Sage Publications.

Gottschalk, R., Davidson, W.S., Gensheimer, L.K. & Mayer, J.P. (1987a) Community-based interventions. In H.C. Quay (Ed.) *Handbook of Juvenile Delinquency*. New York, NY: John Wiley & Sons.

Gottschalk, R., Davidson, W.S., Mayer, J.P. & Gensheimer, L.K. (1987b) Behavioral approaches with juvenile offenders: A meta-analysis of long-term treatment efficacy. In E.K. Morris & C.J. Braukmann (Eds) *Behavioral Approaches to Crime and Delinquency*. New York, NY: Plenum.

Harland, A.T. (Ed.) (1996) *Choosing Correctional Options That Work: Defining the Demand and Evaluating the Supply*. Thousand Oaks, CA: Sage Publications.

Hartman, L.M. & Cashman, F.E. (1983) Cognitive-behavioural and psychopharmacological treatment of delusional symptoms: A preliminary report. *Behavioural Psychotherapy*, **11**, 50–61.

Hayes, S.C. & Follette, W.C. (1992) Can functional analysis provide a substitute for syndromal classification? *Behavioral Assessment*, **14**, 345–365.

Heilbrun, K. & Griffin, P.A. (1998) Community-based forensic treatment. In R.M. Wettstein (Ed.) *Treatment of Offenders with Mental Disorders*. New York, NY: Guilford Press.

Heilbrun, K. & Peters, L. (2000) The efficacy of community treatment programmes in preventing crime and violence. In S. Hodgins & R. Muller-Isberner (Eds) *Violence, Crime and Mentally Disordered Offenders: Concepts and Methods for Effective Treatment and Prevention*. The Hague: Kluwer Academic Publishers.

HM Prison Service (1998) *Criteria for Accrediting Programmes 1998–99*. London: HM Prison Service, Offending Behaviour Programmes Unit.

Hollin, C.R. (1999) Treatment programmes for offenders: Meta-analysis, "What Works", and beyond. *International Journal of Law and Psychiatry*, **22**, 361–371.

Home Office (1996) *Criminal Statistics 1995*. London: Home Office.

Howells, K., Watt, B., Hall, G. & Baldwin, S. (1997) Developing programmes for violent offenders. *Legal and Criminological Psychology*, **2**, 117–128.

Izzo, R.L. & Ross, R.R. (1990) Meta-analysis of rehabilitation programmes for juvenile delinquents. *Criminal Justice and Behavior*, **17**, 134–142.

Lambert, M.J. & Bergin, A.E. (1994) The effectiveness of psychotherapy. In A.E. Bergin & S.L. Garfield (Eds) *Handbook of Psychotherapy and Behavior Change*. New York: Wiley.

Lelliott, P. & Marks, I. (1987) Management of obsessive-compulsive rituals associated with delusions, hallucinations and depression: A case report. *Behavioural Psychotherapy*, **15**, 77–87.

Lipsey, M.W. (1992) Juvenile delinquency treatment: A meta-analytic inquiry into the variability of effects. In T. Cook, D. Cooper, H. Corday, H. Hartman, L. Hedges, R. Light, T. Louis & F. Mosteller (Eds) *Meta-analysis for Explanation: A Casebook*. New York: Russell Sage Foundation.

Lipsey, M.W. (1995) What do we learn from 400 studies on the effectiveness of treatment with juvenile delinquents? In J. McGuire (Ed.) *What Works: Reducing Reoffending: Guidelines from Research and Practice*. Chichester: John Wiley & Sons.

Lipsey, M.W. & Wilson, D.B. (1993) The efficacy of psychological, educational, and behavioral treatment: Confirmation from meta-analysis. *American Psychologist*, **48**, 1181–1209.

Lipsey, M.W. & Wilson, D.B. (1998) Effective intervention for serious juvenile offenders: A synthesis of research. In R. Loeber & D.P. Farrington (Eds) *Serious and Violent Juvenile Offenders: Risk Factors and Successful Interventions.* Thousand Oaks, CA: Sage Publications.

Lipton, D.S., Martinson, R. & Wilks, J. (1976) *The Effectiveness of Correctional Treatment: A Survey of Treatment Evaluation Studies.* New York, NY: Praeger.

Lipton, D.S., Pearson, F.S., Cleland, C. & Yee, D. (1997) *Synthesizing Correctional Treatment Outcomes: Preliminary CDATE Findings.* Paper presented at the 5th Annual National Institute of Justice Conference on Research and Evaluation in Criminal Justice, Washington, July.

Lloyd, C., Mair, G. & Hough, M. (1994) *Explaining Reconviction Rates: A Critical Analysis.* Home Office Research Study No. 136. London: HMSO.

Lösel, F. (1995) The efficacy of correctional treatment: A review and synthesis of meta-evaluations. In J. McGuire (Ed.) *What Works: Reducing Re-offending: Guidelines from Research and Practice.* Chichester: John Wiley & Sons.

Lösel, F. (1998) Treatment and management of psychopaths. In D. Cooke & R.A. Hare (Eds) *Psychopathy: Theory, Research and Implications for Society.* The Hague: Kluwer Academic Publishers.

Lösel, F. & Koferl, P. (1989) Evaluation research on correctional treatment in West Germany: A meta-analysis. In H. Wegener, F. Lösel & J. Haisch (Eds) *Criminal Behaviour and the Justice System: Psychological Perspectives.* New York: Springer-Verlag.

Luborsky, L., Singer, B. & Luborsky, L. (1975) Comparative studies of psychotherapies: Is it true that "Everyone has won and all must have prizes?" *Archives of General Psychiatry*, **32**, 995–1008.

MacDonald, G. (1999) Evidence-based social care: Wheels off the runway? *Public Money and Management*, January–March, 25–32.

MacDonald, G., Sheldon, B. & Gillespie, J. (1992) Contemporary studies of the effectiveness of social work. *British Journal of Social Work*, **22**, 615–643.

Mahoney, M.J. (1991) *Human Change Processes: The Scientific Foundations of Psychotherapy.* New York, NY: Basic Books.

Martinson, R. (1974) What Works? Questions and answers about prison reform. *The Public Interest*, **10**, 22–54.

Martinson, R. (1979) New findings, new views: A note of caution regarding sentencing reform. *Hofstra Law Review*, **7**, 243–258.

Mayer, J.P., Gensheimer, L.K., Davidson, W.S. & Gottschalk, R. (1986) Social learning treatment within juvenile justice: A meta-analysis of impact in the natural environment. In S.A. Apter & A.P. Goldstein (Eds) *Youth Violence: Programs and Prospects*, Elmsford: Pergamon Press.

McGuire, J. (Ed.) (1995a) *What Works: Reducing Re-offending: Guidelines from Research and Practice.* Chichester: John Wiley & Sons.

McGuire, J. (1995b) Reasoning and rehabilitation programs in the UK. In R.R. Ross & B. Ross (Eds) *Thinking Straight: The Reasoning and Rehabilitation Program for Delinquency Prevention and Offender Rehabilitation.* Ottawa: Air Training & Publications.

McGuire, J. (2000) Criminal sanctions versus psychologically-based interventions with offenders: A comparative and empirically-based review. Submitted for publication.

Milton, F., Patwa, V.K. & Hafner, R.J. (1978) Confrontation vs. belief modification in persistently deluded patients. *British Journal of Medical Psychology*, **51**, 127–130.

Monahan, J. (1993) Limiting therapist exposure to *Tarasoff* liability: Guidelines for risk containment. *American Psychologist*, **48**, 242–250.

Morrissey, J.P. (1999) Integrating service delivery systems for persons with a severe mental illness. In A.V. Horwitz & T.L. Scheid (Eds) *A Handbook for the Study of Mental*

Health: Social Contexts, Theories and Systems. Cambridge: Cambridge University Press.

Mulrow, C.D. (1987) The medical review article: State of the science. *Annals of Internal Medicine,* **106,** 485–488.

Nathan, P.E. & Gorman, J.M. (Eds) (1998) *A Guide to Treatments That Work.* New York, NY: Oxford University Press.

Novaco, R.W. (1997) Remediating anger and aggression in violent offenders. *Legal and Criminological Psychology,* **2,** 77–88.

Nuttall, C., Goldblatt, P. & Lewis, C. (1998) *Reducing Offending: An Assessment of Research Evidence on Ways of Dealing with Offending Behaviour.* Home Office Research Study No. 187. London: Home Office.

Palmer, T. (1975) Martinson re-visited. *Journal of Research in Crime and Delinquency,* **12,** 133–152.

Persons, J.B. (1991) Psychotherapy outcome studies do not accurately represent current models of psychotherapy: A proposed remedy. *American Psychologist,* **46,** 99–106.

Persons, J.B. & Silbersatz, G. (1998) Are the results of randomized controlled trials useful to psychotherapists? *Journal of Consulting and Clinical Psychology,* **66,** 126–135.

Petrosino, A.J., Boruch, R.F., Rounding, C., McDonald, S. & Chalmers, I. (1999) *A Social, Psychological, Educational and Criminological Trials Register (SPECTR) to facilitate the preparation and maintenance of systematic reviews of social and educational interventions.* Background paper for the Cochrane Collaboration meeting, School of Public Policy, University College London, July.

Redondo, S., Garrido, V. & Sánchez-Meca, J. (1999) The influence of treatment programmes on the recidivism of juvenile and adult offenders: A European meta-analytic review. *Psychology, Crime and Law,* **5,** 251–278.

Renwick, S.J., Black, L., Ramm, M. & Novaco, R.W. (1997) Anger treatment with forensic hospital patients. *Legal and Criminological Psychology,* **2,** 103–116.

Roberts, A.R. & Camasso, M.J. (1991) The effect of juvenile offender treatment programs on recidivism: A meta-analysis of 46 studies. *Notre Dame Journal of Law, Ethics and Public Policy,* **5,** 421–441.

Robinson, D. (1995) *The Impact of Cognitive Skills Training on Post-Release Recidivism among Canadian Federal Offenders.* Ottawa: Correctional Services of Canada.

Rosenthal, R. (1994) Parametric measures of effect size. In H. Cooper & L.V. Hedges (Eds) *Handbook of Research Synthesis.* New York: Russell Sage Foundation.

Ross, R.R. & Gendreau, P. (Eds) (1980) *Effective Correctional Treatment.* Toronto: Butterworth.

Roth, A. & Fonagy, P. (1996) *What Works For Whom: A Critical Review of Psychotherapy Research.* New York: Guilford Press.

Russell, M.N. (1990) *Clinical Social Work.* Newbury Park, CA: Sage Publications.

Sherman, L., Gottfredson, D., Mackenzie, D.L., Eck, J., Reuter, P. & Bushway, S. (1997) *Preventing Crime: What Works, What Doesn't, What's Promising.* Washington, DC: Office of Justice Programs.

Smith, M.L., Glass, G.V. & Miller, T.I. (1980) *The Benefits of Psychotherapy.* Baltimore, MD: Johns Hopkins University Press.

Sohn, D. (1995) Meta-analysis as a means of discovery. *American Psychologist,* **50,** 108–110.

Tafrate, R.C. (1995) Evaluation of treatment strategies for adult anger disorders. In H. Kassinove (Ed.) *Anger Disorders: Definition, Diagnosis and Treatment.* Washington, DC: Taylor & Francis.

Tarrier, N., Beckett, R., Harwood, S., Baker, A., Yusupoff, L. & Ugarteburu, I. (1993) A trial of two cognitive-behavioural methods of treating drug-resistant residual psychotic symptoms in schizophrenic patients: I. Outcome. *British Journal of Psychiatry,* **162,** 524–532.

Task Force (1995) Task Force on Promotion and Dissemination of Psychological Procedures, Division of Clinical Psychology, American Psychological Association. Training in the Dissemination of Empirically-Validated Psychological Treatments: Report and Recommendations. *The Clinical Psychologist*, **48**, 3–23.

Tennent, G. & Way, C. (1984) The English Special Hospital—a 12–17 year follow-up study: A comparison of violent and non-violent re-offenders and non-offenders. *Medicine, Science and Law*, **24**, 81–91.

Tong, J.E. & Mackay, G.W. (1958) A statistical follow-up of mental defectives of dangerous or violent propensities. *British Journal of Delinquency*, **IX**, 276–284.

Underdown, A. (1998) *Strategies for Effective Offender Supervision: Report of the HMIP What Works Project*. London: Home Office.

Vennard, J., Sugg, D. & Hedderman, C. (1997) *Changing Offenders' Attitudes and Behaviour: What Works?* Home Office Research Study No. 171. London: Home Office.

Watt, B.D. & Howells, K. (1999) Skills training for aggression control: Evaluation of an anger management programme for violent offenders. *Legal and Criminological Psychology*, **4**, 285–300.

Watts, F., Powell, G.V. & Austin, C.V. (1973) The modification of abnormal beliefs. *British Journal of Medical Psychology*, **46**, 359–363.

Whitehead, J.T. & Lab, S.P. (1989) A meta-analysis of juvenile correctional treatment. *Journal of Research in Crime and Delinquency*, **26**, 276–295.

Zamble, E. & Quinsey, V.L. (1997) *The Criminal Recidivism Process*. Cambridge: Cambridge University Press.

Index